GLOBALIZATION,

WLEDGE

AND SOCIETY

GLOBALIZATION, KNOWLEDGE AND SOCIETY

Readings from *International Sociology*

edited by

Martin Albrow and

Elizabeth King

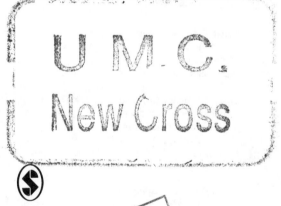

SAGE Publications

London • Newbury Park • New Delhi

in association with the International Sociological Association/ISA

First published 1990

SAGE Publications Ltd
28 Banner Street
London EC1Y 8QE

SAGE Publications Inc
2111 West Hillcrest Drive
Newbury Park, California 91320

SAGE Publications India Pvt Ltd
32, M-block Market
Greater Kailash – I
New Delhi 110 048

British Library Cataloguing in Publication data
    Globalization, knowledge and society: readings from
    International sociology.
    1. Sociology. Methodology
    I. Albrow, Martin II. King, Elizabeth
    301.01

    ISBN 0–8039–8323–9
    ISBN 0–8039–8324–7 pbk

Library of Congress catalog card number 90-061354

Typeset by Megaron, Cardiff, Wales
Printed in Great Britain by Dotesios Printers Ltd,
Trowbridge, Wiltshire

Globalization, Knowledge and Society:
Readings from *International Sociology*

edited by Martin Albrow and Elizabeth King

Contents

Globalization, Knowledge and Society

IS Publication Acknowledgements

1. MARGARET S. ARCHER. Resisting the Revival of Relativism
    Vol. 2, No. 3, pp. 235–250

2. AGNES HELLER. Sociology as the Defetishisation of Modernity
    Vol. 2, No. 4, pp. 391–401

3. PIOTR SZTOMPKA. Conceptual Frameworks in Comparative
    Inquiry: Divergent or Convergent?
    Vol. 3, No. 3, pp. 207–218

4. EDWARD A. TIRYAKIAN. Sociology's Great Leap Forward: The
    Challenge of Internationalisation
    Vol. 1, No. 2, pp. 155–171

5. ORLANDO FALS BORDA. The Application of Participatory-Action
    Research in Latin America
    Vol. 2, No. 4, pp. 329–347

6. AKINSOLA A. AKIWOWO. Contributions to the Sociology of
    Knowledge from an African Oral Poetry
    Vol. 1, No. 4, pp. 343–358

7. M. AKIN. MAKINDE. Asuwada Principle: An Analysis of Akiwowo's
    Contributions to the Sociology of Knowledge from an African
    Perspective
    Vol. 3, No. 1, pp. 61–76

8. O.B. LAWUYI and OLUFEMI TAIWO. Towards an African
    Sociological Tradition: A Rejoinder to Akiwowo and Makinde
    Vol. 5, No. 1, pp. 57–73

9. IMMANUEL WALLERSTEIN. Societal Development, or Develop-
    ment of the World-System?
    Vol. 1, No. 1, pp 3–17

10. ERICH WEEDE. Rent-Seeking or Dependency as Explanations of
    Why Poor People Stay Poor
    Vol. 1, No. 4, pp. 421–441

FOREWORD

If we already lived in a single world society then all talk about globalisation would be in the past tense. Instead, globalisation is the present process of becoming global: globality itself lies in the future, but the very near future. Each major aspect of social reality (the structure, culture and personality of traditional terminology) is simultaneously undergoing globalisation, as witnessed by the emergence of a world economy, a cosmopolitan culture and international social movements.

Through these transformations society is displaying its fundamental morphogenetic nature on the largest possible social canvas, the face of the earth. This defining property, the distinctive capacity of society to change its outward form and internal organisation, has always defeated attempts to find an adequate analogue for it from within it – in mechanism, in organism, in cybernetics or in language. Society has to be grasped in itself, and when it changes radically as now, through a myriad of interaction sequences whose emergent product is globality, sociologists have to respond to the challenge by conceptualising this novel transformation and theorising about it in new ways.

Yet there is always a double morphogenesis involved in large-scale social change. As we collectively transform society, we ourselves are transformed as a collectivity. Globalisation affects everyone since it presents them with a world context which influences them in some of their doings. Equally, we all become global agents because reactions to a single context produce powerful aggregate effects which act back to reshape the world environment. This does not occur equitably or fairly, which is precisely why transnational movements are surfacing as new collective agents, mobilising unprecedented numbers for participation in world concerns. Nor does it happen immediately, for part of the process is a gradual globalisation of consciousness which the sociologist is amongst the first to share.

It is vital that this changing consciousness is grasped reflexively within the international community (inside the ISA) and for us to prompt one another into a full realisation of its implications. For just as we cannot remain the national practitioners that we once were, neither can we hang on to the old tools of the trade, continuing to think and to theorise as we once did.

This reflexivity, which *International Sociology* was founded to foster, leads to new conclusions which in turn point to new commitments. A simple awareness of sociological diversity worldwide will not do, the task is the integration of this diversity. The latter is an active theoretical exercise rather than a passive acknowledgement of global pluralism in sociology. In practice such integration involves four stages – the exposing, the juxtaposing and the synthesising of diversity, which culminates in generating a new variety of social theory. To maximise the cultural representation of sociological ideas from around the world is indeed a necessary but not a sufficient condition for advancing the discipline. In addition, this requires synthetic, syncretic and innovative dialogue between them of a progressive kind.

I would characterise this dialogue as pro-active rather than reactive and egalitarian rather than imperialistic. If this is the case, then two recent

1

developments need treating with charitable caution. Trends towards the 'indigenisation' of sociology were understandably fuelled by reactions against the facile export of models, concepts or theoretical frameworks forged in the more developed world. These represent a proper refusal to import inappropriate conceptual schemes and a principled counter-move to elaborate social theory from the indigenous cultural stock. But such 'indigenisation' can go two ways. If it becomes deeply embedded in the reactive and anti-imperialist mode, there is a danger of regional relativism, of generating incommensurable models which are incommunicable to other parts of the world. Alternatively, indigenous contributions can be pro-active by challenging the supposed universality of propositions, by inducing 'concept stretching' and by injecting new empirical data and theoretical insights. These a genuinely universal sociology would have to incorporate and synthesise through a dialogue entailing reciprocal correction and mutual elaboration.

On the other hand, the recent upsurge of 'post-modernism' in affluent societies rightly discounts the linear spread of modernity and discards blind faith in the modernisation process, which lacks the internal wherewithal to right its own wrongs. Yet this trend too may be a threat to international sociology, because of its 'reactive' elitism: 'elitist' because the curse of necessary labour amidst scarcity has been broken for the very few, and reactive if emancipation is no more than these global consumers toying with stylistic effects. Globalism in sociology must resist both of these elements. Firstly, it must remain tethered to the material finitude of the earth's resources and engage with this reality. The spiritless spirit of ironic idealism cannot be the future lot of humankind, some of whom at least must keep a watching brief on the subsistence of humanity itself. Secondly, if post-modernism indeed reinforces an easy ability to tolerate the incommensurable and the inconsistent, it undercuts the tough endeavour of international sociology which is to render different cultures intelligible to one another, and thus capable of exchanging ideas.

If diversity is to be integrated through progressive sociological dialogue, then this has to be premissed upon interlocution between cultures and that, in turn, means that we have to make the unicity of human nature and the universality of human reasoning our most basic starting points. We predicate unicity, we explore diversity, we elaborate universality. Simultaneously, since this dialogue is about social life in one real world, we need to reclaim reality and focus our discourse on the interplay between humankind and its environment. Relativism and idealism have always been the Scylla and Charybdis on which the sociological enterprise could flounder: Other Minds and Other Worlds are the implacable enemies of international sociology. As Martin Albrow avows later on, 'both the discipline and, infinitely more important, humanity itself have constantly to be reaffirmed as essentially one and indivisible': this is the credo of *International Sociology*. Its profession and practical expression are the point and purpose of the International Sociological Association.

Margaret S. Archer

2

GLOBALIZATION, KNOWLEDGE AND SOCIETY

Introduction

The reason for bringing into one volume 15 papers, all published since 1986 in *International Sociology*, is that they are fine examples of sociology at a new and definite stage in its development.

This is the stage of the *global discipline*, and in three senses:

(a)   carried forward by a worldwide community of scholars and scientists;
(b)   with a focus on the inclusive process of social change, globalisation;
(c)   in the educational role of raising international and global consciousness.

These are not simply ideal aspirations. Much of the work of the International Sociological Association (ISA) proceeds along these directions. Evidence of their actuality is contained in this book. We hope it will be of wide use wherever issues of internationalisation and globalisation are discussed by sociologists and by others who recognise the importance of the social transformation which affects everyone. In particular this collection will help those planning new courses for the students of the 1990s who will not be content with narrow national definitions of their course of study.

The rationale for the new journal

The decision of the ISA, taken in 1984, to establish a second journal was not without risk. Its first journal *Current Sociology* had built a distinguished reputation for its authoritative surveys of specialist fields within the discipline. Was there room for a journal in that apparently small space between ISSC's own *International Social Science Journal*, and the journals of national sociological associations, and at the same time could it approach the standard of its predecessor and companion? Under the circumstances it was an act of faith to found *International Sociology*. But it was faith born of the experience of a number of sociologists which testified to the emergence of a new spirit and new demands.

The same factors resulted in the decisions to hold successive World Congresses in Third World countries in 1982 in Mexico and in 1986 in India. The desire existed to enter into and draw from the full diversity of the world's cultures in shaping a genuinely international discipline.

No one could deny that idealism played a large part in such decisions. The ideas of common humanity, of a world in which people speak to people in peace and friendship, of universal reason, probably have a stronger hold on sociologists than on most professional groups. But there was an interest too, particular to sociology, with its scientific task of understanding social phenomena. Unless the full diversity of human experience is represented in its work, by its own standards it must be defective.

The ISA began as a federation of national associations. Its internationalism was originally part of the reconstructed world order after the catastrophe of the 1939–45 World War. Its multi-culturalism arose out of the experience of representatives of national sociologies as they worked together developing a common understanding of what constituted a truly international sociology.

It was this which prompted the President of the ISA at the time, Fernando Cardoso, in his Foreword to the first issue of *International Sociology* to write:

> In other words, instead of publishing exclusively authors interested in the analysis of socio-cultural diversity across the world, our journal prefers to publish papers by people motivated by their own national and cultural traditions, the summing-up of which will offer to the reader a more global and comprehensive view of contemporary sociology.
>
> (1986 : 1)

Cardoso suggested this stage had been reached through overcoming the dominance of a single paradigm in sociology, American functionalism. In effect, a Western cultural perspective was to be replaced by a new global pluralism. He called, therefore, for a 'balanced editorial policy', publishing authors from diverse regions, ages, sex groups and theoretical orientations.

It is sometimes thought that such a policy must represent the illegitimate imposition of extraneous, even political, criteria on purely scientific work, subordinating truth to positive discrimination for causes which, however worthy, are not in themselves relevant to science.

I sympathise with those who advocate the autonomy of science. But such a criticism betrays a lack of understanding for the rationale of a social science, such as sociology. Truth is not the sole and exhaustive basis for science. Karl Popper used to convince his lecture audience of this at the London School of Economics. Anyone, he would say, who thought science consisted in the accumulation of true facts could be uselessly employed for the whole of their lives in recording the physical features of the room in which they were seated.

Truth is not enough. Theoretical importance, practical relevance, communicability, even economy, are all criteria which are intrinsic and necessary to the pursuit of science. With sociology it is the case that knowledge of a fairly elementary kind of a hitherto neglected sector may be worth far more than the most highly sophisticated measurement of processes already well-known. For instance, who could doubt that a participant observer's record of the experience of an ordinary worker during the Iranian revolution would be worth more than a report of the results of scholastic aptitude tests on pupils in British schools – and that in *scientific* terms? The reasons are clear. In the first case we have scarce information bearing on events which have crucial theoretical significance for work on class, political structure and revolution. In the latter, we are merely replicating well-known methods on different subjects, with an interest perhaps for local educational administrators only.

We know these differences are crucial, but rarely spell them out. But with sociology more than this discriminatory judgement, which can be shared by other sciences, is involved. The reason is that human experience is differentiated. If it were uniform, we would not need sociology. And it is differentiated by time, place and social identity, among other things.

4

This is the reason feminism has a claim on sociology; not because of its political demands, but because women can claim a different experience from men, which they seek to communicate, but to which ultimately they have a privileged access. For this reason we wish to have results from Muslim sociology, from India, or Finland or the Caribbean from those who speak the local languages and have experienced a culture from the inside which the rest of the world cannot know in the same way.

Even in the case of youth I would contend that we welcome papers by younger scholars in our pages not simply for the often observed reason that we need to look after the next generation of scientists. Age cohorts also have their specific experiences. Since the memories of aging people are well recognised by life history specialists, perhaps this fact should encourage editors to look for aged contributors too!

International Sociology then is the product of policy to reflect the nature of the work of the international community of sociologists, a policy to maximise the range of cultural representation, while contributing to the advance of the discipline. But, at the same time, content, theoretical orientation and methodological preferences are left open and we were as ignorant as the next person as to what kind of material would result from our policy.

As it has turned out, the journal in its first four years has rapidly acquired a distinctive character. It clearly does not duplicate national journals. But something more positive than that has happened. It is becoming a forum in which the frame of a global sociological consciousness is debated and at the same time it is coming to reflect the world social processes of which it is a part.

The reason we have collected these papers into one volume and are offering them to the Madrid World Congress is because they record a stage in the development of sociology in which it has become clear that, as an international discipline, it has a specific set of topics and set of discourse partners with a style and approach which justifies the ISA in thinking of itself not just as a federation of national associations, but also as an active worldwide professional association of individual sociologists. The papers in this volume are some of the best examples of this activity. How have we reached this point?

The internationalisation of sociology

Since its beginnings sociology has laboured under grand and universal conceptions of its role. Notions of providing the keystone of the arch of knowledge, of synthesising the other social sciences, or of bringing humanity to full self-consciousness, have never been far from the surface, even if sociologists have often been too embarrassed to display them in mixed company.

Such ideas are regularly self-deceiving for those who hold them. In particular, they tend to conceal real processes of development as such self-assigned tasks are projected back and forward and effectively prevent an appreciation of the history of the discipline.

In fact, if we do take a developmental view of the subject rooted in its real history, there is an interesting story to be told of the interplay between conceptions of its tasks and the location, organisation and ethos of the subject.

While this is too large a theme to expand on here, it must be addressed at least. My contention is that this set of papers, which has been brought together for the occasion of the Madrid World Congress, provides an excellent representation of a stage of development in sociology. They are not simply a random selection which could come from any period. They are part of the new movement of the discipline.

I want to back this claim by proposing an interpretation of the history of our subject which sees it as developing through five stages. All the usual caveats apply: the stages overlap; they have no sharp boundaries; they are not pre-ordained; not every branch of or national sociology may have gone through each and every stage. Having said that, I do believe that there is a detectable sequence, a process not inappropriately called dialectical, as ideas develop in tension with each other and in response to changing social conditions.

Briefly we can identify the following stages: universalism – national sociologies – internationalism – indigenisation – globalisation.

'*Universalism*' was the classical phase of sociology when the aspiration prevailed to provide a science of, and for, humanity based on timeless principles and verified laws. It was the sociology of Comte, Spencer or Lester Ward, inspired by the natural sciences.

'*National sociologies*' was the period of the foundation of sociology on a professional basis in the academies of the Western world, especially in Germany, France and the United States, but also in Italy, Britain, Spain and non-Western countries, such as Japan. The universal aspirations were not expunged, but in these national developments very often professional contacts became confined by national boundaries and the intellectual products similarly took on striking characteristics of the national culture.

The way Weber and Durkheim ignored each other has often been noted, but they were no different from most of their colleagues. The United States was distinct in the way it absorbed European influences, but in a 'melting pot' way which parallelled other social processes in the development of characteristic American culture.

The combination of national sociologies with the residues of universalism produced a conceptual imperialism, a competition between theoretical schemes for exclusive intellectual hegemony which was not so remote from the imperial territorial ambitions of the nation-states associated with the parent culture.

'*Internationalism*' was the response to the collapse of national ideologies and the unmitigated disaster of the World Wars. The scientific cultural and educational aspects of reconstruction were recognised in the establishment of a body like UNESCO, and the association of cultural and political internationalism was taken for granted. It was the climate in which the International Sociological Association was founded in 1949.

From the beginning, this internationalism was double-edged or divided in itself. On the one hand, the increasing worldwide penetration of Western rationality was interpreted through an all-embracing modernisation thesis, especially in the American Parsons version. On the other hand, internationalism as such was central to the ideology of socialist states, was

6

historically based in the proletarian movement and was represented by Marxism.

'*Indigenisation*' was primarily a Third World response, beginning in the 1970s, inspired largely by a 'plague on both your houses' attitude. It is distinguished from the 'national sociologies' by two things. The first is the explicit opposition to the importation of inappropriate models of social science, and especially to terminology and methods developed in and for the First World. The second is an emphasis on the distinctive national cultural tradition and the possibilities of finding inspiration there for new directions in sociology. As S.C. Dube said in 1979, 'It is tragic that the Third World should see itself largely through Western eyes' (quoted by Atal 1981 : 191).

Marxism may have appealed more to this movement than other theories, but as Yogesh Atal has pointed out, that did not make it any more indigenous (1981 : 194). Indeed, it was resistance to foreign products which was a more powerful force and in this respect the movement for indigenisation was not confined to the Third World. Canada, for instance, has experienced a strong Canadianisation movement in sociology.

At the same time, even without an expressed hostility to foreign sociology, the development of national markets within the discipline has been such that the complaint is often expressed in the United States, Britain or West Germany that the subject and its organisation have become more parochial. Often a direct continuity is seen with the period of 'national sociologies'.

These persistent national influences have inspired F.H. Gareau to argue in a stimulating issue of *Current Sociology* (1985, Vol. 33, No. 3) that multinationalism is inherent in the social sciences and that it represents the 'gap betwen promise and reality ... obvious in the distance which separates the universal discourse and the aspiration for the international from a reality which is sectarian and nationalistic' (1985 : 15).

Gareau backs up his case with ample evidence and no one can doubt the local, even parochial, nature of the bulk of sociological work which is produced within national sociologies. However, Nikolai Genov, in his recent collection of papers on national sociologies, has argued that an extreme relativism is not justified (1989 : 9). There is evidence for the emergence of a non-national global sociological discourse.

'*Globalisation*' is the final phase, though not, of course, the ultimate or last that we can foresee or ever will experience. The principle underlying globalisation is neither national nor international, although it is a product of the interaction of the two, and indeed of all four of the previous stages. It results from the freedom individual sociologists have to work with other individuals anywhere on the globe and to appreciate the worldwide processes within which and on which they work.

In this sense the Research Committees of the ISA best represent the principle of globalisation as opposed simply to internationalism. The product of the initiatives of individual scholars, these Committees exchange ideas and work together regardless of national boundaries. The Research Council of the ISA is then based on different principles from the Council of the ISA which consists of national representatives. For the individual sociologist, the inter-

national framework is only a convenience for his or her global scientific interests. It is in response to this that the ISA has increasingly been stressing its services to individual members.

The globalisation of sociology is a facet of what is sometimes called the globalisation of consciousness. It is part of the cultural definition of the global situation which Roland Robertson, in particular, has argued is quite as important as the economy in determining the world historical process (see, especially, Robertson and Lechner 1985). This means that there is a worldwide culture in which people respond to global issues and think in terms which are the products of global communication both through the mass media and in terms of personal interaction. A universal discourse has arisen with multiple interlocutors based in different regions and cultures.

For scientists in general this globalisation is the realisation of the promise of universalism which, unless there is free communication without boundaries and artificial restrictions, can only be an ideal aspiration deprived of content. For sociologists in particular, globalisation means not only that they as scientists can communicate freely; their subject matter has actually been transformed in two ways. In the first place, they are confronted with the full diversity, even babel, of sociological dialects and special visions. Secondly, globalisation is itself a process at a new level of social reality. Global society is a novel phenomenon.

International sociology – a new speciality?

'Global' has become a fashionable adjective. But fashion is also part of reality and there is a real sense in which it is right to emphasise that we are experiencing the creation of global society of a kind and scale which humanity has not previously witnessed. We are indeed seeing the rise of humanity as a collective actor.

In making such large claims, a sense of history is indispensable. So also is an understanding of philosophical ideas. We can then distinguish periods by the prevalence of ideas and their relation to material conditions and social organisation.

We should accordingly distinguish '*globalism*' from '*universalism*'. Both refer to sets of values. 'Universalism' refers to those values which take humanity, at any time or place, hypothetically or actually, as the subject. Both science and religion draw upon universalistic values. Universalism has a long history in Western thought; it also characterises non-Western religions and philosophies.

'Globalism' has a much shorter history. I take it to refer to those values which take the real world of 5 billion people as the object of concern, the whole earth as the physical environment, everyone living as world citizens, consumers and producers, with a common interest in collective action to solve global problems. It is the culmination of changes in value orientations which Ronald Inglehart identified as post-materialism in the 1970s (1977).

But in an important sense 'globalism' is more material than either 'universalism' or 'post-materialism', for it is pervaded by a sense of finitude, of the limits of growth or the earth's resources, by the pressure of population size or the threat of nuclear war. It is therefore a very concrete universalism, moved by the actual sight of starving children in Ethopia, or by data on malnutrition in Bangladesh.

'Globalisation' refers to all those processes by which the peoples of the world are incorporated into a single world society, global society. Globalism is one of the forces which assist in the development of globalisation. But it is only one such force and the relation between it and globalisation is akin to that between universalism and the creation of the United Nations. On its own, universalism could not have been sufficient.

Are we now in a position to talk of a single world society? In my view we are, or at least we are on the verge of it. But it is here where historical perspective is essential. Raymond Aron pointed out that transnational relations had a long history. After all, the Olympic Games are a modern revival of a Greek practice (1966 : 105). Immanuel Wallerstein (and Marx) has emphasised the world creating power of capitalist economic relations going back to the sixteenth century (1974).

Students of international politics have long benefitted from the standard discussion of these issues by Robert Keohane and Joseph Nye (1971). In their view, the extent and scope of transnational relations had by 1970 assumed far greater significance for relations between states than was the case before 1914. By transnational relations they meant interactions across state boundaries not controlled by state foreign policy.

The topics Keohane and Nye covered, from International NGOs to the Roman Catholic Church, from the Ford Foundation to space and ocean research, provided an impressive overview which could be extended in obvious ways now, in particular and especially in the development of mass communications on a global basis and the spread of worldwide social movements. Perhaps globalism itself as a value system is the most important extra ingredient.

It is these extra elements which both confirm the view that transnational relations have taken on a new dimension and justify sociologists in asserting that they have a special contribution to make to the understanding of world society. We can be encouraged in this by recognition from the distinguished French professor of law, Marcel Merle, whose *Sociology of International Relations* (1987) is written out of the conviction that it is sociology which can shed new light on a subject which too often has assumed that relations between states are independent of wider social relations.

Equally, however, Merle points out that sociology has also been too content to stop at state boundaries (ibid. : 7). A recent analysis (Zolberg 1987) wonders how the 'internalist' orientations could ever have held sway when transnational relations have always existed. But we do have to recognise that a global perspective is now qualitatively different from the recognition of regionwide phenomena of previous periods of history.

For this reason we should listen to the call which Wilbert Moore made at an ASA convention as long ago as 1965, for a global sociology, 'sociology of the globe, of mankind' (1966 : 475) in the hope that 'the common features of

9

human existence will be increasingly documented' (ibid. : 476). Additionally, this would involve the recognition that the world is 'a singular system' in minimal senses of sharing an ideology of economic development and drawing on a worldwide pool of options, and also in the sense of 'the life of the individual is affected by events and processes everywhere' (ibid. : 481).

Moore's formulations appear dated now. There is less interest in 'common features', the ideology of economic development has been challenged by those, like S.C. Dube (1988), who call for a genuine social development, and we can express the systemic nature of world society more adequately now than simply by lives being affected by processes elsewhere. For individuals have become self-conscious world actors, organising and responding to events worldwide, and that is true for Muslims, Christians, socialists or capitalists. The case for global sociology is even stronger.

International sociology should be recognised as a sub-area within the discipline, much as we recognise the sociology of industry, religion, or development. I prefer 'international sociology' to 'global sociology', if only because closely related disciplines like economics, law and politics all have similar branches which have long been recognised.

The justification for specifying a new sub-area is the need to group together a range of social phenomena which are not adequately treated at present by being dispersed in a range of specialities. Thus the creation of an international class, international civil servants, managers of multi-nationals, international lawyers, financiers, sportsmen who interact, inter-marry, send their children to international schools is not adequately treated in the study of national systems of social stratification. It is only intelligible as part of the global social system.

An international sociology would bring together related phenomena as diverse as transnational personal relations, cross-cultural marriage and understanding, voluntary associations which cross boundaries, internationalism as a movement, global mass communications, terrorism, multi-national corporations and those large movements which have changed the politics of our time, and are not confined by boundaries – the Green, Peace and Feminist movements.

It is the growth of these phenomena as real features of the social life of individuals which is responsible for the often noted difficulties experienced by comparative sociology. The problems Erwin Scheuch has recently discussed (1989) result from changes which affect the relations of individuals to nation-states and hence also the nature of states and their relations with each other.

The tasks of a global discipline

Moore pointed to a global sociology. He also noted a second sense in which he also used the term 'international sociology', namely to refer to the work of the international body of sociologists (op. cit. : 475). This volume of papers is the product of that community. It is their work which enables us to identify the processes which are creating one world and to suggest that sociology is now in the middle of the period of globalisation.

This period is characterised both by sociologists of different cultures and backgrounds constituting the discipline in a global discourse, and also by global society becoming a key topic for theory and research.

By now, however, we are in a position to acknowledge a third dimension to the globalisation of sociology, namely its educational function. For these transformations of society and sociology extend too to the socialisation process, both in general in education, and specifically in the training of sociologists.

For a considerable time educationalists in the United States have been concerned to internationalise higher education as a response to the leading international role that country has assumed, and they have been concerned by the contradiction between that role and the educational system.

J. Michael Armer alludes to this concern in the introduction he wrote for a collection of resource materials for teaching which he edited for the American Sociological Association, *Syllabi and Resources for Internationalizing Courses in Sociology*:

> In a shrinking world, it is argued, our national security and economic interests rest in part on knowledge about and successful dealings with people, governments and organizations in other nations. The recognition of an increasingly interdependent world and the disadvantages of national parochialism lie at the heart of the widely publicized U.S. Presidential Commission Report on foreign languages and international studies, entitled "Strength through Wisdom: a Critique of U.S. Capability" (Presidential Commission 1975).
>
> (1983 : 2)

That, of course, is an argument from interest, national self-interest, which can easily be represented as an extension merely of American hegemony. But Armer uses two other arguments for internationalising the sociology curriculum which can apply anywhere. The first is from the universalistic values underpinning science, the need to be non-parochial and comparative, and to ignore national boundaries in the pursuit of science.

The other argument is more tough minded, because it recognises that the changing nature of social life worldwide requires change in sociological analysis. Sociologists are adopting a global perspective we can say, precisely because globalisation means that they can no longer seek to explain processes within their own countries by reference only to internal conditions. Actually, we might add that it never was really possible, but globalisation effectively means that societies now cannot be seen as systems in an environment of other systems, but as sub-systems of the larger inclusive world society.

Armer's report grew out of the work of the ASA Committee on World Sociology. These efforts to produce teaching materials with international content are a feature of sociologists' role as agents in the globalisation process. We do not simply report and explain it in our research, nor merely become part of it as we organise ourselves internationally. In incorporating it into our teaching we become active proselytizers.

This volume has been produced because we wish to affirm the active role which sociology has in educating the new world citizens. We believe the papers

11

reproduced here amount to a valuable teaching resource as well as a record of the way sociologists have been working within and on the globalisation process in the 1980s.

As a teaching resource the collection should be useful in providing an international dimension for courses in the philosophy of social science and sociological theory. It will enable teachers in sociology of development courses to highlight what was until recently a submerged issue, namely the development of culture. It will place the problematic of the viability of comparative sociology in a globalised world in the centre of courses of that name.

Finally, we hope that programmes of international studies will find the contribution of sociology to their curriculum, for which there has been growing recognition, is made much more explicit by this book. It is divided into five parts with brief editorial introductions to make the variety of these possible teaching uses obvious.

When this generation of students has progressed out of college and into new roles, we hope this book will still retain some value as a historical document, a testimony in particular to the dedication of all those sociologists who in the 1980s have given unselfishly of their energies to the International Sociological Association and who work for international understanding not simply out of scientific curiosity. Only a very few of them feature as authors here. But we hope that those who do not will feel well represented by those who do. This book is dedicated to them all.

Martin Albrow
Cardiff, December 1989

References

ARMER, J.M. ed. 1983. *Syllabi and Resources for Internationalizing Courses in Sociology*. Washington: ASA Teaching Resources Center.

ARON, R. 1966. *Peace and War: a Theory of International Relations*. Garden City, N.Y.: Doubleday.

ATAL, Y. 1981. 'The Call for Indigenization'. *International Social Science Journal* 33 : 189–197.

CARDOSO, F. 1986. 'Foreword'. *International Sociology* 1 : 1–2.

DUBE, S.C. 1988. *Modernization and Development: The Search for Alternative Paradigms*. Tokyo: UN University/London: Zed Books.

GAREAU, F.H. 1985. 'The Multinational Version of Social Science with Emphasis upon the Discipline of Sociology'. *Current Sociology* 33 (3).

GENOV, N. ed. 1989. *National Traditions in Sociology*. London: Sage.

INGLEHART, R. 1977. *The Silent Revolution – Changing Values and Political Styles among Western Publics*. Princeton: Princeton University Press.

KEOHANE, R.O. and NYE, J.S. Jr. eds. 1971. *Transnational Relations and World Politics*. Cambridge, Mass.: Harvard University Press.

MERLE, M. 1987. *The Sociology of International Relations*. Leamington Spa: Berg.

MOORE, W.E. 1966. 'Global Sociology: the World as a Singular System'. *American Journal of Sociology* 71 : 475–482.

ROBERTSON, R. and LECHNER, F. 1985. 'Modernization, Globalization and the Problem of Culture in World-Systems Theory'. *Theory, Culture and Society* 2 : 103–117.

SCHEUCH, E.K. 1989. 'Theoretical Implications of Comparative Survey Research: Why the Wheel of Cross-Cultural Methodology Keeps on Being Reinvented'. *International Sociology* 4 : 147–168.

WALLERSTEIN, I. 1974. *The Modern World System*. New York: Academic Press.
ZOLBERG, A.R. 1987. 'Beyond the Nation State: Comparative Politics in a Global Perspective', in Jan Berting and Wim Blockmans (eds.), *Beyond Progress and Development: macro-political and macro-societal change*. Aldershot: Avebury. pp. 42–69.

13

TOWARDS A UNIVERSAL SOCIAL SCIENCE

Towards a Universal Social Science

In the long history of social theory the desire to express universal truths has been an enduring feature of reflections on the nature of society. That was true of even the most empirically minded of the great philosophers, of Aristotle or of Ibn Khaldun.

The project of making a science of society, to which the name of sociology has stuck, draws therefore not just upon the prestige of science as it has come to be understood in the modern world, but also upon a longer philosophical concern with truths which all rational people might affirm.

Indeed one of the strongest motives for the development of sociology in the nineteenth century was the belief that a science of society could generate those truths which traditional reflections had failed to produce. Comte's 'stability in fundamental maxims', Spencer's common properties of social aggregates, Durkheim's faith in comparative method all illustrated this belief.

Such trust in the unity of the natural and social sciences, an attitude dubbed 'positivism' by its detractors, has in the twentieth century encountered a number of persisting difficulties.

1. Sciences of nature depend upon identifying a public world independent of the particular impressions of individual investigators. Sociology has found it impossible to disregard the subjective aspect of human experience, even to the extent for some of finding society in the mind.

2. Even where there is a publicly acknowledged sphere, an objective culture, the variety of cultures in the plural rather than a single frame of meaning spanning humanity has appeared as a contrast to the unity of nature.

3. The proliferation of different systems of sociology and the failure to settle on a dominant paradigm have been taken as testimony to the unresolvability of these problems and to an essentially relative nature of sociological propositions whether with reference to time, place or author.

These problems are so deep-seated and enduring that sociologists have learnt to incorporate their personal answers to them in their daily practice and presentation of the discipline. Indeed, it is probably time to see them as something other than problems to be solved. They are rather the constitutive moments of sociological discourse itself. Were they to be 'solved', the subject would be unnecessary. The response they evoke at any one time represents the current state of development of the study of society.

The three papers chosen here are brilliant examples of characteristic 1980s answers to these classic problems. They reflect the changed sociological discourse of the period, with highly nuanced attempts to find unity in diversity, while simultaneously renouncing dogmatism. But the unity which each one finds remains ultimately different from each of the others.

Archer takes issue with the radical relativism of the influential British sociologists of science, Barnes and Bloor. She meets a relativism which arises out of a social theory of knowledge with a universalism which depends on the reassertion of compelling claims of logic and the necessity for allowing for translation. Both in practice depend on the assumption of a common humanity.

The provocative conclusion of Archer's paper makes it clear that the very practice of sociology is dependent on the acceptance of a principle which is equally fundamental to ethics. We may conclude that whatever the diversity of human experience and the variety of facts which social scientists might discover, both the discipline and, infinitely more important, humanity itself have constantly to be reaffirmed as essentially one and indivisible.

Reaffirmation means reconstruction as circumstances change. Agnes Heller captures the dilemma facing sociologists where their attempts to describe and explain the real world necessarily utilise research strategies which reify the ephemeral categories of the life and times of the subject, while at the same time a philosophically informed theoretical analysis penetrates the rationality of action and shows up those categories to be fetishistic. But it is precisely this situation, which Heller defines as modernity, which sociology is bound to interpret. It is the rationalisation process itself, of which sociology is a part, which generates the dilemma which sociologists are bound to face and fail to resolve.

If for Heller rationalisation is the dominating fact of our time, Piotr Sztompka equally finds in globalisation and internationalisation the dominating worldwide processes which transform the practice of sociology. These have in fact provided the cross-cultural frame which earlier naturalistic models of comparative methods, seeking to identify and compare isolated cases, required but were unable to supply. At the same time, the penetration of worldwide processes into every society highlights the preservation of uniqueness and idiosyncratic meaning everywhere in the world. The result is a methodological shift from the search for quantitative regularities to the identification of qualitative differences.

These papers are prime examples of the self-understanding of the sociology of our time. But they are more than that. They demonstrate that the transformations of the society in which we live are represented in the reconstruction of the classic problem of the nature of a social science. Our intellectual advances are measured by the extent to which we can keep up with changes in the world around us.

RESISTING THE REVIVAL OF RELATIVISM

Margaret S. Archer

Relativism has had a long if not particularly distinguished career in the history of social thought. Once upon a time it buttressed the ethnocentric premiss that people in different societies have different 'minds' which think their own kinds of thoughts. Overtly such relativism insisted that the 'natives' were different: covertly this relativism implied that the 'natives' were primitive. Later it bolstered the deterministic premiss of the totally dis-enchanted, namely that nothing but different social milieux determine what ideas are held as truths within them. Here relativism basically joined hands with nihilism, for who could devote themselves wholeheartedly to the pursuit of some parochial verity, unless as unfree agents – local cultural dupes? Later still it provided the ballast for pluralistic tolerance, for the view that different forms of life have their own notions of what makes sense. Here sociologists became eternal tourists but ones who could hazard no generalisations or comparisons about their trips, except perhaps through developing their own academic form of life which, of course, would have the same property of incommensurability as and with any other (Wilson 1979; Hollis and Lukes 1982).

The common thread running through the career of relativism is an imperialistic 'socio-centricity'. It is a careering movement which greedily loots percepts, concepts, truths, reason or logic, tearing them from their rooting in common humanity which abides in the same universe and making a gift of them to 'different worlds' to make what they will of them.

The newcomer is the most 'socio-centric' of all: for the radical relativism contained in the 'strong programme' of Barnes and Bloor (Barnes 1977, 1981; Barnes and Bloor 1982; Bloor 1976, 1978, 1981, 1983) asserts the *social* character and *social* causation of *all* knowledge. Significantly their main focus of interest and illustration has been the sociology of scientific thought. Radical relativism thus undertakes the demagification of science: it is an attempt to storm the twentieth century bastion of universalism, a sort of dissolution of the laboratories in theoretical terms.

By now, of course, a repertoire of responses to the various claims of relativism has been well rehearsed. Essentially these hinge on reasserting the unicity of 'human nature' as a basic axiom of the social sciences. Without endorsing the universal principle of humanity (Grandy 1973) no mode of life can be intelligible at all. In contradistinction, the price of agreeing that actors do inhabit truly 'different worlds' whose principles are matters of local linguistic convention would be the abandonment of any comparative work whatsoever. The rest of this paper defends these principles against the radical counter-attack mounted from the relativist camp.

The 'strong programme' in the sociology of knowledge

The 'strong programme' stakes an explanatory claim for the sociology of knowledge to the entire cultural domain. As with some forms of imperialism its first task is to boot out the present inhabitants, and the candidates for immediate extradition are those philosophers who have misled generations into believing that the truth, rationality, success or progressiveness of knowledge (colloquially known as TRASP) (Collins 1981) had quite a lot to do with people holding it. The 'strong programme' is therefore the anti-TRASP charter. War is declared on the latter in order to defend the fundamental principles of *symmetrical* explanation, namely that the 'same types of cause would explain, say, true and false beliefs' (Bloor 1976 : 5). Nothing about beliefs themselves then plays any part in accounting for why they are held or not (Laudan 1981). (It becomes progressively more difficult to see how the 'strong programme' could be compatible with a realist ontology.)

If all knowledge is socially caused and is social in character, then the ideas held at different times and places are incommensurable. They have no common measure in terms of percepts, concepts, truth, reason or logic for these are all matters of local evaluation.

> The words 'true' and 'false' provide the idiom in which . . . evaluations are expressed, and the words 'rational' and 'irrational' will have a similar function . . . The crucial point is that the relativist accepts that his preferences and evaluations are as context-bound as those of the tribes T1 and T2. Similarly he accepts that none of the justifications of his references can be formulated in absolute or context-independent terms.
>
> (Barnes and Bloor 1982 : 27)

There are *no* such terms.

However, to sustain this 'strong programme' its advocates have to demolish the two propositions which have to date provided other social theorists with *their terms* and their justification for using them comparatively. Specifically then:

(i) Relativists have to deny the invariance of the law of contradiction, whose acceptance has been taken as the touchstone of intelligibility itself. If a member of a social group 'were unable to see that the truth of p excludes the truth of its denial, how could they even communicate truths to one another and reason from them to other truths?' (Lukes 1979 : 209-10) The existence of this logical principle as a non-conventional and trans-contextual criterion has to be categorically denied from within the 'strong programme' for its universality is indeed incompatible with thorough-going relativism. Hence protagonists of this programme maintain that we can really only talk about local preference for the non-contradictory – in local terms.

(ii)   Relativists also have to deny the possibility and necessity of successful translation, since anything more than rough translation for rude purposes is inconsistent with relativism itself. Yet I will argue that translatability is the precondition, first for ascribing ideas to social groups across time and space at all, and secondly for employing logical principles to attribute contradiction or consistency amongst or between alien beliefs. If neither proposition is undermined by the 'strong programme' then the idea of social theory with a strongly comparative character can resist this new onslaught upon it.

I. The invariance of the law of contradiction

Unlike Bloor I believe that Mannheim kept his head rather than losing his nerve (Bloor 1976 : 8) when acknowledging that the universality of mathematics and logic was such that neither could be explained by reference to anything about the specific cultures in which they were adopted. In view of this he quite rightly forewent a thorough-going sociology of knowledge. However, my particular concern is to restore certain logical principles to where Mannheim left them, thus retaining their serviceability in the detection of properties like 'contradiction' and 'consistency' which are essential to the achievement of intelligibility, wherever cultural items are located in time and space, or to the admission that certain beliefs are sometimes mysterious and sometimes indeed unintelligible.

Bloor has provided a detailed attempt to demonstrate that 'mathematics is within the scope of the strong programme, and consequently that all beliefs whatever are within its scope' (Millstone 1978 : 117). With Barnes identical arguments were later extended to logic, re-emphasising the view 'that logical necessity is a species of moral obligation' (Bloor 1976 : 141). The basic argument consists in denying any invariable principles within mathematics, and it is held to be equally applicable to logic: instead both disciplines are socially co-variant. Hence the need for a brief excursion into the former here.

(a) *Alternative mathematics?* Bloor gains elbow-room for socially caused variations in mathematical thinking by noting (contra J.S. Mill) that maths is not a direct 'abstraction' from physical reality because any concrete situation (like pebble sorting) can be 'abstracted' in any number of ways. He then insists (contra Frege) that it is a variety of social conventions which renders any pattern of ordering 'characteristic' to a given society, exactly like traditional patterns of rug weaving (Bloor 1976 : 88 f.) and therefore equally variable between societies (Freudenthal 1979 : 72).

21

The onus is thus on protagonists of the 'strong programme' who conceive of mathematical necessity, and by extension logical necessity, as social institutions, to supply us with convincing examples of 'alternative mathematics' and 'alternative logics'. Alternatives would be ones in which practitioners share a consensus on something we deem erroneous and where they engage in forms of reasoning which 'would have to violate our sense of logical and cognitive propriety' (Bloor 1976 : 95-6). The trouble with their examples in both fields is that these are intended to illustrate *variability*, which they never manage to sustain, whilst these cases always display brute *regularities*, which the relativists never can explain.

Historically the fund of mathematical variation does not begin to match the range of social-cultural variability, yet the former should parallel the latter if indeed it is socially determined. However, Freudenthal's detailed dissection (1979 : 73 and 82) of the examples offered shows that rather than facing the prospect of returning empty-handed, the concept of an 'alternative' is elasticated in advance (Bloor 1976 : 97) and stretches well outside the realm of mathematical necessity to encircle various conventional differences which have no bearing upon it, such as cognitive style, metaphysical implications, and variations in rigour.

One instance of this, particularly relevant to the law of contradiction, is Bloor's discussion of early Greek number theory since he concludes that this illustrates the relativistic status of the whole notion of contradiction. It is considered an 'alternative' because, as the generator of all numbers, 'one' was not regarded as a number itself – consequently resulting in claims about the oddness and evenness of numbers which today would be regarded as false. From this it is concluded that in the Greek classification 'different things will therefore count as violations of order and coherence, *and so different things will count as confusions or contradiction*' (1976 : 98; my italics). But this only follows if the example constitutes a genuine alternative, which it does not. The question at stake here is one of *definitions* (which can readily be accepted as a matter of community consensus) and not alternative conceptions of the validity of mathematical proofs, entailing a reasoning which repudiates 'our' deductive logic but was deemed valid by the Greeks. (The same argument can be used against his most extended example, the polyhedron as a negotiated mathematical concept. Since much of his argument deals with the fact that for a given set of definitions of what constitutes polyhedra, a theorem may be shown not to hold, then the notion of mathematical validity is shared by the negotiators rather than being the subject of negotiation [Bloor 1978]).

Secondly, if we consider proofs themselves, then Bloor's concern to highlight stylistic variations in reaching conclusions only serves to obscure their common core: whilst he expatiates on the variability of methods used, he ignores the stunning *regularity* of the solutions produced by them. For instance, because Diophantus provided specific algebraic solutions rather than general methods of solution, his is hailed as a form of mathematical thinking that is as different from ours 'as the morality or religion of another culture is different to our morality or religion' (1976 : 103). Yet Diophantian solutions entail no violations of logic whatsoever and involve no error. Bloor ignores the latter point by 'not recognizing the simple fact that Diophantus' solutions to his problems, however he may have produced them, and although not general, are *correct*: the numbers cited satisfy the posed conditions'. On his account 'the occurrence of the same results within alternative mathematics' – e.g. Diophantus' and ours – that are all about' different societies, should appear as nothing short of a miracle' (Freudenthal 1979 : 77).

In brief, since neither of these examples fall within the realm of mathematical necessity (which imposes no particular definitions as mandatory and no set style in which problems must be tackled) then they cannot be construed as alternative conceptions of it. Consequently the original corrollary to variability, namely that different things will count as contradictions to those like the early Greeks who were credited with an 'alternative mathematics', has not been sustained either.

(b) *Alternative logics?* Thus it becomes crucial whether the later work with Barnes on logic is any more successful in breaking down either of the main barriers which restrain relativism. In other words, can they deal with the apparent absence of a fund of 'alternative logics' which their 'strong programme' requires, and with stubborn regularities in the principles of logic which seem to deny co-variance with social differences?

As a matter of fact, they claim, people do violate supposedly universal principles (like the law of contradiction) all the time. And these actions therefore withhold universality, compelling necessity or even practical utility from this rule of logic. Thus Barnes and Bloor invite us to 'consider all the familiar locutions we find of pragmatic value in informal speech which appear to do violence to formal logical rules' (1982 : 41). By implication logical variations are everyday occurrences, so thick on the ground that there is no need to appeal to obscure systems of formal logic, invented by academic logicians, as their source of 'alternatives'.

The examples specifically adduced in supposed violation of the law of contradiction are the following locutions: (a) 'Yes and no', (b) 'It was, and yet it wasn't', (c) 'The whole was greater than its parts' and (d) 'There is some truth in that statement' (Barnes and Bloor 1982 : 41-2). These instances, presented as the tip of an ice-berg on which the law of contradiction breaks up daily, must be genuine cases where two propositions, p and not-p are simultaneously asserted to be true. Spurious instances of apparent contradictions have always been easy to generate by simply failing to specify crucial elements like time and place (when supplied then propositions like 'the sun is shining' and 'the sun is not shining' are not contradictories). Now as everyday locutions, all of those above are verbal shorthand, each of them is incomplete, and therefore none of them are fully propositional. Barnes and Bloor argue that their occurrence in discourse is only intelligible in terms of contingent local determinants, as relativism demands, for as deviations from the rules of logic they cannot be explicated by reference to supposedly universal rules. On the contrary, inspection of the four instances cited shows that 'logical contingency' or 'context-specificity' boil down to no more than the specification of omissions, mentioned above, as necessary *before* the universal rule can be applied at all, *and* prior to knowing *whether* it is applicable.

The first two exemplars, 'yes and no', 'it was, and yet it wasn't' obviously had the appeal of (apparently) reproducing the classical form of a logical contradiction – the assertion of p and not-p. However, both are incomplete because they are shorthand responses in a dialogue which has been suppressed. Ask speakers to transcribe their replies into longhand and they may well supply their own specification, thus obviating any violation of the logical rule. Consider the following three questions which could have elicited either locution (1) or (2):

Q1. 'Was a letter expected from your lawyer?'
Q2. 'Is he an architect?'
Q3. 'Was the show a success?'

Now allow the respondent the use of longhand and the contradictories can disappear:

R1. 'Yes my lawyer's letter was expected in the near future, but no I didn't expect it to get here by today.'
R2. He is a qualified architect, but not a practising one.'
R3. It was a very successful production but a commercial diasaster.'

It is not only valid but essential to have shorthand locutions transcribed, for only by examining the longhand version *can it be known whether a rule like the law of non-contradiction is applicable to them.* Often people will use formulae like 'yes and no' or 'it was, and yet it wasn't' to express their inability, unwillingness or unreadiness to advance a propositional statement at all. They are another way of saying 'I'm not sure' and clearly when a locution expresses nothing but uncertainty it cannot count as an instance of contradiction between two propositions which is what violation of the law entails.

Instance (d), 'There is some truth in that statement' could be applied to example (c) 'the whole was greater than its parts', and raises the old problem that we often do talk of propositions being sometimes true and sometimes false whereas the very definition of a proposition excludes this possibility. Traditionally this difficulty is removed by recognising that if a proposition like 'the whole is greater than its parts' asserts that this is *universally* the case, then the existence of any exception to it serves to prove that it is false – *not* contradictory. However, to produce an exception we have to complete the proposition by specifying what kind of whole we are talking about – e.g. a book is not of greater length than the sum of its pages – a completion showing the falsity of the *universal* proposition. Nevertheless, it is true that the volume of frozen water is greater than that of melted ice. Thus when it is said that a

24

statement is sometimes true and sometimes false, what is meant is that expressions like 'the whole' may be completed in some ways which express true propositions and in other ways which express false ones. To say 'there is some truth in that statement' (example (d)) is to volunteer to complete it in both of these ways!

Once again the 'strong programme' confronts its dual difficulty – the absence of common-or-garden variability and the indubitable presence of regularity. On the one hand, Barnes and Bloor concede the general unacceptability of contradictions and acknowledge the 'widespread accept-ance of deductive inference forms and the avoidance of inconsistency' (1982 : 43). Immediately, however, they wheel in biology to explain what *causes* people to avoid inconsistency and thus to take care of the obtrusive regularities, which result from it. Nevertheless, the social is still considered vital (it explains the variable elements) because 'no account of our bio-logically-based reasoning propensities will justify a unique system of logical conventions' (Barnes and Bloor 1982 : 44). On the other hand, the varieties of logical system now appealed to are the various forms of non-standard logic developed in specialised academic contexts and not everyday abrogations of the law of contradiction. Moreover, these instances, like intuitionist logic in the foundations of mathematics, proposals for 3-valued logic in quantum physics and the 4-valued logic of De Morgan implication, fail to impress a firm partisan of the 'strong programme' like Mary Hesse as *alternatives*. She freely admits that 'the possibility of different basic logics is not by itself very cogent, because it may be said that the examples we know of are all parasitic on standard logic' (1980 : 38).

(c) *Alternative paths to intelligibility?* Consequently Hesse supplements the programme with her own argument against any logical principle being a necessary condition of a belief system, without, however, significantly strengthening the relativists' case against the universality of the law of contradiction. Basically she asks how can the rationalist account for cases 'where we *have* found sign systems unintelligible (as in many anthropological and theological examples where the criteria of identity, for example, of men with birds, three persons in one, etc., do not answer to our criteria)' (1980 : 37-8) but which we have eventually come to understand? So the argument goes, here are instances of contradictory beliefs which, according to the rationalist, should be unintelligible, yet we can come to understand them, but without resort to the rules which rationalists claim are indispensable to intelligibility. I shall argue that the two examples, like the Brazilian Bororo's assertion that there are red macaws or the Trinitarian doctrine, do nothing to support her view that our understanding of these cases does not conform in obvious ways to the application of propositional logic or indeed, in the case of metaphors, compares with the (supposed) non-propositional use of language in poetry. On the contrary, the extent to which we can achieve an understanding of either belief is precisely the degree to which they remain

25

obedient to the law of contradiction. (Obviously I am not arguing that only the propositional is coherent and fully accept Sperber's argument (1982) about the incidence of 'pre-propositional' ideas in many societies and areas of discourse. The point is, however, that they will not be intelligible to everyone until completed [see below] and if and when such pre-propositional terms are completed, completion is in conformity with, not abrogation of, the law of contradiction whose invariance is defended here.)

Crocker's reinvestigation of the Bororo (1977) found that the male statement 'we are red macaws' hinged on the facts that these birds are kept as pets by Bororo women and that men are dependent on women, given matrilineal descent and uxorilocal residence. The statement is thus an ironic comment upon the masculine condition (Sperber 1982 : 153) whose understanding involved no extension of 'our language in unpredictable ways' (Hesse 1980 : 38) for we say much the same in English with the metaphor 'henpecked'.

More generally, a claim to have rendered any metaphor or simili intelligible always depends upon 'cashing it in' propositionally (Hollis 1979a : 238). It means identifying at least one aspect of something which is consistent with something otherwise unlike it. Hence the explication of poetry is *not* non-propositional – Burns asserts the truth of his love sharing attractive properties with the rose but also, we can feel confident, the falsity of her 'being prone to black spot' or 'benefitting from mulching'.

The enigmatic statements of the Bororo turned out to be eminently commonsensical when linked to other ideas they had about themselves. Often puzzles are 'invented' by severing these connections. Thus Trinitarianism does become strange indeed if treated as though we had just come across the isolated assertion 'Firmly I believe and truly God is three and God is one'. The rest of Newman's hymn would only deepen the enigma – taken in isolation. Yet Trinitarian doctrine has a vast propositional history and, unlike Hesse, I maintain it is *publicly* understandable, that is intelligible to anyone, (a) through it and (b) not beyond it. The desperate struggles within the early Church (Doceticism or Gnosticism versus Arianism or Sabellianism [Bettenson 1967]) are perfectly comprehensible as attempts to advance consistent doctrine which avoided the *perceived contradiction* of asserting 'three persons in one'. Precisely because the Bishops of the first centuries were clear about the logical rules of intelligibility, they were equally aware that each of the above propositional interpretations, though logically consistent, had unacceptable implications (e.g. the Gnostic Chrisological doctrine reduced the second person to a phantasm *because* of its consistency – 'if he suffered he was not God; and if he was God he did not suffer'). Thus rather than accept any of the doctrines mentioned, the Councils took their stand on a semi-propositional belief, namely a mystery whose 'meaning (i.e. the proper propositional interpretation) is beyond human grasp' (Sperber 1982 : 175).

So, what sense can be made of Hesse's claim that we can extend our understanding and give intelligiblity to that which the faithful themselves deem a mystery? Certainly not through treating the Trinity to any meta-phorical or symbolist interpretation, for such were formally repudiated from the Creed of Nicea onwards. Just possibly (though utterly improbable in this case) an outsider may occasionally come up with a propositional inter-pretation, unthought of but acceptable to 'the natives'. But when this is so, it is a point in favour of logical invariance.

Thus I am arguing that *public* understandability of Trinitarian doctrine is exactly co-extensive with the law of non-contradiction being upheld within it and lapses with its suspension. Everyone can comprehend the doctrine 'before' it is deemed mysterious, but when faith sets in there is no means of comprehension for the outsider other than by being of the faith and sharing its mysteries. Anyone can comprehend 'afterwards', that is when the authority of the apostolic church becomes the basis of the belief. For then the rules of contradiction and consistency came back into play, to identify heterodoxy and define orthodoxy (Bettenson 1967 : 69), and these applications of authoritat-ive doctrine are matters again generally understandable. Public intelligibility then is a thread which breaks with the suspension of the law of contradiction. The suggestion that faith is penetrable is of course perfectly true because it can be embraced, but this does not advance Hesse's case. Since it is nonsense to claim that one professes more than one faith, it is even more nonsensical to predicate an extension of our understanding upon this state of affairs.

Nevertheless, Hesse is ultimately quite willing to grant to the proponents of invariance that there is 'a purely formal similarity of logical structure between belief systems', confident that she has only conceded something 'empty' since 'this says nothing whatever about the *content* of formal logical principles' (Hesse 1980 : 38-9). But my foregoing argument requires nothing more than the acceptance of this purely *formal* similarity of logical structure between belief systems. For *substantive* cross-cultural differences may also be super-ficial, their mere existence provides no direct evidence for relativism. Similarly, advocates of the 'strong programme' could indeed – courtesy again of biology – allow the invariance of the law of contradiction feeling secure that the last thing anyone could do is to employ it as a tool in comparative cultural analysis. For its use is predicated upon the ability to ascribe beliefs to social groups across time and space which depends upon their translatability. Since the relativist denies the possibility of successfully ascribing beliefs through translation, he could grant the universal rule safe in the conviction that one would only be able to use it locally! There is no harm in handing out a tool box, or benefit in receiving one, if the raw materials are then withheld.

II. The possibility of successful translation

Successful translation is a precondition of employing logical principles to attribute contradiction or consistency amongst alien beliefs or between those and our own. Unless we can feel confident in the beliefs we ascribe cross-culturally, nothing can be said about their relations. This confidence rests on the conviction that it is possible to produce adequate translations of the alien beliefs. Yet it is considered misplaced by founders of the 'strong' programme who are well aware that 'an anti-relativist argument' could 'be based simply upon the possibility of successful translation' (Barnes and Bloor 1982 : 39). For it is a necessary condition of a translation being correct that it matches sentences between languages with regard to truth-conditions, but for relativists of course this condition can never be met since what is true for the Nuer is not true for us. Thus, as Newton-Smith puts it economically, 'the possibility of translation entails the falsehood of relativism. By contraposition, the truth of relativism entails the impossibility of translation' (1982 : 114).

The standard rationalist approach to translation, as formulated by Hollis, depends upon the establishment of a bridgehead between two languages, that is 'a set of utterances definitive of the standard meanings of words' (1979a : 238). The investigator has to assume that 'he and the native share the same perceptions and make the same empirical judgements in simple situations', like the cow being in the corn. These simple perceptual situations serve to anchor communication and to get translation going by allowing the researcher to identify standard meanings for everyday native terms, uncomplicated by cultural variables. Each of these key assumptions is denied in the 'strong programme' which seeks to blow up the pass between one language and another. Thus to Barnes and Bloor 'learning even the most elementary of terms is a slow process that involves the acquisition from the culture of specific *conventions*. This makes apparently simple empirical words no different from others that are perhaps more obviously culturally influenced. There are no privileged occasions for the use of terms – no 'simple perceptual situations' – which provide the researcher with 'standard meanings' uncomplicated by cultural variables. In short, there is no bridgehead in Hollis's sense'. (Here the relativists ignore evidential support in areas like basic colour terminology [Berlin and Kay 1969] or geometric forms [Rosch 1977], where the perceptual system appears to determine linguistic categories instead of the other way round. Their arguments then amount to saying that the fact something is red and round plays the same role in leading us to believe that it is and that it isn't.)

Hence, advocates of the 'strong programme' conclude that 'perfect translation cannot exist: there can only be translation acceptable for practical purposes, as judged by contingent local standards' (Barnes and Bloor 1982 : 38). Were the commonsense protest made that the bridgehead serves perfectly well for getting over the Channel and into agreement with any French farmer that 'the cow is in the cowshed'/'la vache est dans l'étable', this kind of relativist could respond *either* by questioning the perfection of the translation *or* by stressing conventions shared by the speakers.

In the first case he could insist that these two sentences were only *pragmatic* equivalents by underlining the lack of precise equivalence between, perhaps, 'cowshed' and 'l'étable', or 'byre' and 'vacherie'. However, this reply does not carry any particular force in relation to *translation* since these terms show regional variations of equal magnitude within the 'same' language (Eng.

'cowshed', Scot. 'byre', Am. 'cowhouse'). Now this fact does not perturb Hollis' argument which is about the 'conditions of the possibility of language in general' (1979a : 230) – so what is true for two languages applies equally to one. But it does raise problems for the 'strong programme', for it carries relativism beyond the endorsement of 'many worlds', each with its own truths, into regress towards decreasingly small worlds, also incapable of exchanging truths. How small? Clearly not 'all English language speakers' – a region then? a community? a neighbourhood? or a small group of like-minded thinkers?

Alternatively, the relativist might suggest that the Common Market is really very parochial: an Englishman, a Scotsman and a Frenchman are all locals (joking cousins) but the 'strong programme' acquires its teeth when it has something on which to cut them, like really alien concepts couched in thoroughly foreign coventions. This seems to be the preferred line of attack since Barnes and Bloor maintain that 'the bridgehead fails as soon as it is measured against the realities of . . . anthropological practice' (1982 : 36). How?

They cite the case of Bulmer's work among the Karam of New Guinea where 'he found that many of the instances of what we would call 'bird' were referred to as 'yakt'. He also found that instances of bats were included amongst the 'yakt', while instances of cassowaries were scrupulously denied admittance to the taxon' (Barnes and Bloor 1982 : 38). These discoveries are taken to mean that the anthropologist had acquired the local culture of specific conventions. In other words, what Bulmer was doing was not the impossible act of translating: instead he was learning Karam conventions until he could pick out 'yakt' as well as they did.

Quite the reverse; the anthropologist had made standard use of the bridgehead in his fieldwork and without it could not have come up with the above translation, which is a quite different achievement from becoming a Karam amongst Karam. Bulmer started by going into the field through his first language (for as we will see a little later, he could not do otherwise), sensibly selected a simple perceptual object 'bird', and soon established a rough correspondence between it and 'yakt'. He could then pinpoint where the two terms did not overlap by proceeding just as Hollis suggests – pointing to a cassowary, saying 'yakt' and receiving a dissent sign, pointing to a bat, saying 'yakt' and commanding assent from the natives. All of which is *only* possible through the use of ostension and correction *in* 'simple perceptual situations'. (Indeed, if Hollis' methods *for* establishing the bridgehead is not on, neither is language learning on the relativists' account.)

The fact that there was imperfect equivalence between the two terms did *not* rule out use of the bridgehead, for there were enough of 'our' birds which were also 'yakt' to get the translation going and take it beyond the point sufficient for 'practical purposes', cropping up in the field, to a specification of the non-overlapping areas between the two classificatory terms. From there the anthropologist could move on to a task – open to the translator but not to the Karam amongst Karam – of trying to explain why there is cross-cultural variation in a classification. Note that Bulmer's paper which the relativists chose to use is entitled '*Why* is the cassowary not a bird?' (1967; my italics). Classifications in our own language change (whales were fish: whales are mammals), but changes in them are not matters of *mere* convention, there are always theoretical reasons for them. Far from the bridgehead argument being 'a plea for a single pure observation language' as the relativists claim (Barnes and Bloor 1982 : 39-40), it is the translator who takes Hesse's 'theory-dependence' of descriptive predicates (1974 : 16 f.) seriously, for only through translation can the theories be explicated and an account of why different ones are held by different language groups be offered – the relativists merely live with the theory, mono-linguistically. They are finally shown up as the real parochial pragmatists. But the possibility of addressing these crucial *comparative* questions, as of translation itself, depends on the existence of a bridgehead – its roughness and readiness are quite immaterial.

Not only will the bridgehead be rough and ready, it will also be floating rather than fixed. We advance with it in crab-like fashion, prepared to accept that the seemingly obvious truths we impute to aliens, in order to make sense of their actions, will undergo endless correction in the light of the evidential consequences of making such assumptions. The bridgehead is made and remade plank by plank – but which planks we change and which assumptions we alter is prompted by the resultant translations now making better sense than did their predecessors based on assumptions just discarded. Success in predicting the words and actions of those being translated confirms that the bridgehead can carry our weight. This is an empirical procedure validated by an empirical criterion (Lukes 1982 : 272).

Indeed, one of the most persuasive forms of substantiation is supremely empirical, namely that we have not yet failed. No anthropologist has yet come home to report the aliens 'incomprehensible' and the supply of tribes is drying up. Yet it remains conceivable that one day we may fail, if not on this earth, at least with extra-terrestrials. Quite rightly this is of no great concern, for the unknown is the unknown and its relationship with *any* theory is identical – simply unknown. Moreover, the appeal to life on other planets does no critical knife work. Take, for instance, Hesse's argument, intended to buttress the 'strong programme', to the effect that all cognitive terminology is 'relative to some set or sets of cultural norms' and that these 'might even *be as wide as biological humankind*, but if so, they would *still not* be rendered absolute or transcendentally *necessary in themselves*' (1980 : 56; my italics) – other worlds, other norms etc. Certainly the rationalist case is expressly and ineluctably predicated upon some version of the 'principle of Humanity' (Grandy 1973). Rationalism is indeed earthbound but this does not mean that it has feet of clay – for the translation of standard inter-galactic (if that is what Hesse's gesticulating E.T.s were emitting) would depend on the generalisability of some 'principle of Intelligent Life', from or to humanity, which thus demonstrated its necessity.

The necessity of translation

Protagonists of the 'strong programme' remain unruffled. They are ready to play their winning card and to demonstrate that they can do without translation altogether. Translation is necessary to the rationalist because without its beliefs cannot be ascribed to people of other places and times, in which case nothing can be said about the formal logical relations between these beliefs. Yet relativists also want to assert things about alien beliefs – very different things like their relationship to local conditions and conventions, but still assertions – so why is translation not equally necessary to them? How can theories be identified as alternatives or indeed known to be incommensurable if translating them is an impossibility? Their answer consists in circumventing the entire translation enterprise and making a direct assault on alien language and culture. As a strategy it could be called 'become as a child' or 'go native'. I shall argue that there are insuperable difficulties preventing the fulfilment of either injunction and that even if these could be spirited away it would not answer the above requirements and obviate the necessity for translation.

Before doing either, however, it is important to stress that quite regardless of whether my arguments prove convincing, their strategy *cannot* be a complete alternative to translation for it can only be attempted with other living people. Of its nature it deals only with the contemporary, with inserting oneself into some current alien context in order to assert its difference. By its nature it cannot then dispose of the necessity of translation when attempting to ascribe beliefs to the majority of cultural agents – for these are the dead. (Advocates of the 'strong programme' should feel bound, in consistency, to eschew pronouncements on the mathematical thought of ancient Greeks, Enlightenment ideas, Romanticism in eighteenth century Europe or the political ideas of Second Empire France, for the combined linguistic skills of these relativist authors could not have been exercised in discourse with the long dead.) However, let us conclude by turning to (i) to the strategy, (ii) to its defects, and (iii) to the reassertion of the necessity of translation.

(i) Hollis had defended the necessity of translation and developed his method of getting it going because where alien beliefs are concerned 'there is no more direct attack on meaning available' (1979b : 214). Barnes and Bloor question his premise and seek a substitute for his procedure. To them

> the fact is that translation is *not* the most direct attack on meaning that is available. It was not available, nor did it play any part at all, in the first and major attack that any of us made upon meaning when we acquired language in childhood. First language acquisition is not a translation process, and nothing that is absent here can be a necessary ingredient in subsequent learning. To understand an alien culture the anthropologist can proceed in the way that native speakers do. Any difficulties in achieving this stance will be pragmatic rather than *a priori*.

(1982 : 37)

Problems now arise because this (questionable) statement about acquiring a second language obfuscates the undoubted truth that the presence of a first language is an ingredient, willy nilly, in subsequent language learning. This leads to difficulties which are indeed *a prioristic* and not just pragmatic.

(ii) As language speakers we simply are unable to become as pre-linguistic children. One's mother-tongue cannot be cast aside, like leaving your shoes at the mosque door. Since all knowledge is conceptually formed (and therefore linguistically enshrined) then acquisition of a second language will inescapably be filtered through the first. Pragmatically, as anyone learning a foreign language knows, the ability to think in it comes fairly late on, *after* one has become proficient enough to stop translating-in-one's head! Theoretically the idea of becoming like the pre-linguistic child is uncomfortably close to the mythological being whom Gellner dubbed the 'Pure Visitor', creatures capable of divesting themselves of their conceptual clothing (1964) and surveying the cultural horizon from a decontaminated vantage point. Since linguistic strip-tease is not on, then it is an impossibility to 'go native' as the strategy recommends. It follows that, *a priori*, there is no alinguistic *entrée* accessible to existing language speakers.

Secondly, even were we to suspend these points for the purpose of argument, it is also the case that given the premises of the 'strong programme', there could be no 'return of the native'. For without the possibility of translation there is no way in which the investigator of alien beliefs who had gone through the business of 'becoming as a child' could then report back what the natives did believe. In other words, not only is there no *entrée*, there would also be no *exit*!

Anthropology would then become a curious study indeed. The role of its professors would reduce to saying 'If you want to understand the X, then go and live with them for five years as I did and then we will talk about the X in the X's language, replete with its conventions, reasons, truths, that is we will then talk together as natives'. It would remain impossible to ascribe beliefs to the natives and communciate these to others. And things get curiouser yet. For if one tries to imagine this capacity to move from one linguistic skin to another, stating and believing one thing in one language and something incompatible in another, then if translation is indeed an impossibility, one could not know that one was doing this oneself! In short, on the 'strong programme', *nothing comparative* can either be privately known or publicly communicated about alien beliefs.

(iii) Hence we come full-circle back to the necessity of translation. For, as Newton-Smith argues, 'if translation lapses so does the ascription of beliefs and the explanation of behaviour in action terms'. It becomes impossible to describe the behaviour of aliens as constituting particular actions or to explain it by reference to the beliefs and desires producing them. Translation cannot be set 'aside as something problematic for a relativist while going on to talk about beliefs and actions as if these notions would remain unproblematic' (1982 : 114).

Thus, if we cannot ascribe beliefs, the end result is that sociology has *no* role to play in explaining action. This must be handed over to behaviourism, materialism or indeed biology – in short anything which excludes reference to the determinate beliefs of human subjects. Thus the 'strong programme' ends up as the vanishing programme. Radical relativism sought to undermine 'Sociology for One World' (Albrow 1987), but taken to its logical conclusion it undermines the discipline altogether. Unless we accept as our basic axiom that 'if the natives reason logically at all, then they reason as we do' (Hollis 1979a), we effectively abolish the *human* subject (in favour of the conditioned or determined humanoid). The Principle of Humanity is well coined: it is not simply a methodological injunction but also an ethical safeguard.

References
ALBROW, M. 1987. 'Sociology for One World'. *International Sociology* 2 : 1-12.
BARNES, B. 1977. *Interests and the Growth of Knowledge*. London: Routledge.
BARNES, B. 1981. 'On the Hows' and Whys' of Cultural Change'. *Social Studies of Science* 11 : 481-98.
BARNES, B. and BLOOR, D. 1982. 'Relativism, Rationalism and the Sociology of Knowledge', in Hollis, M. and Lukes, S. (eds.), *Rationality and Relativism*. Oxford: Blackwell.
BERLIN, B. and KAY, P. 1969. *Basic Color Terms*. Berkeley: University of California Press.
BETTENSON, M. ed. 1967. *Documents of the Christian Church*. Oxford: Oxford University Press.
BLOOR, D. 1976. *Knowledge and Social Imagery*. London: Routledge.
BLOOR, D. 1978. 'Polyhedra and the Abominations of Leviticus'. *The British Journal for the History of Science* 11 : 39, 245-272.
BLOOR, D. 1981. 'The Strengths of the Strong Programme'. *Phil. Soc. Sci.* 11 : 199-213.
BLOOR, D. 1983. *Wittgenstein: A Social Theory of Knowledge*. London: Macmillan.
BULMER, R. 1967. 'Why is the cassowary not a bird?'. *Man* n.s. 2 : 5-25.
COLLINS, H.M. 1981. 'What is TRASP?'. *Phil. Soc. Sci.* 11 : 215-224.
CROCKER, J.C. 1977. 'My brother the parrot', in Sapir, J.D. and Crocker, J.C. (eds.), *The Social Use of Metaphor: Essays on the Anthropology of Rhetoric*. Philadelphia: University of Pennsylvania Press.
FREUDENTHAL, G. 1979. 'How strong is Dr. Bloor's Strong Programme'?'. *Studies in History and Philosophy of Science* 10 : 67-83.
GELLNER, E. 1964. *Thought and Change*. London: Weidenfeld and Nicolson.
GRANDY, R. 1973. 'Reference, Meaning and Belief'. *Journal of Philosophy* 70 : 439-452.
HESSE, M. 1974. *The Structure of Scientific Inference*. London: Macmillan.
HESSE, M. 1980. *Revolutions and Reconstructions in the Philosophy of Science*. Brighton: Harvester.
HOLLIS, M. 1979a. 'Reason and Ritual', in Wilson, B.R. (ed.), *Rationality*. Oxford: Blackwell.
HOLLIS, M. 1979b. 'The Limits of Irrationality', in Wilson, B.R. (ed.), *Rationality*. Oxford: Blackwell.
HOLLIS, M. and LUKES, S. eds. 1982. *Rationality and Relativism*. Oxford: Blackwell.
LAUDAN, L. 1981. 'The Pseudo-Science of Science', *Phil. Soc. Sci.* 11 : 173-198.
LUKES, S. 1979. 'Some Problems about Rationality', in Wilson, B.R. (ed.), *Rationality*. Oxford: Blackwell.
LUKES, S. 1982. 'Relativism in its Place', in Hollis, M. and Lukes, S. (eds.), *Rationality and Relativism*. Oxford: Blackwell.
MILLSTONE, E. 1978. 'A Framework for the Sociology of Knowledge'. *Social Studies of Science* 8 : 111-125.
NEWTON-SMITH, W. 1982. 'Relativism and the Possibility of Interpretation', in Hollis, M. and Lukes, S. (eds.), *Rationality and Relativism*. Oxford: Blackwell.
ROSCH, E. 1977. 'Human Categorisation', in Warren, N. (ed.), *Studies in Cross-Cultural Psychology*, I. Academic Press.
SPERBER, D. 1982. 'Apparently Irrational Beliefs', in Hollis, M. and Lukes, S. (eds.), *Rationality and Relativism*. Oxford: Blackwell.
WILSON, B.R. 1979. *Rationality*. Oxford: Blackwell.

SOCIOLOGY AS THE DEFETISHISATION OF MODERNITY

Agnes Heller

Were it only empirical sociology that we had in mind, the assertion that sociology is the 'diagnosis of modernity' would call for no further explanation. Empirical sociology operates in a time we may refer to as 'the absolute present'. Every research is conducted in the absolute present of 'now'. The genesis of any institution or community is a matter of interest only in so far as it is present in the memory of the members of the institution or community *now*. Moreover, every research is conducted in a particular 'here' and each and every 'here' is located in modern societies. When a research is conducted in a pre-modern social setting or in a pre-modern enclave of modern society we speak of 'anthropology' or 'ethnology' and this is not only a matter of vocabulary. However, the correctness of the introductory assertion is not quite so self-evident when we are referring to theoretical sociology. This is because theoretical sociology is an admixture of philosophy and sociology. No theoretical sociology which is not at the same time a philosophy is conceivable. But there is a constant tension between the philosophical and sociological aspects of theoretical sociology, and the tension is due to a divergence of the inherent logics of the two objectivations. Philosophy can be conscious of the time-space co-ordinates of its coming-to-existence; philosophy of history always is. But even if philosophy understands itself as historically rooted, its truth claim is and remains absolute: even if philosophers reflect upon the *locus* of their discovery, they formulate their truth *sub specie aeternitatis*, being in all times and with a message for all times. Philosophy has a tradition which goes back to ancient times and the rules of the game had therefore been set long before the dawn of modernity and cannot be undone unless the genre of philosophy itself is abandoned. Sociology as a genre, however, is the offspring of modernity and it wears the birthmark of modern parentage. Its mission is to understand the specificity of the modern world to which it belongs. The various sociological theories cope with this tension in different ways, but there is one thing in common in all of them. They

35

all formulate generalised statements they claim to be valid *sub specie aeternitatis*, and then all apply these statements, as a kind of meta-theory, to their particular theory of modernity. The dividing line between all pre-modern societies, on the one hand, and modernity, on the other hand, can be defined in different terms but the juxtaposition of pre-modern and modern societies is always essential. Pre-modern societies are contrasted to modernity first and foremost as a device to present the genesis and specific character of modernity in all its implications.

A leading contemporary sociologist, Niklas Luhmann, has contrasted pre-modern and modern societies in the following terms. Pre-modern societies were structured by stratification, whereas modern society is structured by the division of functions. Luhmann, in fact, juxtaposes functionalist society (the modern) to stratified society (the pre-modern). Thus, he challenges two kinds of sociology of knowledge: that of Mannheim and that of the phenomenological tradition. In the period when society was in the stage of transformation from the stratified model to the functionalist, social science was not yet possible. This is why social problems proper were understood and reflected upon in the framework of philosophical anthropology. If we disregard his systems-theoretical explanation and consider his diagnosis alone, it is clear that Luhmann has only spelt out, if in an extreme fashion, the common element in all theories of modernity. In juxtaposing labour and capital, Marx referred to the two basic functions of capitalist (modern) society. In emphasising the rationalisation of institutions in modernity, Weber too illustrated the functionalist character of this society. The organic division of labour in Durkheim is a functionalist concept of the division of labour. Similarly, Mannheim argued that in modern times a social function, that of the intellectuals, and not a class position, engenders true knowledge of totality. In Habermas, the critique of functionalist reason is one of the major tasks of modern communicative rationality. The difference between all these theories, systems-theories included, can be located on three levels. Firstly, functionalism can be regarded as one, but not the only, characteristic of modernity; secondly, functionalism can be acclaimed, treated with ambiguity or rejected outright; thirdly, the possible transcendence of a functionalist society can be either envisaged or dismissed. However, in all such cases the functionalist character of modern society is regarded as at least one, if not always the exclusive, foundation of modern social science, including sociology.

In pre-modern societies no sociology, as social science, was needed in order to formulate a true theory of society; philosophy performed this task admirably. The understanding of society from Plato to Hegel was by no means inferior in kind to the understanding of modern society by sociological theories. Sociology emerged precisely because philosophy alone cannot perform the same task in a functionalist society. Just as sociology needs to have a philosophical paradigm and a philosophical meta-theory, so too philosophy, if it wants to say anything relevant about modern societies, must be complemented with a sociological theory. Functionalist society places several important methodological constraints on philosophy. Sociological theory, and sociology generally, provides the wherewithal to cope with these methodological constraints.

The exigencies of our historical present are thus twofold. On the one hand, there is the historical exigency we share with each and every historical present: we can only conceptualise our present historical consciousness in each and every philsophy or theory we formulate. Moreover, we become conscious of the historical character of our consciousness; as far as the latter is concerned, we all are Hegelians or Marxists. In this respect we do differ from pre-modern actors and thinkers: even if their ideas were embedded in their particular present to the same extent, they were unaware of this circumstance, whereas we are aware of it from the start. Even hermeneutics, a philosophical enterprise so remote from those of Hegel or Marx, takes its point of departure from the historicity of consciousness. On the other hand, the methodological constraints I mentioned are due to the divided character of the historical consciousness of each and every individual in a functionalist society. (This consciousness is divided in the sense that its manifestations demand a different method in philsophy and social theory.)

In philosophy we can rely upon our good intuition as a final resort. Of course, good intuition is not a gift of heaven, it presupposes knowledge in the field we intuit. On what kind of knowledge is philosophical intuition based? It is based, firstly, on the knowledge of the lives, concerns, ideas and behavioural patterns of everyday actors, and secondly, on the knowledge of previous and contemporary philosophies. These two sources of knowledge are blended with the personal life experience of the philosopher, and if this is the case, good intuition may be the outcome. Good intuition does not, however, make a philosophical system for the new insights have to be properly conceptualised, and all assertions have to be argued for rationally. But as a starting point, good intuition suffices.

Aristotle, the author of the most complete social and political theory thus far known, was born in a stratified society. He shared the life experience of the stratum of 'free citizens'. Yet even in his lifetime, there were divergences in the form of life of free citizens, though all of them shared certain ideas about the idea of a 'good life' for the hierarchy of common values was, more or less, fixed. All free citizens performed, or could perform, more or less the same functions in the body politic; the division of technical and economic functions was only beginning to emerge. When Aristotle offered his idea about the good life he could rightly assume that he knew perfectly well the life patterns, concerns, ideas of all free men (irrespective of the technical or economic functions some of them may eventually have had to perform). He could also assume that this idea of the good life is but the perfected image of the understanding of the good life held by all free men. When he offered a theory of the state and economy, he could rightly assume that he had offered a perfected image of state and economy which every free person could and would share on the grounds of their intuition and rational argumentation. Intuition may be sufficient for creating philosophy or art works even in far less homogeneous societies. Lucien Goldmann, in his unjustly forgotten *opus magnum*, *The Hidden God*, made a case for the existence of a so-called 'group consciousness' in the times of French absolutism. It is not necessary to subscribe to the notion of 'group consciousness' to accept his conclusions in terms of which if a historically relevant social stratum, community or group shares a form of life, and thus a total life experience, the single member of this group can still intuit and thereby produce a body of knowledge or an art work expressing the shared life experience of this group to an extent which surpasses in clarity, radicality and homogeneity, the actual ideas of the other members of the group. And it is exactly this procedure that has become highly problematic in modernity, and outright impossible in modern social theory. Goldman himself became increasingly aware of the constraints of modernity, and was finally led to the conclusion that the concept of 'group consciousness' cannot be rationally applied to our epoch.

The modern question is not 'how true knowledge can be achieved', but 'how scientific knowledge is possible'. As is well-known, it was Kant with the epistemological foundation of natural sciences firmly in his mind who first posed the question in a modern form. The question of 'how social science is possible' was raised subsequently, with attempts to provide answers appearing ever since. Outlining a typology of the answers is beyond the scope of this study; it is only the theoretical implications of the question itself that will be addressed.

Let me reiterate: the production of meaningful world-views becomes a particular function in a functionalist society. People allocated to perform this function are called intellectuals. Sociologists (and social theorists) are intellectuals allocated to perform the function of practising 'social science'. They are educated by, and active within, particular institutions. Their life-experiences, ways of thinking and values may be divergent, but even the divergence itself emerges out of a commonly shared attitude different from the attitude of all people who perform social functions other than the creation of meaningful world-views. If 'practising social science' becomes a particular function, social theorists cannot obtain a true insight into society by relying on their own intuition alone. There is no reason to assume that in producing an 'image' about society as a whole or about particular social institutions, the result of intuition would be, or even could be, recognised as true by people who perform other social functions, operate with different kinds of knowledge, and within different kinds of institution. The social scientist does not know intuitively much about the life-experiences, ways of thinking or values of others; he or she can offer a true theory of society only after having acquired this knowledge. To a degree then, other subjects have to be treated as objects of research. There is no sociology without a measure of reification; scientific methodology includes reification. This circumstance does not arise as a problem for sociologists of a positivist persuasion, nor does it for systems theorists. However, this circumstance raises serious problems in all other schools of sociology, and not only for moral reasons. The question to be raised is whether true knowledge of society is possible at all if subjects are treated as objects. With this in mind I want to formulate the dilemma of sociology as it appears to me.

In modern (functional) society no true knowledge of society (sociology or social theory) is possible without the reification, at least to a certain degree, of subjects (actors). Philosophy, true to its tradition, does not, however, reify subjects (actors). But all social theories are in fact conceived under the aegis of a philosophical paradigm, a philosophical meta-theory. Sociology (social theory) has to cope with this dilemma; and in fact, even empirical sociology has, often unaware of its own philosophical presuppositions, become increasingly entangled in the above mentioned dilemma.

In what follows, I shall discuss the dilemma first as it appears in empirical sociology, and from there I shall proceed to social theory proper.

(a)   Empirical sociology collects relevant information about institutions, communities and strata of which the investigator is not a member. In organising a relevant survey, the investigator must assume that the members of the institutions, communities or strata in question can provide him or her with information he or she cannot otherwise achieve, and that the ideas, opinions and intuitions of the members of the group differ from his or her own. If this is not assumed, the survey is irrelevant as a survey: it serves only as a fake device to legitimise the intuitions of the sociologist. Of course, the empirical sociologist can operate with a preliminary hypothesis, under the proviso that the hypothesis can be proved false in the course of investigation. A self-abandonment to the opinions, ideas, intuitions of the members of groups or institutions other than those of the sociologists is a precondition of a good survey.

The opinions collected by the sociologists are opinions of subjects (actors), but these subjects are treated as objects by the sociologists. The subjects under scrutiny are no interlocutors: they answer, but do not ask, questions. They answer specific questions which are assumed to be relevant from the perspective of the sociologist, a member of another institution. Answering questionnaires is in itself an 'abnormal' situation for the members of the institutions under investigation. The 'abnormality' of the situation influences the subject-object to a greater or lesser degree. Partly as a result of the abnormality of the situation, partly as a result of the fixed character of the questions and the impossibility of a real dialogue, the answers will not completely express the opinions, ideas and the intuitions of the questioned subjects. What is called an 'uncertainty relation' in physics is obviously present in empirical sociology: the means of obtaining information influences the subject-object who provides information.

Nowadays efforts are made to circumvent the 'uncertainty relation' in empirical sociology though none can be completely successful. One can combine the survey with 'in-depth interviews', or, alternatively, the sociologist can pretend to be a member of the group or institution under scrutiny, and act, behave and intuit as such a member. One can engage in an 'in-depth interview' with each and every member of a group only if the group (institution) is very small, something which is definitively excluded in the case of basic groups or institutions of society. The same holds true of pretended membership. One can join the workforce in a factory, but the observations performed in a particular factory will hardly provide any relevant knowledge of opinions, forms of life and intuitions of 'factory workers'. Moreover, one cannot even guess whether or not 'factory workers' have any opinion, form of life or intuition in common at all. This is so primarily because, while the sociologist can become a member of an institution, he or she will not share thereby the way of life of other members outside the institution. Secondly, this is so because the very fact that he or she is a sociologist, influences his or her intuition. He or she is a member in order to observe; he or she cannot take for granted what others take for granted. Finally, the feigned membership of the sociologist poses serious moral problems: he or she will become a kind of 'spy' and, in principle, can misuse this situation by betraying confidence. But even if he or she does not (if he or she finally discloses his or her identity and achieves the consent of other members of the group to the publication of his or her findings), he or she nevertheless still treats other members of the group as objects. Even if the moral problem can be solved, the epistemological-methodological problem cannot. The reification of the subject can be counterbalanced, but it cannot be completely overcome.

(b)   The problem social theory proper is confronted with seems to be much more serious. In the final analysis, empirical sociology is able to reach the subject (the interrogated person), even if the subject is more or less reified in the process of investigation. However, theoretical sociology operates with generalised concepts of social structure or action. The individual subjects disappear with their opinions, ideas and intuitions behind these categories. Even if subjective aims, opinions, ideas and motivations are considered to be relevant (which is not always the case), they are not discovered or located but imputed. The social theorists first conceive a conception of the functioning of institutions, and then impute motivations, ideas and opinions to the members of those institutions or structures with which they are involved. It was Schutz who made this critical point against Weber. According to Schutz, Weber confused 'in order to' motives with 'because' motives; he inferred the motivation of action from the act already accomplished. Schutz's remark is quite correct, nonetheless, his criticism is irrelevant. In this context, the Lukacsian notion of 'imputed consciousness', if freed from its particular connotations, can be put to use. No theoretical sociologist can completely circumvent the procedure of imputing consciousness. Since no institution can function without people making them function, even extreme structuralists who treat the subject as an epiphenomenon, like Althusser, must impute consciousness to members of institutions. This is evidently even more valid in the case of certain versions of action theory.

One could obviously argue that social theories, precisely because of the imputation of consciousness, are less prone to the fallacy of reifying subjects than empirical sociology. One can reify individual subjects, not, however, social institutions for they are by definition non-subjects but objects (objectivations). Adorno, for example, did argue that the minds of individual subjects in modern capitalist society had already been reified, so that empirical sociology is guilty of a double reification: that of the method of investigation and that of accepting reified subjects as sources of true information. If Adorno's assertion is completely true, we are not entitled to speak of an 'uncertainty relation' in empirical sociology. However, the assumption that the minds of contemporary actors are completely reified, can only be true if the minds of the persons who make this statement are not reified, which cannot be the case if the mind of all contemporary actors is reified; therefore the statement itself cannot raise any truth-claim. Sociology and social theory are only possible then if the minds of our contemporaries are not seen as being completely reified. Although a critical assessment of collective opinions, ideas and intuitions is always necessary (and always involves a process of methodological reification), the critical assessment is based on the assumption that the members of any institution have some true opinions to offer.

True enough, theoretical sociology does not reify individual subjects for it does not deal with them directly. However, methodological reification cannot be circumvented in social theories either. As mentioned, theoretical sociology operates with generalised concepts of social structure and action. As far as they are sociological concepts proper (and not philosophical notions), they encompass social functions. Even if human relationships do not necessarily appear as relations among things, they do appear necessarily as relations among social functions. In a functional society, there is no other way to offer true knowledge about this particular society but through interpreting social relations as relations among social functions. In order to grasp the structural and action patterns of modern society, social science has to operate with fetishistic categories. Marx, the great critic of commodity fetishism, was no exception to this rule either. Labour as social function and capital as social function are not identical with the sum total of subjects of the cluster 'industrial workers', on the one hand, and with the sum total of subjects of the cluster 'capitalists', on the other. The concept of class, if it refers to modern, socio-economic classes, and not to castes and estates, is a fetishistic category. This is why the problem of designating the class position of social actors has remained unresolved in the Marxist tradition. If the concept referred to human relations, and human relations alone (relations among conscious subjects), the question 'who belongs to this or that class' would not and could not even have been raised. No one has seen it significant to ask the questions such as: Who belongs to the citizenry of a city state? Who is a serf? Who is a slave? Who is untouchable? – for these categories are not fetishistic, they refer to human relations (of equality or domination) alone. Indeed, Marx was the one who detected the emergence of fetishistic categories in modernity, if only in one dimension. But he was not less prone to operating with fetishised notions simply because he wanted to recommend a true theory of modern (capitalist) society.

The easiest way to exemplify the fetishistic character of our scientific notions is to examine a concept such as 'the state'. In pre-modern times philosophers asked who the state was: Aristotle, for example, defined the state as the 'sum total of citizens'. By contrast, modern social theory and sociology does not ask *who* the state is, but rather *what* the state is. The state is no longer supposed to be a sum total of definable persons, or a relationship between such persons. The question 'what is the state?' itself indicates that 'the state' is understood as a system or sub-system which performs a variety of functions in relation to 'civil society' or to other sub-systems of modern society. It further indicates that persons, and even various institutions active within the system, perform circumscribed functions under systemic constraint. But even if the state is understood as a system or sub-system, the simple question 'what is the state?' cannot be answered in a straightforward way. Habermas, for instance, has isolated a political sub-system (the system of power), but it would be a hasty conclusion to identify the state with this sub-system. Thus, oppositional parties might belong to the system of power but do they 'belong' to the state? To mention only one qualification, they do not participate in the monopoly of the legitimate use of force, the very characteristics Weber believed to be the function common to all modern states. Certain authors, among them Hannah Arendt, identify sometimes the government with the state (Arendt had in mind here only states with a two-party system). But if the government is the state and the government is elected, can we state, which sounds absurd, that the state is elected as well? Does the electorate belong to the state or not? Is bureaucracy the 'general estate' of the state, as Hegel believed, and as Weber was still very close to believing? In times when we could still ask who the state was, everyone knew exactly what the state was. In modern times, when we ask what the state is, we cannot find any unanimity. This is not a 'failure' of modern sociology, rather the outcome of increasing systemic complexity in modernity to which Luhmann refers or, to use Weber's expression, of the increasing rationalisation of modern institutions.

What was stated of the concept of 'state' can equally be stated of all concepts utilised by sociology (or social theory). Marx was right in emphasising that 'the market' is a fetishised category but so is, as we have seen, social class, 'civil society', 'economy' and the like. In order to arrive at non-fetishised categories, we would need to unambiguously identify the members of the groups and institutions captured by these categories. For example, if we do not refer to 'the state' as such, but rather speak of judiciary, legislative and executive powers as Montesquieu did, we know exactly what these powers are, for we know exactly who these powers are. We can state that parliament comprises legislative powers and we mean thereby the sum total of MPs; we have also identified one major function of the state, namely, legislation. But as long as we operate with the general (and fetishistic) concept of state, we cannot completely perform this reduction to particular functions. When in pre-modern times theorists referred to 'crafts', there was no doubt in their minds that they were speaking about the activity of craftsmen. But whose activity is industry? Whose activity is economy? Who belongs to civil society? These questions cannot be reasonably answered. We can answer the question who (how many) belong to this or that party, but we cannot answer the question who (how many) belong to the multi-party system. The question is wrongly posed and right questions can be asked as soon as we start to operate with fetishistic categories.

But if this is so, and if modern sociology (and social theory) must operate with fetishistic categories in order to raise relevant questions, how can sociology (and social theory) assert anything about human action at all? If we speak of action, we must speak of actors, that is to say subjects, moreover individual subjects. Collective action is nothing but the 'outcome' or 'aggregate' of the decisions of individual subjects. And even if the norms and strategies of action are intersubjectively constituted, the consensus is the outcome of the consent of each and every individual subject. Were sociology (or social theory) unable to cope with human action, it would be unable to grasp rationality as well. For rationality and non-rationality are attributes of action, and action alone (today we would also include speech acts). But rationality of action is a decisive characteristic of modernity. Consequently, if sociology (social theory) cannot explain or interpret rationality in modernity, it cannot explain (interpret) modernity at all.

The explanation (and interpretation) of human action (praxis) is a primordial, traditional task of philosophy. 'Rational action' (praxis) is by definition a non-reified category, for the actor (the subject) is the author of his or her action. Whether action is defined as moral action, political action or contemplation, whether it is attributed to *energeia*, 'practial reason', to good understanding or to speech, it was and has remained a philosophical construct. If we refer to the performance of a function as to an action, we conceive this performance under the guidance of a philosophical paradigm (or meta-theory).

After a detour we have returned to the dilemma of sociology, although on a more concrete level. Sociology (as social theory) must provide true knowledge about modern society. Modernity is characterised by increasing rationality and by increasing rationalisation. One can offer true knowledge about rationalised institutions (or the complexity of rationalised systems) only if one operates with reified (fetishistic) categories. One can only offer true knowledge about rational action if one performs social analysis under the guidance of a defetishised (or non-fetishistic) philosophical paradigm (or meta-theory). Social science, as a true account of modernity, is only possible if these two tasks can be performed within a common theoretical framework.

Sociologists can of course eliminate any genuine philosophical paradigm and construct their meta-theory from blocks of reified categories. Positivist theories do in fact embark on this course. Thus society will appear as quasi-nature, as a realm of necessity, of quasi-natural laws, of 'laws of development', of self-producing systems, of subjectless structures. Such theories embrace rationalisation without account for rational action; this is why they cannot provide a basis for true knowledge of modernity.

Alternatively, sociologists can eliminate the use and application of all reified categories and construct a social theory out of the blocks of a philsophical meta-theory. Philosophies of 'praxis' and mere action theories embark on just such a course, and society, here, will appear as the sum total of individual and collective actions. In this presentation, everything is in flow, everything is possible, everything depends on will and consciousness. Such theories embrace rationality without account for rationalisation; this is why they too cannot provide true knowledge of modernity.

Both Marx and Weber recognised the exigency of accounting for both rationalisation and rationality. Marx imputed consciousness to a reified category (class) and made a reified entity the rational actor of modernity. Weber typified action and, as we know from Schutz's criticism, imputed typical motivations (consciousness) to actors from the perspective of the accomplished act. Put bluntly, he reified action itself. But finally Schutz fared no better himself. Although he proved that the Weberian solution does not stand the criticism of a philosophical theory of consciousness accounting for the actions of individual-real subjects, when it came to providing a grounding for sociology, Schutz too ended up constructing 'ideal types' himself. The only thing he finally proved is that in the world of our 'consociates' we do not need social science to achieve true knowledge. However, even at the level of everyday life, that of face-to-face encounters, intuition cannot be the basis of true knowledge once we move away from the milieu we were born into and thus from that which we 'take for granted'. We know that in empirical sociology we inevitably reify subjects though this occurs, to a degree, in face-to-face encounters as well. Forms of life in modernity, if there are such, are pluralistic and fragmented so that we cannot understand them via pure insight. Schutz was aware of this difficulty and this is why he finally accepted a solution he had first challenged.

The best attempt so far to solve the problem can be found in the social theory of Habermas. It accounts for both rationalisation and rationality and terms them 'system-rationality' and 'communicative rationality'. His philosophical meta-theory accounts for communicative rationality, whereas his systems-theory accounts for the rationalisation of functionalist society. The philosophical theory also provides the critique of functional reason (of the system). Although social theory is subjected to a philosophical paradigm, methodologically they remain worlds apart (on the one hand, a theory of speech acts and consensus, on the other hand, the method of 'reconstruction'). Apart from the philosophical problems inherent in the communication paradigm and the consensus theory of truth, which we cannot tackle here, it should be remarked that this divergence in method leads to his sharp division between 'social integration' and 'system integration'. This is why Habermas is still entangled in difficulties which, as far as the functioning of systems is concerned, are positivist in nature.

To conclude, sociology (both empirical and theoretical, although in different ways) is the exigency of our historical age, modernity. Social sciences which raise a truth claim in their endeavours to grasp modernity have to account for both rationalisation and rationality. They have to combine systems theory and action theory. They have to operate with fetishistic (reified) categories, and they must reify actors methodologically, but they will only become true theories if they proceed to perform this task under the guidance of a philosophical paradigm (or meta-theory) which defetishises (or de-reifies) human subjects, action, speech, consciousness.

CONCEPTUAL FRAMEWORKS IN COMPARATIVE INQUIRY: DIVERGENT OR CONVERGENT?*

Piotr Sztompka

Incommensurability of concepts

One of the perennial methodological riddles of comparative sociology is the incommensurability of concepts[1]. The plurality, variety and heterogeneity of meanings encountered in human societies repeatedly engenders the query so aptly phrased by C. Osgood: 'When is the same really the same? When is the same really different? When is different really the same? When is different really different?' (Przeworski and Teune 1970: 11).

The problem has deep ontological roots and related methodological implications, which have been recognised and pursued within the rich tradition of humanistic sociology, from Max Weber to Alfred Schutz and beyond. The crux of the matter is that human societies and all they are made of – actions, institutions, groups, organisations, roles, and what not – are endowed with shared meanings by their members, and in this sense produced, created, constructed. As contemporary authors put it: 'every society can be seen as a precariously put together fabric of meanings by which human beings seek to find guidance for their lives' (Berger and Kellner 1981: 74). 'Meaning complex', 'relevance-structure', 'life world', 'axionormative system', 'cognitive map', 'collective self-interpretation' are just some of the terms used by sociologists to grasp this fundamental peculiarity of the social world, distinguishing it clearly from the extra-human domain. In the words of A. Schutz:

> The world of nature, as explored by natural scientists, does not 'mean' anything to the molecules, atoms and electrons therein. The observational field of the social scientist, however, namely the social reality, has a specific meaning and relevance structure for the human beings living, acting and thinking therein.
>
> (Schutz 1975: 272-3)

*This paper was presented at the thematic session 'The Trans-National Meaning of Concepts' of the 82nd Annual Meeting of the American Sociological Association in Chicago, August 17-21, 1987.

The same idea is crucial for F. Znaniecki's 'humanistic coefficient':

> The scientist who wants to study ... actions inductively must take them as they are in the human experience of those agents and re-agents; they are his empirical data inasmuch and because they are theirs.
>
> (Znaniecki 1969: 221)

The methodological significance of this peculiarity is obvious in *any* sociological investigation which – by necessity – approaches the meaningful world, already pre-constituted, pre-structured, pre-articulated, pre-interpreted by its participants. The sociologist has to order what is already ordered, to map what is already mapped, to interpret what is already interpreted.

The resulting methodological dilemmas, encountered to some extent in every sociological inquiry, are even more acute when a researcher faces alien, foreign societies or cultures, with their idiosyncratic, seemingly bizarre, conceptual conventions. This has always been a predicament of social anthropologists who, by the very nature of the job, deal primarily with 'primitive societies', 'savage cultures', 'illogical mentalities' etc. It is not by accident that the involved philosophical and methodological debate on ethnocentrism and relativism has been conducted mainly by social anthropologists or philosophers inspired by the experience of social anthropology[2].

But the gravest consequences of the meaningful constitution of social reality appear only when several distinct societies are studied by means of a comparative method. It is only in the context of comparative research that the problem of the incommensurability of concepts receives its full formulation. If every human society is a peculiar, self-contained universe of meanings devised by its members, is inter-societal comparison at all possible? Aren't we comparing uncomparables? How to raise oneself above the uniqueness and specificity of the cases studied? Where to seek for some common denominators of divergent worlds? How to construct a platform from which to appraise the variety of human societies, so to speak, from afar and from the outside[3]? Some answer to these and similar questions has to be given by every self-critical, methodologically aware comparative researcher. Most often the answer is only implicit:

> Part and parcel of the sociologist's enterprise is comparison. If the sociologist compares different societies and their divergent meaning systems, he *ipso facto* assumes that there is a plane on which such comparison is possible, and this assumption is part of his relevance structure while doing sociology. There is a further implication to this – namely, that *all* human societies and meaning systems have some things in common.
>
> (Berger and Kellner 1981: 72)

But is this assumption justifiable? Anyway, it certainly cannot be taken for granted, and requires precise explication.

In the practice of comparative research, the problem of incommensurability emerges already in the phase of data-gathering. For example, it becomes manifest when questionnaires are addressed to respondents from disparate societies, for whom seemingly similar questions appear to have quite diverse connotations. Or when common indicators are construed for cross-cultural purposes, but acquire quite different denotations in various societies. Or when variables are specified and scales devised, which turn out to measure quite discrepant dimensions in various social and cultural contexts. Such and similar difficulties have often been discussed in methodological literature under the label of reliability and validity of concepts, and several technical remedies were proposed by means of operationalisation, precisation, definition, elucidation, formalisation of concepts. Even though I am a little suspicious of the positivistic overtones of such attempts[4], I do not feel competent to enter the debate at this level.

There is another level, much more neglected and, to my mind, crucial. I mean the theory-building phase of comparative inquiry; the formulating of explanatory propositions and proposing theoretical explanations of data. How does the riddle of incommensurability affect sociological theorising? Here not much of substance can be discovered in methodological literature. Reason enough to take up this question as my exclusive concern in the discussion below.

Societal versus sociological concepts

At the level of theory construction, the crux of the issue is a duality of concepts with which a sociologist has to deal. As was emphasised before, the subject-matter, human society, is infused with meanings by societal members; it is articulated in terms of specific concepts by the participants in social life, who assign certain sense to their own actions, institutions, groups, organisations and the like. Such concepts, which I shall call *societal*, are constitutive components of social reality. As E. Gellner puts it:

> Concepts and beliefs are themselves, in a sense, institutions amongst others; for they provide a kind of fairly permanent frame, as do other institutions, independent of any one individual, within which individual conduct takes place.
>
> (Gellner 1970: 115)

Sociological theory is, at least in part, *about* such concepts; they fare in the *explanandum* of a theory.

But there are also different concepts, couched by sociologists for identifying, describing and – most importantly – explaining social phenomena. They are *sociological* concepts. Sociological theory is formulated *in terms of* them; they appear in the *explanans* of a theory[5].

Societal and sociological concepts make up two distinct universes of discourse. In the inimitable poetics of A. Schutz:

> The thought objects constructed by the social scientist, in order to grasp ... social reality, have to be founded upon the thought objects constructed by the common-sense thinking of men, living their daily life within their social world. Thus, the constructs of the social sciences are, so to speak, constructs of the second degree, namely constructs of the constructs made by the actors on the social scene, whose behaviour the social scientist has to observe and explain in accordance with the procedural rules of his science[6].
>
> (Schutz 1975: 273)

The dilemmas of comparative inquiry stem both from the plurality, variety and heterogeneity of ways in which members of various societies envisage social reality to which they belong, and from the plurality, variety and heterogeneity of ways in which sociologists envisage social reality from the perspective of various theoretical orientations with which they identify. Thus, the problem of incommensurability may be rephrased and specified by means of two distinct questions:

- for the level of societal discourse: are *trans-societal meanings* available? can common denominators be found for the variety of particular, local, 'situated' societal conceptual frameworks?
- for the level of sociological discourse: are *trans-theoretical meanings* available? can common denominators be found for the variety of particular theoretical orientations with their characteristic sociological conceptual frameworks?

Uncritical ethnocentrism and its twin – theoretical dogmatism – pretended to solve the riddle by arbitrary *fiat*: it is the perspective of my own society or of my own theory which are the ultimate measuring rods of other societies and other theories; they provide the only rational, or true, or right, or valid, concepts. It took time to unravel the excesses and fallacies of ethnocentrism and dogmatism, only to land in the trap of radical relativism and theoretical anarchism. As witnessed all too often in intellectual history, the pendulum has swung back too far to the other extreme. Thus, it is often claimed nowadays that societies and cultures constitute mutually impermeable worlds, and that their societal concepts are fundamentally divergent. Each has a sense only in its native context, and each is equally valid as another[7]. And it is also claimed that sociological theories constitute mutually closed intellectual domains, and that their sociological concepts are totally disparate. Each has a sense only in the context of native theory, and each is equally valid as another[8]. Here, the issue of incommensurability is treated as a fundamental, ineradicable obstacle to comparative inquiry. Neither trans-societal, nor trans-theoretical concepts are to be found, as they are always embedded in concrete contexts – of societies or of social theories, respectively.

I find the position of radical relativism and theoretical anarchism equally untenable as the ethnocentrism and dogmatism they have replaced. My refutation of them, and my search for the third way, opening new directions and new perspectives for comparative research, is grounded in a rather unorthodox argumentation. Namely, I will abandon traditional logical, formal or philosophical considerations and turn instead toward factual, substantive, historical circumstances obtaining at the end of the twentieth century. In the long discussions of relativism, one important sort of relativism was somehow forgotten: the necessity to discuss methods in relation to the subject-matter studied. And it was overlooked that, while debates on comparative method were going their merry way, society itself underwent profound changes.

I will claim that the actual historical tendencies, both in the social world and in the sociological world, work toward growing convergence and commensurability of societal as well as sociological concepts. The trans-societal and trans-theoretical concepts are more and more available, the riddle of incommensurability is getting resolved, and new emphases and opportunities for comparative inquiry present themselves. This is the claim in a nutshell. Now, let me proceed to give at least an outline of a proof.

Globalisation of society and internationalisation of sociology

To simplify matters, I propose to think in terms of extreme, polar types, providing only very rough approximations to complex historical realities. It will be enough for my purpose, as I wish only to suggest some overall, general tendencies.

One extreme case is the social world made up of numerous, heterogeneous, differentiated, isolated, self-contained units: tribes, clans, ethnic groups, nations, states and the like. And – at the sociological level – the world made up of mutually exclusive and conflicting schools, or even academic sects. This is, roughly, the world facing the founders of sociology in the nineteenth century, as well as the classics of social anthropology at the beginning of the twentieth century. The world for which the problem of incommensurability is very relevant indeed, at both levels – societal and sociological.

But, since that time, the world has undergone tremendous changes. Two persistent trends which I wish to single out, because of their implications for the problem of incommensurability, may be called the globalisation of society and the internationalisation of sociology.

Under the impact of various economic, political and technological developments, and particularly the revolution in communications and flows of information – the social world has almost literally shrunk, coming closer to what M. McLuhan calls a global village (1964), I. Wallerstein a world-system (1974, 1980) and C. Tilly 'our own, single-network era' (1984: 61). At the same time, the social world has changed the typical modes of its internal articulation or structuralisation. Due to growing worldwide interconnectedness of societies, several social phenomena have acquired a truly global scale. According to C. Tilly:

> A sensible rule of thumb for connectedness might be that the actions of powerholders in one region of a network rapidly (say within a year) and visibly (say in changes actually reported by nearby observers) affect the welfare of at least a significant minority (say a tenth) of the population in another region of the network. Such a criterion indubitably makes our own world a single system; even in the absence of worldwide flows of capital, communications, and manufactured goods, shipments of grain and arms from region to region would suffice to establish the minimum connections.

(Tilly 1984: 62)

Differentiation into local communities, tribes, clans, ethnic groups, nations, even states, has lost at least some of its former significance. Their borderlines have become more fluid, and much more comprehensive wholes have emerged as crucial – political and military blocks, regions, economic areas, global networks – most often of a vertical, hierarchical rather than horizontal structure, with clearly demarcated centres and gradations of peripheries or dependencies. E. Tiryakian (1985: 118-134) addresses this tendency as one aspect of the processes of de-differentiation, J. Naisbitt (1984) includes it among his pervasive 'mega-trends', E. Gellner observes: 'The requirement that societies be seen as

51

unities is unsatisfiable for most societies in the modern world, and in view of their size, complexity, and in view of the difficulties of delimiting "societies"' (1970: 118-9). I put all those tendencies together under the label of globalisation[9].

What happens to societal meanings and concepts entertained by the common people in such a globalised world? Obviously, they undergo far-reaching uniformisation due to double mechanisms. First, the actual experiences, ways of life and social conditions become more alike. And, second, even if they remain different, the knowledge of foreign experiences, ways of life, social conditions becomes more accessible – through travel, tourism, mass media, personal contacts. Provincial ignorance turns into a more cosmopolitan imagination. Similarity of actual experiences, or at least access to information about alien experiences, opens up the actual, or at least vicarious, possibility of either re-living or imagining a multiplicity and variety of possible social arrangements. What social anthropologists called the contextual reinterpretation or relativisation becomes available as daily practice for common people. Consequently, their meaning-systems, conceptual frameworks and relevance structures undergo mutual accommodations. Even if they still differ in beliefs and interpretations, members of various societies begin to understand each other instead of talking past each other. The trans-societal meanings emerge not as a result of methodological tricks, but of a real historical process. The problem of incommensurability of societal concepts becomes definitely less acute than before.

The parallel process is occurring at the level of sociological community and affects the character of sociological concepts. Sociology becomes globally recognised as a valid mode of inquiry, as legitimate discipline with more or less similar scope and method[10]. What F. Gareau (1985) calls 'global communication systems' among sociologists are established and institutionalised by means of international associations, journals, conferences etc. Local, national or regional specificity is becoming ever more tenuous and is gradually replaced by differences of theoretical and methodological orientations, embracing scholars from various countries or parts of the world[11]. And in the domain of sociological theories themselves a similar, unifying tendency seems to reign, with the characteristic emphasis on 'theoretical openings' (Eisenstadt and Curelaru 1976), 'dialectic synthesis' (Sztompka 1979b), 'disciplined eclecticism' (Merton 1976), or 'multidimensional approaches' (Alexander 1982, 1987). For the present purposes I cover all those trends by the term internationalisation of sociology.

What happens to sociological meanings and theoretical concepts used by sociologists in such an expanding international academic milieu? Obviously they also pass through the process of uniformisation: homogenisation of perspectives and mutual accommodation of relevance structures. First of all, there is a growing canon of concepts taken out of particular theoretical contexts, and recognised as common by sociologists of all theoretical or methodological persuasions, as indispensable tools of the sociological trade[12]. And, second, there is a growing pool of synthetic, multidimensional concepts bridging the gap between various theories, comprising components originating in different theoretical traditions[13]. As a result, trans-theoretical meanings become widely available. The problem of the incommensurability of sociological concepts loses some of its earlier urgency.

The paradox of comparative research

To repeat, if my diagnosis of historical trends has any merit, then the problem of incommensurability at both levels – of societal and of sociological concepts – seems to be fading away. One of the major obstacles to comparative inquiry is getting overcome by the historical changes in the very subject-matter of comparative research, and in the constitution of investigating communities. On the face of it, the chances of comparative studies seem better than ever. But here we stumble upon a baffling paradox.

Let us remind ourselves of the famous 'Galton's problem': the observation by the British statistician that valid comparison requires mutually independent and isolated cases, and therefore cultural diffusion, cultural contact, culture clash or outright conquest – with their consequent borrowing, imitation, migrations etc. – invalidates the results of comparative studies[14]. If this was true of Galton's epoch of 1889, it is even more true a century later when the interdependent, closely interlinked global world-system is becoming a reality. The same historical forces, which eliminate the problem of incommensurability, make Galton's problem more immediate and pressing. Comparative research seems in principle easier, but unfortunately basically unattainable.

Luckily, in all this argument there is one important 'if'. There is really no way out and the paradox is truly damaging only if one assumes that comparative inquiry has just one possible mode and one possible format – it is predestined to follow the logic of quasi-experimentation. This assumption is unfounded. The comparative method is not of a piece, and allows for large variety. The mode and format of comparative inquiry has to be matched to the realities of the world subjected to such study. In the dramatically changed world of the twentieth century, the goals and directions of comparisons must be different from those in the societies of the nineteenth century in which the comparative method originated and acquired its early codifications.

To bring this specificity of contemporary comparativism into focus, we must put it against the background of other possible research options. This requires a brief excursus toward a systematic typology of some alternative forms of comparative inquiry.

Uniformity in variety or uniqueness in uniformity?

The rationale of such typology is found in the observation that the ultimate goal of comparative inquiry, like any sociological inquiry, is the formulation of true propositions about society. In turn, the sociological propositions, like any scientific propositions, may be analysed in terms of three distinct dimensions. First is the scope of applicability: the delimitation of an area or a system (by historical, geographical criteria) within which a proposition is found to hold. This dimension ranges from maximum inclusiveness (e.g.

on Earth) to extreme exclusiveness (e.g. only in Burkina Faso). Second is the scope of objects: the delimitation of a class or a category of entities (by typological criteria) to which the proposition refers. This dimension ranges from the widest universality (e.g. human beings) to the narrowest specificity (e.g. workers in the cotton industry). Finally, the third dimension is the scope of predicates: the delimitation of properties and traits attributed by a proposition to certain objects. This covers the scale from the greatest generality (e.g. reward) to full concreteness (e.g. wage)[15].

The focus of comparative inquiry may vary accordingly: it may be mainly concerned either with modifying the scope of applicability, or with changing the scope of objects, or with altering the scope of predicates. And, what is most important for our considerations, the directions of those attempted modifications may differ too. In some cases it is the extensive direction: the point is to widen the scope of applicability (e.g. to speak not only of Burkina Faso but of African societies), or the scope of objects (e.g. to speak not only of workers but of the labour force), or the scope of predicates (e.g. to speak not only of theft but of crime). In short, the attempt is to seek for commonalities and uniformities among variety. There is a cognitive gain in extending the range of systems, entities or traits covered by the proposition (its systematising power with respect to diversified phenomena; ability to subsume them under common regularities), but only at the cost of lower informational content (its interpreting power). We know *about more*, but we know less, in the sense of detail, concreteness and specificity.

But the direction of comparative inquiry may be quite the opposite: intensive rather than extensive. The point then is to narrow down the scope of applicability, or the scope of objects, or the scope of predicates: to delimit it more precisely, and to find out more about cases included – their individual traits, specific qualities and concrete characteristics. In short, the attempt is to seek for divergences, uniqueness among uniformity. For example, we want to know why it is only *in Poland* that the Church is so strong among other Eastern European countries; or why it is *young, educated workers* who are most prone to rebel against oppressive political systems; or why *economic grievances* are most likely to mobilise social movements. The gain in informational content (interpreting power) is paid by the loss of comprehensiveness (systematising power). We know more, but *about less*. Unfortunately, as so often in life, one can't have it both ways.

Combining and cross-tabulating two criteria - the focus and the direction of research – we arrive at the six-fold typology of comparisons, and corresponding modes of comparative inquiry: (1) encompassing, (2) universalising, (3) generalising, (4) individualising, (5) specifying, (6) particularising. This is represented by means of the scheme shown in Figure 1.

The rationale of traditional comparative method was to seek uniformities in the sea of differences; to show that certain regularities hold in other societies as well, or that they hold for other categories of people, or that they extend to other social characteristics. This was inspired by a naturalistic methodological creed; an attempt to imitate the logic of experiment. It was

Modes of Comparative Research

		The focus of comparative research		
		Scope of applicability	Scope of objects	Scope of predicates
The directions of comparative research	Seeking uniformities	Encompassing comparisons	Universalizing comparisons	Generalizing comparisons
	Seeking uniqueness	Individualizing comparisons	Specifying comparisons	Particularizing comparisons

also encouraged by the cognitive situation, in which plurality, heterogeneity, variety and relative isolation of separate societies was the reality of the day. What was really baffling and problematic was the discovery of commonalities; the diversity could be easily taken for granted.

The globalisation of the social world brought about the complete reversal of the cognitive situation. What really becomes baffling and problematic is the preservation of enclaves of uniqueness amid growing homogeneity and uniformity. At the same time, methodological creeds are also radically changed, with the widespread anti-naturalist backlash and the ascendance of the humanistic, interpretive, qualitative, 'soft' approach. In sum, the emphasis shifts to the alternative types of comparative inquiry: seeking uniqueness among uniformities, rather than uniformity among variety. Thus, in individualising comparisons the point is now to unravel the peculiarities of a given country, or area, or region, by contrasting it with others[16]. In specifying comparisons the point is to delimit as precisely as possible a category of people exhibiting certain motivations, possessing certain attitudes, being prone to certain actions etc., by contrasting them with other people. In particularising comparisons, the point is to make as concrete as possible the set of traits characteristic for people of a certain kind – be it motivations, beliefs, attitudes etc., by contrasting them with less typical traits.

Needless to add, I find these uses of comparative method patently fit for the realities of contemporary social world, and most commendable for various methodological reasons. Not the least important for the present discussion is the fact that in the context of uniqueness-seeking comparisons the riddle of incommensurability finally transforms the methodological predicament into a research opportunity. Namely, the remaining, residual specificity of conceptual frameworks becomes a subject-matter worthy of studies both in its own right, and as an aspect or indicator of some wider uniqueness. If we detect enclaves of peculiar, idiosyncratic societal meanings amidst the growing uniformity of the social world, or if we detect enclaves of peculiar, idiosyncratic sociological meanings held to by some sociological communities in spite of the growing internationalisation of sociology – it will raise serious questions and require systematic explanation by comparative sociologists, or sociologists of sociology respectively.

The additional heuristic bonus of such research into the peculiarities of meanings is that it sensitises the scholar to the historical dimension of the social world; it inevitably invokes a historical perspective. The idiosyncratic meanings cannot but be treated as the accumulated crystallization of former social experiences – particular historical fates of a given society or a given academic community. The only reasonable explanation of the divergences of meanings in an otherwise convergent – globalised and internationalised – world is the history of past divergences; the varieties and peculiarities of unique chains of historical tradition.

The shift of emphasis from the uniformity-seeking to uniqueness-seeking comparisons is just a symptom of a wider intellectual development: taking sociology away from the misleading cognitive patterns of natural science (epitomised by the logic of experiment), toward more relevant patterns of history and humanities (epitomised by the logic of interpretation) (see Sztompka 1986). To this paradigmatic shift the reformed comparative research has much to contribute.

Notes

1. In the appraisal of a contemporary commentator 'this problem is the one whose importance is least doubted by thoughtful anthropologists of every point of view. Most behavioural scientists from other disciplines also give it great weight' (Naroll 1968: 267).

2. Some recent examples would include: Hollis and Lukes (1982); Jarvie (1984); Wilson (1984 [1974]); Gellner (1985).

3. An obvious parallel to Galileo's problem of where to find a support for the lever to move the globe from its orbit.

4. Just an example from Przeworski and Teune (1970: 12): 'Most problems of uniqueness versus universality can be redefined as problems of measurement'. I doubt it. More fundamental issues are at stake.

5. More about my understanding of a theory as an explanatory structure in Sztompka (1979a: 173-94).

6. The complicating fact is that the two universes – of societal and sociological meanings – are not strictly isolated, but rather interpenetrate each other. Sociological concepts are often infused with common-sense connotations, and societal concepts sometimes borrow connotations from scientific, sociological language. As Jarvie (1972: 171) depicts it: 'the difference of depth between the maps of ordinary chaps and the maps of sociological chaps is not yet very great. Social scientists are constructing maps which include the maps of other chaps as part of the landscape. But their maps also overlap, to a considerable extent, with those of ordinary people who co-inhabit the society with them'. For analytical purposes I have nevertheless to abstract from this difficulty and proceed with the discussion at two levels - of societal and sociological concepts – treated separately.

7. This kind of 'sociological solipsism' seems to me close to the position taken by P. Winch (1958).

8. One can encounter such a standpoint in some of the earlier works of J. Habermas.

9. This is not an evolutionism in disguise. I do not assume any necessity or inevitability of this process. It simply happens to be the case in the twentieth century. And this contingent development happens to have implications for the methods of social studies. This is all that is claimed here.

10. Just one of more spectacular instances of this trend is the recent career of sociology in China.

11. Instead of differentiating Polish, German, French, or American sociologists, it is much more meaningful to speak about functionalists, ethnomethodologists, Marxists, phenomenologists, exchange theorists etc.

12. It is hardly remembered any more that standard sociological concepts – like group, community, norm, value, role, institution, status, action, nation etc. – originated in specific sociological theories. Their link with them is completely severed.

13. For example, the concepts of a class, alienation, anomie, rationality, development, progress and many more.

14. Naroll (1968: 258-262) discusses some aspects of Galton's problem.

15. I develop such an analysis of sociological propositions in a Polish article (Sztompka 1974: 51-86). It was presented at the World Congress of Sociology at Toronto in 1974.

16. I borrow the term from Tilly (1984) who uses it with reference to a similar type of historical comparison.

References

ALEXANDER, J.C. 1982. *Theoretical Logic in Sociology*, Vol. 1. London: Routledge & Kegan Paul.

ALEXANDER, J.C. 1987. *Twenty Lectures*. New York: Oxford University Press.

BERGER, P.L. and KELLNER, H. 1981. *Sociology Reinterpreted*. Garden City: Anchor.

EISENSTADT, S.N. and CURELARU, M. 1976. *The Form of Sociology: Paradigms and Crises*. New York: Wiley.

GAREAU, F.H. 1985. 'The Multinational Version of Social Science with Special Emphasis upon the Discipline of Sociology'. *Current Sociology* 33 (3).

GELLNER, E. 1970. 'Concepts and Society', in Emmet, D. and MacIntyre, A. (eds.), *Sociological Theory and Philosophical Analysis*. New York: Macmillan.

GELLNER, E. 1985. *Relativism and the Social Sciences*. Cambridge: Cambridge University Press.

HOLLIS, M. and LUKES, S. 1982. *Rationality and Relativism*. Oxford: Blackwell.

JARVIE, I.C. 1984. *Rationality and Relativism*. London: Routledge & Kegan Paul.

McLUHAN, M. 1964. *Understanding Media*. New York: McGraw-Hill.

MERTON, R.K. 1976. 'Structural Analysis in Sociology', in *Sociological Ambivalence and Other Essays*. New York: Free Press. pp. 109-44.

NAISBITT, J. 1984. *Megatrends*. London: Futura.

NAROLL, R. 1968. 'Some Thoughts on Comparative Method in Cultural Anthropology', in Blalock, H.M., Jr. and Blalock, A.B. (eds.), *Methodology in Social Research*. New York: McGraw-Hill.

PRZEWORSKI, A. and TEUNE, H. 1970. *The Logic of Comparative Social Inquiry*. New York: Wiley.

SCHUTZ, A. 1975. *On Phenomenology and Social Relations*. Chicago: University of Chicago Press.

SZTOMPKA, P. 1974. 'O prawach socjologicznych' ('On Sociological Laws'). *Studia Socjologiczne* 3: 51-86.

SZTOMPKA, P. 1979a. 'Strategy of Theory-Construction in Sociology', in Wiatr, J. (ed.), *Polish Essays in the Methodology of the Social Sciences*. Dordrecht: Reidel. pp.173-94.

SZTOMPKA, P. 1979b. *Sociological Dilemmas: Toward a Dialectic Paradigm*. New York: Academic Press.

SZTOMPKA, P. 1986. 'The Renaissance of Historical Orientation in Sociology'. *International Sociology* 1 (3): 321-38.

TILLY, C. 1984. *Big Structures, Large Processes, Huge Comparisons*. New York: Russell Sage.

TIRYAKIAN, E.A. 1985. 'On the Significance of De-differentiation', in Eisenstadt, S.N. and Helle, H.J. (eds.), *Macro-Sociological Theory*. Beverly Hills: Sage. pp. 118-34.

WALLERSTEIN, I. 1974/1980. *The Modern World System*, 2 vols. New York: Academic Press.

WILSON, B.R. ed. 1984 [1974]. *Rationality*. Oxford: Blackwell.

WINCH, P. 1958. *The Idea of a Social Science and its Relation to Philosophy*. London: Routledge & Kegan Paul.

ZNANIECKI, F. 1969. *On Humanistic Sociology*. Chicago: University of Chicago Press.

INTERNATIONALISING SOCIOLOGY

Internationalising Sociology

The process of internationalisation is Janus-faced. It looks both ways. Looking outwards, the simplest case was colonisation, in which one culture penetrated and dominated another. But in a world of nation-states the interaction between them generates new and supervening social units which react back upon the states themselves.

The development of sociology in the twentieth century has itself been a facet of that overall process of internationalisation and has shared in its contradictory tensions. Before 1914, the discipline, like the colonial powers, took upon itself a universal task, the production of a science of society, with all times and peoples as part of its remit. In fact that task was conceived within and coloured by distinct national cultures and French, German, Italian and American sociologies all bore characteristic traits.

The recent volume edited by Nikolai Genov, *National Traditions in Sociology* (Sage 1989), shows that these national sociological cultures remain as distinct as ever. At the same time we know, at the very least from the vitality of the International Sociological Association and its research committees, that there is a complex network of international activity.

The interrelation of these processes has long been well understood by organisational sociologists. We need only recall Alvin Gouldner's famous distinction between locals and cosmopolitans. The cosmopolitans work to maximise their external contacts and to create new ventures across boundaries. Even as they do so, the locals strengthen their power base within the organisation. In a sense, both are winners if their organisation continues to grow.

The contradictions and tensions between internationalisation and the development of national sociologies should therefore be understood as part of an overall process of development. Edward Tiryakian's paper exemplifies a consciousness of and involvement in that process as he seeks to bring American sociology to a greater awareness of the need to look outwards.

The justifications he advances for his appeal themselves provide an interesting overview of a sociologist's sense of the importance of the process of internationalisation. It is the actual development of transnational global structures which impresses him as the dominant factor in requiring a renegotiation of the content of the sociology curriculum in American colleges.

There is additionally a specifically American vantage point from which Tiryakian speaks. It is as a world power that the United States requires graduates with 'international competency', 'a general knowledge of the world scene'. We can discern here a good example of the feedback effects of successful cultural, political and economic expansion upon the originating social structure. The contradiction is, of course, that this very success may reinforce an opposite tendency, namely ethnocentrism, and it is against this which Tiryakian directs his argument.

The Latin American vantage point occupied by Orlando Fals Borda provides us with a quite different perspective on the same processes. In his case he seeks to import theories and methods in such a way that they can serve the interests of exploited groups and classes. But in fact what are imported, Marxist, phenomenological ideas, insights from Ortega y Gasset or Foucault, are rapidly subordinated to the developing counter-discourse initiated in the Third World which is participatory action-research and which Fals Borda's own *Historia Doble de la Costa* exemplifies.

Fals Borda lists four main techniques which arise out of participatory action-research: collective research; critical recovery of history; valuing and applying folk culture; production and diffusion of new knowledge. These are combined with more traditional sociological and anthropological research practices and communicated at different levels to involve not only intellectuals but the grass-roots and exploited classes as well.

The quotation from Francis Bacon, 'knowledge is power', which Fals Borda makes, enhances the clarity with which we can recognise the fact that he and Tiryakian are indeed each concerned with the intellectual and social impact of internationalisation and with ensuring that sociology provides an adequate response for the purposes of particular social groups within the confines of their own cultural settings.

The call for elites in the United States to be more sensitive to the processes of worldwide social change is matched by efforts in Colombia, Nicaragua and Mexico to generate a knowledge and consciousness which will defend local populations against the insensitivity of elites from the developed world.

In neither case, however, will things be left as they were. The change process in which both are implicated transforms sociology even as, and in part through their agency, the new lessons are learnt, students, researchers and publics acquire new consciousness, and they respond in new ways to the emerging structures of their time. The internationalisation of sociology is the product of the discourses which arise around the worldwide process of social change.

SOCIOLOGY'S GREAT LEAP FORWARD: THE CHALLENGE OF INTERNATIONALISATION*

Edward A. Tiryakian

1. Introduction

This paper takes as given that (a) the level of international competency in the United States, even among America's elites (in both the private and the public sector), is substantially less than it should be in terms of our national interest as a competing world power, one whose hegemony is under severe pressure, economically as well as politically, and (b) the level of international competency among American students of sociology (graduate and under-graduate) is considerably below what might be an acceptable figure, given the nature of sociology as a comparative discipline that seeks to present systematic information and theoretically grounded interpretations of modern societies.

By 'international competency', a term that has received some recognition (Commission on International Education, n.d.), I will mean a general knowledge of the world scene so as to be able to have an environmental context for actions, events and situations that receive world recognition and that have world import. By 'general knowledge of the world scene', in turn, I mean a basic knowledge of world geography, world demography, world history, world economy (including gross parameters of the international division of labour and/or the interrelatedness of regional economies), world politics and intersocietal processes and exchanges. If we take all these aspects together, it will be few individuals indeed who have international competency. We might loosen the criteria to signify by international competency:

* Prepared for the Global Knowledge Project, David Wiley coordinator, Committee on World Sociology, American Sociological Association.

knowledge (geographical, demographical, historical, etc.) of two or more regions other than the one in which the actor's country of origin is located, or perhaps, to dilute the standards of competency even more, knowledge of one region other than that of the actor. No matter which of the above standards are invoked – and we might call them 'high', 'medium' or 'low' levels of international competency – I suspect that the majority of undergraduate majors, graduate students, *and quite likely, the sociology faculty in the United States*, would fall below the threshold mark.

If I have mentioned graduate students and faculty in the same breath as undergraduates, it is because the three are interrelated. The point is obvious but deserves to be made. The problem of increasing international competency in sociology is not simply a question of introducing more comparative materials in the undergraduate curriculum. It is that, but it is more than that. It is also increasing the international competency and awareness of graduate students who will be tomorrow's teaching and research faculty. And, of course, it is also increasing acceptance and support among the majority of American academic sociologists that international competency *is* and ought to be of vital importance to the discipline, not simply an exotic frosting.

My academic career has been limited to the university setting, but of course, sociology is also taught at colleges, either four-year or two-year ones. I will try in this paper to make recommendations that may be useful to the spectrum of institutional settings in which sociology is taught, but it does make a difference as to whether the undergraduate programme is given in a college or at university where graduate training is also part of the setting. Where the latter is the case, increasing the international competency of the undergraduate curriculum may be facilitated or obstructed by graduate teaching assistants. If the graduate students either are from other countries or have done field work outside the United States as part of their, say, doctoral research, they can add in classroom discussions an important cross-national perspective to substantive materials; further, the instructor in charge of the course would do well to invite such a teaching assistant to give a lecture to the course on comparative aspects of a given topic, to complement readings that pertain to the United States. On the other hand, if the ethos of the department is such that graduate students are implicitly steered to doing research solely on American data sets and discouraged from doing overseas field research, then they are of little assistance in increasing awareness of the global scene among undergraduate majors.

Perhaps, by virtue of the experience of being a teaching assistant in a course where the instructor can make the comparative emphasis a salient one, a graduate student may be proselytised to the merit of developing an international or cross-national perspective in her research. At this point, the faculty person will have the question of providing adequate support, intellectual and financial. Intellectual support means not only encouraging a graduate student to think comparatively about a project or theme that might be of interest as doctoral research, but also to facilitate an informal on-going intellectual exchange between students and possibly faculty, and not just in sociology but from other departments (anthropology, political science, perhaps history and economics). Financial support will mean seeking external funding that provides travel and support for an overseas stay. My limited experience in recent years has been that contrary to what one might think, given severe cutbacks in social science programmes in federal agencies, finding financial support for students wishing to do research outside the United States is not an acute problem. What is an acute problem is to find adequately prepared and trained sociology graduate students! Most of our graduate students lack language facility to do research abroad (except in English-speaking areas) and lack knowledge of the social milieu for which funding may be available; this is a reflection of the fact that the language requirement has been discarded from graduate training. Worse, they lack professional motivation to do research overseas.

So much for a digression on graduate students, but they are a key link between undergraduates and faculty, and attention about upgrading the international competency of undergraduates should give consideration to these background intermediaries. But let me concentrate on the under-graduate side of internationalising the sociology curriculum, since that is my main concern.

My first recommendation is that in planning how to internationalise sociology, the faculty make an *assessment of available resources*. Resources may be grouped under three categories: material, institutional and human. By *material resources* I include on-going programmes at one's institution that may facilitate students obtaining overseas experience (e.g. study abroad programmes, exchange programmes with foreign universities, etc.). I also include, of course, the compilation of instructional materials, syllabi, readers and other such printed matter that can be used in course preparation (e.g. Adams and Waldman 1983; Armer 1983). These should be thought of as initial stimuli that can be utilised once the crucial decision of internationalising the sociology curriculum has been reached.

By *institutional resources* will be meant both resources available within one's academic institution (e.g. the presence of a Center of International Studies, films available for classroom use, etc.) and outside the academic institution: for example, corporations in the town, city or state where the college is located – corporations that have an international dimension; or in the public sector, state agencies that seek foreign investments or foreign markets.

By *human resources* I mean persons at one's institution who may have specialised knowledge of social conditions in foreign regions or specific countries, or if not specialised knowledge, then first-hand experience in the everyday life of persons living in such regions or countries. Such persons may be thought of as potential 'informants'. Again, human resources may well include persons living in proximity to the academic institution who have first-hand knowledge of some areas or countries – for example, refugees from

Southeast Asia, immigrants/refugees from Central America and the Caribbean, and so forth.

If I suggest such an inventory of resources, it is because these will be an important support system for whatever academic attempt one will undertake. To devise a course having an international component or focus is not difficult, but to develop an interest and a commitment among undergraduate students (or graduates ones for that matter) does involve the ability to mobilise certain resources other than sheer intellectual ones, such as reading assignments. In my judgement, if one does bother to make an assessment of the three sorts of resources that be mobilised or utilised, then practically anywhere in the United States a considerable latent support system can be identified that would undergird curriculum innovations of the sort to be discussed here.

2. *Internationalising the Sociology Curriculum*

In the face of the enrolment crisis which has beset sociology nationally, there are different adaptive modes of response which departments have tried. One mode is to weather the storm by doing 'business as usual', not seeking structural changes in the undergraduate curriculum, and simply doing (better) what one has been doing before the enrolment inflation of the late 1960s to early 1970s, and before the enrolment deflation of the late 1970s to early 1980s. A second mode has been to adapt the curriculum to students' concern that what they take be instrumental in landing a job, and this may mean reorienting the curriculum to better training in research methods and applied sociology (Watts, Short and Schultz 1983 : 47-61). A third mode that I know of, but with just a few brave souls attempting it, such as Farganis at Vassar (1983), is to upgrade the introductory course by making it an introduction to the most exciting theoretical issues and figures of the discipline (such as the classical triumvirate of Durkheim, Weber and Marx).

What I wish to suggest here is a fourth mode, namely to provide an international/comparative concentration within the sociology major. I will only sketch out what this concentration might have as key components, and of course, modifications would have to be made depending upon departmental circumstances, availability of resources and the like.

Let me begin by following up a proposal made by Gerhard Lenski (1983, 1984a) that introductory sociology be (like Gaul and so many other things) made into three. In this formulation, Lenski suggested (1983 : 157) there be a separate (a) *macro* (the study of total societies and of the world system), (b) *micro* (the impact of societies on the individual) and (c) *meso* (the student's own society and its institutions) course. I would like to focus on just the macro introductory, leaving aside the merit and feasibility of the tripartite scheme and of the other two avenues of introducing sociology.

As a preliminary consideration let me suggest, to be mildly provocative, that sociology's distinctiveness as a discipline rests upon two great insights/ premises fashioned by a host of our tribal ancestors. At the micro level, sociology posits the *internalisation* of society in the development process of the human being (without which self-reflexivity would be impossible). At the macro level, sociology posits the *systemic* nature of social institutions, that is, the interrelatedness and interdependence of units into an on-going whole whose properties cannot be deduced from any one single unit *and* whose properties are subject to transformations over time stemming from endogenous and exogenous factors. Perhaps we can summarise both of these insights/premises into a single compound statement: 'No man is an island unto himself; and neither is any social institution'. By extrapolation, if in a given physical setting social institutions come to cohere so as to form a recognised nation-state (i.e. a socio-political actor recognised as such by other such actors having political legitimation), then macro sociology may be viewed in a complementary manner. On the one hand, it may be viewed as dealing with the processes operative within nation-states that interrelate these structurally and dynamically into a social system, either by voluntary or coercive means or a combination thereof.

On the other hand, macro sociology may have a more encompassing, 'global' perspective, namely, as dealing with the structure and dynamics of relations between clusters of countries (such clusters having a certain collective identity, political, cultural, or otherwise) and, ultimately, with relational structures between clusters tending in the modern period to develop into one broad, interrelated global system. It follows that if this is the case, important features of social phenomena occurring within a given country or nation-state must in part be accounted for by 'exogenous' factors, that is, by interrelationships between those phenomena, their societal setting and those of other societies. I trust that these remarks will be seen, upon reflection, as sociological 'common sense', for they are simply an extension of the customary sociological standpoint. The only radical aspect of this, is that I am suggesting we make this as the basis for introducing sociology to students.

What might the syllabus of such an introductory course look like? The *aim* or *purpose* of the course should emphasise that this is designed to introduce students to the field of sociology which deals with large-scale social phenomena and their global interdependence and manifestations. The course intends to give students a sociological orientation to the contemporary world scene, viewed as an evolving network of nation-states, and to provide students an orientation to the comparative nature of sociology, its theoretical and methodological traditions. Other such statements indicating the macro dimension of this introductory course could be stated.

Regarding textbooks, this is of course a matter of preference. As far as I am aware, there is not presently a textbook structured along the lines of a global orientation. But some introductory textbooks have more of a macro and/or comparative emphasis than others. To be suggestive, and only suggestive, one might consider as an appropriate text – if one is inclined to use a textbook in introductory sociology – Lenski and Lenski, *Human Societies* (1982) for its macro/evolutionary emphasis, or two texts having more comparative materials than most: Westhues, *First Sociology* (1982) and Spencer and

Inkeles, *Foundations* (1985). This may reflect that Westhues and Spencer reside in Canada. Actually, I would encourage using alternatives to textbooks, unless by unanticipated good fortune the macro introductory course drew such large numbers of students as to warrant multiple sections and make a textbook a desirable uniform standard reading assignment, readily accessible. Let me suggest some alternatives to having a textbook as the mainstay of the course.

First, I think it might be important to spend the initial meetings in laying out the conceptual frame of reference of macro sociology, in particular, that emphasis dealing with transnational and international components of the world scene. In some ways, Wilbert Moore's paper of 20 years ago (Moore 1966), if not programmatic of the new macro sociology, is at least mildly prophetic and could be used as a lead-off reading assignment. Following this initial orientation to sociology as a study of interrelated social systems, etc., it would seem well to spend three or four weeks on giving students the broad parameters of the *spatial-temporal* context of the world scene, since human action, including the action of large-scale social systems, is always framed or grounded in a spatial-temporal context. Concretely, I mean exposing students to the rudiments of world history and human geography. Readings might be selected from such works as McNeill (1971), for world history, and De Blij (1971) for geography. It is here that human resources of one's institution can be involved in the form of guest lectures by historians, geographers, demographers, and others. Historians would be invited to provide concisely an orientation to the world's major historical doings, on an area or regional basis, at least in the past 500 years which is, in terms of Weberian and Marxist orientations alike, the temporal frame of the 'modern' period. Geographers and demographers (if instances of both can be located within one's institution or nearby) would be asked to provide an orientation to the major human ecosystems of the world, population distributions, their habitats, their resources and major modes of adaptation to the environment.

It is only after such an orientation that a sociological approach to the international scene should be undertaken. If a text is not used, it might prove rewarding to use a macro orientation that is consistent and integrated. Daniel Chirot's *Social Change* (1977), which has affinity (but not identity) with a world-system political economy approach, is eminently readable and would provide useful reading materials for a couple of weeks. This can be complemented, supplemented, or foiled by a work with a different, more 'idealistic' orientation than that of political economy, namely Parsons' *The Evolution of Societies* (1977).

Both of these works have a tacit Western emphasis, and do not give major attention to a very salient fact about the modern world, namely the intrusion and domination on a rather systematic basis by Western nation-states (and here I would include Russia) of non-Western peoples and societies. That is, a very major aspect of the transformation of the modern world is the effective colonisation of the Middle East, Asia, Africa and the Western Hemisphere by

Europeans and their progenies overseas. The modern world has been fashioned by the *interaction* of relatively economically advanced, predominantly industrialised, politically unified and autonomous Western nation-states with, for the most part, (outside Asia) small-scale, agrarian, predominantly rural societies; this interaction, backed up by technological and military superiority of the former forced the latter into varying states of dependency. Formally politically dependent social units became linked with Western nation-states in a colonial system.

The above remarks may seem banal, if not a truism of modernisation. But perhaps less obvious is that the social systems which resulted from this interaction, that is, colonial societies, have *sui generis* characteristics that cannot be deduced from the properties of Western countries or non-Western countries *ante* modern colonialism. The nature of economic, political, religious and other institutions, even the nature of social identity, differs in colonial societies from comparable sets of social and socio-psychological phenomena in either Western 'modern' societies or in non-Western 'traditional' societies. Since this is not the occasion to discuss colonial societies as such, I will refrain from the temptation of a long digression. But I will not refrain from saying that if we want sociology majors to have an understanding of the world scene, they must have an awareness that most of the world bears a heavy imprint of a colonial burden/legacy. Naivety on this topic is not only an affliction of undergraduates, it is also a common undiagnosed ailment of most sociologists who write introductory textbooks.

To rectify this at the very beginning of a student's introduction to sociology, I would recommend that an important section be devoted to the colonial situation, the colonial social system and how this has an effect on the nature of social relationships. The sort of readings which might be used here would be at the psycho-social level: the first work of Fanon, *Black Skin, White Masks* (1967) and the more recent, brilliant study of Said, *Orientalism* (1979). Both of these can be used to show how the 'construction of reality', and more specifically, the 'construction of personality' has a societal function in a colonial context of (Western) domination; more structural readings of colonial and post-colonial situations might be found in the early but still useful volume edited by Wallerstein (1966) and later works by Goldthorpe (1975) and Alavi and Shanin (1982).

At this point in the introductory course, I would provide students with a learning experience of a different nature, but one that will assist them in learning to pay attention to the world scene from a standpoint other than is customary, namely, to view the world scene from the perspective of other world actors besides the official American stance and that provided by major mass media. The single experience which I have found over the years provides students with an ineluctable appreciation and awareness of 'the other' (and after all, the etymology of sociology is derived from the science of 'the other') is the *field experience*.

By that I mean students spending for a week or two several hours (say in lieu of class contact hours) in the town, city or village near the academic institution and trying to do some participant observation of persons or different life-styles or social class or ethnicity than the student's familiar world. It was very effectively put in the year-long introductory course in Social Relations at Harvard (then called 'Soc. Rel. 10') by Leon Bramson when he was in charge of organising the course, many years ago. Readings were done in the classic study of William Whyte, *Street Corner Society*, and students then had the task of finding their way to the North End of Boston, spending several hours in this Italian neighbourhood, writing up their observations and interactions with the urban dwellers and discussing their notes in class. Having participated in that course as a faculty associate, I have been sold ever since in giving undergraduates field experience not only in introductory sociology but in almost any substantive course above it. I find this is one of the best ways of getting students to be ego-involved with the materials, that is, to have a feel for being producers of sociological knowledge, not simply passive consumers.

In terms of field experience in an introductory course which might be instrumental in relating to the international scene, one could use vintage participant observation studies of a very varied kind: Laurence Wylie's sensitive *Village in the Vaucluse* (1974); and Banfield's *The Moral Basis of a Backward Society* (1958) are community studies done in Europe by American social scientists, while Gans' *Urban Villages* (1962) and Liebow's *Tally's Corner* are equally fine domestic studies also done with a participant observation orientation. Any one of these, or any other current favourites, can be used as background models to give students a grasp of the sort of information and data that may be gathered in the field. The experience itself will sensitise students to seeking to understand how the everyday world is structured, perceived and understood by actors operating in a different cultural, physical and socio-economic environment from that of the everyday world of students.

I would also propose that the introductory course make a provision to appeal to the student's *past*. Before expanding this, let me suggest that if we want sociology undergraduates to become more competent in international affairs, we must appeal to their own *interest*, and not simply to some vague idealistic line that 'it is part of a liberal arts curriculum to have knowledge of the world scene, etc.'. And what I want to indicate is that a concentration in macro/global sociology should make the case that such a concentration is to the student's interest – past, present and future. The introductory course may be a useful vehicle for tapping at the student's *past*.

Every person in the United States, with few exceptions, has a socially identifiable ethnic and/or racial status. This entails the carrying of a social baggage which may be more or less burdensome, more or less in the consciousness and awareness of the actor. I would suggest that as a project for an independent paper, one that would provide an important component of the term grade, each student seek to find something about (a) the society and social milieu from whence originated her/his ancestors at the time of coming to the United States, (b) that society and social milieu today (in terms of regime, economy, social stratification, etc.) and (c) the major intervening social processes and structural changes that took place in the society or setting of origin from the period of emigration/immigration to the present. This, of course, is a task which might well be appropriate for a master's paper or even doctoral research, and in making the assignment in an introductory course, one must be realistic as to what one expects students to be able to achieve. But it should give students an experience of major importance. It may give them an exposure to oral history, if they have parents or grandparents who can provide information about the locale from when emigrating to he United States. In the case of students whose families have been here for more than, say, three generations, it will still provide them with the occasion to learn about social history.

As a result of this assignment, students should also gain familiarity with an area of the contemporary world setting and its situation today – whether that is Ireland, or Norway, or West Africa, or Puerto Rico, or Mexico, or Hong Kong, or Pakistan, or Quebec, or Poland, etc. In uncovering the past, that is, one's ethnic roots, students will find relational ties with other parts of the globe today. Hopefully, this should lead to a sustained interest and increased awareness in at least one other part of the world scene.

I would also recommend wherever appropriate the use of *films* to sensitise students to the everyday life in the modern world as it is experienced in other geographical settings, preferably *not* anthropological films of exotic settings and peoples living in a 'primitive' environment which is seemingly cut off from the world historical process. I mean films more like 'The Battle of Algers' or 'Xala', or even 'Gandhi', that can depict colonial and neo-colonial situations, but by no means do I wish to suggest they be confined to the Third World (domestic or overseas). In my opinion, sociology has to catch up with anthropology in making effective classroom use of films and other visual media.

These, then, constitute my major recommendations for what might go into an introductory course in sociology having the international scene as its emphasis.

A second course in the global concentration programme I am proposing is a topical course on *major international issues and problems*. This course would be particularly effective when co-taught by a sociologist and another colleague from a different department, such as a political scientist or a macro economist. Such a course has been successfully given at Duke University by my colleague Gary Gereffi and a description of the syllabus is available in Armer and Goodman (1983 : 123-134). I am sure that a great many colleagues and universities have developed or are developing similar interdisciplinary courses on global issues (Soroos 1983; Tulchin 1984), but I am not sure if sociologists are everywhere taking the lead in having the chief responsibility for organising such a course. I am advocating that they do so and that such a course would be a very logical part of an undergraduate curriculum in sociology: essentially it would be the macro/global equivalent of courses in 'social problems'. In fact, it may be quite possible to take the typical content of a 'social problems' course and make it comparative and global. For the purpose of illustration, if one of the social problems treated is that of 'drug addiction', a global perspective would situate that problem historically and cross-nationally (e.g. the forcible introduction of opium in China in the nineteenth century), examine global variations in the nature and incidence of drug addiction today and consider economic and social structures involved in the international traffic in drugs, etc.

I would suggest that such a topical course on global issues and problems might begin with the theme of *the global crisis*, both because of the real urgency of having Americans understand deteriorating socio-economic conditions abroad as much as at home, and because the theme of 'global crisis' is one which will indicate to students that sociology is alert to real-life concerns of the world scene. Among core readings that could be assigned here would be the volumes put out, respectively, by The Brandt Commission (1983); by Amin et al (1982); and by Tiryakian (1984).

Finally, irrespective of the contents, this course would do well to get students to start reading some of the informed, non-specialised journals that deal with world affairs, such as *Foreign Affairs, World Policy Journal* and *World Press Review*. If possible, students with some linguistic ability should be encouraged to make oral reports or prepare written papers that would document some global issue by means of periodicals written in languages other than English. An important learning experience comes from seeing how a certain global issue is perceived and formulated in countries outside the United States, hence the merit of encouraging students to read papers published outside the United States. Even English language editions of newspapers and periodicals published abroad will generate an international awareness among students they would not have if they stick to the American press and television for their way of looking at the world scene.

The first two courses sketched out in the preceding pages are intended for underclassmen (albeit they should be attractive electives for students concentrating in other departments). For sophomore and junior concentrators in sociology, I would propose a required course that might be entitled 'Comparative Analysis in Sociology' or just 'Comparative Sociology'. This course would have as its basic purpose imparting to students methodological training in large-scale comparative research in diachronic and synchronic analysis. It would be a complement to standard undergraduate courses in 'Research Methods', which usually do not examine the societal or historical matrix of sociological data gathering and analysis.

Much of the orientation readings in such a course can be taken from several volumes explicitly devoted to comparative sociology as such, beginning with Marsh (1967) and going on to Vallier (1971), Armer and Grimshaw (1973) and Armer and Marsh (1982). Students can then be exposed to more recent macro-comparative materials and methodological discussions, for example, those found in Lenski (1984b) and Hopkins and Wallerstein (1982). Depending upon the calibre of students and their motivation, I would also urge the assignment (in part if not in whole) of major substantive sociological studies that make extensive use of historical data. The classic figure is Max Weber, particularly his comparative studies of religion, civilisation and modernity. As a bold step, why not assign *The Protestant Ethic and the Spirit of Capitalism* alongside with *The Religion of India* or *The Religion of China*? (of course, one student can be assigned *The Protestant Ethic*, one *India*, and a third *China*, with the entire class discussing the comparative features and logic of Weber's specific studies). On the contemporary scene, Eisenstadt's study of empires (1963) and the more recent ones of Skocpol (1979) on endogenous and exogenous factors common to successful revolutions and Baltzell (1979) on differentials in the development of Boston and Philadelphia, are the sort of first-rate studies that illustrate the richness of comparative sociology. During this course, students should either get specific assignments or be asked to do independent readings in journals that have a comparative focus, for example, *Comparative Studies in Society and History* and the *International Journal of Comparative Sociology*.

Let me add that if at one's institution there is available to students a secondary major in international studies, comparative area studies or the like, then the comparative analysis course in sociology should get visibility outside the department as a course that can give students a methodological training they would not otherwise obtain. This will be beneficial to the course in attracting students who already have some interest in the international sphere (and might perhaps attract first majors who might otherwise be attracted to other departments); it will also be beneficial to the students in giving them certain conceptual tools and technical skills that will appeal to prospective employers and professional schools. If the 'Comparative Sociology' ('Comparative Methods of Analysis', etc.) course can be cross-listed, it might make it an even more stimulating classroom situation if the course can be co-taught with a colleague from another department, such as history, anthropology or political science. A substantive topic might be the focus for some weeks, one that would allow comparisons between the incidence and nature of a social phenomenon in the United States and the same phenomenon in another setting. Again, just to be suggestive, one might look at the industrial setting in Japan and the United States to account for differences in productivity, or national policy towards autochthonous populations in the United States, South Africa and Australia, etc., and the sociologist and her/his colleague could make explicit how each would approach the topic methodologically.

The methodological training of students concentrating in the international sphere should not be limited to the course I have just indicated. They should be encouraged to take a course in field research, if that were available in anthropology, one in historiography, if available in history, and of course, courses in research methods and statistics for the social sciences (presumably

73

available in sociology). However, these opportunities may not be available and may be best thought of as further training for a master's degree (which I will briefly touch on later).

Before we get to the senior year, there are a couple of aspects of the concentration in the macro/global sociology curriculum that I would like to mention. First, it is my observation over the years that a good number of students at college like to spend some time abroad, usually in their junior year; however, unless my perception is erroneous, most of those who go abroad are in the humanities rather than the social sciences, and in any case very few if any sociology major takes a junior year abroad programme. I like to think that the new introductory course and the global issues course would stimulate interest in students to spend time abroad and experience a different setting. The person(s) responsible for the concentration in macro/global sociology should encourage and assist in this, not only in providing information, but also in assistance to the students. By 'assistance to the students', I mean several things. One is that the department should be willing to give course credit to students who might do some supervised research in the course of a summer semester or year abroad (even if the supervision is done at a distance, with the student writing up his/her experiences in the form of a journal or gathering some quantifiable data that can be analysed upon his/her return). Second, the coordinator for macro/global sociology, or some other departmental figure (such as the director of undergraduate studies) should seek to find for undergraduate concentrators training experience outside the classroom with firms or agencies that have some interest in the international scene. The training experience could be either remunerated (e.g. summer employment) or not (e.g. internships), depending upon the circumstances.

It is here again that making an extensive inventory of locally available resources can prove rewarding. For example, an internship may be worked out with a state agency which sends trade missions abroad and/or which acts as host for trade missions from abroad; a multinational corporation may have its headquarters in the state in which the academic institution is located and can provide summer employment in its branch office in Mexico or in Scotland; the municipality has a social welfare bureau that requires part-time workers to interview families recently arrived from the Philippines, Hong Kong and Vietnam. It is these and myriad other possibilities of relating students to different socio-cultural settings, either during the academic year or during summers, that should be thought of as part of the total experience a sociology department can offer concentrators in the international scene.

As to the senior year, I would propose here a seminar, on a topic of the instructor's choice, which would be required of all concentrators (but open to others). It would be well if the seminar allowed the opportunity, perhaps in the early weeks, for students who have gathered data in the field over the summer or during their junior year abroad to address the topic in terms of how the topic might appear to persons in the setting where they did their extra-curricular work. The topic might have comparative and timely aspects, as well as, if possible, allow for research on the part of students.

Again, let me suggest a couple of possibilities. Suppose that the academic institution is located in a state marked by growing unemployment in the steel or textile industry, and suppose further that various figures (spokesmen for the industry, political representatives, etc.) have been saying that there is need to restrict imports if further cuts in the domestic labour force are to be avoided. This situation could well provide the basis for a sociology seminar in the international sphere, since obviously the unemployment of American factory workers is interrelated with economic development outside the United States. The seminar could spend some time discussing the nature of the American industrial setting, factors of productivity, management-workers relationships and so forth; it would also take up from what other countries are imports coming and what the industrial scene is that or those exporting countries. Students in the seminar should have the experience of utilising not only aggregate data available from published sources (World Bank reports, Department of Commerce publications, etc.) but also data that might be obtained directly by interviewing management and union officials, factory workers, unemployed workers, etc.

A second possible topic might be one like 'Migrants and Refugees', which would examine domestic and transnational aspects of the subject. As of this writing (1984) there is pending in the United States a major legislation concerning the regulation of migration into the United States (the Simpson-Mazzoli Immigration Reform and Control Act). In several states there is an important seasonal migration of farm workers, with a labour force consisting of a considerable number of alien migrant workers. Students in the seminar might collaborate on a study of the problem of foreign migrant workers and their relation to local communities, not only in the state in which the academic institution is located, but also nationally and cross-nationally (for example, the status and situation of alien or 'guest' workers in different countries in Western Europe, or in the Middle East).

Further, the seminar should also examine the economic and political situation of migrant workers (and other immigrants) in their country of origin. After all, some persons who leave one country to go to another may do so for either or both, economic and political reasons. The seminar should consequently examine not only economic migrants to the United States, but also political refugees, or persons seeking political asylum. An important variable here is how the United States government defines certain groups. Thus, if the United States has friendly ties with country X in Central America, it may deny 'refugee' status to persons seeking entry under that rubric, but allow this to persons coming from country Y, defined officially as unfriendly.

In dealing with these and related aspects of the general topic, including international aspects of migration and refugees, students would learn a lot about the agricultural business in the United States, about the politics of legislation, and about the nature of linkages of the United States to various other countries who are, wittingly or not, 'exporting' population to America. I think this is an excellent way of making undergraduates appreciate the significance of the many facets of the sociological study of migration.

Perhaps not all topics for a senior seminar can exploit local resources, but in any case, the senior seminar should give students the opportunity of writing a term paper which allows them to explore analytically and empirically an aspect of the interdependence of the modern world. Preferably, the seminar topic and the term paper should drive home the point that global interdependence and interrelatedness have real consequences on the lives of people, including real people with whom students have had contact.

3. Conclusions

I have earlier mentioned that internationalising sociology, by means of a concentration in sociology, should appeal to students' interest in terms of their past, present and future. The *past*, I have suggested, may be personalised in the focus on ethnicity and the interrelationships between the United States or the North American setting and the historical societies from which students' families originated. The *present* should come out of courses on global issues and the senior seminar (as well as getting students to read regularly journals and magazines that have a heavy content of global affairs). What about the *future*?

Besides the obvious point that the interrelatedness and interdependence of the world means that the well-being and survival of one part of the world affects the well-being and survival of all parts, including the United States, and besides the corollary that as a world power the economic and political activities of the United States have a disproportionate impact on other parts of the world, there is a more personal consideration that pertains to the future of students. I would here invoke a material interest, namely that majoring in sociology with a concentration in the international/global sphere can provide strong assets and background skills for employment in companies and agencies that have a vital stake in international matters. These are bound to increase in coming years, whether the domestic economy is on an upswing or a downswing, whether liberals or conservatives are in office.

I have no doubt that there would be a demand for undergraduate majors who have had a concentration in the international sphere. What is needed is for the sociology faculty to realise that this is one way of revitalising the undergraduate curriculum and in getting bright and socially aware students to take sociology courses that they might otherwise shun. But it will entail some serious work and coordination with other departments, perhaps even with some other professional schools that might be part of the academic institution (e.g. a Business School, a Law School, etc.).

Whether or not the work entailed in developing such a concentration is worth it or not is, to be sure, a gamble. To add to the gamble, let me suggest that if the academic institution in question has a graduate programme, the sociology department might think of offering a combined B.A./M.A. degree for those undergraduate concentrators in macro/global sociology who opt for a fifth year, one in which they would prepare a master's thesis and take graduate courses that might complete their methodological and theoretical training in both sociology and ancillary departments. The advantage of this degree would be to enhance employment opportunities in the public or private sector, by providing a higher level of supervised training than just the B.A.

One last point to be raised is why should the sociology profession encourage the internationalisation of the curriculum? Quite aside from the fact that sociology ought to play an important role in the social science curriculum of any academic institution, there is a more fundamental reason. I would like to argue that the sociological concepts we have been brought up with, our tools of analysis, our basic frame of reference, have been developed in the context of a certain historical epoch, the epoch of industrial and state formation. The major actors on the scene were actors on the domestic scene, public and private actors. The social landscape on which they moved, cooperated and struggled for a place in the sun was the landscape of the self-contained nation-state. But that landscape is rapidly changing today, certainly in part because of technological revolutions that are interrelating the world, and also because of economic and cultural changes that also increase international networks and interrelatedness.

All this leads me to my ultimate conclusion. Namely, if the current academic crisis for sociology involving enrolments is that somehow we are not perceived as 'relevant' for undergraduates, there is a more serious side to the crisis, which Touraine (1984) has very cogently exposed. It is that of the relevance of sociology in general today in representing social life and modernity. We are near the point of exhausting our intellectual capital based on 'modern' Western industrial societies, and of the everyday life self-contained in these entities. If macro sociology is to be relevant in the next century, it must drop the parochialism of implicitly confining itself to intra-state phenomena, it must develop the concepts and the grammar to deal with the transnational scene and transnational structures and processes of change. It must, in brief, in its graduate training and professional research, commit itself to a 'great leap forward'.

References

ADAMS, Jan S. and WALDMAN, Marilyn eds. 1983. *Transnational Approaches of the Social Sciences*. Lanham, Md. New York and London: University Press of America.

AMIN, Sami, ARRIGHI, G., FRANK, A.G. and WALLERSTEIN, I. 1983. *Dynamics of World Crisis*. New York and London: Monthly Review Press.

ARMER, Michael and GRIMSHAW, Allen D. eds. 1973. *Comparative Social Research: Methodological Problems and Strategies*. New York: Wiley.

ARMER, J. Michael ed. and GOODMAN, Neal R. comp. 1983. *Syllabi and Resources for Internationalising Courses in Sociology*. Washington, D.C.: American Sociological Association Teaching Resource Center.

ARMER, J. Michael and MARSH, Robert M. eds. 1982. *Comparative Sociological Research in the 1960s and 1970s*. Leiden, Netherlands: E.J. Brill. (Originally published as Volume 22 of the *International Journal of Comparative Sociology*.)

BALTZELL, E. Digby 1979. *Puritan Boston and Quaker Philadelphia.* New York: Free Press.

BANFIELD, Edward C. 1958. *The Moral Basis of a Backward Society.* New York: Free Press.

BRANDT COMMISSION 1983. *Common Crisis North-South: Co-Operation for World Recovery.* Cambridge, MA: MIT Press.

CHIROT, Daniel 1977. *Social Change in the Twentieth Century.* New York: Harcourt, Brace.

COMMISSION ON INTERNATIONAL EDUCATION n.d. *What We Don't Know Can Hurt Us.* Washington, D.C.: American Council on Education.

DE BLIJ, Harm J. 1971. *Geography: Regions and Concepts.* New York: Wiley.

EISENSTADT, S.N. 1963. *The Political Systems of Empires.* New York: Free Press.

FANON, Frantz 1967. *Black Skin, White Masks.* New York: Grove Press. First published in French in 1952.

FARGANIS, James 1983. 'Social Theory as Introductory Sociology: A Humanities Perspective'. National Endowment for the Humanities. Education Division. Grant 20015.

GANS, Herbert 1962. *The Urban Villagers. Group and Class in Life of Italian-Americans.* New York: Free Press.

GOLDTHORPE, J.E. 1975. *The Sociology of the Third World. Disparity and Involvement.* Cambridge: Cambridge University Press.

HOPKINS, Terence K. and WALLERSTEIN, Immanuel eds. 1982. *World-Systems Analysis. Theory and Methodology.* Beverly Hills: Sage.

LENSKI, Gerhard 1983. 'Rethinking the Introductory Course'. *Teaching Sociology*, 10 : 153-168.

LENSKI, Gerhard 1984a. 'Sociology, Anthropology, and the Study of Human Societies'. *Teaching Sociology*, 11 : 335-340.

LENSKI, Gerhard 1984b. *Current Issues and Research in Macrosociology.* Leiden, Netherlands: E.J. Brill.

LENSKI, Gerhard and LENSKI, Jean 1982. *Human Societies: An Introduction to Macrosociology.* 4th ed. New York: McGraw-Hill.

LIEBOW, Elliot 1967. *Tally's Corner.* Boston: Little, Brown.

McNEILL, William H. 1971. *A World History.* 2nd ed. New York: Oxford University Press.

MARSH, Robert M. 1967. *Comparative Sociology: A Codification of Cross-Societal Analysis.* New York: Harcourt Brace & World.

MOORE, Wilbert E. 1966. 'Global Sociology: The World as a Singular System'. *American Journal of Sociology*, 71 : 475-482.

PARSONS, Talcott 1977. *The Evolution of Societies.* (Ed. with an introduction by Jackson Toby.) Englewood Cliffs, N.J.: Prentice-Hall.

SAID, Edward W. 1979. *Orientalism.* New York: Vintage/Random House.

SKOCPOL, Theda 1979. *States and Social Revolutions.* Cambridge: Cambridge University Press.

SOROOS, Marvin S. 1983. 'The Study of Global Issues'. *SASASAAS (South Atlantic States Association of Asian and African Studies) Review*, 8 : n.p. (Published at Appalachian State University, Boone, N.C.).

SPENCER, Metta and INKELES, Alex 1985. *Foundations of Modern Sociology.* 4th ed. Englewood Cliffs, N.J.: Prentice-Hall.

TIRYAKIAN, Edward A. ed. 1984. 'The Global Crisis: Sociological Analyses and Responses'. *International Journal of Comparative Sociology*, special issue, 25, Nos. 1-2. (Also published as a paperback by E.J. Brill, Leiden, Netherlands.)

TOURAINE, Alain 1984. 'The Waning Sociological Image of Social Life', in E.A. Tiryakian ed: 'The Global Crisis: Sociological Analyses and Responses', *International Journal of Comparative Sociology*, 25, Nos. 1-2, in press.

TULCHIN, Joseph S. 1984. 'Global Issues', *Office of International Programs Nesletter*, Spring issue, n.p. Chapel Hill, N.C.: University of North Carolina.

VALLIER, Ivan ed. 1971. *Comparative Methods in Sociology. Essays on Trends and Applications.* Berkeley: University of California Press.

WALLERSTEIN, Immanuel ed. 1966. *Social Change. The Colonial Situation.* New York: Wiley.

WATTS, W. David, SHORT, A.P. and SCHULTZ, C.C. 1983. 'Applied Sociology and the Current Crisis'. *Teaching Sociology*, 11 : 47-61.

WESTHUES, Kenneth 1982. *First Sociology.* New York: McGraw-Hill.

THE APPLICATION OF PARTICIPATORY-ACTION RESEARCH IN LATIN AMERICA*

Orlando Fals Borda

Interest in Participatory Action-Research (PAR) has grown worldwide due to its pertinence to the initiation and promotion of radical changes at the grassroots level where unsolved economic, political and social problems have been accumulating a dangerous potential. PAR claims to further change processes in constructive non-violent ways due to its emphases on awareness-building processes, although it does anticipate revolutionary action in cases of collective frustration or belligerent reactionary violence applied at base levels and groups.

Such processes of radical change include scientific research, adult education and political action combined. That it can be done has been ascertained through a series of studies undertaken in many Third World countries by local scholars and activists. In Colombia, PAR studies started in the 1970s on the Atlantic Coast where further work has been completed in recent years. Some of these studies were sponsored by Canada's International Development Research Center (IDRC) and Bogotá's Punta de Lanza Foundation. Their results are now in published form under the title *Historia Doble de la Costa* (The Double History of the Coast) in four volumes (Fals-Borda 1979-1986).

The title of this work tells something of PAR methodology. It is a 'double history' because it is written in two styles or languages which run simultaneously on opposite pages: one for the non-initiated reader, presented in literary form; and the other for cadres' training, presented in conceptual and theoretical terms, being a sociological interpretation of the literary text. The purpose of this dual style is to assure popular comprehension of analytical messages and to raise levels of consciousness. The 'double history' is now

*Based on fieldwork sponsored by Canada's International Development Research Center, the International Labour Office (Geneva) and the Punta de Lanza Foundation (Bogotá), 1980-86. Collaborators included Malena de Montis, Alvaro Velasco, John Jairo Cárdenas, Félix Cadena, Victor Negrete, José Galeano, Salvador García and Bertha Barrogán. This article was translated from the Spanish by Brian Mallet.

amply utilised by people concerned with progress and development on the Atlantic Coast and elsewhere.

Another recent attempt has involved the comparative field approach with PAR. This had never been done until 1982 when teams of researchers applied the same frame of reference in their respective countries (Nicaragua, Colombia and Mexico) among tri-racial rural communities. This effort, under the sponsorship of the International Labour Office (Employment and Development Department, Geneva) was published in book form (Fals-Borda 1985) with the title, *Conocimiento y poder popular: Lecciones con campesinos de Nicaragua, Colombia y México* (Knowledge and People's Power: Lessons with peasants in Nicaragua, Colombia and Mexico). (An English version is being published by The Indian Social Institute, New Delhi.)

The coastal IDRC research as well as the comparative ILO study with PAR have helped in clarifying basic methodological and technical issues related to this type of work with and for grassroots units. They confirmed that PAR, as stated above, is not exclusively research oriented, nor only to adult education or political action, but that it encompasses all these aspects as three stages or emphases not necessarily consecutively. They are combined into an experiential methodology, a process of personal and collective behaviour occurring within a satisfying and productive cycle of life and labour. This experiential methodology for life and labour implies the acquisition of serious and reliable knowledge upon which to construct power for the poor and exploited social groups and their authentic organisations. In this connection, *people's power* may be defined as the capacity of the grass-roots groups, which are exploited socially and economically, to articulate and systematise knowledge (both their own and that which comes from outside) in such a way that they can become protagonists in the advancement of their society and in defence of their own class and group interests.

The aims of this combination of knowledge and power are: 1) to enable the oppressed groups and classes to acquire sufficient creative and transforming leverage as expressed in specific projects, acts and struggles; and 2) to produce and develop socio-political thought processes with which popular bases can identify. The evaluation of these aims is done in practice by examining the results obtained in PAR projects, not by abstract reasoning or rules.

It is obvious that these aims go beyond the academic traditions which have emphasised value neutrality and a positivist objectivity as prerequisites for 'serious science'. PAR does not negate the need for discipline and continuity in accumulating and systematising knowledge, and it hopes to draw such qualities from academe. However, it would induce a reorientation in teleological terms that would lead into more integrated academic and popular, or common-sensical, knowledges so that a new type of 'revolutionary science' (in Kuhnian terms) becomes a real possibility, not only a felt necessity. As this is still in the making, the polemical nature of such a possibility is readily granted, and it is hoped that everyone involved will be able to profit from it intellectually and humanly.

Within such polemics and limitations, the application of this methodology for productive life and labour in Mexican, Nicaraguan and Colombian rural communities in recent years has allowed progress to be made in the examinations of two important theoretical problems: 1) the implications that the perception of reality and the contemporary world have on personal and collective *everyday behaviour*; and 2) the effects which the people's conscious struggle may have on improving existing standards of life and labour; and in order to accomplish, defend and promote revolutionary changes in society through internal and external mechanisms of *countervailing power* exercised against exploitative systems.

Obviously, distinctions must be taken into account between the revolutionary condition of Nicaragua and the 'representative democracies' of Mexico and Colombia, even though these 'democratic' systems are in crisis. The PAR approach has proved to be supportive of the Nicaraguan Revolution, an indication that the latter's cultural, social and economic components have replication and projection value elsewhere in the continent. However timely, this is not a new discovery, but the recent shared experience with PAR in the three countries (and elsewhere) underlines the importance of two broad lessons concerning the establishment and exercise of people's power in fieldwork and adult education: 1) how to interact and organise for such purposes; and 2) how to recognise oneself and to learn in such contexts.

At first sight it may appear that there is nothing new in these two lessons. Many observers would claim that such theses are implicit in the current literature on social and economic development, yet there are significant differences in the way the proposed elements of organisation and cognition are conceived in the two approaches of developmentalism and participation as herein presented.

The main difference lies in their ontological conceptions. The developmentalist discourse, as is well known (Foucault's thesis of the archaeology of knowledge can help us in this respect), involves dealing with the concepts of poverty, technology, capital, growth, values, and so forth, as defined from the standpoint of rich, developed countries (where in fact the concept of development was first proposed), a discourse organised into a coherent intellectual whole for the purpose of rationalising and defending the worldwide dominance of those rich and powerful societies.

The participatory discourse or counter-discourse, on the other hand, initiated in the Third World – quite probably as an endogenous dialectical response to the actions of the developed world – postulates an organisation and structure of knowledge in such a way that the dominated, underdeveloped societies articulate their own socio-political position on the basis of their own values and capacities and act accordingly to achieve their liberation from the oppressive and exploitative forms of domination imposed by opulent (capitalist) foreign powers and local consular elites and thus create a more satisfactory life for everyone. In this way a more human *Weltanschauung*, or world outlook, could be fashioned.

81

This creative balance, or positive confrontation, may be necessary today in order to halt the destructive forces being unleashed in the world, though not of course through the wishes of the poor and the destitute: the arrogant arms race, flagrant injustices, squandering and egotistical oligarchies, monopolistic trends, rampant abuse of nature and man. PAR can make an important contribution in this field in which knowledge and action are combined for social progress.

Participation and organisation

Our first lesson – learning to interact and organise – is based on the existential concept of *vivencia* (experience or *Erlebnis*) proposed by the Spanish philosopher José Ortega y Gasset. Through actual experience of something we intuitively apprehend its essence, we feel, enjoy and understand it as reality, and we thereby place our own being in a wider, more fulfilling context. In PAR such an experience is complemented by another one: that of *authentic commitment* resulting from historical materialism and classical Marxism (Eleventh Thesis on Feuerbach: 'Philosophers should not be content with just explaining the world, but should try to transform it').

This combination of experience and commitment allows us to decide for whom such knowledge is intended: the base groups themselves. Moreover, such a concept of experience recognises that there are two types of animators or agents of change: those which are external and those internal to the exploited classes and units. Such agents are unified in one sole purpose (telos), that of achieving the shared goals of social transformation.

Both types of animators (internal and external) contribute their own knowledge, techniques and experiences to the transformation process. Since these elements of knowledge result from different class conformations and rationalities (one Cartesian and academic, the other experiential and practical) a *dialectical tension* is created between them which can be resolved only through practical commitment, that is, through *praxis*. But the sum of knowledge from both types of agents permits the acquisition of a much more accurate and correct picture of the reality which we want to transform. Therefore academic knowledge plus popular knowledge and wisdom may give as a result a total scientific knowledge of a revolutionary nature (and perhaps another paradigm) which destroys the previous unjust class monopoloy.

This dialectical tension in praxis leads to the rejection of the asymmetry implied in the subject/object relationship which characterises traditional academic research and most tasks of daily life. According to participatory theory, such a relationship must be transformed into a subject/subject one. Indeed, the destruction of the asymmetric binomial is the kernel of the concept of participation as understood in the present context and in other aspects of the daily routine (family, health, education, politics, etc.).

Thus *to participate* means to break up voluntarily and through experience the asymmetrical relationship of submission and dependence implicit in the subject/object binomial. Such is its authentic essence.

Let us review one example from fieldwork related to these concepts. The Co-ordination Commission of El Regadio (Nicaragua), which was set up at the beginning of our experience, had to become fully acquainted with the research, ensure that the census of the community was properly carried out and help in the analysis and correction of its results. The researchers noted, however, that the members of the Commission began to complain of headaches, backaches, stiff necks, etc. precisely when greater intellectual reflection was required. The latent intention was that the external animators should give the 'correct answers'. As they did not lend themselves to such purposes, tense moments of silence arose as the members of the Commission waited for the answer, or indulged in trivial conversation and jokes.

If they had adopted other guidelines on research and action, our researchers could easily have assumed the role of these indispensable leaders 'normally' expected by the peasants of El Regadio. However, the animators insisted that the peasants should analyse their own patterns of dependency, authoritarianism and paternalism inherited from the traditional exploitation systems of the past which continued to flourish there despite the revolution of 19 July 1979. Together with the results of the census, this historical and social self-analysis offered the community another excellent opportunity to take a look at itself. It was the first time that the inhabitants had done this, and so their history 'acquired a face of its own' in a process similar to that which had occurred among the Otomis of El Mezquital (Mexico). In this way the process of change in El Regadio became more dynamic and the people could undertake new tasks for their own development with more effectiveness and confidence.

If the old habits of submission and dependency had not been broken in El Regadio, the community census would have failed because the interviewees would have given false answers. Resistance and suspicion disappeared when it was seen that the interviewers themselves were from the community and were trained *in situ* by the animators (using 'socio-dramas' among other techniques), thus establishing a direct subject to subject relationship. 'If people from other places had come to do it, the investigation would have failed because there are persons here who believe that most outsiders come just to steal', the Commission rightly concluded.

In the case of Nicaragua there was no difficulty in training community cadres and interviewers in *simple methods* of registering, counting, systematisation and data analysis. Thus the concept of 'research' was demythologised. It was no longer seen as something magical or difficult, as if it were an exclusive monopoly of 'experts' and 'academics'. The demystification of research and its replacement by subject-to-subject analysis also occurred in Puerto Tejada (Colombia) when the housing conditions of the poor were examined. This process strengthened the confidence of the communities to get on with the task of asserting their claims. Nevertheless, care had to be taken that the newly trained cadres did not adopt the superior attitudes of exploitation and allow themselves to become pivotal men, just because of the training which they had received and which, in one way or another, made them different from the rest. When this selective training was not done carefully, its results were counter-productive.

Obviously not everything which goes by the name of participation today is in fact of a participatory nature. There are voluntary and vertically imposed aspects of this process which should be taken into account in present-day processes of political and social action. In particular, national and international politicians have been prone to base their philosophy of popular participation on Samuel Huntington's limited definition of it as 'acts affecting governmental decision-making' (Huntington and Nelson 1976). Of course, this is not participation at all according to PAR standards (since it is not the government which is the final referent, but the peoples themselves), a fact which is recognised by critical political scientists such as Seligson and Booth (1979) and Gran (1983), who admit the real-life complexities of the participatory process.

Neither is Jaroslav Vanek's 'participatory economy' entirely satisfactory for the Third World peoples (in spite of Vanek's well-intentioned remarks that the powerful may learn 'something fundamentally good' from the poor and weak to achieve 'a better balance of respect among nations'), because his analysis is limited to equilibrium and convergence theories deeply rooted in the developmentalist discourse; the latter is failing precisely because it has achieved only a selective assimilation of what is 'fundamentally good' in the dependent countries (Vanek 1971).

PAR principles on interaction and organisation in praxis lead on to other important consequences, namely, that PAR induces the creation of its own field in order to extend itself in time and space, both horizontally and vertically in communities and regions. It moves from the micro to the macro level and thus acquires a political dimension. The final *evaluation or applied criteria* of the methodology revolve on this political dimension and the opportunity which it offers for making theory concomitant with action.

In addition to the central ideas of culture and ethnicity, special importance is accorded to the concept of *region* (within the context of social formation), as a key element in the PAR interpretation of reality. Exploitative traditional structures are thus better understood, as are the alliances of forces toward revolutionary conjunctures which may be forged under new leadership or by enlightened vanguards. Catalytic external agents play a crucial role in linking up the local dimension to regional and, at a later stage, to the national and the international levels. The particular and the general, social formation and mode of production, may thus be synthesised in this manner.

The open-ended nature of these struggles, as seen in the three countries studied, shows that ebbs and flows are unavoidable because of personal failures by animators and cadres, official repression, internal and external conflicts, ecological rhythms, and lack of material resources. These factors cause the communities to fall victim to the structural violence of the old order (seigneurial or capitalist) of poverty, exploitation, oppression and

84

dependence. To persist at every level and over the long term is therefore an integral ingredient of PAR, and of the endogenous lesson of the organisation of the popular bases.

Let us see how incipient processes of theorisation and political militancy in our cases have developed and opened up new opportunities for working the resulting countervailing power for base groups in regions.

During a local housing crisis commissions set out from Puerto Tejada (Colombia) to seek the solidarity of neighbouring municipalities. However, the breaking of local boundaries was never so dramatic as on that day when, from the mountains of Cauca and Nariño in the south of the country, an 'Indian march' (of Paeces, Guambianos and Gran Cumbal) arrived with their traditional costumes and flutes on their way to Bogotá to denounce the constant persecutions of which they were the victims, and to have the rights of the Indian people respected. The Indians and blacks, in an unusual way, made a sacred pact to fight their common oppression. Everybody in the town came out to receive the visitors with floats, music and dancing, cheering, posters and fireworks. Thus the bases were laid for future investigations and co-ordinated actions by their respective organisations.

The holding of a Regional Assembly was another important step towards further strengthening this encouraging process of internal and external regional relations. Delegates from six different parts of Northern Cauca were present, with their respective studies and papers on local problems. From this Assembly there emerged the first sure indications that it would be possible to establish a regional political movement which would be set within an autochthonous cultural reality.

Meanwhile, the people of Cauca and Valle del Cauca discovered that there were similar independent and critical groups and movements in other Colombian departments (Tolima, Cundinamarca, Cordoba, Sucre, Antioquia and Caqueta). Their first contacts were nervous and unsure. However, little by little relations became warmer among these local groups and movements until they saw that it was both possible and necessary to reach a supra-regional level of activity by establishing the formal bases for a national 'popular movement'. The first convention of this movement took place in Bogotá on 24-25 September 1983, two years after the first local contacts had been established. This 'popular movement' was not born as a political monolith: it has neither hierarchies nor chiefs, but is a pluralist and many-sided body. It has already managed to co-ordinate civic and regional movements at the national level, and has continued to reinforce the same process in cultural, scientific, social, economic, religious and other spheres. It is hoped that by maintaining their autonomy and leadership these movements would coalesce towards the common political goal of achieving substantial changes in the fabric of Colombian society.

It is significant that in Colombia this process has led to the organisation of a movement rather than a political party as such, and that the procedure adopted has been *from the bases upwards* and from the periphery towards the centre, rather than the contrary, as has usually been the case with traditional parties, including those of the left. There was resistance on the part of local groups to 'founding a party', something which they had seen fail so many times before in regional capitals through decisions taken by intellectuals cut off from the bases. Any eventual party was seen more as a result of the process and work with the bases rather than an imposing guide to carry out the tasks in hand.

Upholding the organisational and interactive efforts of PAR – the mechanisms of people's countervailing power – can also reach the international level. Indeed, there already exist in several world capitals important support institutions for this type of work and which are responding to this special (and perhaps unexpected) challenge from the Third World. They are non-governmental organisations, private foundations, sympathetic ministries, ecclesiastical bodies, alert United Nations agencies whose positive support calls for an awareness on the part of participatory researchers to preserve the freshness of the PAR approach as an original input from the world periphery.

Moreover, many writers and thinkers from the dominant countries are also responding to the need to understand these new intellectual and political trends which are coming from the world periphery and harmonise them with their own schemes of explanation and action. Hence the contributions of work on historical economic theory (Feder 1976; Frank 1978; Barraclough 1982); the countercurrents in the sciences (Capra 1983; Berman 1981; Nowotny 1978); the new emphasis on political processes from the bottom up (Gran 1983; Wolfe 1981; Pitt 1976; Galtung 1980; Castells 1985); critical epistemology (Oquist 1978; Moser 1982); applied hermeneutics (Himmelstrand 1978); radical adult education (Hall 1977; de Schutter 1981; Swantz 1980); problem-oriented social science (Pearse 1980; Taussig 1986; Comstock 1982; Goulet 1977); and the convergent work on social intervention and action (Touraine 1978) as well as on world systems versus dependence theories (Wallerstein 1979; Seers 1981).

Perhaps we have all been drawing closer, each in his or her own way in the face of the scientific, political and moral crisis facing the world today, towards the expression of a new kind of socio-political discourse based on revalued concepts such as participation, endogenesis, regionality, and power as we have tried to define them in this study and which would replace and supercede the current concepts of development, underdevelopment, integrated rural development, nationality, and growth per se, that is the concepts which have dominated international literature since at least 1949 in support of the views from rich countries, but which are now in crisis.

Techniques for knowledge and power

The second lesson – which proposes the experiences of learning to know and recognise ourselves as a means of creating people's power – has a certain phenomenological basis.

86

It starts with the thesis that science is not a fetish with a life of its own or something which has an absolute value. As amply demonstrated, science is a cultural product with specific human purposes and implicitly carries those class biases and values which scientists hold as a group. It therefore favours those who produce and control it, although its present institutionalised development may in fact be developing into a phase threatening humanity. For this reason it is theoretically possible to conceive of alternative ways of science, such as a people's science to exist as an endogenous process. People's science may be formally constructed in its own terms, and perhaps it could serve as a corrective to certain destructive tendencies of the predominant inhuman forms of science. The knowledge thus acquired, properly system-atised, would serve the interests of the exploited classes. This people's science would converge with the so-called 'universal science' of academe to the point where a totalising paradigm would be created which would incorporate the newly acquired systematised knowledge.

Under these conditions, it is obvious that *forms and relationships of knowledge production* should have as much, or even more, value than forms and relationships of material production. As Md. Anisur Rahman (1985) has pointed out, the elimination of exploitation patterns at the material or infrastructural level of a society does not assure, by itself, that the general system of exploitation has been destroyed or that poverty, ignorance, and injustice have been overcome. It becomes necessary to eliminate also the relationship governing the production of knowledge, production which tends to give ideological support to injustice, oppression and the destructive forces which characterise the modern world. It is only in this manner that the classic Baconian axiom, 'Knowledge is power' can be fully understood; and when the exploited classes require such an understanding that they take a decisive step not only towards their own liberation, but towards that of the other social classes threatened with global destruction.

This creative process of responsible all-embracing and useful knowledge-making does not take as its point of insertion the pedagogical method implied in the early Freire treatises but dialogical research oriented to the social situation in which people live. For this reason, it begins with the question 'Why is there poverty?' the answer to which may lead simultaneously to greater awareness, social research and political praxis.

Ideally in such cases the grass-roots and their cadres should be able to participate in the research process from the very beginning, that is from the moment it is decided what the subject of research will be. And they should remain involved at every step of the process until the publication of results and the various forms of returning the knowledge to the people are completed.

As has been done in practice, such a participatory task gives precedence to qualitative rather than quantitative analysis, without losing sight of the importance of explanatory scientific schemas of cause-and-effect. In this realm, participatory researchers have faced the dilemmas of employing affective logic involving the heart versus dialectical logic with cold-headed laboratory analysis. As a rule we have followed Pascal's dictum, 'The heart has its *reasons* which the reason does not at all perceive', much as in William Bateson's ideal that scientific work can reach its highest point when it aspires to art (cf. Berman 1981 : 197). If emotion and reason have their own precise algorhythms, their discovery is not beyond human efforts as has been done with musical logic, for example, and with men of letters and aesthetes who have been able 'to think with the heart' (Hofmannsthal, Gide, Mann), a possibility recognised for the sciences (and practised) by Einstein, Russell and Whitehead (*Principia Mathematica*), among others.

With these general objectives in mind, we found that our Mexico, Nicaragua and Colombia experiences indicated that the following *techniques* resulting from the practice of PAR are useful in the establishment of people's countervailing power and in aiding adult education.

1. *Collective research.* This is the systematic use of information collected and systematised on a group basis, as a source of data and objective knowledge of facts resulting from meetings, socio-dramas, public assemblies, committees, fact-finding trips, etc. This collective and dialogical method not only produces data which may be immediately corrected or verified but also provides a social validation of objective knowledge which cannot be achieved through individual methods based on surveys or field work. In this way confirmation is obtained of the positive values of dialogue, discussion, argumentation and consensus in the objective investigation of social realities.

Let us give some illustrations of this technique.

People's assemblies in Puerto Tejada were held at least twenty times. They became a sort of social arena in which the people discovered themselves and their history. There were several modes in such collective recognition: 1) that of individuals as acting and thinking people; 2) the past in relation to the present; 3) the legitimacy of the struggle to destroy the bourgeois values of crime and sin; 4) the causes of injustice and exploitation and the identification of those responsible; 5) the people's capacity to decide, act and transform themselves collectively.

The assemblies became a sort of 'public trial' in which the people acted as judge and where the proceedings concerned the reasons for injustice. Evidence was presented to the assemblies in the form of witness accounts, documents, technical opinion from friendly experts, etc. on the basis of which the sugar planters were indicted and ordered to return the land they had abusively taken. In this dynamic way the people of Puerto Tejada took over for themselves a well-known bourgeois ritual and gave it a different meaning and content.

The combination of study and practice, when done in this collective and dialogical way, implies the idea of a service to the community. It is altruistic knowledge. Thus in El Mezquital the inhabitants hoped that the outside investigators 'would show the people how their training could be applied to the problems of real life'. This expectation was closely connected with the Indian communal tradition. In this way the periodicity of meetings increased;

88

communal first-aid kits, maize mills, and family kitchen gardens were established; defective wells were repaired; buildings were roofed and pine trees planted in school yards.

The same effects, at another level, were seen in the 'census data socialisation' meetings which took place in El Regadio. Through comments and analysis at these meetings the people not only corrected the data and filled in the gaps (they knew each other quite well) but also gave meaning to the collected information, so that the successive steps of the economic and political development of this region could then be established (see Fals-Borda 1985 for details of this process).

The final work on the local history of El Cerrito (Colombia) was another collective experience which was indispensable for the proper completion of the task. All the inhabitants were summoned to listen to the first draft of the text. It was there – with some persons answering, others correcting – that the final orderly and polished text emerged and which was then sent to the printers as part of the local PAR experience.

2. *Critical recovery of history.* This is an effort to discover selectively, through collective memory, those elements of the past which proved useful in the defence of the interests of exploited classes, and which proved useful and which may be applied to the present struggles to increase awareness. Use is thus made of oral tradition, in the form of interviews and witness accounts by older members of the community possessing good analytical memories; the search for concrete information on given periods of the past kept in family coffers; data columns and popular stories; by ideological projections, imputation, personification and other techniques designed to stimulate the collective memory. In this way folk heroes, data and facts were discovered which corrected, complemented or clarified official or academic accounts written with other class interests or biases in mind. Or completely new and fresh information was discovered and which was of major importance to regional and national history, all with the purpose of upholding people's power.

In the case of Puerto Tejada, pertinent historical results became quickly evident. The first attempts at critical recollection during the communal forum saw the re-emergence of an ideal of freedom dating back to the time of the courageous runaway black slaves who had colonised the neighbouring region of La Perezosa on the Palo river. It was a recollection which had been repressed by subsequent exploitation, when the whites established their cattle ranches and extended them by violence, destroying the free black villages which had thrived in that region.

But the feeling of being free, which had characterised the old Palo villages, re-emerged in unexpected ways during the forum. It was as if a sleeping volcano had suddenly become active. Some elders recalled the life of authentic heroes of the region like Crucito (a local Robin Hood), Fidel and José Ignacio Mina (Sinecio), Sixto and Ciro Biáfara, and Natanael Diaz. They had been exceptional crusaders who had fought since the beginning of the present century with their black groups for the possession of lands which the estate owners still wanted to wrest from the people. They were indeed real men who knew how to value their freedom! By comparison, the present situation of town life was hateful and incomprehensible. Critical collective memory called for something more concrete to be done to correct such injustices, because if their grandparents had been able to fight the 'whites' before with relative success, why could they not also? History thus gained a new meaning from these new glimpses of truth and power, namely that not only could the facts be remembered, but that they could also be converted into a catapult for a better communal life.

The free settlement of the former slaves thus emerged from the past and became an ideal of freedom for the entire Northern Cauca. This was not all. As cocoa had been the principal product for trade and economic survival during that heroic period, the plant became the local symbol of freedom. At the same time, its historical counter-symbol clearly emerged in dialectical opposition: the sugar cane as a sign of evil, represented by the plantation owners who were destroying the traditional ways of life by taking over the land of the peasants.

In the same fashion, Don Silvestre in El Cerrito (Colombia), together with other elders, became one of the few sources of trustworthy historical facts about the region. His inimitable stories explained how the village was founded on the shores of a lagoon, with recognised legal rights to the use of the fertile plains in which staple crops were grown. Formal law protected the peasants, although it was constantly ignored by the powerful land-owners of Coardoba whose aim was to increase their herds selfishly. They wanted the same territory as the peasants.

The struggle had begun decades ago, towards the end of the last century and the beginning of the present century. Its sparks did not spare the new hamlet of El Cerrito. It was history which had been forgotten and buried, until 1972 when a piece of participatory research was carried out with the then powerful peasant movement. Some of the heroes and heroines who had defended the interests of the working classes during the 1920s, were fortunately still alive: Juana Julia Guzmán among others, now old, poor and sick. She had worked shoulder to shoulder since 1918 with Vicente Adamo, an immigrant Italian labourer who organised the first workers' struggles in Monteria and its surrounding districts.

Juana Julia held the key to the critical, untapped historical knowledge of those years. She had not wanted to share it with local conservative or liberal politicians who constantly urged her to tell her story. She only relented when she saw that her own class had re-emerged in the peasant movement which had inspired her in her youth and took part herself in the new struggle, attending meetings and assemblies along with the others. Juana Julia's presence in the peasant meetings was like seeing history in the flesh. In these special circumstances her word carried the additional magic of real experience and the weight of the exciting experiment which had defeated the land-owners of the coast for the first time. In the same way, it can be said that the rediscovery of

Juana Julia (and other contemporary figures) was one of the ideological factors which most stimulated the struggle for land between 1970 and 1976 in Córdoba. The legal possession of the marshes and lagoons by the people was at last established in El Cerrito through pressure from the peasants on the Colombian Institute of Agrarian Reform (INCORA).

Another advantage gained from the 'recovery' of Juana Julia Guzmán was that she also opened the coffers where she kept the material souvenirs of her past struggles. In spite of the ravages of time and damp, they contained the first treasures of a genuine people's museum, like the silk armbands with the 'three eights' (a socialist aspiration of the period), pictures of Adamo, the Monteria Workers' House, the first public hospital, members of the first organised trade-unions. They were indispensable elements (we call them 'data columns') to understand past events, the antecedents of the present struggle carried on by the grandchildren of those who figured in the old yellow documents or in the faded photographs of an epoch resurrected from the past in these family coffers.

All this systematic research activity carried out in collaboration with the local people – with data columns, the recovery of popular figures and heroes, ideological projections, imputations, and personifications – took place outside academic institutions. Official and academic historians had completely ignored the existence of Vicente Adamo and the socialist workers' organisations of the 1920s. But this grass-roots corrector of official history completed and illustrated it in a critical manner, putting it to the service of poor people so that they too could acquire a respectable identity and a collective ego through the recognition of their tradition and their own history. The PAR ideal of opening new ideological and scientific perspectives of popular origin in the Atlantic coast of Colombia was thus fulfilled. The same happened in Mexico and Nicaragua.

3. *Valuing and applying folk culture.* In order to mobilise the masses, this technique is based upon the recognition of essential or core values among the peoples in each region. This allows account to be taken of cultural and ethnic elements frequently ignored in regular political practice, such as art, music, drama, sports, beliefs, myths, story-telling, and other expressions related to human sentiment, imagination, and ludic or recreational tendencies.

Two social groups have distinguished themselves in Nicaragua by their enthusiastic and loyal dedication to the onerous revolutionary tasks: women and young teachers, that is, those young people with a minimum level of education and who have only recently become literate. This is understandable. They are among the most haunted victims of the economic and social systems which predominate throughout most of the world and who have found, in the revolutionary adventure, a genuine outlet for their creativity hitherto frustrated by injustice, exploitation and prejudice.

In El Regadio women were considered dolls, good for making tortillas and cooking beans. Hardly anyone recognised their important role as 'anchors' in society, although they were the centre and often the main support for their families. But with the revolution, women found in the educational committees (CEP) a way of leaving home and kitchen. They discovered how to break their routine and organise themselves to defend their interests. They began to speak about less trivial matters and to seek ways of overcoming existing poverty. Their task was how to transform the CEPs into something more productive, such as a useful sewing class, for example, and from there to proceed to the acquisition of a sewing machine which the community would share. Debates of this kind could finish in 'subversive' talk, as happened with the subject of machismo in public dances. How was it that married men, but not married women, could go alone to these dances? Armed with this dynamic and critical approach to such double moral standards, Nicaraguan peasant women became a motor for social and revolutionary change, and displayed an almost monopolistic activism in the new processes.

For their part, recently literate young Nicaraguans have experienced a spiritual elation which has made them more altruistic than before. They dedicate themselves to the educational campaigns with 'body and soul'. For them, there are no fixed timetables nor family duties. Their spirit of sacrifice is absolute and they are the driving force of the revolutionary wheel. A temptation to which they are sometimes exposed is to make pupils feel the weight of their newly found knowledge – their newly acquired authority as teacher of the people – and to become somewhat domineering.

However, in this they are simply imitating the oppressive educational models which they had seen applied before in the local school or nearest village. In such cases they fail to break the subject/object binominal and prefer to bully adult pupils who cannot understand, let us say, what the dactylic stress is. But imagination can come quickly to their aid, by recourse to shared experiences. Then they can explain that the dactylic stress in any given word is like a 'triple play' in baseball. Everyone can understand this and proceed to the next lesson.

Through such *feelings* it is possible to understand the primal forces of people's culture and symbols. They are like an affective logic. In Puerto Tejada, when he spoke of the historical origins of the enclosures of the runaway slaves of the Palo river, Ño Didacio expressed the same idea: 'Negro culture is not just a culture of evocation; it is not a question of memory but of feelings'. His sentiments led him to revive the old 'dance of the knives', a half-dead musical folk expression the meaning of which could only be recaptured in the mobilising context of the People's Civic Movement of Northern Cauca, with its challenge to the municipal bosses. Through the importance which it attached to local culture in this way, the movement experienced the greatest political gains of its short history. It had managed to give voice to the soul of the people.

Another important popular recreative expression which is recoverable for action through research – at least among the coastal people of Colombia – is that of *story-telling*: tales, legends, parables, fables, anecdotes, riddles and puns. Even refined gossip, viewed as information, may be useful as a means of positive mobilisation. All these elements of oral culture may be exploited as a new and dynamic political language which belongs to the people, as we saw in El Cerrito and Puerto Tejada, especially those forms which already contain an implicit protest intention. This is the case for example with the well-known tales of 'Uncle Tiger and Uncle Rabbit' which narrate the impudence and skills of a defenceless little animal (the peasant) confronted with a dangerous beast (the boss) and which display a powerful sense of latent resistance against the injustices which characterise the production relationship. On the Colombian coast (as in other regions), story-telling and other expressions of oral tradition are among the most effective ways for keeping alive the people's culture and their core values. Story-telling refuses to die because, if it did, the peasant people would die with it.

These cultural processes operating within the heart of the community are an active force which allows the knowledge of the people to ferment in a vast cauldron or melting pot, and build up the incredible resources of resistance which characterise the popular struggles in the three countries.

Feelings, imagination and the sense of play are apparently inexhaustible sources of strength and resistance among the people. These three elements have a common basis which cannot be ignored in the struggle to promote mobilisation and people's power in our countries: religious beliefs. Here are some examples.

The death of a child during the invasion of the sugar plantation outside Puerto Tejada and the bravery of its mother – together with the practices and beliefs implicit during the funeral wake – were events which stopped the army in its tracks when soldiers attempted to occupy and burn the huts of the new district. The spectre of the 'little angel' lying dead and the hypnotic rhythm of the *alabao* (ritual music), more than the presence of the national flag which had been hoisted there, made the troops respect the invasion.

A witch added his secret power to the fight against a land-owner who did not want to give up his excess land to the peasants of Córdoba. The witch's services must have been effective judging by the eventual success, and his support had an important moral and psychological effect among the popular masses. Another witch is still being consulted in Villapaz, not far from Puerto Tejada, to see if the course of a river can be changed so as to recuperate public land and avoid floods, which are the objectives of a new local civic movement.

Something similar can be said with regard to health protection practices based on the knowledge of medicine-men and herbalists in the peasant communities of the three countries. These are serious and systematic class-ificatory practices, as can be seen in Ixmiquilpan and other Otomi settlements in the valley of El Mezquital. Such revaluation endeavours have had an extra-ordinary effect on Otomi peasant behaviour and on their campaigns to defend their economic and cultural heritage. The same can be said for San Agustin Atenango (Mexico) where the community 'doctor', the dispenser of the empir-ical scientific knowledge which he holds as *Tata Yiva*, or 'lord of the powers', is the permanent guardian of the core values of his ancient community.

All this and much more can and should be examined and better understood with a view to establishing countervailing action. If the basic culture and values of the peasants are selectively harnessed to the popular struggle, and if negative alienation is properly contained, an unconquerable force is thus created which would lead to the establishment of an authentic and deep-rooted people's power based on imagination and feelings, capable of transforming unjust structures of the dominant society.

4. *Production and diffusion of new knowledge.* This technique is an integral part of the research process because it is a central part of the feedback and evaluative objective of PAR. It recognises a division of labour among and within base groups. Although PAR strives to end the monopoly of the written word (which as a rule is an elitist phenomenon), it incorporates various styles and procedures for systematising new data and knowledge according to the level of political conscience and ability for understanding written, oral or visual messages by the base groups and public in general.

Four levels of communication are established depending on whether the message and systematised knowledge are addressed to preliterate peoples, cadres and intellectuals. They require that a good PAR researcher should learn to address all four levels with the same message in the different styles required, if he or she is to be really effective in the written, auditory or visual communication of the thought or message. Nevertheless the actual need for articulating abstract theory and concepts is still retained for level four. This carries the danger that intellectuals hold onto their traditional monopoly and dominance unless they become truly organic with the people and acknowledge their real commitment to base groups and their struggles.

Other efficient forms of communication based on a 'total' or intentional language include the use of image, sound, painting, gestures, mime, photo-graphs, radio programmes, popular theatre, video-tapes, audio-visual material, poetry, music, puppets and exhibitions. Finally, material forms of organisation and economic and social action by base groups, such as in the organisation of cooperatives, trade-unions, leagues, cultural centres, action units, workshops, training centres, etc. as a result of pertinent studies carried out.

There is an obligation to return this knowledge systematically to the communities and workers' organisations because they continue to be its owners. They may determine the priorities concerning its use and authorise and establish the conditions for its publication and dissemination.

This systematic devolution of knowledge complies with Gramsci's objective of transforming 'common' sense into 'good' sense or critical knowledge ('revolutionary science' as a new paradigm) which would be the sum of experiential and theoretical knowledge. It thus transcends Mao Tse-Tung's principle of 'from the masses to the masses' in that it recognises the capacity of the masses to systematise the data discovered, that is, to participate fully in the entire process, with their own organic intellectuals from the beginning to the end.

To succeed in these endeavours requires a shared code of communication between internal elements and external agents of change which leads to a common and mutually understandable conceptualisation and categorisation. The resulting plain and understandable language should be based on daily intentional expressions and be accessible to all, avoiding the airs of arrogance and the technical jargon that spring from usual academic and political practices, including ideological elements from the current (and increasingly discredited) developmentalist discourse.

These PAR techniques do not exclude a flexible use of other practices deriving from sociological and anthropological tradition such as the open interview (avoiding any excessively rigid structure), census or simple survey (on rare occasions mail questionnaires), direct systematic observation (with personal participation and selective experimentation), field diaries, data filing, photography, cartography, statistics, sound recordings, primary and secondary source materials, notarial, regional and national archives. Cadres ('resource persons') should not only be equipped to handle these orthodox techniques responsibly but also know how to popularise them by teaching the activists simpler, more economic and controllable methods of research, so that they can carry on their work without being dependent on intellectuals or external agents of change and their costly equipment and procedures.

Thus with all these ways and techniques, advancement and transformation of oppressed peoples can be made possible in several applied fields: in adult education, in political and civic action, in socio-economic advancement, and other types of fieldwork. Additional current experiences are enriching this approach and challenging non-committed academic ways in established institutions. In this manner perhaps PAR may contribute to help build a better world for everybody with justice and peace.

References

BARRACLOUGH 1982. *A Preliminary Analysis of the Nicaraguan Food System*. Geneva: UNRISD.
BERMAN, M. 1981. *The Reenchantment of the World*. Ithaca: Cornell University Press.
CAPRA, F. 1983. *The Turning Point*. New York: Bantam.
CASTELLS, M. 1985. 'Urban Problems and Social Change', in Fals-Borda, O. (ed.), *The Challenge of Social Change*. London: Sage.
FEDER, E. 1976. *Strawberry Imperialism*. The Hague: Institute of Social Studies.
FRANK, A.G. 1978. *Dependent Accumulation and Underdevelopment*. London: Macmillan.
GALTUNG, J. et al. 1980. *Self-Reliance: A New Development Strategy?*. London: Bogle-L'Ouverture.
GOULET, D. 1977. *The Uncertain Promise*. New York: IDOC.
HIMMELSTRAND, U. 1978. 'Action Research and Applied Social Science', in Punta de Lanza (ed.), *Crítica y política en ciencias sociales* 1. Bogotá: Punta de Lanza.
HUNTINGTON, S.P. and NELSON, J.M. 1976. *No Easy Choice: Political Participation in Developing Countries*. Cambridge, Mass.: Harvard University Press.
MOSER, H. 1982. 'The Participatory Research Approach on Village Level'. Unpublished paper. Münster: University of Münster.
NOWOTNY, H. et al. 1978. *Counter-Currents in the Sciences*. Dordrecht: Mouton.
OQUIST, P. 1978. 'The Epistemology of Action-Research'. *Development Dialogue* 4 : 10-17.
PITT, D. ed. 1976. *Development from Below*. The Hague: Mouton.

SEERS, D. 1981. *Dependency Theory: A Reassessment*. London: Frances Pinter.
SELIGSON, M.A. and BOOTH, J.A. 1979. *Political Participation in Latin America: Politics and the Poor* 2. New York: Holmes and Meier.
TAUSSIG, M. 1986. *Shamanism, Colonialism and the Wild Man*. Chicago: University of Chicago Press.
TOURAINE, A. 1978. *La voix et le regard*. Paris: Seuil.
VANEK, J. 1971. *The Participatory Economy*. Ithaca: Cornell University Press.
WALLERSTEIN, I. 1979. *The Capitalist World Economy*. Cambridge: Cambridge University Press.
WOLFE, M. 1981. *Elusive Development*. Geneva: UNRISD.

Selected Bibliography on PAR

BRANDÃO, C.R. 1981. *Pesquisa participante*. São Paulo: Editora Brasiliense.
BRANDÃO, C.R. and FALS-BORDA, O. 1986. *Investigación participativa*. Montevideo: Instituto del Hombre.
COMSTOCK, D.E. 1982. 'Participatory Research as Critical Theory: The North Bonneville, USA Experience'. Paper presented at Evergreen State College, Olympia, Washington.
DA SILVA, M.O. 1886. *Refletindo a pesquisa participante*. São Paulo: Cortez Editora.
DE SCHUTTER, A. 1981. *Investigación participativa: Una opción metodológica*. Pátzcuaro: CREFAL.
DE SILVA, G.V.S. et al. 1979. 'Bhoomi Sena, a Struggle for People's Power'. *Development Dialogue* 2 : 3-70.
DE VRIES, J. 1980. *Science as Human Behavior: On the Epistemology of Participatory Research Approach*. Amersfoort: Studiencentrum.
ERASMIE, T. and DUBELL, F. eds. 1980. *Research for the People, Research by the People: An Introduction to Participatory Research*. Linköping: University of Linköping.
FALS-BORDA, O. 1981. 'Science and the Common People'. *Journal of Social Studies* 11 : 2-21.
FALS-BORDA, O. 1985. *Conocimiento y poder popular: Lecciones con campesinos de Nicaragua, Colombia y México*. Bogotá, Madrid, México: Siglo XXI Editores.
FALS-BORDA, O. 1979-1986. *Historia doble de la Costa* 1-4. Bogotá: Carlos Valencia Editores.
FERNANDES, W. and TANDON, R. 1981. *Participatory Research and Evaluation: Experiments in Research as a Process of Liberation*. New Delhi: Indian Social Institute.
FORUM INTERNATIONAL D'ACTION COMMUNAUTAIRE 1981. 'La Recherche-Action: enjeux et pratiques', *Revue internationale d'action communautaire* 5 : 5-45.
FUGLESANG, A. and CHANDLER, D. 1986. *Participation as Process: What we can learn from Grameen Bank, Bangladesh*. Oslo: NORAD.
FUNDACION PUNTA DE LANZA 1978. *Crítica y política en ciencias sociales* 1-2. Bogotá: Punta de Lanza.
GAJARDO, M. ed. 1985. *Teoría y práctica de la educación popular*. Pátzcuaro: OEA, CREFAL, IDRC.
GAVENTA, J. 1980. *Power and Powerlessness: Quiescence and Rebellion in an Appalachian Valley*. Urbana: University of Illinois Press.
GIANOTTEN, V. and DeWIT, T. 1985. *Organización campesina: El objetivo político de la educación popular y la investigación participativa*. Dordrecht: Centre for Latin American Research and Documentation.
GRAN, G. 1983. *Development by People*. New York: Praeger.
HALL, B. and GILLETTE, A. 1977. *Participatory Research*. Toronto: International Council for Adult Education.
INTERNATIONAL COUNCIL FOR ADULT EDUCATION 1981. 'Participatory Research: Development and Issues'. *Convergence* 14 : 3-51.
KERALA SASTRA SAHITHYA PARISHAD 1984. *Science as Social Activism: Reports and Papers on the People's Science Movements in India*. Trivandrum: KSSP.
LeBOTERF, G. 1981. *L'enquête participation en question*. Condé-sur-Noireau: Ch. Corlet.
LOPEZLLERA, L. ed. 1984. *Estrategias de organizaciones de base en la crisis regional*. México: SID, CRES.
MAX-NEEF, M. 1981. *From the Outside Looking In: Experiences in Barefoot Economics*. Uppsala: Dag Hammarskjöld Foundation.

MOSER, H. and ORNAUER, H. eds. 1978. *Internationale Aspekte der Aktionsforschung.* Munich: Kösel-Verlag.

MUSTAFA, K. 1983. *Participatory Research and Popular Education in Africa.* Dar-es-Salaam: African Participatory Network.

OAKLEY, P. and MARSDEN, D. 1984. *Approaches to Participation in Rural Development.* Geneva: International Labour Office.

PARK, P. 1978. 'Social Research and Radical Change'. Paper presented at University of Massachusetts, Amherst.

PARRA ESCOBAR, E. 1983. *La investiagación-acción en la Costa Atlántica: Evaluación de la Rosca.* Cali: Fundación para la Comunicación Popular.

PEARSE, A. and STIEFEL, M. 1980. *Inquiry into Participation: A Research Approach.* Geneva: UNRISD.

RAHMAN, Md. A. ed. 1984. *Grass-Roots Participation and Self-Reliance: Experiences in South and South East Asia.* New Delhi: Oxford and IBH.

RAHMAN, Md. A. 1985. 'The Theory and Practice of Participatory Action Research', in Fals-Borda, O. (ed.), *The Challenge of Social Change.* London: Sage.

RUDQVIST, A. 1986. *Action Research and the Peasant Movement in Colombia.* Uppsala: University of Uppsala, Department of Sociology.

SWANTZ, M.L. 1980. *Rejoinder to Research: Methodology and the Participatory Research Approach.* Dar-es-Salaam: Ministry of National Culture and Youth.

SWEDNER, H. 1983. *Human Welfare and Action Research in Urban Settings.* Stockholm: Delegation for Social Research.

THIOLLENT, M. 1985. *Metodologia da pesquisa-ação.* São Paulo: Cortez Editora.

VILAS, C. 1985. *Entre la producción de lo nuevo y la reproducción de lo viejo: Educación, ideologia y poder popular en Nicaragua.* Managua: Centro de Estudios Económicos.

VIO GROSSI, F. 1981. *Investigación participativa y praxis rural.* Lima: Mosca Azul.

WIGNARAJA, P. ed. 1983. *Grass Root Initiatives in Developing Countries and UNDP Project Planning and Implementation.* Rome: Society for International Development.

ZAMOSC, L. 1986. 'Socioalogos y campesinos: Estudio comparado de dos casos en Colombia', in Foro Nacional por Colombia, *La investigación-acción participativa en Colombia.* Bogotá: Foro por Colombia.

CREATING INDIGENOUS SOCIOLOGIES

Creating Indigenous Sociologies

Sociology as a professional research-based activity underpinned by its institutionalisation as an academic discipline is a twentieth century Western product. Social theory in the sense of coherent reflections on the nature of society has a much longer history and worldwide incidence.

Social theory informed by empirical observation has occurred more rarely, but even so pre-modern and non-Western societies have produced it often enough to suggest that the capacity to develop sociology, or something like it, is not limited to present Western versions. We only have to think of the extensive references to the social arrangements in Greek city-states which Aristotle's *Politics* contained, or of Ibn Khaldun's science of civilisation (*Ilm Al Umran*) with its systematic history of Arab society, to remind ourselves of this fact.

The conditions for generating sociology are not confined therefore to the importation of Western ideas and it is this which encourages scholars in the developing world to look to their own traditions of thought for independent inspiration in analysing their own societies. The ambition to create indigenous sociologies has developed *pari passu* with the rejection of dependency on the developed world.

But there are irremediable differences which distinguish this sociological movement from the examples from pre-modern cultures. It takes much of its impetus from reaction against dominant modes of thought. It does not operate within an unstructured setting. The Arab, Chinese, Muslim, African or Latin American scholars today are as likely to derive inspiration for indigenisation from the aspirations of national sociologies in advanced societies as from their own. Canadian sociology may reject the hegemony of the sociology of the United States, Welsh may reject British, or Basque, Spanish.

In other words, it is impossible to divorce the drive for indigenous sociologies from the overall processes of internationalisation and globalisation. Such implications are contained even in the phrase 'the indigenisation of sociology'. To make something indigenous is as self-contradictory as giving someone freedom. It must in essence already be there.

This should be even more apparent when we reflect on the fact that 'indigenisation' is something which has been promoted by international conferences and supported by bodies such as the International Social Science Council. For instance, papers on this theme were given at the X. World Congress of Sociology in Mexico City in 1982 in a session organised by Akinsola Akiwowo. (Some have been published in *International Sociology*, 3, 1988, 155–199). 'Indigenisation' carries all the difficulties and ambiguities of 'development aid'. The extent to which it represents an outside imposition is always open to question.

What is, however, unquestionable is that, under the banner of indigenisation, sociologies with distinctive national characteristics have developed and that the discourse of the discipline has correspondingly been enriched. Each time this happens there is a test of the limits of universalism and communicability in sociology. For it is clear that the newly developed indigenous sociology is as anxious to communicate its insights and findings in such a way that they may be absorbed by the world community of sociologists as it is concerned to be heard within its parent culture. But that in itself is a tension within the national sociology.

Readers of *International Sociology* have been fortunate in being able to follow the development of a particular argument around indigenisation among Nigerian sociologists and philosophers. The three papers assembled here surrounding Akiwowo's claims for a Yoruba sociology represent the basis for a case study which can reveal the cross-currents which exist in any such claims anywhere. They should therefore make particularly useful source material for teachers and students of this subject.

Akiwowo turns to folk culture as the source for propositions of an explanatory kind which might be used in future sociological studies within an African setting. The particular source he uses is traditional oral poetry recited by the Yoruba people when a new human settlement is founded, the *Ayajo Asuwada*. Within it is contained a myth of creation, called *Alasuwada*, which Akiwowo interprets as expressing a number of universal principles which can be used to generate sociological type propositions.

Makinde seeks to build upon the foundations Akiwowo has laid in the previous and other papers. He stresses that *asuwada* is a philosophical and teleological principle, one which contains the ideas of purposiveness and unity. At one level it is realised in the very basis of any society. At another level it is realised in the application of profound knowledge for the improvement of the human condition in the work of social scientists, philosophers, natural scientists or ordinary people. This is Akiwowo's concept of *ifogbontaayese*.

Lawuyi and Taiwo acknowledge the folk basis for the concepts which Akiwowo and Makinde develop, but they remain unconvinced that they have demonstrated they can serve as the basis for sociology. In particular they charge Akiwowo and Makinde with basically being concerned to find Yoruba equivalents for English concepts and they call for rigour and precision in real Yoruba sociological concepts.

Yet Lawuyi and Taiwo's demand is itself justified by reference to Aristotle and notions of essence, which they hold are implied by the idea of *asuwa*. They accept the possibility of a Yoruba sociology, but explicate it in terms of Western philosophy.

There is no resolution in sight for these problems. All we know is that the scope of the argument continues to extend over time and cultures.

CONTRIBUTIONS TO THE SOCIOLOGY OF KNOWLEDGE FROM AN AFRICAN ORAL POETRY*

Akinsola A. Akiwowo

Over the whole of Africa, creation is the most widely acknowledged work of God. This Concept is expressed through saying that God created all things, through giving Him the name of creator (or Moulder or Maker), and through addressing Him in prayer and invocations as the Creator. We have abundant examples of what African people say concerning the creative activity of God, and a few of these will suffice here.

John S. Mbiti 1970 : 50.

Introduction

A study of the history of sociology in nations that are either ideologically diverse or similar, such as, for example, the USA, the USSR, Bulgaria and Hungary[1] may reveal significant lessons for professing sociologists in Africa. Among these lessons may be how linguistic and metaphysical representations of knowledge may enter into the development of what George Homans (1967) calls 'the body of general explanatory principles' of the social sciences. Bodies of such explanatory principles may consist of many approaches to the discovery of general relationships between elements of human behaviour. In sociology, approaches are identified by different names: the paradigmatic, the metaphorical, the allegorical, and so on, are examples. For each approach an example can be cited to illustrate it; but there is not enough time in this paper to engage in such illustrations.[2]

The principal aim of this paper is to contribute to a general body of explanatory principles by demonstrating how some ideas and notions contained in a type of African oral poetry can be extrapolated in the form of propositions for testing in future sociological studies in Africa or other world societies.

In order to reach this end, this paper will attempt to do three things. It will present a large portion of a translation into English of a Yoruba oral poetry

* *Previously entitled 'Ayajo Asuwada: An Oral Poetry on the Doctrine of Creation: with contributions to Sociology of Knowledge'. A seminar paper prepared for presentation on 19th May 1986 under the auspices of the Institute of Cultural Studies and Department of African Languages and Literatures, University of Ife, Ile-Ife, Nigeria.*

103

called *Ayajo Asuwada*. This poetry is usually recited, according to the informant, at a rite-of-consecration called *akintelu*, performed when a new human settlement is to be founded in the Ikoyi section of the Osun Division in Oyo State[3] of Nigeria. It will present interpretative ideas and thoughts that came to mind from reflecting, several times, upon the meanings of the language of the oral poetry. Finally, the paper will set forth a number of propositions inductively inferred from the doctrine of creation contained in the oral poetry as a probable sociological theoretical framework.

The Asuwada Myth of Creation

Initially we had chosen to entitle this paper, *Alasuwada: A Myth of Creation*, but later events made us change it to the one on the title page. The term 'doctrine', which has been introduced, has this dictionary definition: 'What is taught; body of instruction; religious, political, scientific, etc.: belief, dogma, or tenet'. For our purpose we accept for the meaning of 'myth', 'purely fictitious narrative usually involving supernatural persons, etc., embodying popular ideas on natural phenomena, etc., allegory . . . fictitious person or thing' is relegated to a less central role.

From these definitions of both 'myth' and 'doctrine' the grounds for their choice can be perceived.[4] The object of our investigation is both a myth of creation, called *Alasuwada*, and what it teaches about the creation of the Earth and everything in it, including man. It is obvious that both doctrine and 'myth' can be classified sociologically under the broad terms 'belief system'. Myths and their doctrines are the subject of keen interest to social scientists because of their relevance to social theory. Quite recently, three American sociologists – Beth B. Hess, Elizabeth W. Markson and Peter J. Stein (1982) – observed that the French sociologist Emile Durkheim, while looking into the nature of social life itself, has noted that beliefs emerge from human interactions and that religion and society are coterminous (exist together). Further, they noted that without going so far as to claim that society worships itself, 'the social scientist must pay attention to the particular structure of a society and its culture to understand why certain beliefs and rituals are elaborated' (Hess et al 1982 : 402). Hess and her colleagues also discussed how certain belief systems may be linked to the economic uncertainty experienced by people operating a certain type of economy; while other beliefs may be linked to the important ritual functions performed by females in an agriculturalist society. Thus, they see not only religions as reflections of the social system, but also suggest rather convincingly that 'If one were to classify societies on the basis of belief systems rather than mode of subsistence, it is the industrial nations that are more simple in their rituals and belief systems' (1982 : 402). In this paper we hold the view that by paying attention to certain beliefs and rituals, it is possible to arrive at an understanding of a society.

Before concluding these introductory remarks, it is right to advance the following two points of view:

(a)   Many African societies, such as the Igbo, Kikuyu, Yoruba, and Zulu, for example, are indeed complex, highly developed societies when belief system, and that includes myths and rituals, instead of mode of subsistence system, is used as a criterion of classification.

(b)   *Alasuwada*, a body of doctrines of creation in oral poetry form, may be confidently described as '*a vision of the future*' which, according to Hess et al, provides a sense of destiny that 'unifies all true behaviours and gives meaning to both individuals' existence and human history' (401).[5]

As an aid to the presentation of the doctrines, the text of the *Alasuwada* Oral Poetry, which comprises 176 lines, has been divided into two main sub-divisions: the spoken poetry and the song poetry. There are eight poems in the spoken poetry, while the song poetry has only one main poem consisting of six verses. Verses 1 to 3 of the second sub-division form the lead song. Verses 4 and 5 together form the *Akogbe* (song and chorus), while Verse 6 is an *Egbe Orin* (chorus song).

Furthermore, for ease of treatment, we present only the text in its English translation. By 'treatment', here we mean simply putting down in prose the gist of one's understanding of the oral poetry. Such a treatment has its own limitation and on no account should it be regarded as the only possible interpretation of the verses of the oral poetry. We have endeavoured to be as faithful to the Yoruba text as possible in the course of interpretation.

Main Themes in the Alasuwada Oral Poetry

Lines 1-6 of Poem One

1.   Teeming heads congregate at the grove of *Ogun*.

2.   The anthill is the *morere* of the *eerun*.

3.   *Asuwa* is the *morere* of humankind.

4.   It was with the principle of *asuwa* that the Heavens were established.

5.   It was with the principle of *asuwa* that the Earth was created.

6.   In *asuwa* forms all things descended upon the Earth activated by purpose.

Interpretation: In these six lines, the *Alasuwada* Oral Poetry begins with a declaration of a principle, called *asuwa*, by which all things on and in Earth and the Heavens were created (*da*) and given form.

Lines 7-10:

7.   Complete and actuated for a purpose was *iwa* at its first emanations.

8. It was by *asuwa* that *Ori* was formed in order to be the Father of all.

9. Perfect, complete, and actuated for a purpose was *iwa* at first emanations.

10. For a set purpose was *iwa* when it poured down upon Earth.

Interpretation: Three stages in the process of creation are identified by the author of this oral poetry. The stages are represented in Yoruba as *igba iwa se* (when *Iwa* first emanated); *igba iwa gun* (When *Iwa* was complete and perfect), and *igba iwa ro* (when *Iwa* poured down on Earth like rain). Here, we are told that the archetype *Ori*, called *Origun*, was formed according to the principle of *asuwa*. And Origun was created to be the 'father' of all *Ori* on Earth.

11. *Origun* was the source of *Oluiwaaye*.

12. While *Baba-asemuegun-sunwon* was the emanate of *Oluiwaaye*.

13. *Olofin Otete* was the emanate of *Baba-asemuegun-sunwon*.

14. *Olofin Otete* it was who used a basketful measure of dust particles to create the Earth.

Interpretation: Four Divinities are named and introduced in these four lines in terms of their pristine essences: *Origun*, *Baba-asemuegun-sunwon*, and *Olofin Otete*. They are introduced in the order and source of their emanations; that is, in the order in which one springs from the other.

Lines 15-25:

15. *Olofin Otete* it was who proscribed the cultivation of *igbikugbin*.[7]

16. In this Father's soil.

17. *Igbinkugbin* is death.

18. *Igbinkugbin* is loss.

19. *Igbinkugbin* is *ewe-ina*.

20. *Igbinkugbin* is *yeesi*.

21. *Igbinkugbin* is *anragba* leaf.

22. *Igbinkugbin* is *Yemoro*.

23. *Olofin Otete* carried the basket of soil particles

24. And created *ile ife* (terra firma).

25. All goodness together formed an *asuwa*.

Interpretation: Here the focus is on the creation of the Earth under the supervision of *Olofin Otete*. Note that creation is presented as a specific demonstration of the principle of *asuwada* (purposive clumping of diverse *iwa*). The Earth is also seen as a haven for implanting and cultivating goodness. The declaratory statement '*Ire gbogbo Diasuwa*', which runs through the rest of the poetry, is introduced here.

Lines 26-53:

26. When the assembly of hairs was complete,

27. They took over the head.

28. When the assembly of hairs on the beard was complete,

29. They became *ojontagiri*.

30. When the clumping of trees was complete,

31. They became forests.

32. When the *eruwa* grasses were completely assembled,

33. They became savannah.

34. The *agbon*, when they assembled completely,

35. They uphold the roofing of a house.

36. When the *ita* assembled completely,

37. They covered the face of the Earth.

38. *Girigiri* is never absent

39. In the habitat of the *aladi*.

40. *Girigiri* is never absent

41. In the *agiriyan* of the *eerun*.

42. *Alasuwada* I invoke you

43. To send *iwa-susu* down

44. To bear to me all *ire gbogbo* (common good).

45. *Origun*, begot *Baba Asemuegun-sunwon*,

46. *Olu-iwaaye* begat *Baba Asemuegun-sunwon*,

47. *Baba Asemuegun-sunwon* begat *Olofin Otete*.

48. *Otete*, you are *Alasuwada*.

49. *Asuwa*:

50. *Asuwa*:

51. Permit all *gbogbo ire* compressed together to issue forth to ward me.

52. *Asuwa*:

53. *Asuwa*:

Interpretation: In these lines, three basic abstractions are introduced: *iwa-susu* (bunched existence) and *ire-gbogbo* (all existing good collectively viewed) and *gbogbo ire* (all good individually viewed). *Iwa-susu* is the independent variable. There is in this poem a causal relationship between *iwa* (existence, being, character), and *ire* (goodness); between *iwa-susu* (a collectivity of existence or beings, or characters) and *ire-gbogbo* (the sum total of goodness) and *gbogbo ire* (common good). The source of all earthly forms of *iwa-susu* is the divine being called *Olofin Otete*. He or She is addressed as *Alasuwada* (The Author of all things).

Poem Five, Lines 56-70

56. *Asuwa* is what the *oyin* are.

57. *Asuwa* is what the *ado* bees are.

58. The *eeran* leaves grow in asuwa.

59. *Asuwa* is what broomsticks form;

60. It is in *asuwa* that the *eeran* leaves grow in the *aare*.

61. *Asuwa* is what the *elegiri* birds form;

62. It is the coming together of a multitude of men

63. That we know as warfare.

64. It is as *asuwa* that one encounters the grassland,

65. It is as *asuwa* that locusts invade a farmland.

66. *Alasuwada*, it is You I call

67. To send all goodness to me:

68. All forms of *aisuwa*, depart from me:

69. It is from *Alasuwada* that I emanate.

70. I am he who is begotten of *Alasuwada*.

Poem Six, Lines 71-87

71. In countless number, the *yindinyin* throngs their habitats;

72. In countless number, swarms the *Yaya* in the hills,

73. In several *asuwa* the termites colonise their mounds,

74. In several *asuwa* we encounter the *ekunkun* by the riverside.

75. It is as *asuwa* that we find the *labelabe* by the waterside.

76. It is as *asuwa* that we meet the *oore* in the swamp.

77. It is as *asuwa* that we behold the *lamilami*.

78. The leaf called *adosusu* is never found singly.

79. In *asuwa* – far as the eyes behold –

80. We encounter the *Erimi* tree.

81. In *asuwa*, we encounter the *egbele* fish at sea.

82. In *asuwa* – far as the eyes behold –

83. We encounter the crustaceans in the ocean.

84. In *asuwa* – far as the eyes can see –

85. We meet the *eegun*: *Akaranba* is the cognomen of *eegun*;

86. Which, when they feed in a school

87. All other fishes follow in their trail.

Interpretation: These selected lines from the Spoken Poems Five and Six list types of life forms, or beings, which continue in-being as a result of their conformity with the principle of *asuwa*. Among the life-forms are *oyin* (bumble bee), *ado* (honey-bee), the human hair, trees, grasses, ants, leaves, birds, locusts and even man-made *asuwa*, such as broomsticks, and a corps of fighting men.

Poem Seven, Lines 90-100

90. *Origun Olu-iwa-aye*.

91. Help me to achieve my goal.

92. *Ela*: you are the offspring of *Alasuwada*!

93. There is no *Alasuwada* like *Origun*!

94. *Origun*, you are *Alasuwada*!

95. The sediments of last year are found in the river.

96. Performing their sacrificial rites in the undergrowths.

97. *Ela wooro-wayi!*

98. *Origun*: come forth and collect *sus-iwa-da* for me.

99. *Ela wooro-wayi!*

100. You are the *Alasuwada!*

Interpretation: In these lines, the Oral Poet demonstrates his communion with *Alasuwada*. He declares his faith in the unfailing working of the principle of *asuwa* in every community of life-forms, particularly in the operation of the principle in the community the poet has formed with *Alasuwada*.

In the following poems, lines 101-118, there is an impressive description of a moment of the down-pouring of myriads of life-forms, described metaphorically as *iri* (dews), upon the Earth. The down-pouring is likened to the falling of the dews upon the plains of the Earth (*iri tu wili, tu wili*). This poem also contains a statement of Time as a moment, a reference point, in the outpouring of life. Here, Time is given the generic name of *Ojo*, which is often translated into English as 'Day'. But the oral poet says:

Lines 101-118:

101. 'Dews pour lightly, pour lightly,[8]

102. Dews pour heavily, pour heavily,

103. Dews pour heavily so that you may pour lightly.'

104. Thus *Ifa* was consulted for *Olofin Otete*.

105. Who would pour myriads of existences down upon the Earth

106. On the day he was to receive the *ado* of existence

107. From the hands of *Olodumare*;

108. On the day, he was to release

109. Existences on the Earth,

110. One particle of dust became

111. A basketful measure of dust.

112. A basketful measure of soil became the earthcrust.

113. Dews pouring lightly, pouring lightly

114. Were used in moulding our earthly home;

115. Dews pouring hearily, pouring heavily

116. Were used to mould the Earth.

117. So that *ire-gbogbo* may multiply upon it.

118. *Ire-gbogbo* took the shape of *asuwa*.

Interpretation: A moment in the infinitude of the dawn of creation witnessed the pouring of myriad forms of existence onto the Earth like dews. By the phrase 'a moment at the dawn of creation', we mean the moment when the notion of time dawned in human consciousness. Time is merely a point of reference in infinitude. It is *ojo*. Among these myriads of outpourings were the *Okanlerinwo Irunmole* – the 401 humans first to people the Earth.[9]

Lines 129-138, from '*Orin Osuwa*', Stanza 3:

We now come to the most significant event after the creation of life forms: the introduction of *aisuwa* by *Yankangi* into the natural order. The intended message in this short small passage is not easy to grasp.

129. There is no luckless head in a companion of travellers.

130. For *ire-gbogbo* is in form of *asuwa*.

131. *Yankangi*[10] alone it was

132. Who strayed for a moment from his companion,

133. Was said to have stolen *iru* to eat[11]

134. From Mother *Olugamo*'s tray in Heaven.

135. *Asuwa!*

136. *Asuwa!*

138. *Iiree mi.*

139. *Asuwa!*

Interpretation: This passage deals with the ontology of Error, or moral offence, in the world, which began when *Yankangi* strayed away from *ire-gbogbo* in order to steal *iru* (a kind of seed), from the Divine Mother called *Olugamo*. The true meaning of these metaphorical statements elude one at this point. Is the allusion to the stealing of *iru* analogous to the act of eating the forbidden apple in the mythical Garden of Eden in the Hebraic myth of creation composed by Moses? It is probably an analogous doctrine of the first sin in the Christian religion, except that *iru* is a seed and food condiment, which is sometimes used to symbolise 'assortment', separation into lots, differentiation and fragmentation.

111

More lines from the *Akogbe* (song verses) 147-154:

147.　There is no luckless head in the domains of *Ife*.

148.　It is not-being-in-tune-with-other-heads that is the problem.

149.　*Ire-gbogbo* is in the form of *asuwa*.

150.　Yet it is from the only-and-only-one *Origun* in *Orun*

151.　That each earthly *Ori* branches,

152.　*Ire-gbogbo* is in the form of *asuwa*.

Thus:

153.　If one *ori* improves

154.　Its improvement will affect two hundred others.

Interpretation: From this stanza of the song, there is the expression of a law of social harmony in human communities and the evil social consequences of self-alienating behaviour. The verses conclude with what experimental psychologists, like Lippit, Polansky and Rosen (1952) in their study of collective behaviour, would label as *emotional contagion*. In the study of collective behaviour by Western psychologists, and sociologists, it has been established that a person's behaviour may serve as an unintended model for others. That is, one person may initiate another's behaviour without any such intention on the part of the first person. In the *Alasuwada* doctrine, one 'initiator' of *ire* (goodness) may have a maximum of 200 'recipients'; for an emotional state of goodness spreads among members of the community.

Conclusion From the experiences derived from several observations of our artistic and religious predecessors, we inductively infer that there is a universal principle of *asuwa*, according to which everything was created alone but by which nothing continued-in-being alone. All things continue-in-being as communities, throughout the whole realms of nature from ants to elephants, from algae to whales, from plants to giant forest trees; man-made objects continue-in-being in communities or systemic wholes, from dyads to congregations, from families to nations. It is this community of creatures that is the substance of *goodness*. The whole earth is a macro-community in which human settlements of varied sizes and densities are micro-communities.

According to the principle of *asuwa* there was no error at the emanations of earthly beings. Error, 'sin', or self-alienation, was introduced into the natural order when *Yankangi* inadvertently turned his back against his original community to be alone in order to enjoy alone the provision that was intended for the common good. Self-alienation, called *aisuwa*, was the first prototype of Error or Sin, of what we regard in sociology as social deviation, or social pathology. Each human being, if he or she so desires, with faith, may establish and continue-in-being in fellowship with the source of his or her being, but it is imperative for the common good that there be always sodality among all elements in creation.

Derived Propositions of Relevance to Sociology

We bring this paper to an end by shifting attention from the attempts of the poet of the *Ayajo Asuwa* myth of creation to define and illustrate, with wide-ranging examples, the principle of *asuwa*, or *asuwada*. Attention is now on the following propositions which, we hope, will invite the serious, even if critical, interest of Nigerian social scientists in particular, and anthropologists or sociologists in general. The propositions are of a general nature. They are intended to be statements of relationships between some significant elements of the subject matter of sociology, namely human society. These propositions are derived from the several interpretations which have already been given to the translated Yoruba text of the oral poetry in the preceding pages.

The propositions are as follows:

1. The unit of social life is the individual's life, being, existence, or character.

2. Although each human being is metaphysically a unique emanation – an *emi* – of a Divine Being, yet each individual's life, as a corporeal self, needs the fellowship of other corporeal selves to feel and be whole and complete.

3. The corporeal individual, essentially, cannot continue-in-being without a community.

4. Since the social life of a group of individual beings is sustained by a spirit of sodality, any form of self-alienation for the purpose of pursuing a purely selfish aim is, morally speaking, an error or sin.

5. A good society, in an axiological sense, is one which recognises the uniqueness of each life's authentic nature and its right to self-expression and self-actualisation.

6. A genuine social being is one who works daily, and sacrifices willingly, in varying ways, his or her cherished freedom and material acquisitions for self-improvement as well as for the common good. For without one, the other cannot be achieved.

7. Every individual, as may be observed within the diverse contexts of social life in Africa, is capable of being an initiator or a recipient of true (good) or erroneous (bad) conduct.

8. The social worth of an individual within his or her community can be measured by the qualitative value of the differential between types of conduct he or she has initiated or received.

9. A social scientist in the Nigerian Universities who studies with a view to acquiring an understanding of people and society in Africa and to planning effectively to develop the quality of life in both westernised and historical communities may find that he or she needs to work with this derived conceptual scheme of *iwa*, *ihuwasi*, *isesi* and *ajumose* as these apply to a single actor or to a plurality of actors in the community's social life.

Notes

1 In a recent paper, accepted for the XIth World Congress Sociology Research Committee on the History of Sociology to be held in August 1986 in New Delhi, India, the author compares to a limited extent historical factors in the development of sociology in Great Britain, France, the United States of America, the Soviet Union, Hungary, Bulgaria and the West African sub-region. It was, however, Edwin Arthur Burtt, Catholic theologian and physical scientist, who brought to my attention the usefulness and difficulties attendant upon the use of translations of poetic products of medieval European thinkers as a basis for constructing the metaphysical foundations of modern physics. The poetical product which is named *Ayajo Asuwada* comes, according to David Agboola Adeniyi, from the Odu by Orunmila entitled *Ogunda-sa*. I accept responsibility for the translation of *Ayajo Asuwada* with its miscueings of meanings.

2 The concept of 'approach', as used in sociological studies, was viewed by Stefan Novak in 'Philosophical Schools and Working Methods in Social Science', *International Social Science Journal* 1984, 102 (Vol. XXXVI, No. 4) : 587-601, as both theory and methodology. The interplay of theory with methodology and vice versa as developed by Novak provides not only some key approaches developed in the sociological enterprise, he also illustrates them.

3 This does not mean that the performance of Akintelu rites is confined to this section of Yoruba-speaking people.

4 The term 'credo' can be used as a synonym for 'doctrine' in this paper.

5 Abiodun Adewale, Ife Philosophy graduate, Class 1978, in a discussion once speculated that *Alasuwada* is the Yoruba name for what in Western thought is known as 'the most transcendental order'. He was of the opinion too that '*Alasuwada* has a metaphysical identity and its power could be invoked metaphysically'. His guess and opinion are one of the possible ones.

6 These lines in their Yoruba are as follows:
1. *Asekun-suwada nigba Iwa se.*
2. *Asuwa la fi da Ori tii se Baba won nigba Iwa se.*
3. *Origun, Asekun-suwada nigba Iwa gun.*
4. *Asuwada nigba ti Iwa ro.*

7 One of the most difficult concepts to translate into English, in this *Ayajo* poetry is *Igbinkugbin*. It could mean a plant that is not intended to be planted in a particular soil.

8 In *Sixteen Great Poems*, UNESCO 1975, Wande Abimbola writes about the importance of *iri* (dews) in Yoruba thought: 'For the Yoruba, dew, known to them as *iri*, is more than ordinary water. It serves to refresh man and his environment. It helps both plants and animals to regain lost energy. It is therefore some times more beneficial to plants than the heavy downpour of rain, which is so characteristic of much of Yorubaland. In contrast to rain, dew is very gentle and without any harsh effects whatsoever. There is even a type of dew known as *iri-aimo* which falls almost without anyone knowing that it is falling until one sees particles of water on leaves and other objects exposed to it. Dew, in contrast to other harsh and opposing objects of nature, is therefore symbolic of life, continuity, fertility and regeneration. It is an indispensable element of life – a substance without which the opposing forces of nature would have destroyed themselves leaving the Earth itself in utter chaos and nation' (412).

In this *Ayajo Asuwada* poetry the dew (*iri*) symbolises the chemicalisation of the Earth's crust.

9 According to the Reverend David Onadele Epega, in his *The Mystery of Yoruba Gods* (n.d.), of the first cohort of 401 souls sent to inhabit the Earth, 200 of them committed some heinous crimes – not mentioned – that their names were placed under the curse of the unspoken names forever. The *orisa* we know today were not among those anathematised.

114

¹⁰ *Yakangi*, often known as *Yangi* is the pristine name for *Esu Elegbara*. According to David A.
Adeniyi (1975), *Olugamo* is our Mother-in-Heaven, while *Ela* is our Father-in-Heaven. In our
view *Olugamo* could be a shortened form of *Olu-gun-amo* (One-who-kneads-clay-together).
Probably it is the clay which *Ajalamo* used in moulding *Ori* in the mythical account of
Efuwape, that *Iya Wa Olugamo* kneads.

¹¹ The full symbolic meaning of *Iru* in Yoruba secular and sacred thought is yet to be
investigated.

Glossary of Yoruba Terms and Selected English and Latin Translations
(Listed alphabetically)

1. *Ado* honeybee

2. *ado* a small gourd used to store powder or drug

3. *Adosusu* a type of leaf which is never found growing singly

4. *Agbon* hornet, wasp

5. *Agiriyan* an ant-hill

6. *Aisuwa* incapable of clumping together, with other beings, inability to
   fuse existences; self-alienation

7. *Ajumose* action based upon consensus, or common knowledge

8. *Akogbe* any type of song – and – repeat song

9. *Aladi* small black ants which make nests on trees

10. *Alasuwada* The Great Being who creates all existences in groups for a
    purpose. Also individuals who are in positions to make things happen

11. *Anragba* a type of poisonous leaf

12. *Asesese-sunwon* balanced at the time of creation

13. *Asuwa* (pronounced ah-shoo-wah) either the process of coming together
    for a purpose; or one who brings existence together to form a new entity

14. *Baba Asemuegun-sunwon* literally 'Father who selects and makes all
    things perfect and balanced'

15. *Eeran* a type of good fodder grass

16. *Eerun* a type of brown ant

17. *Egbe Orin* the Chorus of a song

18. *Ekunkun Pandanus candelabrum* a tropical forest tree

19. *Elegiri* small birds in flock

20. *Ela* the divinatory name for 'The Saviour'

21. *'Ela wooro wayi!'* An exclamation which can be compared to 'Halleluyah'

22. *Erimi* another type of tropical forest tree

23. *Eruwa* grassland

24. *Ewe-ina* another name for the twiner called *esisi*: a stinging leaf

25. *Girigiri* readiness in good time

26. *Girigiri* an imitation of the noise made by the feet of a large number of people or animals

27. *Ihuwasi* the mode of expressing life toward other lives

28. *ile-ife (not Ile – Ife)* the ever-widening *terra firma*

29. *Iru* African locust bean

30. *isesi* the mode of action employed in relating to other beings

31. *Ita* a yellow type of ant found in equatorial lands

32. *Labelabe* a species of grass with razor-like edges which grows inside shallow rivers

33. *Lamiilami* dragonfly

34. *Mogun* a sacred place where the worshipper of *OGUN*, the god of iron and war, assemble

35. *Morere* any place where two or more individuals converge to deliberate or worship

36. *Odu* a corpus of African oral tradition in the Yoruba language of West Africa

37. *Ojontagiri* something to reckon with

38. *Olodumare* God, the Ominipotent and Omniscience

39. *Olofin-Otete* Ruler of the palace of infinite spaciousness

40. *Olugamo* The Divine Being (female) who cuts the clay out of which man is fashioned

41. *Oluiwaaye* Lord of Earthbound existences

42. *Oore [Cyperus articulatus]* a sedge grass used in making mats

43. *Ori* literally 'head'; it could also mean mind

44. *Ori-Orun* The One and Only metaphysical Archetype of the head

45. *Origun* the complete head; or The One Perfect Mind

46. *Orisa* god, or goddess

47. *Orun* heaven

48. *Orunmila* an African sage, scientist and medical practitioner (14th-15th Century)

49. *Owo* a broom made from the midrib of palm tree leaflets *(elaeisis guineensis*

50. *Oyin* bee

51. *Yaya* any species of ants that live in anthills other than termites

52. *Yeesi,* sometimes pronounced as *esisi* a species of twiners or trailers with stinging hairs

53. *Yemoro* a type of poisonous plant that can cause physical disability when taken

54. *Yindin-yindin* another species of ants

Bibliography

Note: Although all of these works were referred to while writing the paper, not all of them were cited in the text.

A. Books

ABIMBOLA, W. 1975. *Sixteen Great Poems.* Paris: UNESCO.

BEIER, H.U. 1955. 'The Historical and Psychological Significance of Yoruba Myths'. *ODU, Journal of Yoruba and Related Studies* 1 : 17-25.

BIOBAKU, S.O. 1955. 'The Use and Interpretation of Myths: 1. Myths and Oral History'. *ODU, Journal of Yoruba and Related Studies* 1 : 12-17.

BURTT, E.A. 1967. *The Metaphysical Foundation of Modern Physical Science: A Historical and Critical Essay.* London: Routledge and Kegan Paul.

EPEGA, Rev. D. Olarinwa 1964. *IFA, Amona Awon Baba Wa.* Lagos : The Patriarchate.

EPEGA, A.D. Onadele ca. 1924. *The Mystery of Yoruba Gods,* Pars I and II. Imole Oluwa Institute, Ode Remo, Nigeria.

HESS, B.B. et al 1982. *Sociology.* New York: Macmillan.

HOMANS, G.C. 1967. *The Nature of Social Science.* New York: Harcourt, Brace and World.

LIPPIT, R., POLANSKY, N. and ROSEN, S. 1952. 'The Dynamics of Power', *Human Relations* 5 : 37-64; cited in *Handbook of Social Psychology,* Vol. II, 1954 (edited by Gardner Lindzey). New York: Addison-Wesley.

MBITI, J.S. 1970. *African Religions and Philosophy.* New York: Doubleday.

NOVAK, S. 'Philosophical Schools and Working Methods in Social Science'. *International Social Science Journal* 102 (Vol. XXXVI, No. 4) : 587-601.

TEMPLES, Rev. Placide. *Bantu Philosophy.* Paris: Presence Africaine.

B. Tape Transcription and Translation

ADENIYI, D.A. 1975. *Alasuwada, lati Enu Alagba.* Ibadan: Institute of Arican Studies, University of Ibadan.

AKIWOWO, A.A. 1981. *Ayajo Asuwada: An Oral Poetry* (English translation of a Yoruba Tape Transcription). Ile-Ife: University of Ife. 7 pp. Quarto

UNIVERSITY OF
WOLVERHAMPTON
Harrison Learning Centre

Title: Researching social life
ID: 7608262799

Title: Approaches to audiences : a reader
ID: 7621735123

Title: Communication theory reader
ID: 7620930178

Title: How to research
ID: 7620214359

Total items: 4
16/03/2006 13:29

Thank You for using Self Service.
Please keep your receipt.

Overdue books are fined at 40p per day for
week loans, 10p per day for long loans.

ASUWADA PRINCIPLE: AN ANALYSIS OF AKIWOWO'S CONTRIBUTIONS TO THE SOCIOLOGY OF KNOWLEDGE FROM AN AFRICAN PERSPECTIVE

M. Akin. Makinde

Introduction

In an earlier volume of this journal (1986b : 343-58), Professor Akiwowo published a paper entitled 'Contributions to the Sociology of Knowledge from an African Oral Poetry'. As it turned out, the 'Contributions' were in fact Akiwowo's since, before him, the oral poets were not aware of the relevance of their poetry to the sociology of knowledge. Thus, the contributions, if any, of those poems to the sociology of knowledge were as a result of Akiwowo's discovery.

The purpose of the present paper is to give further interpretations of Akiwowo's discovery, particularly of the most valuable concept in his work – *asuwada* – which later develops into a principle of sociation. As I have had the privilege to present a paper on Akiwowo's novel idea in an organised symposium at the University of Ife[1], I think it is necessary to point out that Akiwowo's idea is more fully developed in other writings that should be made known in the present paper[2].

At the University of Ife, Akiwowo, a well-known Nigerian sociologist, has for some time undertaken a study of sociology from the perspective of African culture and philosophy. The strength of his analysis rests on his interest in philosophical thought, or what Afghani calls 'philosophic spirit'[3]. According to Akiwowo:

> In our Department of Sociology and Anthropology at the University of Ife, there is a definite appreciation among us members of the contributions which African

philosophical ideas . . . can make to the growth of our discipline. This was especially so
for some of us who are doing research work in the sensitive areas of medical sociology,
political sociology, industrial sociology and mass communication.

(Akiwowo 1983a : 25-6)[5]

From my own observation, the above quotation demonstrates clearly
Akiwowo's recognition of the part philosophy has played in the development
of social theories, and the need for 'philosophic spirit', or what the Yoruba call
emi arojinle (spirit of profound thinking), in any serious intellectual enterprise.
As the present paper unfolds. it shall be pointed out that the concept of
Ifogbontaayese, which I have interpreted as essential to the unity of
knowledge, can be derived from the principle of *asuwada* as enunciated by
Akiwowo. Both concepts originate from Akiwowo's work.

African Oral Poetry and the Ayajo Asuwada

In the Yoruba tradition *ayajo* is a kind of poem, but is more especially
known as incantation which is recited, in addition to that given by Akiwowo
(1986b : 344), by *Onisegun* and *Babalawo* during the performance of
ceremonial rites or on the occasion of healing the sick[5]. In the sense Akiwowo
uses the term, *ayajo* refers to the poetic words as well as the totality of the
poem in which *asuwada*, as a myth of creation, is contained (Akiwowo 1986b :
344). It is from this 'myth' or 'doctrine' that Akiwowo develops what I call a
philosophical principle of *asuwada*. When this principle is related to man in
society we get what Akiwowo calls *asuwada eniyan* (*asuwada* of persons or
human beings) as opposed to *asuwada eranko* (*asuwada* of lower animals)
(1983a : 16-8). It is at this stage that the *asuwada* principle which governs all
nature is seen also as a principle of sociation or human society. Hence
'*alasuwada*, a body of doctrine of creation in oral poetry form, may be
confidently described as a 'a vision of the future' which, according to Hess et
al, provides a sense of destiny that unifies all true behaviours and gives
meaning to both individuals' existence and human history' (1986b : 345)[6].

The *ayajo asuwada* is to unravel this doctrine of creation which, when
properly interpreted verse by verse, leads Akiwowo to his derivation of nine
'propositions', eight of which I call axioms (following Spinoza's philosophical
method in his *Ethics*) that are of great 'relevance to sociology' (1986b : 353-4).
The last of these propositions, which is not an axiom, is an injunction to
African social scientists to apply 'philosophic spirit', or *emi arojinle* to the
study of their societies (1986b : 354). Of the eight axioms, the first three deserve
our attention because they are, in my judgement, the most fundamental
axioms concerning the principle of *asuwada* as related to 'the subject matter of
sociology, namely, human society' (1986b : 353).

Axiom 1: The unit of social life is the individual's life, being, existence, or
character.

Axiom 2: Although each human being is metaphysically a unique
emanation – an *emi* – of a Divine Being, each individual's life, as a corporeal

120

self, needs the fellowship of other corporeal selves to feel and be whole and complete.

Axiom 3: The corporeal individual, essentially, cannot continue-in-being without a community.

The other axioms are more or less connected with these, while all of them are derived from Akiwowo's interpretation of the Yoruba oral poetry – *ayajo asuwada* – which is also known as *alasuwada* oral poetry (1986b : 344-5).

In other publications, Akiwowo provides a detailed analysis of the concept of *asuwada*. According to him, the concept, *asuwada*, is derived from *Iwa* (a state of being, existence, or character in a perpetual state of development; *Suwada*, to come together or coexist for a common end or purpose) and *asu-iwa-da* (literally meaning that which kneads or moulds *Iwa*, ie., beings, states of existence or characters so that they can live together in harmony for a purpose or common end). Thus it is often said: '*asuwada eniyan ni awon ti on nsu iwa da tabi awujo eniyan ti nsuwada*', literally meaning 'man-made mode of existence'[7].

Behind the *asuwada* principle is a philosophical presupposition character-ised as teleological by which *asuwada* represents the idea of purposiveness in nature. It is also a principle that governs all nature. In this respect, there is *asuwada eniyan* as well as *asuwada eranko*, ie. *asuwada* of persons and of lower animals respectively, although Akiwowo's concern is with the former dealing with the human beings and society. For this reason, *asuwada* is seen as a conscious purpose as it exists in human beings[8]. It may also be regarded as a highly evolved derivation of natural condition or property which Edmund W. Sinnot calls 'directiveness' (1961 : 46). This 'directiveness' or 'purposiveness', which characterises living organisms on its conscious side implies the existence of a parallel between individual human beings and society as individuals-writ-large, both rich in ideas, inspirations, intellectual subtleties and emotions. Thus Akiwowo's concept of *asuwada* finds its philosophical bearing in Sinnot's work, especially for the purpose of constructing a satisfying life in philosophy and society. As Sinnot points out:

> the suggestion that man's physical life grows out of the basic goal seeking and purposiveness found in all organic behaviour and that this, in turn, is an aspect of the more general self-regulating and normative character evident in the development and activities of living organisms is, at least, worth serious consideration.

> (Sinnot 1961 : Preface)

Note that the first axiom stresses the importance of *iwa* (character) as 'the unit of social life'. The *alasuwada* oral poetry provides some lines to suggest the 'goodness' of *Iwa* (character), also personified as 'being', in the concept of *asuwada*, ie., the process of coming together for a purpose, or one who brings existence together to form a new entity. Thus line 7 of the oral poetry says: 'complete and actuated for a purpose was *iwa* at its first emanation', and line 25: 'All goodness together formed an *asuwa*' (1986b : 345, 346). The '*Asuwada* principle is then the purposive clumping of diverse *iwa*' (characters or beings) on earth, while the earth is seen as 'a heaven for implanting and cultivating goodness' through individual *iwa* (1986b : 347).

The Yoruba often say *iwa'lewa* (character is beauty)[9]) and *'iwa ni orisa, bi a ba ti wuu si ni nfi ngbe ni'* (character is like a deity: it assists us in the way we use it in life). *Iwa*, therefore, suggests the most significant aspect of the 'goodness' in individual human beings and consequently the moulding of individuals and society. This is why the Great Being who creates all existences in groups for a purpose is known as *Alasuwada* (Akiwowo 1986b : 350). This purpose, of course, is for living together in a community for a common good.

> All things continue-in-being as communities, through the whole realms of nature from ants to elephants, from algae to whales, from plants to giant forest trees; man-made objects continue-in-being in communities of systematic wholes, from dyads to congregations, from families to nations. It is this community of creatures that is the substance of goodness.
>
> (Akiwowo 1986b : 352)

As it has been noted above, the most fundamental aspect of the *asuwada* principle is the concept of *iwa*, 'complete and actuated at its first emanation'. The principle of *asuwada* then makes it clear that 'there was no error at the emanation of earthly beings' (ibid.), and this is to say that in its first emanation, the principle of *asuwada* was pure, without any admixture of 'error' or 'sin'. But human beings themselves introduced 'error' or 'sin' into the natural order, thus creating what is now known as self-alienation or *aisuwada*, or what the sociologists now regard as 'social deviation' or 'social pathology' (Akiwowo 1986b : 352-3). 'Each human being, if he or she so desires, with faith, may establish and continue-in-being, but it is imperative for the common good that there be always sodality among all elements in creation' (ibid.).

It is important here to note the affinity of *asuwa* to the Yoruba concept of *ori*. Line 8 of the *Alasuwada* oral poetry states thus: 'It was by *asuwa* that *ori* was formed in order to be the Father of all' (1986b : 346). In Yoruba philosophical thought *ori* is known as the bearer of human destiny of earth[10] : 346). One's success or failure is determined according to one's choice of *ori* (good or bad) in heaven. And *ori* (inner or metaphysical head) is also known as the 'guardian spirit'. From Akiwowo's interpretation of the *ayajo* oral poetry, a new dimension has been introduced to the Yoruba concept of *ori*. *Ori* was formed according to the principle of *asuwa* (Akiwowo 1986b : 346). While this suggestion is consistent with the idea that *asuwada* is a principle governing all nature (including human society and human destiny), it may fail to explain why certain choices of *ori* lead to success and why others lead to failure, unless the purposive nature of the *asuwada* principle is to be seen as leading to two opposite directions: goodness and evil in the destiny of man and society. But the principle of *asuwada* seems to show that man is inherently good and that he exists for the purpose for which he and everything were created – goodness, which we may conceivably describe as one essential characteristic of the destiny of the human being as presupposed by the *asuwada* principle.

122

My own assessment of the inclusion of *ori* in Akiwowo's discussion of the *asuwada* principle is that it creates unnecessary difficulty in the system. Philosophically speaking, the relation between both concepts will be difficult to justify. As it is, the issue of the metaphysical concept of *ori* and its relation, if any, to *asuwada*, needs to be clearly worked out so as to bring into clearer focus its relevance, if any, to the *asuwada* principle.

What I am trying to argue here is that if *ori* can be subsumed under the *asuwada* principle, then the latter should be regarded as an ultimate presupposition according to which an individual choice of *ori* and his or her destiny is made. And if this is so, whether we should further assume that an adherence to the *asuwada* principle leads one to a good choice of *ori*, and hence 'goodness', as the positive characterisation of *iwa* (ie. individual *iwa hihu*, or behaviour) or a violation of this principle leads to a bad choice of *ori* and hence to *aisuwa* (the opposite of *asuwa*) as the negative characterisation of *iwa*. But then if, according to the Yoruba philosophical thought, *ori* as the bearer of human destiny on earth is chosen in heaven and only brought to fruition on earth[12], it will appear that this concept is logically prior to that of *asuwada*, so that an individual's adherence to, or violation of, the *asuwada* principle on earth would have been determined, in advance, by his or her choice of good or bad *ori* in heaven, ie. prior to birth. In this case it could be argued that an adherence to, or violation of, the *asuwada* principle depends on the kind of *ori*, good or bad, an individual had chosen in heaven, or the relationship of *ori* to the *asuwada* principle could be such that a good *ori* was 'formed' or chosen for the purpose of 'goodness' inherent in the *asuwada* principle, while a bad *ori* was 'formed' or chosen for the purpose of evil inherent in *aisuwa* or *aisuwada*, both of which manifest themselves in human behaviours and human societies on earth. In this sense evil and *aisuwa*, the opposites of good and *asuwa* respectively in man and society, are deviations from the *asuwada* principle. Perhaps the notion of *aisuwa* corresponds to the evil aspect of *iwa* (character) and this may mean that, with *aisuwa*, the concept of *iwa* in its original form breaks down, and consequently the very principle of *asuwada* itself, particularly as it relates to human beings.

What is not clear is that if *ori* was formed according to the principle of *asuwa* or *asuwada*, how we are to account for the social relation between this principle and the concept of *ori* which is seen as the bearer of human destiny, and whether individual human destiny points to the destiny of a society or nation, since individual destiny and that of society or nation are governed alike by, and subsumed under, the *asuwada* principle. One way is to see *ori* itself as an embodiment of *iwa* (in both *asuwa* and *aisuwa*) so that, while a good *ori* corresponds to *iwa* in its positive sense as goodness of character or being, a bad *ori* corresponds to *aisuwa*, ie. *iwa* in its negative sense as evil. But in all it appears that the concept of *aisuwa* (one of the characteristics of a bad *ori*) which negates the goodness of *iwa* and *asuwa* may provide an explanation for a breakdown of the very principle of *asuwada* and consequently of the degeneration of human society. Something of this nature is anticipated in

Akiwowo's interpretation of the *Akogbe* song, verses 147-154 (Akiwowo 1986b: 352). From the stanzas of this song 'there is the expression for a law of social harmony in human communities and the evil social consequences of self-alienating behaviour' (ibid.). One important discussion by Akiwowo on the 'evil social consequences' of social deviation or *aisuwa* is the possible breakdown of society which, in my judgement, is one of the consequences of the violation of the *asuwada* principle.

Asuwada and the Human Society: Ajobi and Ajogbe

Elsewhere in his discussion on the 'Ontogeny of Sociality' (Akiwowo 1983a : 15-8), Akiwowo tries to explain his concept of *asuwada* in relation to human society from the point of view of ethology, or the field which studies animal society. Peter H. Klopper has talked about 'aggregation, or *asuwa* among lower animals' in his *Perspectives in Ethology* (1973) (Akiwowo 1983a : 15), and has discussed in great detail the social life of animals in another work[12]. The first work is referred to by Akiwowo but the second work seems to me equally important for our understanding of the different applications of the concept *asu-iwa-da* (*asuwada*) as the principle governing all nature, including human and animal associations. In Akiwowo's thought *suwa-da* stands for the concept of sociation; *a-suwa-da* for association, and *ai-suwa-da* for dis-sociation[13], or what he calls 'self-alienation'. All these concepts are applicable in ethology to the society of human beings (*asuwada eniyan*) as discussed by Akiwowo and that of the lower animals (*asuwada eranko*) as discussed by Klopper and contrasted to human association by Akiwowo.

Asuwada as a principle of human association manifests itself in *asuwada eniyan* (*asuwada* of persons). Specifically, *asuwada eniyan* refers to what Akiwowo calls 'the sociality of man' (Akiwowo 1983a : 16). By sociality he means:

> the quality or fact of being able to live and grow in communities; the quality or fact of being able to establish companionship and mutual converse, in the *Orunmilaist* perspective it is simply the quality of being able to *suwada* (come together for a common end; to coexist). The perspective clearly distinguishes between *asuwa* (coexistence) and *asuwada* (the fact of being together for a purpose). Both animal and human *asuwa* require no overt response to one another though it has survival values for the members. In the language of the ethologist, *asuwa* can be said to be mere 'kinetic aggregation'. It does not require the exercise of a free-will response to the physical or social environment. By contrast, *asuwada*, or social aggregation results from the free-willed response of one individual person to another. It is species-oriented, and leads to the emergence of various types of social categories such as the dyad, the triad, the quad, families, poor groups, complex organizations, tribes and various kinds of societies.

> (Akiwowo 1983a : 16-7)

In this regard, what we perceive in the world around us as members of a society, or as a 'cultural animal' (to borrow a phrase from Robin Fox [1970 : 31-42]) is, in Akiwowo's view, largely influenced by the beliefs, values and world-view which, as members of a specific *asuwada eniyan*, we share in common in our environment (Akiwowo 1983a : 17).

The concept of *asuwada* may therefore be seen as a principle of unity which sustains the very concepts of the family and society known by Akiwowo as *ajobi* and *ajogbe* respectively. In Akiwowo's doctrine, both the concepts of *ajobi* and *ajogbe* are manifestations of the *asuwada eniyan*. The relationship of *asuwada eniyan* to social theory and organisation is suggested in a passage from his writing: 'The primordial forms of *asuwada eniyan*, that is human society, are *ajobi* and *ajogbe* whose English equivalents are *consanguinity* and *co-residentship* respectively' (Akiwowo 1983a : 18). While anthropologists define consanguinity as the facts of lineal and collateral relationships based upon blood and birth, co-residentship is defined by Akiwowo as 'the fact of sharing same or contiguous shelter whether or not the sharers are related by blood' (ibid.).

From the above point of view other derivative concepts are suggested: *alajobi*, which is defined as 'that which sustains all kinds of lineal and collateral relationship', while *alajogbe* is 'that which sustains persons or individualised groups who are living together under one roof or in contiguous shelters in a locale' (ibid.). By definition, therefore, *ajobi* is the unit-idea of social groups in an African society, the most fundamental of which is the person or individual in the *ajobi* group, and sustained by *iwa*, ie. character of being. It refers to the family not as individuals but as a unit or group of closely related persons by blood or birth (nuclear family), or related families (extended family) or several units or groups of related families in a house, compound or village. *Ajobi* also refers to members united by birth or blood who live separately at distant villages, towns, or even other regions of the world or a people in diaspora (Akiwowo 1983a : 19).

By my own interpretation of Akiwowo's indigenous theory of society *ajobi* represents the concept of the nuclear family or related families (extended family) as indicated above, while *alajobi* represents the individuals in the family or related families sharing a common bond under similar environmental and social conditions. *Ajobi*, then, is the first sign of human sociality, the irreducible unit of society. From this it follows that a society, or *ajogbe*, is made up of the smallest units of social groups known as *ajobi* consisting, so to say, of individuals virtually united by the 'ties of consanguinity'. This organic conception of Akiwowo's indigenous theory of society – an African society – thus recognises *ajogbe* both as the coming together of several *ajobi* or families, on the one hand, and as individuals-writ-large, on the other, with the latter seen as, and perfectly consistent with, what Sorokin describes as society or *ajogbe* in its 'super-individual reality', its 'natural origin and spontaneous existence' (1928 : 195). Thus interpreted as 'super-individual reality' or individuals-writ-large *ajogbe* consists of *alajogbe*, ie. people living together from different kinds of *ajobi* (families) all united by a common purpose, as suggested by our understanding of the *asuwada* principle, and particularly of *asuwada eniyan*. In this respect, *alajobi* ascends to the larger group of *alajogbe* in order to achieve its true purpose in *ajogbe* or society. The concepts of *ajobi* (family) and *ajogbe* (society), therefore, represent, in varying degrees, the forms or manifestations of *asuwada eniyan* (*asuwada* of persons) as opposed to *asuwada eranko* (*asuwada* of lower animals). As forms of *asuwada eniyan* Akiwowo maintains that *ajobi* and *ajogbe* are distinctive social relationships and social processes with established observable patterns (Akiwowo 1983a : 20).

The Breakdown of Ajobi and the Making of Ajogbe

We have seen that in Akiwowo's thought both *ajobi* (family) and *ajogbe* (society) are manifestations of the *asuwada eniyan*, particularly as it relates to human association. We have also shown that *ajobi* is the first and smallest unit of social groups, and that each family or social group is made up of individuals. A family may now be defined as an aggregate of individuals of like minds united by, and for, a common purpose. From this a society may also be defined as an aggregate of different families or social groups in a community, sharing a belief, custom, hope and aspiration and united by culture. In all, the common principle is that of *asuwada*, particularly *asuwada eniyan*. This applies to individuals (*enia*), family (*ajobi*) and society (*ajogbe*) all of which, according to Akiwowo, have body and soul (1983a : 18), and exist for a purpose by virtue of the *asuwada* principle. By virtue of the *asuwada* principle, such concepts like 'bond' (by birth or blood) and 'unity' which are naturally related to *alajobi* and *alajogbe* respectively do suggest goodness: love, tolerance, peaceful coexistence, spirit of brotherhood and all the good things which are associated with *iwa*. All this tends to suggest that, in a society or *ajogbe* (also described by Akiwowo as goal-seeking [ibid.]) people will, or ought to, always live together in peace and harmony, with each *alajogbe* exhibiting the right and natural social behaviour. The same situation is expected in the social behaviour of each *alajobi* in the family structure.

However, Akiwowo perceives the 'total breakdown of the ties of consanguinity'. According to him, 'in spite of its appeal, *ajobi* bonds get attenuated even to the point of seeming non-existence' (1983a : 19). It is this circumstance that leads to the shifting of emphasis from *ajobi* to *ajogbe* as we now have it. Some conditions which have damaged the *ajobi* bonds are provided from the history of African peoples. Among these, as given by Akiwowo, are the linkage of local economies to the markets in Europe during the eighteenth century, a situation which 'led to the acquisition of profitable forms of money, sudden social upheavals which led to the physical separation of blood relations' and forced people to depend on strangers for help and means of living. 'Commerce and paper money enabled people to easily acquire wealth through one's initiative and efforts, without dependence on one's blood relations. While the successful ones among blood relations became successful by acquiring more money with which they bought new things and married attractive and influential young women around them, the less successful ones were forced into competition or envy' (ibid.). Thus sibling rivalry arose among members of *ajobi* groups. And finally:

As soon as the social process of competition, envy, and conflict over the visible means to success were universally established among *alajobi* members, a new form of social bond called *ore* (friendship) emerged. It was not based upon blood relationship nor marriage but on simiiarity of *iwa* (individual's mode of expressing his or her being). Friends could live in one or the other's home, and take part in the life of the household except in the rites of the household. The physical structure of the household changed to accommodate the increased population by adding dwelling units as a new optimum was reached. A household became therefore a fold of such added unit. Thus it is clear that it was not everyone who lived in the same household that constituted an *ajobi* since the folks in a household may include lineal and collateral relations, alien residents, friends, migrant workers, and so on. Together, these social elements form the *ajogbe* (the co-residentship) with a distinctive set of *eewo* (taboos), forms of interactions, persistence and discontinuities.

(Akiwowo 1983a : 20)

According to Akiwowo, the Yoruba express the breakdown of *ajobi* in the following expression: *Ko si alajobi mo o, alajogbe lo ku u* (there is no more *alajobi* in the relationship of human beings; only *alajogbe* is left) (1983a : 10). Now, in so far as *asuwada* is a principle which governs all nature, including human nature and human association, and is easily recognisable in the human species in the forms of *ajobi* and *ajogbe*, it appears that the breakdown of *ajobi*, which is one of the forms or manifestations of *asuwada eniyan*, implies a breakdown, or a misapplication, of the *asuwada* principle. In this connection I submit that a breakdown or misapplication of the *asuwada* principle leads to what Akiwowo calls, in various terminologies, 'self-alienation' or 'social pathology' (1986b : 352-3) – all of which are negations of *iwa* and hence of the concept of *asuwada* itself. The very concept of *aisuwa* which, according to Akiwowo, is 'the first prototype or Error or Sin' (ibid.) either in the individual family (*ajobi*) or society (*ajogbe*) can also be seen as the negation or violation of *asuwa* or *asuwada* – a principle governing human societies. In the above sense we can now read further into the *asuwada principle* and suggest that, from it the idea of a society's or nation's constitution is derived, especially as a constitution is seen as an instrument 'governing human behaviour and the interrelationships between individual citizens' in a society[14].

So far Akiwowo's discussion is limited to the breakdown of *ajobi* which, in his interpretation, has enhanced the significance of the coming together of different *alajobi* (persons from different unrelated families) to strengthen the hitherto loose bonds between them. This situation has been used to explain the reason for the 'new bond' between hitherto unrelated families in human societies, and particularly in a multi-ethnic and multi-religious society like Nigeria. Although Akiwowo did not go beyond the total breakdwon of *ajobi*, I am proposing that in as much as 'the primordial forms' of *asuwada eniyan* are *ajobi* and *ajogbe*, and in as much as the breakdown of *ajobi*, or 'the ties of consanguinity', has been ascertained – a breakdown that leaves us with *ajogbe* only – it is not unreasonable to suggest that what happened to *ajobi* can, and will, happen to *ajogbe* in the final analysis, and precisely for much the same reasons. In either case, it could be said that the principle of *asuwada*, as originally proposed by Akiwowo, has broken down.

127

The idea of a breakdown or degeneration of society is not new in the history of thought. In his *Republic*, Plato was concerned about the society of his time, just as Akiwowo is about his own society, with social and political generation as well as their degeneration or breakdown. At no time in our history of social thought is the discussion of social degeneration more relevant to African societies than the present age when all the vices, 'sins', 'errors' or *aisuwa* (greed, competition, envy etc.), which led to Akiwowo's breakdown of *ajobi* are daily multiplied at the level of *ajogbe* or society. What this seems to suggest is that, although the *asuwada* principle is a rational principle, the defective nature of the human being's character and behaviour (*aisuwa*) makes it an ideal principle. Surely if Plato's ideal of a just and organised society was founded on the principle that the human being as a rational animal ought to use reason, or what an African social and political philosopher describes as 'mental magnitude' (Awolowo 1968 : Ch. 9; Makinde 1987b : 3-13) societies might have existed and been run according to rational principles. In such societies, *alajobi* amd *alajogbe* might have lived peacefully together in their respective *ajobi* and *ajogbe* in accordance with the principle of *asuwada eniyan*. Under this ideal situation the question of social degeneration presumably would not arise, for philosophers would easily have been kings or kings philosophers.

In Plato, for instance, reason takes the place of *asuwada eniyan* and certainly not that of *asuwada* of the lower species whose behaviours are governed mainly by appetite. But when appetite, greed, unhealthy rivalry, corruption, nepotism, mediocrity and all the things that answer the name of *aisuwa* are made to govern reason or *asuwada* as a principle, then reason succumbs to the ignoble parts of man and society, just as *asuwada* succumbs to *aisuwada* of persons and society under similar conditions. And this inevitably leads to a breakdown or degeneration of *iwa* as it relates to the individual human being, *ajobi* (family) and finally *ajogbe* (society). My contention, therefore, is that the collapse of reason in Plato and *asuwada* in Akiwowo both lead to a total breakdown of natural order, first in the individual, then in *ajobi* and finally in *ajogbe* or society as the super-individual reality or individuals-writ-large.

One question can now be raised. If *ajogbe* or society can, and must, break down as *ajobi* does; and if it is true that the breakdown of *ajobi* leaves us with only *ajogbe*, what then takes the place of *ajogbe* after it has degenerated like its maker, *ajobi*? That is to say if, according to Akiwowo, with the total breakdown of *ajobi* only *alajogbe* is left, what is left after *ajogbe* has broken down? An answer to this question seems to suggest a line of action. But then no action should be taken unless we know precisely what the action is against and what it hopes to achieve. The purposive character of this action may very well suggest another variation in the *asuwada* principle, ie. a variation that suggests a self-correcting or regulating measure in the application of this principle. As I have pointed out somewhere else[15], one of such self-correcting measures is *revolution*. But an intellectual, non-violent, means seems to have been suggested in Akiwowo's concept of *Ifogbontaayese*.

Ifogbontaayese and the Unity of Knowledge

I have suggested that if *ajobi* can break down in Akiwowo's sense, then, *ajogbe*, to which the breakdown of *ajobi* leads, can also break down. This is what I mean by the degeneration of society, a situation that has become a common feature in many societies of the world, particularly in the Third World countries of Asia, Africa and Latin America. But even then the industrialised nations of the world have their own social problems. Technological revolution has created complex problems in the highly industrialised societies. High technology has led to an era of violence, electronic surveillance and erosion of privacy. The computer revolution has gradually replaced human labour, forcing able-bodied people out of jobs and thus reducing people's self-esteem. Military technology has continued to create psychological fear in the human mind in all societies of the world, with the daily threat of the possibility of nuclear war and the destruction of the human race and civilisation[16]. From this it becomes obvious that in any society even scientific and technological achievement must be brought under social control if the human being, the creator of the monster known as technology, must enjoy the fruits of scientific intelligence. For this reason, there is a need for man to emphasise the social responsibilities of science and technology[17]. This may involve the coming together of intellectuals from different departments of knowledge for the purpose of improving not only the material lot of human beings, but the general condition of humanity in societies. Instead of allowing science and technology to control us, we, as social animals and creators of technology, should control the achievement of science and technology and their impact on modern societies. But this suggests to us the working together of natural scientists and social scientists, historians, theologians and other scholars in the humanities and the life sciences. It is this working together of scholars from various departments of knowledge for the purpose of improving the world and humanity that catches the spirit of *Ifogbontaayese*, or unity of knowledge, for a common purpose – the survival of humanity and civilisation.

By *Ifogbontaayese* Akiwowo means, literally, 'using wisdom to remake the world', and uses it as an indigenous concept of sociology or theory of society (Akiwowo 1983a : 4). In the wider context of which I am using it, by *Ifogbontaayese* is meant, roughly in the Yoruba philosophical thought, the conscious employment of human knowledge, reason and wisdom for the understanding and improvement of the world (both the mental and the physical), of the human relationship to the physical world and to fellow human beings, and the improvement of the general condition of people on earth. According to my own philosophical interpretation of *Ifogbontaayese*, it involves *arojinle* (profound thinking) in all the intellectual disciplines, with the possibility of the unity of knowledge in Herbert Spencer's sense [18], or, in the sense in which we often talk of the unity of the sciences[19]. In so far as a person lives in one society or the other, his or her fate in the modern world is to be determined, not only by contributions to knowledge in science and technology but by contributions to knowledge in the social sciences, medicine (orthodox and traditional), the humanities, the arts and other areas of human knowledge. This situation points to the interrelatedness of human knowledge in its diverse fields.

Since the practical goal of all knowledge involves, or should involve, the human need for survival, and the survival instinct of the human being compels the choice of life rather than death on earth, the positive goal of any useful knowledge must be the one which seeks knowledge as something to be used only to human advantage. And this is to say that all knowledge must aim at improving the world and the general condition of humanity by means of what we now call *Ifogbontaayese*, a concept which refers not only to the natural sciences (as dealing with the physical world and the entire universe), the life sciences (as dealing with what Popper calls 'terrestrial phenomena' as opposed to physics which has universal application)[20], but also and, perhaps, most important of all, the social sciences which deal with the relationship of human beings on earth (which of course includes persons from all fields of knowledge: the natural scientists themselves, the social scientists, the medical scientists, the philosophers, the artists, the historians, the theologians, and even the ordinary man in the street) and their social, economic and political behaviours. This makes social science a wider subject than all the other disciplines including, of course, science and technology. Our position rests on the fact that the subject matter of social science includes even the natural scientists themselves as well as intellectuals from other disciplines. And it is from this point of view that I have argued elsewhere that the science of the future may turn out to be social science[21].

Thus, when the Yoruba say *arojinle ni taa ye se* (profound thinking improves the world and mankind)[22], we recognise this fact not only in the social sciences but in all disciplines and from the perspective of the unity of knowledge. *Ifogbontaayese*, therefore, provides the sound theoretical background for the unity of knowledge or unity of the sciences, all for the purpose of making societies of the world better places to live in. Technology has in fact created its own problems for modern societies. If we take this as one of the reasons for the degeneration of modern societies then *Ifogbontaayese* must be seen as one important antidote against societal problems. The spirit of *Ifogbontaayese* seems to have been reflected in John Gray's lecture on human happiness. According to John Gray:

> If the power by which we exist has implanted in man a desire to associate himself with others of his own species, which is evidently the case, society is the natural condition of mankind. If then societies produce the most overwhelming evils, and give to man the power of exercising over man cruelty, it is certain, either that God has created man for wretchedness, or that man has yet to learn the principles on which societies must be founded to render him happy.
>
> (Gray 1825 : 5)

Akiwowo's concept of *ifogbontaayese* is an 'African pragmatic view of knowledge'. Construed in this sense it may very well be the final realisation of the *asuwada* principle, and the ultimate aim of human reasoning that can, and must, be recognised in the very concept of *asuwada eniyan* if humanity is to be rendered humane and happy in societies of the modern world. This much is evident from the fact that '*asuwada eniyan*', according to Akiwowo, 'is also the physical expression of a non-physical design whose main object is to bring goodness to all humanity (1983a : 15). Having been thus recognised, I think the concept of *ifogbontaayese* should be seen as a necessary concept for the development and improvement of society and the general condition of humanity, irrespective of the individual's intellectual discipline, and also irrespective of caste, creed, colour or ideological differences – all of which have, in recent years, created social confusion locally and on the global scene.

In one of his unpublished works Akiwowo puts forth an argument for indigenisation of sociological thought as follows:

> The idea is that sociology can benefit from home-grown ideas contained in African oral literature so as to lessen the danger of depending entirely upon Western concepts and theoretical assumptions.

(Akiwowo 1983a : 4)[23]

And he goes further to say:

> Nigerian social scientists in general and sociologists in particular have an obligation of recycling what are elements in our world views into their explanatory and analytical studies of present or future social conditions of existence, and to the development of new knowledge about this and other societies.

(ibid.)

The present paper has validated Akiwowo's argument and contention, for not only has he succeeded in showing, through his work, that 'sociology can benefit a great deal from indigenous African ideas as contained in oral tradition and literatures', but also that other disciplines can benefit as well. As he himself has pointed out, the theoretical aspect of his preoccupation with indigenous theories may be called 'fruitful alternatives' to Western theories of society, and the practical aspect, 'conceptualised' as *ifogbontaayese*, 'deals with the application of sociological insights to the problems of social welfare and social development' (ibid.). From our own interpretation we have broadened this concept to encompass all the fields of human knowledge.

We conclude, therefore, that in line with 'proposition 9' of his 'derived propositions of relevance to sociology' (1986b : 354)[24], a proposition that is perfectly consistent with our last two quotations from his work above, Akiwowo's elucidation of *Ayajo Asuwada* shows clearly what African intellectuals can do with oral poetry and oral tradition as well as other indigenous concepts from which, it now appears, a great deal of ideas and knowledge can be discovered. The crucial point is how Akiwowo's pioneering effort, as demonstrated by his 'home-grown ideas', would be sustained by his African academic colleagues as well as his Western readers in the field of sociology in particular, and social science in general.

131

Notes

[1] A symposium held in honour of Professor Akinsola Akiwowo on the occasion of his retirement from the University of Ife, February 24, 1987, on the theme 'Social Theory and the African Reality'. The paper in which I discussed some of the novel ideas of Akiwowo and pointed out his challenges to other African intellectuals was entitled 'Social Theory and Social Relevance: An African Intellectual Tradition and the Social Construction of Reality' (1987a).

[2] For elaborate discussions on the concept of *Asuwada* as a principle of sociation, see Akiwowo's two important papers (1983a, 1986a). See also Akiwowo (1983b).

[3] The idea of 'philosophic spirit' as 'intellectual spirit' is attributed to Jamaludin Afghani, a well-known Muslim reformer (1838-1897), by S.H. Alatas (1977 : 11). By philosophic spirit Afghani means 'the spirit of inquiry, the sense of the enchantment of the intellectual pursuit and the reverence for scientific and rational knowledge' which he thinks 'are not widespread in the developing societies'. This implicit suggestion of 'intellectual indolence' was conveyed in my recent paper (1986a).

[4] Apart from his considerable influence in the Department of Sociology and Anthropology at the University of Ife, Professor Akiwowo is the founder and leader of the Alada Study Circle (ASC) of the same University of which Rowland Abiodun (Department of Fine Arts), Olufemi Morakinyo (Department of Mental Health) and the present writer (Department of Philosophy) are active foundation members. The circle also publishes the *Journal of Cultures and Ideas* (JCI) with Akiwowo as its current Editor-in-Chief.

[5] *Ayajo* and other forms of incantations like *Ase*, *Afose*, *Olugbohun* etc., which are usually recited from memory during some healing process by traditional healers, are contained in my lecture (1984a). The issue is also well discussed in another of my papers (1987c). For a related discussion on the traditional healing system based on *Odu-Ifa*, 'an ancient but well preserved form of Oral Literature' among the Yoruba of Nigeria, see Olufemi Morakinyo (1983).

[6] *Alasuwada* is also referred to as 'the author of all things' (Akiwowo 1986b : 348).

[7] I am indebted to Professor Akiwowo who made some of his thoughts available to me, written in the form of notes, during one of our conversations. This is apart from a large volume of manuscripts he is compiling for future publication.

[8] From the same conversation and notes.

[9] For an interesting discussion on this subject, see Rowland Abiodun (1984, 1983). Rowland Abiodun's work (1984) has led to the naming of a German Institute as Iwalewa Institute, an institute for encounters with the cultures of Africa, Asia and the Pacific at the University of Bayreuth in West Germany.

[10] See, for instance, Makinde (1985), and his other papers (1984c, 1983).

[11] See, for instance, Wande Abimbola (1976, 1971).

[12] See, for instance, Peter H. Klopper (1974 : 149-70).

[13] From my conversation with Akiwowo.

[14] This point, which is perfectly consistent with, and derivable from, the *asuwada* principle – particularly as it governs the human society (*asuwada eniyan*), was made by Akinola Aguda, Director of the Nigerian Institute of Advanced Legal Studies, University of Lagos in his lecture entitled 'Law as an Instrument of National Unity' delivered at a maiden session of the Bendel State Civil Service Forum, and published in *The Guardian* (1987, April 28, 30 and May 4 : 13, 19 and 17 respectively).

[15] I refer to my paper (1987) in Note 1 above.

[16] The issues raised here are well discussed in my paper (1984b).

[17] I have treated this issue in greater detail elsewhere (1986b).

[18] See, for instance, Malcolm Guthrie (1882). For related discussions on this issue in recent time, see a collection of articles (Jantsch 1981).

[19] The idea of the unity of the sciences which, to me, implies the idea of the unity of knowledge is a laudable one, although it is not uncontroversial. Some philosophers do see the unity of the sciences as the unity of methods. See, for instance Popper (1961 : 130-43; 1969 : 47-53).

[20] From my conversation with Popper in his home in Fallowfied, Buckinghamshire, England in December 1972.

[21] This view is strongly expressed in my paper (Bodurin, ed. : forthcoming).

[22] From one of the lyrical poems of Lanrewaju Adepoju, the *Ewi* metaphysical poet and social critic, in his 1987 musical record entitled *Eto Ominiyan* (Human Rights), No. LALPS 134, distributed by Leader Records Ltd., 7 Shipeolu Street, Palmgrove, Lagos, Nigeria.

[23] Cited by Akiwowo (1983a : 4).

[24] This proposition, which I have called an injunction rather than an axiom, reads thus: 'A social scientist in the Nigerian Universities who studies with a view to acquiring an understanding of people and society in Africa and to planning effectively to develop the quality of life in both westernised and historical communities may find that he or she needs to work with this derived conceptual scheme of *Iwa, Ihuwasi, Isesi* and *Ajumose* as these apply to a single actor or to a plurality of actors' in the community's social life'.

References

ABIMBOLA, W. 1971. *La notion de personne en Afrique Noir* (The Yoruba Concept of Human Personality). Paris: Centre National de la Recherche Scientifique.

ABIMBOLA, W. 1976. *Ifa: An Expository of the Ifa Literary Corpus.* Ibadan: Oxford University Press.

ABIODUN, R. 1983. 'Identity and the Artistic Process in Yoruba Aesthetic Concept of Iwa'. *Journal of Cultures and Ideas* 1 (1) : 13-30.

ABIODUN, R. 1984. 'Der Begriff des *Iwa* in der Yoruba Aesthetic'. *Tendenzen* 146 : 62-68. (Translated by U. Beier from the English 'The Concept of Iwa in Yoruba Aesthetic'.)

AGUDA, A. 1987. 'Law as an Instrument of National Unity'. *The Guardian*, April 28, 30 and May 4 : 13, 19, 17.

AKIWOWO, A. 1983a. *Ajobi and Ajogbe: Variations on the Theme of Sociation.* Inaugural Lecture Series 46. Ile-Ife, Nigeria: University of Ife Press.

AKIWOWO, A. 1983b. 'Understanding Interpretative Sociology in the Light of the Oriki of Orunmila'. *Journal of Cultures and Ideas* 1 (1) : 139-157.

AKIWOWO, A. 1986a. 'Asuwada Eniyan'. *Ife: Annals of the Institute of Cultural Studies* (University of Ife) 1 : 113-123.

AKIWOWO, A. 1986b. 'Contributions to the Sociology of Knowledge from an African Oral Poetry'. *International Sociology* 1 (4) : 343-358.

ALATAS, S.H. 1977. *Intellectuals in Developing Societies.* London: Frank Cass.

AWOLOWO, O. 1968. *The People's Republic.* Ibadan: Oxford University Press.

FOX, R. 1970. 'The Cultural Animal'. *Encounter* XXXV (1) : 31-42.

GRAY, J. 1825. *A Lecture on Happiness.* London: Sherwood, Jones and Co.

GUTHRIE, M. 1882. *Mr. Spencer's Unification of Knowledge.* London: Trubner & Co.

JANTSCH, E. ed. 1981. *The Evolutionary Vision: Toward a Unifying Paradigm of Physical, Biological, and Sociocultural Evolution* (AAAS Selected Symposium 61). Boulder, Colorado: Westview Press.

KLOPPER, P.H. 1974. *An Introduction to Animal Behaviour: Ethology's First Century.* Englewood Cliffs: Prentice-Hall.

MAKINDE, M.A. 1983. 'Immortality of the Soul and the Yoruba Theory of Seven Heavens (Orun Meje)'. *Journal of Cultures and Ideas* 1 (1) : 31-59.

MAKINDE, M.A. 1984a. 'African Philosophy, Culture, and Traditional Medicine'. First Fulbright Hays Lecture, Ohio University, Athens, Ohio, USA on May 2. Revised and expanded version to be published in a book under the same title (forthcoming 1988). Athens: Ohio University Press.

MAKINDE, M.A. 1984b. 'The World and its Enemies: A Philosophical Perspective'. Unpublished paper presented at the International Conference on George Orwell's 1984 and its Implication for Life Today, Ohio State University, Columbus, Ohio on May 4-6. Forthcoming under a new title 'George Orwell's 1984 and After: A Study in Societal Psychology and the Impact of Technology on Human Values'. *Ibadan Journal of Humanistic Studies.*

MAKINDE, M.A. 1984c. 'An African Concept of Human Personality: The Yoruba Example. *Ultimate Reality and Meaning* 7 (3) : 189-200.

MAKINDE, M.A. 1985. 'A Philosophical Analysis of the Yoruba Concepts of Ori and Human Destiny'. *International Studies in Philsophy* XVII (1) : 53-69.

MAKINDE, M.A. 1986a. 'Technology Transfer: An African Dilemma', in Murphy, J.W., Mickunas, A. and Pilot, J.J. (eds.), *Underside of High Technology* : 177-89. London: Greenwood Press.

MAKINDE, M.A. 1986b. 'Science, Technology and Human Values: A Perspective of the Paradox of Progress. Unpublished paper, 33 pp., quarto.

MAKINDE, M.A. 1987a. 'Social Theory and Social Relevance: An African Intellectual Tradition and the Social Construction of Reality'. Unpublished paper presented at the symposium 'Social Theory and the African Reality', University of Ife, Ile-Ife, Nigeria on February 24, 1987.

MAKINDE, M.A. 1987b. 'Mental Magnitude: Awolowo's Search for Ultimate Reality, Meaning and Supreme Value of Human Existence'. *Ultimate Reality and Meaning* 10 (1) : 3-13.

MAKINDE, M.A. 1987c. 'Cultural and Philosophical Dimensions of Neuro-Medical Sciences'. *Nigerian Journal of Psychiatry* 1 (2) : 85-100.

MAKINDE, M.A. Forthcoming. 'Man and the Problem of Society: In Defence of Social Science', in Bodunrin, P. (ed.), *Philosophy in Africa*, Vol. 2. Ile-Ife: University of Ife Press.

MORAKINYO, O. 1983. 'The Ayanmo Myth and Mental Health Care in West Africa'. *Journal of Cultures and Ideas* 1 (1) : 61-92.

POPPER, K.R. 1961. 'The Hypothetical-Deductive Method and the Unity of Social and Natural Science', in Popper, K.R., *The Poverty of Historicism* : 130-43. New York: Harper & Row. Reprinted in Krimerman, L.I. (ed.), *The Nature and Scope of Social Science: A Critical Anthology* : 47-53. New York: Appleton-Century-Crofts.

SINNOT, E.W. 1961. *Cell and Psyche: The Biology of Purpose*. New York: Harper and Row.

SOROKIN, P.A. 1928. *Contemporary Sociological Theories*. New York: Harper & Row.

TOWARDS AN AFRICAN SOCIOLOGICAL TRADITION: A REJOINDER TO AKIWOWO AND MAKINDE

O.B. Lawuyi and Olufemi Taiwo

In his paper on 'Contributions to the Sociology of Knowledge from an African Oral Poetry', Akiwowo (1986b) raised a question which appears as important to us: can we do sociology in African idioms? The study of the history of sociology in such ideologically diverse societies like the United States of America, the Soviet Union, Hungary and Austria points to the intrusion of linguistic and metaphysical representations of knowledge into the development of what George Homans (1967) calls 'the body of general explanatory principles' of social sciences. So why not also attempt to explain African realities from their linguistic and metaphysical constructions?

Makinde (1988) seems to agree with Akiwowo that it is indeed possible to do sociology in African languages. To him, Akiwowo (1986b) teaches African, and indeed other, scholars not only to break with common representations but also concretely to root their research in African culture and philosophy. African sociology is to be deployed against commonsense. On this view what matters is *emi arojinle* (spirit of profound thinking), that is, a rational development of sociology.

In this paper we accept that it is possible to do sociology in African languages. But we have to specify the concepts for doing sociology in African languages, clarify their meanings, suggest their interrelationships in thought and practice, and show how they can be used to understand social phenomena. However, neither Akiwowo and Makinde have sufficiently clarified their concepts for doing sociology in Yoruba. Hence their concepts, as they stand, are unsuited for sociological use. We wish to acknowledge that there is an everyday basis for the use of the concepts they have identified. But, as we shall argue presently, they never adequately specify how we can move from the everyday basis to doing sociology. Their explication of the concepts they have identified is fuzzy.

135

We direct attention to some neglected possibilities inhering in the conceptual discoveries made by Akiwowo, especially those relating to the importance of language, philosophy, and sociological theory to the development of indigenous sociological theories and paradigms. The focus is on four principal concepts which Akiwowo has appropriated from Yoruba language as pylons upon which to erect a sociological theory informed by the peculiar historical experiences and linguistic categories of an African people – the Yoruba. The concepts are those of *Asuwada*, *Ajobi*, *Ajogbe* and *Ifogbontayese*, which will be clarified presently. These four concepts are the ones around which Makinde's article (1988) is organised. Indeed, Makinde essays to provide further interpretations of the *asuwada* principle and its derivative forms of *ajobi*, *ajogbe* and *ifogbontayese*. We treat each concept in turn.

The Asuwada principle

We argue in this section that Akiwowo inaugurated and Makinde compounded some indistinctness regarding the usage of *asuwada*. According to Akiwowo, he came upon the concept of *asuwada* in his attempt to see whether there are Yoruba equivalents for 'sociology' and 'society' (Akiwowo 1986a : 114). He proposes the concept of '*imo nipa asuwa eniyan*', and that of '*asuwa-eniyan*' for 'sociology' and 'society' respectively. It is in the process of explicating the manifold determinations of these concepts that, we argue, Akiwowo inaugurated the indistinctness we alluded to. How did this come about?[1]

In '*Asuwada-Eniyan*' (Akiwowo 1986a), Akiwowo extracts the concept of '*asuwada*' from an *Odu Ifa* called *Osa-Guda* or *Alasuwada* (1986a : 115). He points out in the 'Contributions' article that '*ayajo asuwada*' is 'a myth of creation' and part of the object of that article was to investigate what this myth 'teaches about the creation of the Earth and everything in it, including man' (1986b : 344). It is arguable that it is the *ayajo asuwada* that one should focus on. What is the content of *ayajo asuwada* and what does it teach about the creation of the Earth and everything in it, including human beings?

Ayajo asuwada teaches that everything on Earth is created by the creator (*Alasuwada* – the one who *suwada*). But each thing on Earth is created with a purpose which it seeks to attain when it *su'wa* and it is this purpose which constitutes the principle of its being. Support for this contention is drawn from the *Odu Ifa* called *Osa-Guda* or *Alasuwada* (see Akiwowo 1986a : 116–7; 1986b : 345–7). According to the *ayajo asuwada*, when interpreted as a myth of creation, all things *are* in so far as they *su iwa*. Akiwowo infers from this myth the principle which actuates all things. He concludes:

Ese-Ifa wonyi fi han ni pe ni asuwa ni a ti da gbogbo eda inu aye ati aye paapaa. Nitori naa ni o fi je wi pe igi inu igbo, irawe odan, eja inu omi, koko inu odo, eye ojo orun, awon orisirisi eera ile ati beebee ni a da ni asuwa, asuwa ni igba iwase.

(Akiwowo 1986a : 118; also 1986b : 345)

(These poems of Ifa show that it is in *asuwa* that all earthly creatures as well as the Earth itself are created. This is why it is that all trees in the forest, all (leaves) grasses in the plains (savannah), fish in the ocean, aquatic flora, birds in the sky, varieties of ants and the like were created in *asuwa* in their first emanations.)

(Our translation)

On the above, *asuwada* is a story about creation, about origins, about how something came about on Earth. At the same time, *asuwa* is the principle of things and that in virtue of which different things assume different forms (Akiwowo 1986b : 345). What exactly is involved in this principle and what its implications are will be examined presently. For now we want to state a different version of the *asuwada* principle in Akiwowo.

In his inaugural lecture Akiwowo asserted that 'From the Orunmilaist view, a human being is an *asuwa* (a physiological organism) which is capable of forming and being an *asuwada* (social organism). That is, human beings possess the capacity which makes it possible for them to form purposive and purposeful bonds and to live together as one entity (Akiwowo 1983 : 12). On this conception *asuwada* is not to be understood as the principle of creation but a state of being *in potentia*. Given that human beings are *asuwa* which can *suwada*, the manifold ways in which they *suwada in concreto* depend on what purposes they have for *suwada*-ing and these purposes which they seek to realise when they *suwada* are external to their being *in potentia*. For it is not absurd to say that human beings are *asuwa*, even though the movement towards forming *asuwada* is aborted by some supervening occurrence.

Moreover, as Akiwowo himself sees it, the movement from being an *asuwa* to being an *asuwada* is mediated by the mutual *isesi* of individuals who cohere in a single social formation bound by common rules or standards of behaviour. Mutual *isesi* is what gives rise to the network which he calls '*Asuwada*' or the purposeful knitting together of conscious beings for the attainment of a goal. In the case of conscious human beings, the purpose of such a knitting together is social. Hence, according to this view, that which is called human society is what we call '*asuwa eniyan*' (Akiwowo 1983 : 13).

The two senses of *asuwada* that we have identified in Akiwowo are different and yield different implications for our understanding of 'being'. On the first conception, *asuwada–1* as a myth of creation tells us only why there is something in the world rather than nothing: there is something rather than nothing because things are made to be by their creator. But it is a different question why things are the way they are. It might be that the principle of their specific forms of being is derivable from the principle of creation *per se* but it remains distinct and separate from the latter.

On the second conception, Akiwowo insists that things are the way they are because they are *asuwada–2*. They are *asuwada–2* because they clump together for a purpose. In the specific case we are interested in, human beings are *asuwada–2* because they clump together for a purpose and the context within which they clump together is society (*asuwada–2 eniyan*) and the purpose and goal of *asuwada–2 eniyan* are stated as follows:

137

(a) *Ire aiku* (the value of good health till old age);
(b) *Ire owo* (financial security, or *ire oko-aya*, the value of intimate companionship and love);
(c) *Ire omo* (the value of parenthood); and
(d) *Ire abori ota* (the value of assured self-actualisation).

(Akiwowo 1983 : 13–4)

There is yet a third conception of *asuwada* in Akiwowo's writings. This is to be found in a section of his inaugural lecture on the 'Ontogeny of Sociality'. He writes:

> By sociality we mean the quality of being able to live and to grow in communities; the quality or fact of being able to establish companionship and mutual converse, in the Orunmilaist perspective is simply the quality of being able to *suwada* (come together for a common end; to coexist). The perspective clearly distinguishes between *asuwa* (coexistence) and *asuwada* (the fact of being together for a purpose).

(Akiwowo 1983 : 16)

There is a point of similarity between this third conception and the second because on the third sense, to *suwada–3* is to come together for a common end. However, a differentia is introduced when he supplies an additional gloss on what it is to *suwada: to coexist*. Akiwowo appears to believe that to coexist and to come together for a purpose are coeval with one another. They are not. Hence our identification of a third sense of *asuwada–3*. The difference in the English translation is obvious. But even in Yoruba the difference is clear. An *asuwa* is one who *su iwa* and the focus is on *the subject* of *iwa susu*. On the other hand, *asuwa–2* refers to a mode of being and means roughly 'the state of being together'. Thus a thing can be an *asuwa–1* (one who *su iwa*) alone, whereas it cannot be *asuwa–2* unless in the community of other things: *asuwa–2* is the state of being together, whereas *asuwa–1* is what each of them is on its own.

Furthermore it is one thing to *suwada–1* (to coexist) and another to *suwada–2* (to be together for a purpose). There is no doubt that human beings *suwada–1* (coexist) in manifold structures in society. However, it is not persuasive that they necessarily *suwada–2* (coexist for a purpose). The view that society has a purpose which it seeks to attain is one that has undergone considerable strictures in the history of sociological theory (see Popper 1961; Watkins 1957; Hayek 1944; Weber 1949). If Akiwowo wants to rescue this theory and cite it as a promising African alternative theory of sociological explanations, he should defeat those strictures.

When we turn our attention from society to various social categories and aggregates which make it up, we find that it is not every time that individuals *suwada–1* (coexist) that they *suwada–2* (coexist for a purpose). Individuals *suwada–1* when they are travelling on a bus or when they are in the market-place but one may not suggest that they *suwada–2* for a common purpose. Individuals *suwada–2* for a common purpose when they consciously come together in the aftermath of seeking out individuals of similar inclination with whom they form social categories like clubs, societies, etc., with set aims and objectives. On such occasions we do not merely affirm of them that they *suwada–2* we would say that they *suwada lati, fun apere, da egbe kan sile* (come

138

together, say, to found a club). In other words, the idea of purpose is not an inherent element of the concept of *asuwada*. It is problematic to claim that the concept of *asuwada*, in any of the senses we have identified, is, without further explication, undergirded by a philosophical presupposition of purposiveness in nature as claimed by Makinde (Makinde 1988 : 63).

The upshot of what we have said so far is to show that Akiwowo's concept of *asuwada* is characterised by an indistinctness which renders it, as it stands, unhelpful for sociological analysis. This is not to say that the concept is worthless or that it does not hold any promise of further development and fruitful application in social analysis. We should not be construed as saying that Akiwowo and Makinde misunderstood the concept. Nor are we suggesting that the concept is not suitable for sociological use. Our point is that much work is needed to suit the concept for sociological or philosophical application. In addition there must be awareness of the fuzziness of the concept in its current usage as well as evidence of a serious effort at clearing this fuzziness before any one goes on to build sociological or philosophical analysis on it. It is to be hoped that our identification of various senses of the concept will contribute towards clearing the fuzziness of which we speak.

The absence of an awareness of, and serious effort to clear, the fuzziness afflicting Akiwowo's concept of *asuwada* is the singular flaw in Makinde's essay (Makinde 1988) which seeks to advance further interpretations of Akiwowo's conceptual discoveries. The equivocations in Akiwowo assume tremendous proportions in Makinde's work. The fuzziness in Akiwowo is augmented in Makinde by several shifting usages of *asuwada*.

Makinde variously calls *asuwada*: (1) 'a philosophical principle of asuwada . . . which governs all nature', but which as 'related to man in society . . . is a principle of sociation or human society' (Makinde 1988 : 62); (2) 'a philosophical presupposition characterised as teleological by which *asuwada* represents the idea of purposiveness in nature' (Makinde 1988 : 63); (3) ' . . . an ultimate presupposition according to which an individual choice of *ori* and his or her destiny is made' (Makinde 1988 : 65); (4) ' . . . a principle of unity which sustains the very concepts of the family and society known by Akiwowo as *ajobi* and *ajogbe* respectively' (Makinde 1988 : 67); (5) an ideal rational principle made so by the defective nature of the human being's character and behaviour (Makinde 1988 : 70). We do not wish to assert that there may not be any connections among the five senses of *asuwada* that we have identified in Makinde's paper. What we affirm is that Makinde, too, seems innocent of the shifts in his usage of *asuwada* and does not appear to consider the possibility that Akiwowo's concepts suffer from the fuzziness we pointed out above. Had he averted his mind to this fuzziness, he himself would not have so easily fallen victim to the same flaw which we next argue vitiates the execution of the task he set himself in his paper. Let us take some instances of this vitiation.

On the second sense of Makinde's *asuwada* he accepts as unproblematic Akiwowo's explication of *asuwada* as a teleological principle. He avers:

> According to [Akiwowo], the concept, *asuwada*, is derived from *Iwa* (a state of being, existence or character, in a perpetual state of development; *Suwada*, to come together or coexist for a common end or purpose) and *asu-iwa-da* (literally meaning that which kneads

or moulds *Iwa*, i.e., beings, states of existence or characters so that they can live together in harmony for a purpose or common end). Thus it is often said: '*asuwada eniyan ni awon ti on nsu iwa da tabi awujo eniyan ti nsuwada*', literally meaning 'man-made mode of existence'.
(Makinde 1988 : 63)

He interprets *suwada* as 'to come together or coexist for a common end or purpose'. The *asuwada eniyan* is the conscious purpose which exists in human beings. An analysis of the concept of *asuwada* would, however, reveal the equivocations to which we already referred but did not elucidate. Our analysis, if successful, would show that Makinde's exposition is unclear and falls prey to conceptual confusions which have their roots in his failure to apprehend the indistinctness which marks Akiwowo's concepts.

We concur in the view of both Akiwowo and Makinde that the concept of *asuwada* is derived from *Iwa*. That is the extent of our concurrence. *Iwa* is translated as state of being, existence or character. It seems to us that both Akiwowo and Makinde believe that 'being', 'existence' and 'character' are somewhat interchangeable, and they both settle for 'character' as what *Iwa* is. So when Akiwowo says 'The unit of social life is the individual's life, being, existence, or character' (Akiwowo 1986b : 353), Makinde glosses that '*Iwa* (character) [is] the "unit of social life" ' and that 'The *alasuwada* oral poetry provides some lines to suggest the "goodness" of *Iwa* (character), also personified as 'being', in the concept of *asuwada*, i.e., the process of coming together for a purpose, or one who brings existence together to form a new entity' (Makinde 1988 : 63).

In the remainder of his paper Makinde translates *Iwa* as 'character' and 'character' was complete and actuated for a purpose at its first emanation. The purpose for which *Iwa* was actuated is 'goodness'. Makinde does not tell us whether 'goodness' is external to *iwa* or *iwa* is itself 'goodness' towards which all things tend. If 'goodness' is external to *iwa* then it is the case that the possession of *iwa* is a means to goodness and *iwa* is not its own justification. However, if '*iwa*' and 'goodness' are coterminous, then *iwa* is that to which all things tend and it is not itself referred to anything else. The second interpretation does not fit the general tenor of Makinde's analysis. The following passage might suggest that Makinde adopts the second interpretation:

> But the principle of *asuwada* seems to show that man is inherently good and that he exists for the purpose for which he and everything were created – goodness, which we may conceivably describe as one essential characteristic of the destiny of the human being as presupposed by the *asuwada* principle.
>
> (Makinde 1988 : 64)

Since there is no account of 'goodness', and since he keeps referring to good *iwa* and bad *iwa*, we shall take it that he does not want to identify '*iwa*' with 'goodness'. At another point in the paper he refers to '*iwa*' in its positive sense as goodness of character or being . . . ' (Makinde 1988 : 65).

Nevertheless, the first interpretation is not clearly articulated and the result is confusion about the status and, hence, the significance, of *iwa* considered separate from whether it is good *iwa* or bad *iwa*. In as much as it is not otiose to talk of good *iwa* and bad *iwa*, '*iwa*' and 'goodness' are not coterminous; unless

140

of course we mean by 'goodness' something above and beyond what is suggested by 'good *iwa*'. The onus to make this clear lies on Makinde and it is one he does not discharge in his paper.

We have dwelled at length on the different conceptions of *asuwada* because Akiwowo and, following him, Makinde place much store by the concept itself. We look next at the twin concepts of *ajobi* and *ajogbe* which Akiwowo calls 'the primordial forms of *asuwada eniyan*'.

Ajobi and ajogbe

In this section we shall argue that whereas *ajobi* and *ajogbe* hold some promise as concepts with which to unravel in part the evolution of sociality, Akiwowo's articulation of the concepts, and Makinde's interpretations of them, are inadequate for the redemption of this promise. There are two reasons for this. One, the concepts are, like that of *asuwada*, indistinct and Akiwowo shifts in his usages. As before, Makinde fails to apprehend the indistinctness. Two, Akiwowo's conceptions and Makinde's further interpretations yield some implausible explanations of particular phenomena they look at.

In his inaugural lecture (Akiwowo 1983), Akiwowo avers that *ajobi* and *ajogbe* are the primordial forms of *asuwada eniyan*. *Asuwada eniyan* he there referred to as 'human society'. The English equivalents for *ajobi* and *ajogbe* are consanguinity and co-residence respectively. *Ajobi* (consanguinity) refers to 'the facts of lineal and collateral relationships based upon blood and birth' (Akiwowo 1983 : 16). People are *ajobi* who are 'members of a family or of a group of related families, in a house, in a compound of dwellers, units in a village, town and so on' (Akiwowo 1983 : 16–17). The derivative concept *alajobi* describes that intangible spirit which binds the *ajobi* and in virtue of which these lineal and collateral relationships are defined and sustained. *Alajobi* supplies the criterion of identity as well as a measure by which relationships based on it are validated. The material element of *ajobi* is in blood and birth. Had Akiwowo remained with the preceding characterisation of *ajobi*, the concept would have had boundaries. But when he proceeded to say that on 'the Orunmilaist perspective of mankind, all human beings, regardless of race, colour and religion belong to a primordial *alajobi* and, therefore, share the *ajobi* bond' (Akiwowo 1983 : 17), he eliminated the boundaries of the concept and generated confusion. If we all form one vast primordial *ajobi*, how could we then affirm that we belong to different *ajobi*? What would we say accounts for the diversity of *ajobi* in the world, and even in specific societies? After all Akiwowo does not say that it is absurd to speak of diverse *ajobi* in the world.

It could be that Akiwowo means different things by *ajobi* when affirmed of the human race and when affirmed of diverse subspecies of the human race.[2] It still would remain to explain the nature of the primordial *ajobi* of which the diverse *ajobi* in the world are instances and what the principle of differentiation of different *ajobi* is. There may be possible explanations of the latter, but Akiwowo does not give us any.[3] We propose, for the reasons just stated, to examine *ajobi* as a bounded concept. So understood *ajobi* is a form of *asuwada eniyan*; that is, an *ajobi* is a form of social group.[4]

Ajobi is a form of social group. It embodies a structure of reciprocal expectations on the part of its members. It supplies a principle of social regulation and organisation specifying rights and forebearances for those who constitute it. There are duties and obligations which *ajobi* owe one another and there are things *alajobi* forbids members to do to or with the person and possessions of one another. There are times when the *ajobi* breaks down and *alajobi* is violated or negated. The conditions for such breakdowns and the reasons for them supply some indices for affirming that such a society is in the throes of change.

Ajogbe (co-residence), on the other hand, refers to 'the facts of sharing same or contiguous shelter whether or not the sharers are related by blood' (Akiwowo 1983 : 18). On this construal, what defines an *ajogbe* and separates it from *ajobi* is that those who are *ajogbe* are related not by any sanguinary bonds but by the fact that they live together under one roof or in contiguous shelters. Once you remove the shared shelter(s) you have dispersed an *ajogbe*. It does not matter what has brought the *ajogbe* together or how they were brought together. What matters is that an *ajogbe* might consist entirely of total strangers, whereas strangers cannot be members of an *ajobi*. *Alajogbe* is the spirit which informs and structures the reciprocal relations and mutual expectations of those who co-reside in an *ajogbe* and these latter are different from those of *alajobi*.[5]

Akiwowo starts out by saying that both *ajobi* and *ajogbe* are primordial forms of human society. This means that both are coordinate in time without having one precede the other and that society at the beginning manifested one or both of the forms. Later he seems to introduce a sequence into their emergence, such that *ajobi* is first and *ajogbe* is a later form of sociation. How is this translation effected? Persons and groups of persons from time to time negate, deny or break asunder the bonds of *alajobi* between them and others. Many factors may be responsible for this: irruption of individualism into a hitherto collectivist ethos, material differentiation in society among *ajobi*, competition, envy, etc. The consequence is the emergence of new forms of social bond, e.g., *ore* (friendship) and, most important for our purposes, *ajogbe* (see Akiwowo 1983 : 20). It seems to be the case that rather than being a primordial form of sociation, *ajogbe* emerges with the breakdown of *ajobi*. This was the interpretation Makinde was led to.

> By my own interpretation of Akiwowo's indigenous theory of society, *ajobi* represents the concept of the nuclear family or related families (extended family) . . . , while *alajobi* represents the individuals in the family or related families sharing a common bond under similar environmental and social conditions. *Ajobi*, then, is the first sign of human sociality, the irreducible unit of society.
>
> (Makinde 1988 : 67)

The passage just quoted from Makinde represents a shift in meaning away from Akiwowo's usage of *ajobi* and *alajobi* respectively. It is our view that Makinde's interpretation is confused and it compounds the fuzziness in Akiwowo's characterisation of the two terms. Whereas similar environmental and social conditions are not essential for *ajobi* to obtain, Makinde incorporates them. In addition, it is wrong to say, as Makinde does, that *alajobi* represents the individuals in the family or related families. For, as we pointed out above, *alajobi* is the intangible bond in virtue of which individuals constitute an *ajobi*. We do not say that individuals are *alajobi*; we say instead that they are '*ebi*' and '*molebi*' (i.e., sons/daughters of a common *ebi*).

Most importantly, by reducing *ajobi* to a nuclear family or related families, it was very easy for Makinde to interpret *ajogbe* as society which is made up of 'the smallest units of social groups known as *ajobi* consisting, so to say, of individuals virtually united by the "ties of consanguinity" ' (Makinde 1988 : 67). What this means is that an *ajogbe* is the coming together of different kinds of *ajobi* and *alajogbe* then refers to 'people living together from different kinds of *ajobi* (families) all united by a common purpose . . . ' (ibid.). Makinde cannot claim fidelity to Akiwowo for his latter claim.

In the works by Akiwowo in which he elucidated the concepts of *ajobi* and *ajogbe*, nowhere does he refer to *ajogbe* as society. Society is *asuwada eniyan* and *ajobi* and *ajogbe* he calls variously forms of sociation (Akiwowo 1983 : 23), 'distinctive social relationships and social processes with established observable patterns' (ibid. : 20). Moreover, Makinde's interpretation of *alajogbe* as people living together from different kinds of *ajobi* is undermined by the fact that there may not be an *ajobi* in an *ajogbe* and a common purpose is not one of the constitutive elements of an *ajogbe*. *Ajogbe* is simply co-residence whose essential attribute is a common shelter or contiguous shelters in a locality (ibid. : 18). For all of these reasons we contend that Makinde is merely offering *his* indigenous theory of society, which may or may not be good, cloaked under the rubric of further interpretations of Akiwowo's discoveries. Makinde is welcome to his views in so far as he makes it clear they are *his* and he defends them as such.

It is true that Akiwowo asserts that *asuwada eniyan* is the coming together of diverse *iwa* for a purpose. However, to conflate *alajogbe* and *asuwada eniyan* is to compound the fuzziness in Akiwowo's usages. The other problem is that it introduces a subordinate–superordinate relationship between *alajobi* and *alajogbe* which is not supported by Akiwowo's initial assertion that *ajobi* and *ajogbe* and their derivatives are primordial forms of *asuwada eniyan*. The introduction of a hierarchical relationship between *ajobi* and *ajogbe* comes also with a temporal sequence, such that *ajobi* is primary, while *ajogbe* is secondary. Not only that, it turns out that *ajogbe* arises from the breakdown of *ajobi*. At one level Makinde says that ' . . . *alajobi* ascends to the larger group of *alajogbe* in order to achieve its true purpose in *ajogbe* or society' (Makinde 1988 : 67–8). The metaphor of ascent suggests improvement – *ajogbe* is superior to *ajobi* and it represents the 'coming together of different *alajobi* (persons from different unrelated families) to strengthen the hitherto loose bonds between them' (Makinde 1988 : 69). At another level, he talks as if *ajogbe* is inferior to *ajobi* since *ajogbe* is constituted on the ruins of *ajobi* and there is an implicit recognition that people would rather have *ajobi* than *ajogbe*, hence the lament, '*ko si alajobi mo o, alajogbe lo ku u*' (there is no more *alajobi* in the relationship of human beings, only *alajogbe* is left) (Akiwowo

1983 : 10). All these interpretations do not cohere easily in one set. Meanwhile, by the time we get to this point in Makinde's essay we see that the author has without justification distanced himself sufficiently from the original meaning of *ajobi* and *alajobi* in Akiwowo's writings to support our contention that he is not offering further interpretations of Akiwowo. Here is Makinde:

> We have seen that in Akiwowo's thought both *ajobi* (family) and *ajogbe* (society) are manifestations of the *asuwada eniyan*, particularly as it relates to human association. We have also shown that *ajobi* is the first and smallest unit of social groups, and each family or social group is made up of individuals. A family may now be defined as an aggregate of individuals of like minds united by, and for, a common purpose.
>
> (Makinde 1988 : 68)

Compare Akiwowo:

> ... *ajobi* refers to members of a family, or a group of related families or several groups of related families, in a house, in a compound of dwellers, units in a village, town and so on. *Ajobi* also refers to members united by birth and blood who live separately in distant villages, towns, or regions of the world or a people in diaspora.
>
> (Akiwowo 1983 : 18–9)

A reference to purpose or like minds is absent in Akiwowo's depiction of *ajobi*.

What is absent in Makinde is an awareness that *ajobi* and *ajogbe* are social processes distinguished by their different principles of identification and of norms of social behaviour. Regardless of purpose, people are *ajobi* in as much as they have consanguinary ties. These ties are used to identify members of an *ajobi* and these ties ground a structure of mutual expectations among the members and an appeal to *alajobi* is taken as justification for and validation of particular behaviours.

Similarly, those who are *ajogbe* start out as co-residents – sharing the same shelter or contiguous shelters. This has a different structure of expectations from that of an *ajobi* and, equally, from that of strangers who meet occasionally either in the market or at social functions. There are forms of behaviour forbidden by *alajogbe* and there are those that are justified and validated by *alajogbe*. Members of an *ajogbe* might deepen their ties in such a way that they simulate an *ajobi*. On the other hand, disruptive factors might so attenuate *ajobi* bonds that an *ajobi* is marked by forms of behaviour that are more germane in an *ajogbe*. Additionally, *ajobi* and *ajogbe* may coexist with individuals switching roles in accordance with which of the rules they find themselves in at different times. So, contrary to Makinde's interpretations, *ajobi* and *ajogbe* may coexist and individuals may enjoy concurrent membership in both at any one time. This way we preserve Akiwowo's original description of *ajobi* and *ajogbe* as 'variations on the theme of sociation' with each one possessing 'different fractions of sociation' (Akiwowo 1983 : 23) without hierarchising them.

The source of the numerous problems we have identified in the works by Makinde and Akiwowo can, in our opinion, be traced to the general nationalist animus which informs their theoretical labours. Even though they may deny it, both Akiwowo and Makinde are concerned to show that there are Yoruba equivalents of philosophical and sociological concepts prevalent in English. Their aim is to show that the Yoruba language too possesses words which can double as sociological and philosophical concepts. Whereas one may not fault the effort to find Yoruba equivalents of English concepts, one surely must cry foul when the identification of these Yoruba equivalents is presented as discovery of sociological theories and philosophical doctrines. It is one thing, and an easy one at that, to say that sociology *can be done* in Yoruba. It is quite another and infinitely more difficult thing to *do* sociology in Yoruba.

It could be that all that Akiwowo and Makinde are concerned to show is that sociology can be done in Yoruba. Perhaps they have merely offered us pointers in the direction of fruitful equivalents in everyday Yoruba for the technical concepts of sociological analysis and philosophical reflection in English. At this modest level one must applaud Akiwowo's discoveries. Indeed, one must acknowledge that Akiwowo is sometimes tentative when he offers his discoveries to those who are interested in creating an indigenous tradition in sociological theory. Even this occasional tentativeness can nowhere be found in Makinde's paper. When Makinde talks of his (Makinde's) 'own interpretation of Akiwowo's indigenous theory of society . . . ' (Makinde 1988 : 67), he abandons Akiwowo's tentativeness. He conveys the impression that Akiwowo has not merely offered us evidence that everyday Yoruba has a basis for sociological analysis. He writes as if Akiwowo has actually done sociological analysis in Yoruba and has given us an indigenous theory. We do not dispute the claim that Akiwowo's discoveries show that the everyday basis for sociology is there in Yoruba. What we deny is that either of our interlocutors has given us a sociological theory in Yoruba.

Doing sociology in Yoruba requires, in addition to the identification of words that can serve as concepts, a rigorous demarcation of the boundaries of such concepts and of their derivatives, considerable sophistication at theory construction. It demands analyses of the structures of social interaction, the norms and values which inform social relations and people's understanding of them. There also must be the accumulation of vast amounts of empirical data regarding Yoruba language and culture. That Makinde, for instance, is guilty of a lack of sufficient grounding in the Yoruba language is evidenced in his discussion of *ajobi* and *ajogbe* which we already criticised. That both Akiwowo and Makinde do not take language seriously can be seen in their shifting usages of their central concepts: *asuwada, asuwa, asuwada eniyan*.

We conclude this section by offering in a nutshell what we think a more promising interpretation of *asuwa* and its derivative concepts would look like. Let us go back to the *ayajo alasuwada*.

2. *Agiriyan ni Morere eerun.*
   The anthill is the *morere* of the *eerun*.
3. *Asuwa ni Morere eniyan.*
   Asuwa is the *morere* of humankind.
4. *Asuwa da aye.*
   It was with the principle of *asuwa* that the Earth was created.
5. *Asuwa da orun.*
   It was with the principle of *asuwa* that the Heavens were established.

145

6. *Asuwa daa sile* (Akiwowo 1986a : 116).
   In *asuwa* forms all things descended upon the Earth activated by purpose. (Akiwowo 1986b : 345)
56. *Asuwa ni t'oyin.*
   Asuwa is what the *oyin* are.
57. *Asuwa ni t'ado.*
   Asuwa is what the *ado* bees are.
58. *Asuwa leeran n hu ninu oko.*
   The *eeran* leaves grow in *asuwa*.
59. *Asuwa ni tosusu owo.*
   Asuwa is what broomsticks form.
60. *Asuwa leeran n hu ninu aare.*
   It is in *asuwa* that the *eeran* leaves grow in the *aare*.
61. *Asuwa ni ti Elegiri* (Akiwowo 1986a : 117).
   Asuwa is what the *Elegiri* birds form (Akiwowo 1986b : 348).

In the lines we have cited from Akiwowo, what stands out clearly is that the concept of *asuwa* is pointing to something which is characteristic of whatever it is that is supposed to be *asuwa*. We now try to unearth the key to understanding what this something is. We have already mentioned that there is a basic ambiguity about the concept of *asuwa* (see p. [7] above). First, we have *asuwa–1* (one who *su iwa*). Here the emphasis is on the pronomial subject – 'The one who . . . '. Second, we have *asuwa–2* (being in a state of *isuwa*). Here the emphasis is on the quality of being – a particular form of being rather than on the subject who does something. To see even more clearly the importance of this effort at disambiguation, the negation of each version yields different statements. The negation of *asuwa–1* (one who *su iwa*) is *alaisuwa* (one who does not *su iwa*). But the negation of *asuwa–2* is *aisuwa* (not being in a state of *isuwa*). Neither Makinde nor Akiwowo make it clear in their writings which of the two senses of *asuwa* they are employing at any particular time.

Both Akiwowo and Makinde appear to be unaware of the ambiguity we just described. At least there is no evidence of such an awareness in their articles. Even if we suppose that their shifting usages of the *asuwa* concept portray an implicit recognition of the ambiguity, they do not realise the far-reaching implications of the ambiguity. Hence they fail to consider either the ambiguity or its implications. Perhaps their lack of awareness best explains the absence of efforts at disambiguation. We attempt to disambiguate the *asuwa* concept.

Asuwa–1 and *asuwa–2* share a common etymological root in *Iwa*. As Wande Abimbola points out:

> The word *iwa* is formed from the verbal root *wa* (to be, to exist) by the addition of the deverbative prefix *i*. The original meaning of *iwa* can therefore be interpreted as 'the fact of being, living or existing'.
>
> (Abimbola 1975 : 393)

We propose to use Abimbola's explication as the basis of our own interpretation.[6] An understanding of the root *iwa* holds the key to the disambiguation of *asuwa*. *Iwa* is Being *sans* determinations. All things that are have *iwa* (being). However, each thing is in accordance with its peculiar form of being. For each thing is a particular with its own identity and attributes which define it. The sum total of those attributes which define each thing, which make it what it is, and in the absence of which it will not be what it is but something else, is what we generally refer to as the *essence* of the thing. Sometimes these attributes refer to what Aristotle would call the *erga* (characteristic activities) of the thing. For instance, for Aristotle, the *erga* of human beings consist of contemplation and the best form of life that human beings could have is the contemplative life (*bios theoretikos*). There are forms of existence which are most appropriate for particular beings.

Each *iwa* (being) has an *essence* which defines it and differentiates it from other beings. There are forms of life which are most appropriate for particular *iwa* (being). We are suggesting that the *asuwa* concept is better understood as a principle of the essence of beings which supplies us with criteria of identity and differentiation of beings from other beings. For example, when Akiwowo writes that '*Asuwa* is what the *oyin* are', '*Asuwa* is what the *ado* bees are', 'The *eeran* leaves grow in *asuwa*', etc., he is pointing at the *essence* of *oyin*, *ado* bees, *eeran*, etc., and at the form of life that approximates this essence.

We have said that *asuwa–2* is a form of being in which beings congregate or coexist with one another. When it is said that something is *asuwa–2*, what is meant is that that thing does not exist singly but rather in togetherness with others of its kind. Even though he grounds it differently, it is our belief that Akiwowo presaged an interpretation like ours when he avers:

> . . . [T]here is a universal principle of *asuwa*, according to which everything was created alone but by which nothing continued-in-being alone. All things continue-in-being as communities, throughout the whole realms of nature from ants to elephants, from algae to whales, from plants to giant forests; man-made objects continue-in-being in communities or systemic wholes, from dyads to congregations, from families to nations.
>
> (Akiwowo 1986b : 352)

What Akiwowo appears to be saying is that it is the essence of beings to continue-in-being as communities – *iwa susu* is the best form of life for beings in the world; hence it is predicated of things that they are *asuwa–2*. But the *asuwa eniyan* is different from the *asuwa eranko*. *Ajobi* and *ajogbe* are *asuwa eniyan* (forms of life of human beings), whereas they are not *asuwa eranko* (forms of life of animals). Thus gregariousness is part of the essence of human beings and society is the most appropriate form of life for the realisation of this essence.

The strengths of an essentialist interpretation are many. We mention only two. In the first place, by understanding *asuwa eniyan* as the form of life best suited to the human essence, we are able to answer the question why we cannot live as monadic individuals. Furthermore, all those forms of life, e.g., atomistic individualism, widespread aggression and private appropriation of socialised production, can all be said to be subversive of the human essence and therefore stand condemned. Although it is part of the essence of human beings to be *asuwa–2*, i.e. exist in the community of other human beings, part of the reason that this is so is that human beings are *asuwa–1*, i.e. those who *are*, or *clump* together, and it is only in clumping together that we become human beings, so that *asuwada eniyan–1* (those who *su iwa* to become human

147

beings) and *asuwada eniyan-2* (the form of being peculiar to human beings) complement each other. This leads us to the second major strength of an essentialist interpretation of *asuwa eniyan.*

Iwa is often interpreted as character, good behaviour and the like. Wande Abimbola broaches the root of this interpretation when he asserts:

> It is my impression that the other meaning of *iwa* (character, moral behaviour) originates from an idiomatic usage of this original lexical meaning (i.e. 'fact of being, living or existing'). If this is the case, *iwa* (character) is therefore the essence of being. A man's *iwa* is what can be used to characterise his life especially in ethical terms.
>
> (Abimbola 1975 : 393–4)

The kernel of truth in Abimbola's impression is that *iwa* can supply an axiological standard by which we apply moral epithets to human behaviour. What is absent is an awareness that we need a middle term between *iwa* as an ontological category and *iwa* as a value epithet. We believe that an essentialist reading can yield this middle term. Although we cannot develop the argument in this paper, it will go along the following lines.

The form of life that is most appropriate to a thing is one that allows the full efflorescence of the thing's essence. A form of life in which a thing's *iwa* (being) coincides with its *essence* is the best form of life of the thing. The greater the gulf between a thing and its essence, the less suited is its form of life to its essence. Thus if we know the *erga* of a thing, the more its *iwa* is not an embodiment of these *erga*, the more we will say that its *iwa* is not good and vice versa. A being has *iwa rere* where its being approximates its essence. The middle term is supplied by the essence and it supplies us with some evaluative criteria. For instance, *aisuwa*, which is the negation of *asuwa-2* will be an *iwa buburu* for *eniyan* whose essence is *asuwa ni awujo awon ti o nsu'wa* (to be together in the company of other human beings). This leads us to the final part of this essay; a consideration of the sociology of knowledge, or what Akiwowo terms *ifogbontayese.*

Ifogbontayese and the sociology of knowledge

The thrust of *ifogbontayese* is change in the social order. This change can be effected through an ability to discern and make critical judgements. In Akiwowo's definition, *ifogbontayese* is the application of wisdom to remake the world (Akiwowo 1983 : 4). By implication, the existing order is not good enough. This conclusion follows naturally from his observation that society is becoming more and more individualistic; that there is a shift from the communalistic ethos of the indigenous African social structure to a focusing upon the role of individuals in the cultural context, and on describing such temporal processes like the institution of knowledge and knowledge-gathering, which constitute the activities of individuals. For Akiwowo there must be a return to the indigenous culture for identity creation and the construction of the criteria of relevant knowledge.

Our view is that Akiwowo's account of the sociology of knowledge assumes a cultural reversibility. The assumption of reversible 'time' impels us to intrinsic processes of culture by drawing upon the terms and concepts of this very culture: history is, by necessity, an auto-reflexive view of the cultural being on her/his own culture. Knowledge is not only a transcendent phenomenon but also a notion so thoroughly culture-bound as to be useless beyond Yoruba or African societies. Hence not only would Yoruba myths make sense to the Yoruba, in relation to one another, a more profitable thing to do is to look for their relevance to local development. Makinde's position is slightly different.

In his analysis of Akiwowo's contribution to the sociology of knowledge from an African perspective, Makinde seems to agree with Akiwowo that the issue in the development of any society is the kind of knowledge of its people, of the environment, and of aspirations and expectations that are promoted by the culture of the society. But Makinde sees this knowledge as more nearly embodying the norms of 'profound thinking' than the wisdom one. Consequently, while he does not disagree with Akiwowo on the substance of change, he advocates a different means relying more on philosophical thoughts than on traditional values and ideas. The two may not correspond to each other. A profound thinking can actually lead to a condemnation of traditional values.

For Makinde, Nigerian societies in general have remained relatively unchanged, even after colonial intervention. Although the people are not lacking in wisdom, there is no profound thinking about how to improve their world. Therefore, the practical goal of knowledge in these societies must be to survive in a rapidly changing world. To this end, the positive goal of any useful knowledge is to develop appropriate technology, while being sensitive to the implications of such technological development for human values. The need for sensitivity is conditioned by the fact that no society survives purely on technological knowledge. Rather, they also need philosophical thoughts on the 'conscious employment of human knowledge, reason and wisdom for the understanding and improvement of the world, of the human relationship to the physical world and to fellow human beings, and the improvement of the general condition of people on earth' (Makinde 1988 : 71). Invariably the stress is on an interdisciplinary approach to problem-solving as the weakness of one approach can be corrected by the strength of the other within the general framework.

If, therefore, we understand Makinde correctly, his target of attack is the emphasis on technology as a means of improving the human environment and welfare. We do not see this as flowing from Akiwowo's work; instead it reflects on and captures the essence of Makinde's own interest in his society (see Makinde 1986a, 1986b, 1987). We must grant though that most of the African societies have remained underdeveloped technologically. The reason for this is partly the negative effect of technology in a society where such technology is still rudimentary and partly the impact of conflicting ideologies held by the people.

For the sociology of knowledge, the role of ideology and belief systems in the systematic structuring of knowledge cannot be overemphasised. Yet, nowhere in Makinde's work was the issue of ideology and belief systems treated. The presumption that technology is 'bad' is of little systematic importance to general knowledge. We need to know in what ways and contexts a knowledge is 'bad'; we must also be able to recognise the depth sufficient to make a knowledge profound.

The African reality must be grasped as a dynamic reality responding to both internal and external pressures. Every aspect of the knowledge system is contaminated by this dynamism. A partial spin-off of this dynamism is that the development of African knowledge, scientific or social, is processual and gradual, and is built from experiences – since Africans have always attempted to develop their technologies along the line of their situational and ecological experiences. They are not backward-looking; they adapt to changes in their environment. From this point of view we cannot stress the unity of knowledge too much. Variations and change in the organisation, transmission and evaluation of knowledge are realities that cannot be ignored.

Akiwowo and Makinde seem to have simplified the reality of Africans by thinking that the acquisition of the relevant knowledge is a precondition for the solution of all problems society might face. They ignore the larger question of the restrictive influence of social knowledge itself on the process of intellectual growth, and the role of human activity in the genesis and structuring of cognitive capabilities. Knowledge is used differently by the different segments of society. As such, how a society selects, classifies, distributes, transmits and evaluates a knowledge it considers 'good' or 'bad' invariably reflects both the distribution of power and the principles of social control.

The clue to social knowledge is supplied by the essence which defines and structures social groups and their interactional processes (including those of their members). The essence cannot be determined a priori in so far as the essence of a social organism does not betray itself except in acts, behaviours and thought systems. But then, once the essence is known, the identification with it and the attempt to promote it could lead to socio-technological innovation, to the complex problem of individuality and collectivity, to the acts which promote self-esteem and social change. Of course, it may well be that when local knowledge is evaluated from this standpoint, the conclusion is that the 'being' does not approximate the 'essence'. The task of the social scientist in this situation would then be that of bringing the being and the essence into phase; that is, harmonising the individual and the collective, particularism and nationalism, etc., through the educational media.

In all, given that cultures are endlessly various, so also is human nature. A renewed interest in the sociology of knowledge must grapple with the integration of essence and being as dynamic aspects of socio-cultural phenomena. The acquisition, interpretation, and utility of knowledge, given the above, become reflexive and critical. They become co-extensive with developing a truly human, truly relevant, society.

Notes

1. We cannot pronounce on the chronological order of Akiwowo's writings. It appears to us that the dates on which they are published are not reliable indicators of when they were written. For example, Akiwowo 1986b contains freely translated portions of the oral poetry in Akiwowo 1986a without any indication of the relationship between the two.

2. We are grateful to the Editor of this journal for suggesting this possible interpretation.

3. He does explain the breakdown of the African *ajobi* into diverse *ajobi* but not that of the primordial global *ajobi* into different racial/regional *ajobi* (see Akiwowo 1983 : 19–20).

4. We say 'social group' instead of Akiwowo's 'society' because it will only generate confusion to interpret *ajobi* as a form of society because *ajobi* occurs within society and society is made up of several *ajobi*.

5. Unfortunately, neither Akiwowo nor Makinde tells us what precisely are some of the duties, obligations and entitlements entailed by membership of *ajobi* and how they differ from those of *ajogbe*. Some might think that such an account is not important. However, we insist it is because when Akiwowo says that co-residence is 'the fact of sharing same or contiguous shelters whether or not the sharers are related by blood', he leaves open the possibility that members of an *ajobi* who are otherwise related by blood may cohabit an *ajogbe*. If this is possible, then we need to know the differentia between the cohabitation, which occurs under *ajobi* and that typified by *ajogbe* for co-residence could take place in both forms.

6. We wish to point out, though, that Abimbola too quickly abandons this basic meaning of *iwa* for that of *iwa* as 'character' or 'moral behaviour' (Abimbola 1975 : 393).

References

ABIMBOLA, W. 1975. 'Iwapele: The Concept of Good Character in Ifa Literary Corpus', in Abimbola, W. (ed.), *Yoruba Oral Tradition*. Ile-Ife: Dept. of African Languages and Literature, University of Ife. pp. 389–420.

AKIWOWO, A. 1983. *Ajobi and Ajogbe: Variations on the Theme of Sociation*. Inaugural Lecture Series 46. Ile-Ife: University of Ife Press.

AKIWOWO, A. 1986a. 'Asuwada Eniyan'. *Ile: Annals of the Institute of Cultural Studies* (University of Ife) 1 : 113–23.

AKIWOWO, A. 1986b. 'Contributions to the Sociology of Knowledge from an African Oral Poetry'. *International Sociology* 1 (4) : 343–58.

HAYEK, F.A. 1944. *The Road to Serfdom*. Chicago: University of Chicago Press.

HOMANS, G.C. 1967. *The Nature of Social Science*. New York: Harcourt, Brace and World.

MAKINDE, M.A. 1986a. 'Technology Transfer: An African Dilemma', in Murphy, J.W., Mickunas, A. and Pilot, J.J. (eds.), *Underside of High Technology*. London: Greenwood Press.

MAKINDE, M.A. 1986b. 'Science, Technology and Human Values: A Perspective of the Paradox of Progress'. Unpublished paper.

MAKINDE, M.A. 1987. 'Mental Magnitude: Awolowo's Search for Ultimate Reality, Meaning and Supreme Value of Human Existence'. *Ultimate Reality and Meaning* 10 (1) : 3–13.

MAKINDE, M.A. 1988. 'Asuwada Principle: An Analysis of Akiwowo's Contributions to the Sociology of Knowledge'. *International Sociology* 3 (4) : 61–76.

POPPER, K.R. 1961. *The Poverty of Historicism*. London: Routledge and Kegan Paul.

WATKINS, J.W.N. 1957. 'Historical Explanation in the Social Sciences'. *British Journal for the Philosophy of Science* 8 : 104–17.

WEBER, M. 1949. *The Methodology of the Social Sciences*. New York: The Free Press.

ONE WORLD SOCIETY

One World Society

The idea of one humanity is as old as coherent social thought. But it was as an idea for potential realisation or as an ideal to be striven for that it captured the attention of philosophers. To that extent the expansion of Western society from the sixteenth century appeared rather to emphasise the difference between the actual and the ideal. Cultural diversity and often mutual unintelligibility seemed to characterise the real world. Comparative method took on a centrality within sociology precisely as a response to this experience.

It is the reality of social development which has changed this situation. Since the Second World War there has been an increasing recognition among sociologists that the world's population is enveloped by a single world social system. 'Society' as such comes to comprise a multitude of 'societies' which, in the context of the larger system, can only find a highly conditioned and relative autonomy, largely as closely entwined nation-states.

Possibly nothing separates the sociology of the second half of the twentieth century so much from the sociology of the first half as the different starting point for the study of development. In the first half there was still a deep attachment to evolutionary ideas in which different cultures were thought to be able to find their own route up a scale of social complexity.

The theory of modernisation, inspired in part by Weberian ideas of the peculiarity of Western rationalism, represented a transition to the later period. Modernisation appeared as a kind of secularised missionary activity, in the narrowest sense the extension of the American dream. As such it was a ready target for Marxist critique. It was represented as an ideological expression of political interests, repressive of the legitimate aspirations of poor countries and above all neglectful of real dynamics underlying the creation of a single world economy, namely the globalisation of capital.

The most famous phrase summing up this conception of the shape of a new world order was André Gunder Frank's 'the development of underdevelopment'. It expressed the widely received view that internal authentic development in non-Western societies was thwarted by their incorporation into the global capitalist economy and their consequent dependency. It was an approach generalised for the overall historical development of capitalism in Immanuel Wallerstein's world-system theory.

There was something particularly appropriate, then, that it was a paper by Wallerstein reprinted here which became the first article in the first issue of *International Sociology*. He has done more than anyone else in the last twenty years to insist that the world-system is the necessary framework within which any explanations of contemporary social and economic processes must be placed. That insistence is also a challenge to much of contemporary sociology as his critique of the idea of society contained in that article demonstrates. It is the reification of that idea which for him represents an obstacle to a full appreciation of the direction of world development.

That challenge is, however, being met. Moreover, it is being met in such a way that the dominant interpretation of one world as the product of capitalist

155

processes is being modified by an emphasis on other forces. A valuable account of these shifts in emphasis is contained in the recent *Handbook of Sociology*, edited by Neil Smelser (Sage 1988; Chapter 22, 'Development and the World Economy', by Peter B. Evans and John D. Stephens, 739–773).

Evans and Stephens argue that in recent years a comparative political economy has developed as the choices before and varieties of different national responses to the international system have been given far more attention. They also identify two powerful new tendencies which are likely to compete for the interpretation of processes of development, namely a new interest in cultural approaches, and secondly, the increasing use of models of rational individual behaviour.

The three other articles in this section represent those new tendencies. Erich Weede adopts an approach which is consistent with neo-classical micro-economic theory to explain why poor people stay poor. In doing so, he challenges the assumptions of dependency theorists. Far from internationalisation being the source of poverty and dependency, he argues that the dismantling of national barriers to trade, and the reduction of state involvement in the economies of less developed countries, would reduce the incentives to seek collective privilege. Moreover, the dismantling of barriers and privileges in developed countries would do more than anything else to allow poor countries to compete successfully.

The papers by Dhaouadi and Abaza and Stauth both consider the cultural dimensions of underdevelopment in the Arab world. Dhaouadi attributes a sense of cultural inferiority and a deterioration of self-esteem in the third world to Western domination. Abaza and Stauth go further and suggest that the very call for self-assertion represented by the demand for indigenisation is a product of interaction with the West and of the importation of Western ideas of the essential and authentic tradition.

SOCIETAL DEVELOPMENT, OR DEVELOPMENT OF THE WORLD-SYSTEM?*

Immanuel Wallerstein

The theme of this German Sociological Congress is 'Sociology and Societal Development'. This title includes two of the most common, most ambiguous, and most deceptive words in the sociological lexicon - society *(Gesellschaft)* and development *(Entwicklung)*. That is why I have entitled my talk in the form of a question, Societal Development or Development of the World-System?

Society of course is an old term. The *Oxford English Dictionary* (OED) gives twelve principal meanings to it, of which two seem most relevant to our present discussion. One is 'the aggregate of persons living together in a more or less ordered community'. The second, not very different, is 'a collection of individuals comprising a community or living under the same organisation of government'. The OED has the merit of being an historical dictionary and therefore indicating first usages. The first usages listed for these two senses are 1639 and 1577 respectively - hence, at the beginning of the modern world.

Looking in German dictionaries, I find the *Grosse Duden* (1977) offers the following relevant definition: *'Gesamtheit der Menschen, die unter bestimmten politischen, wirtschaftlichen und sozialen Verhältnissen zusammen leben'*, followed immediately by these examples: 'die bürgerliche, sozialistische

* Prepared for the 22nd German Sociological Congress, October 9-12, Dortmund, on the theme: 'Sociology and Societal Development'. I acknowledge the very perceptive comments of Terence K. Hopkins on an earlier draft, which helped me clarify my arguments considerably.

Klassenlose Gesellschaft'.[1] The *Wörterbuch der deutschen Gegenwartssprache* (1967), published in the GDR, gives a rather similar definition: *'Gesamtheit der unter gleichartigen sozialen und ökonomischen sowie auch politischen Verhältnissen lebenden Menschen'*, and it follows this by various examples including: *'die Entwicklung der (menschlichen) Gesellschaft ...; die neue sozialistische, kommunistische Gesellschaft; die Klassenlose Gesellschaft...; die bürgerliche, kapitalistische Gesellschaft'*. It precedes this definition with a notation that reads: *'ohne Plural'*.[2]

Now, if one regards these definitions closely, which are probably typical of what one would find in most dictionaries in most languages, one notes a curious anomaly. Each of the definitions refers to a political component which seems to imply that each society exists within a specific set of political boundaries, yet the examples also suggest that a society is a type of state defined in terms of less specific, more abstract phenomena, with the last-mentioned dictionary specifically adding 'no plural'. In these examples, 'society' is modified by an adjective, and the combined phrase describes the kind of structure which a 'society' in the other usage, that of a politically-bounded entity, is said to have. This latter usage of society can then take a plural, whereas the former cannot.

Perhaps you see no anomaly here. Yet I would like to start by endorsing the opening remark of one of the first serious attempts in modern social science to treat this matter. It is a German attempt, Lorenz von Stein's largely forgotten work on *Der Begriff der Gesellschaft und die soziale Geschichte der Französischen Revolution bis zum Jahre 1830*.[3] Stein says in the Introduction that *'Der Begriff der Gesellschaft gehört...zu den schwierigsten in der ganzen Staatswissenschaft...'* (1959 I : 12).

Why does Stein talk of *Gesellschaft* as a concept in *Staatswissenschaft*? To be sure, one answer is that *Staatswissenschaft* was the term then in use in Germany that included the domain of what today in Germany is called *Sozialwissenschaften*, although the boundaries of the two are not identical. The use of the term *Staatswissenschaften* in nineteenth-century Germany, but not in England or France, is itself a significant phenomenon, reflecting an understanding of the social sciences from the vantage point of what I would call a semi-peripheral state, but one outside the cultural circle of the hegemonic power. Yet this is not the whole answer. *Gesellschaft* is a concept of *Staatswissenschaft*, and 'the most difficult one', because, as is clear from Stein's work itself, the concept 'society' has its meaning for us primarily (even only) in the classic antinomy, society/state. And this antinomy in turn has its origin in the attempt of the modern world to come to grips with the ideological implications of the French Revolution.

158

Monarchs had been ousted before 1792, and/or forced by rebellions to change the constitutional structures of their regime. But the legitimation of such changes had previously been sought in the existence of some illegitimate act or acts of the monarch. The French Revolution was not justified on this basis, or at least came not to be so justified. Instead, the revolutionaries asserted with some vigour a new moral or structural basis on which to assign legitimacy, the concept of the popular will. As we know, this theoretical construct swept the world in the two centuries that have followed the French Revolution, and there are few today who contest it, despite all the attempts of conservative theorists from Burke and de Maistre on to disparage the doctrine, and despite the numerous instances in which popular sovereignty has been de facto ignored.

There are two problems with a theory that sovereignty resides in the people. First of all, we must know who and where are the people, that is who are and ought to be the 'citizens' of a 'state'. I remind you that the central term of honorific address in the heyday of the French Revolution was *'Citoyen'*. But it is the 'state' which decides who are the 'citzens', and in particular decides who are the full-fledged members of the polity. Even today, nowhere is every resident of a state a citizen of that state, or a voter in that state. The second problem is how one knows what the popular will is. This is of course even more difficult than the first problem. I do not believe it is very much of an exaggeration to say that a very large part of the historical and social scientific enterprise in the nineteenth and twentieth centuries has been one vast attempt to solve these two problems, and that the key conceptual tool that has been used is the idea that there exists something called a 'society' that is locked into a complicated, partially symbiotic, partially antagonistic relationship with something called the 'state'. If, however, you feel (as I do) that after 150 or so years we have not resolved these problems very well, perhaps the reason is that we have not given ourselves very adequate conceptual tools. Of course, if this is so, one would have to analyse why this has occurred, and I will come to this matter.

Let us now look briefly at the other term of our title, which is 'development'. Development too has many, many meanings. The one in the OED most relevant to its usage here is as follows: 'the growth or unfolding of what is in the germ: (b) of races of plants and animals'. The OED traces this usage only to 1871, to a work of social science in fact. Tylor's *Primitive Culture*, Volume I. Tylor is cited as saying: 'Its various grades may be regarded as stages of development or evolution, each the outcome of previous history'. Development, the OED adds, is 'the same as evolution'.

We get something similar in the German dictionaries. The *Grosse Duden* seems to avoid almost all usages in our sense until it comes to the compound

'Entwicklungsgesetz' which it tells us refers to *'Wirtschaft und Gesellschaft'*.[4] The GDR dictionary similarly treats the matter indirectly, through an example, *'die kulturelle, gesellschaftliche, geschichtliche, politische, ökonomische, soziale Entwicklung unseres Volkes'*[5].

The English definitions make it abundantly clear how tied this usage in social science is to the doctrine of biological evolution which emerged in the latter half of the nineteenth century. This is of course true of German as well. Duden's *Das Fremdwörterbuch* defines the *'Entwicklungsgesetz'*, a direct borrowing from English, as follows: *'Theorie der Entwicklung aller Lebewesen aus niedrigen, primitiven Organismen'*[6].

If we now combine the two terms, as you have done in the title of this congress (not at all in an unusual fashion), and talk of 'Societal Development', we seem to be dealing with how some entity (an entity that is not the state, but also is not divorced from the state, and usually one sharing more or less the same boundaries as the state) has evolved over time from some lower to some or more 'complex' state of being.

Where then is the 'germ' from which one can trace this evolution, and how far back can one trace it? Let me mention briefly two possible examples of a 'society' and ask some naive questions about them. One example I will take is German society. The second example is Puerto Rican society. I do not plan to review the abundant literature of scholarly and public debate on these two instances. This would be a monumental task in the case of the German example, and not such a small one in the case of the Puerto Rican example. I merely want to show that there are some very elementary problems in using the concept 'society' in either instance. I know that these two cases have their peculiarities, and that some may say they are somehow not 'typical' or 'representative'. But one of the realities of history is that every example is specific and particular, and I frankly am skeptical that there are any representative 'instances' anywhere. So I chose these because you know the German case, and you may be intrigued by the Puerto Rican case, which most of you probably do not know.

Let me ask the simple question, where is German society? Is it within the present boundaries of the Federal Republic? The official answer seems to be that today there are *'zwei deutsche Staaten'* (two German States) but only *'ein Volk'* (one nation). So the one 'nation' or 'people' seems to be defined, at least by some, as including both those persons found in the Federal Republic and those in the GDR.

What then about Austria? Are Austrians part of German 'society', of the German 'people'? Austria was only briefly, from 1938 to 1945, formally incorporated into the German state. Nevertheless, as you know, in the middle of the nineteenth century, Austria's incorporation into a then only potential

German state was widely discussed as a distinct possibility. There seems to exist a long nationalist tradition, or at least one long nationalist tradition, that would define Austria as part of German society.

Despite this, the official answer to my question, 'Is Austria part of German society?', today seems to be no - but only today. That is, because of the efforts of the present-day Federal Republic to dissociate itself morally from the Third Reich, itself associated with *Anschluss*, any suggestion that Austria is not and will not always be a separate state (and therefore nation? therefore 'society'?) is distinctly frowned upon, both in the Federal Republic and in Austria. But if a 'society' is something which 'develops' out of a 'germ', how is it possible that a mere political event, the outcome of the Second World War, or further back the outcome of the Austro-Prussian War of 1866, could affect the definition of the social space of German society? After all, a 'society' is supposed to be different from a state, a sort of underlying and developing reality, at least in part against and in spite of the state? If, however, every time we change state boundaries we change the boundaries of 'society', how can we argue that the legitimacy of a government provided by a 'society' is different from the legitimacy of a government provided by a state? The concept of 'society' was supposed to give us something solid on which to build. If it turns out to be mere putty, which we can reshape at will, it will do us precious little good - little analytical good, little political good, little moral good.

If the German case is one in which there are today two, perhaps three, sovereign 'German' states, the Puerto Rican case seems virtually the opposite. As against a society with several states, here may be a society without any state. Ever since the sixteenth century there has been an administrative entity called Puerto Rico, but at no point in time has there ever been a sovereign state, a fully recognised member of the interstate system. To be sure, the United Nations does debate from time to time whether there ever will be one in the future, and so of course do the inhabitants of Puerto Rico.

If there is no state at all, how do we define the 'society'? Where is it located? Who are its members? How did it come into existence? These, as you may immediately intuit, are political questions that have given rise to much passion. Recently, this intellectual controversy has been reopened in an unusual way by José Luis González who in 1980 published a book entitled *El país de cuatros pisos*. González is a man of letters who considers himself a Puerto Rican nationalist. The book, however, is a polemic against certain Puerto Rican *independistas*, and in particular against Pedro Albizu Campos, not because they stood for independence, but because they based their claims on a totally wrong analysis of what is Puerto Rican 'society'.

González starts, in the best tradition of Max Weber, with an observed anomaly. Of all Spain's colonies in the Western Hemisphere, Puerto Rico alone has never obtained an independent status. How come? His answer revolves around his belief that Puerto Rican 'society' precisely did *not* evolve out of some 'germ'. He suggests an alternative analogy: Puerto Rican 'society' is a house of four stories, each story being added at specific historical moments. The first story is that created in the sixteenth to eighteenth centuries, mixing the three historical 'races': the Taína (or indigenous Carib Indians), the Africans (brought over as slaves), and the Spanish settlers. Since the Taína were largely wiped out and the Spaniards were few in number and often only temporary residents, the Africans came to predominate. 'Hence my conviction, expressed on various occasions and disconcerting or irritating to some people, that the first Puerto Ricans were in fact Black Puerto Ricans.' (González 1980 : 20)

It was only in 1815 that this ethnic mix changed in Puerto Rico. In 1815, the *Real Cédula de Gracias* opened the island to refugees from the various other Hispano-American colonies that were in the midst of wars of independence - and not only to Spaniards loyal to the Crown, but to English, French, Dutch, and Irish persons as well. Note well the date: 1815. It is the year of Napoleon's definitive exile, the founding of the Holy Alliance, the enthronement of British hegemony in the world-system. In addition, in the course of the late nineteenth century, Puerto Rico was the recipient of a recorded further wave of immigration, coming primarily from Corsica, Majorca, and Catalonia. Hence, by the end of the century, says González, a second story had been erected by these white settlers of the nineteenth century, and they constituted in Puerto Rico a 'privileged minority' (p.24). Thus, continues González, it is not true, as Albizu Campos and others had claimed, that when American colonisation began in 1898, Puerto Rico had a homogeneous 'national culture'. Quite the contrary, it was a 'people divided'.

González uses this fact to explain the differential response of Puerto Ricans to U.S. colonisation, which created the third story. To simplify his argument, he argues that the *hacendados* at first welcomed the Americans since they thought that the U.S. intended to incoporate them eventually as part of the U.S. bourgeoisie. When it became clear within ten years that this was not to be, the 'privileged minority' turned to nationalism. Meanwhile, the Puerto Rican working class had initially also greeted favourably the U.S. invasion, but for opposite reasons. They saw it as opening the door to 'squaring their accounts' (p.33) with the land-owning classes, who 'were seen by the Puerto Rican masses for what they in fact were: foreigners and exploiters' (p.35).

And then there is the fourth story, that constructed not as a result of the initial cultural 'Northamericanisation' but rather as the result of the economic transformations beginning in the 1940s. It led initially to a 'modernisation-within-dependency' (p.41) of Puerto Rican society, but then subsequently to system a the 'spectacular and irreparable breakdown' (p.40) of this fourth story in the 1970s. González does not discuss directly the further complication, that since the 1940s there has also been a massive migration of Puerto Ricans to the continental United States, and that today a substantial proportion of all Puerto Ricans were born and live outside Puerto Rico. Are these latter still part of Puerto Rican 'society', and if so for how long will this be true?

I cite González not to debate the future of Puerto Rico, nor merely to remind us of the profound social divisions in our so-called societies, which are to be sure class divisions, but ones often (even usually) overlain with and linked to ethnic divisions. Rather, I cite the Puerto Rican case, as I did the German case, to underline the changing and debatable definitions of the boundaries of a 'society' and to the close link such changing definitions have with historical events which are not products primarily of some 'development' *intrinsic* to the 'society'.

What is fundamentally wrong with the concept of society is that it reifies and therefore crystallises social phenomena whose real significance lies not in their solidity but precisely in their fluidity and malleability. The concept 'society' implies we have before us to analyse something that is a tangible reality, albeit to be sure a 'developing' one. In fact what we have before us is primarily a rhetorical construct, and therefore, as Lorenz von Stein says, a 'difficult concept' of *Staatswissenschaft* (that is, in this case, of political philosophy). We do not, however, have an analytical tool for the summation or dissection of our social processes.

One of the underlying elements of world social science for the last 150 years has been a particular reading of modern European history. This reading of history is not limited to professional historians and social scientists. It constitutes a deep layer of our common culture, taught via the secondary school system to all, and simply assumed as a basic structuring of our comprehension of the social world. It has not been the subject of major controversy. Rather it has been the *common* property of the two major principal *Weltanschauungen* of the last century, liberalism and Marxism, which otherwise have stood in stark opposition one to the other.

This reading of history takes the form of an historical myth which comprises two main statements. The first statement is that, out of a European medieval feudal world where seigniors ruled over peasants, there arose (emerged, was created) a new social stratum, the urban bourgeoisie, who first economically undermined and then politically overthrew the old system (the *Ancien Régime*). The result was a market-dominated capitalist economy combined with a representative political system based on individual rights. Both the liberals and Marxists described European history in this way; they also both applauded this historical process as 'progressive'.

163

The second statement in this historical myth is most clearly captured in the book by Karl Bücher, *Die Entstehung der Volkswirtschaft*, in which Bücher distinguishes three successive stages of European economic history - *geschlossene Hauswirtschaft, Stadtwirtschaft*, and *Volkswirtschaft*.[7] The key element here, the one in which Bücher represents the liberal-Marxist consensus, is the perception of modern history as the story of widening economic circles, in which the major jump was to go from a 'local' economy to a 'national' economy, a national economy located of course in a national state. Bücher underlines the connection insisting that *"die Volkswirtschraft das Produkt einer jahrtausendelangen historischen Entwicklung ist, das nicht älter ist als der moderne Staat* (1913 : 90)[8]. Note incidentally once again the term 'development'. Bücher brings out explicitly the spatial implications that are implicit in the generic, descriptive categories found in the works of many other major figures of nineteenth-century social science: Comte and Durkheim, Maine and Spencer, Tönnies and Weber.

I think both of these statements comprising the dominant historical myth of modern European history are great distortions of what really happened. I will not discuss here why I believe the concept of the rise of a bourgeoisie, which somehow overthrew an aristocracy, is more or less the opposite of what really happened, which is that the aristocracy reconverted itself into a bourgeoisie in order to salvage its collective privilege. I have argued this case elsewhere (Wallerstein 1982). I prefer to concentrate my attention on the second myth, that of the widening circles.

If the essential movement of modern European history was from town economy to national economy, from the local arena to the national state, where does the 'world' come into the picture? The answer is essentially as an epiphenomenon. National states are seen as spending a portion of their time and energy (a relatively small portion for the most part) on *inter*-national activities - international trade, international diplomacy. These so-called international relations are somehow 'external' to this state, this nation, this 'society'. At the very most, some might concede that this situation has been evolving in the direction of the 'internationalisation' of the economy and of the political and cultural arenas, but only very recently (since 1945, or even since only the 1970s). So, we are told, there may now be, 'for the very first time', something we can call world production or a world culture.

This imagery, which frankly seems to me more and more bizarre the more I study the real world, is the heart of the operational meaning of the concept, the 'development of society'. Allow me to present to you another imagery, another way of summarising social reality, an alternative conceptual framework, which I hope can be said to capture more fully and more usefully the real social world in which we are living.

164

The transition from feudalism to capitalism involves first of all (first logically and first temporally) the creation of a world-economy. That is to say, a social division of labor was brought into being through the transformation of long-distance trade from a trade in 'luxuries' to a trade in 'essentials' or 'bulk goods', which tied together processes that were widely dispersed into long commodity chains. The commodity chains consisted of particular linked production processes whose linkage made possible the accumulation of significant amounts of surplus-value and its relative concentration in the hands of a few.

Such commodity chains were already there in the sixteenth century and predated anything that could meaningfully be called 'national economies'. These chains in turn could only be secured by the construction of an interstate system coordinate with the boundaries of the real social division of labor, the capitalist world-economy. As the capitalist world-economy expanded from its original European base to include the entire globe, so did the boundaries of the interstate system. The sovereign states were institutions that were then created within this (expanding) interstate system, were defined by it, and derived their legitimacy from the combination of juridical self-assertion and recognition by others that is the essence of what we mean by 'sovereignty'. That it is not enough merely to proclaim sovereignty in order to exercise it is illustrated well by the current examples of the 'independent' Bantustans in South Africa and the Turkish state in northern Cyprus. These entitities are not sovereign states because the other members of the club of sovereign states (in each case with one single exception, which is insufficient) do not recognise them as sovereign states. How many recognitions, and whose, it takes to legitimate a claim to sovereignty is unclear. That there is a threshold somewhere becomes evident when we observe how firmly Morocco stands opposed to the wish of the majority (a bare majority, to be sure) of members of the Organization of African Unity (OAU) to admit the Sahraoui Arab Democratic Republic to full status in this regional interstate structure. Clearly, Morocco feels that a recognition by the OAU would create pressure on the great powers, and the claim might thereby pass the threshold.

It has been the world-system then and not the separate 'societies' that has been 'developing'. That is, once created, the capitalist world-economy first became consolidated and then over time the hold of its basic structures on the social processes located within it was deepened and widened. The whole imagery of going from acorn to oak, from germ to fulfilment, if plausible at all, makes sense only if it is applied to the singular capitalist world-economy as an historical system.

It is within that developing framework that many of the institutions we often describe quite mistakenly as 'primordial' came into existence. The sovereignty of jurisdictions became ever more institutionalised, as (and to the degree that) some kind of social allegiance evolved to the entities defined by the jurisdictions. Hence, slowly, and more or less coordinate with the evolving boundaries of each state, a corresponding nationalist sentiment took root. The modern world-system has developed from one in which these 'nationalisms' were weak or non-existent to one in which they were salient, well-ensconced, and pervasive.

Nor were the nations the only new social groupings. The social classes, as we have come to know them, were also created in the course of this development, both objectively and subjectively. The pathways of both proletarianisation and bourgeoisification have been long and sinuous, but above all they have been the outcome of world-scale processes. Even our present household structures - yes, even they - are constructed entitities, meeting simultaneously the double need of a structure to socialise the labor force and one to give this labor force partial shelter against the harsh effects of the work-system.

In all of this description, the imagery I am employing is not of a small core adding on outer layers but of a thin outer framework gradually filling in a dense inner network. To contrast *Gemeinschaft* und *Gesellschaft* in the way conventionally done not only by German but by all of world sociology is to miss the whole point. It is the modern world-system (that is, the capitalist world-economy whose political framework is the interstate system composed of sovereign states) which is the *Gesellschaft* within which our contractual obligations are located. To legitimate its structures, this *Gesellschaft* has not only destroyed the multiple *Gemeinschaften* that historically existed (which is the point normally stressed) but has created a network of new *Gemeinschaften* (and most notably, the nations, that is, the so-called societies). Our language thus is topsy-turvy.

I am tempted to say we are really going not from *Gemeinschaft* to *Gesellschaft* but from *Gesellschaft* to *Gemeinschaft*, but that is not quite right either. Rather it is that our only *Gesellschaft*, the capitalist world-economy (and even it is only a partially-contractualised structure) has been creating our multiple, meaningful *Gemeinschaften*. Far from *Gemeinschaften* dying out, they have never been stronger, more complex, more overlapping and competing, more determinative of our lives. And yet never have they been less legitimate. Nor have they ever been more irrational, substantively irrational, and this is precisely because they have emerged out of a *gesellschaftliche* process. Our *Gemeinschaften* are, if you will, our loves that dare not speak their names.

Of course this is an impossible situation and we find ourselves amidst a worldwide cultural rebellion against these pressures all around us, one which is taking the widest of forms - the religious fundamentalisms, the hedonisms of withdrawal and the hedonisms of total self-interestedness, the multiple 'countercultures', the Green movements, and not least the seething of really serious and really powerful anti-racist and anti-sexist movements. I do not mean to imply that these diverse groups are at all the same. Far from it. But they are the common consequence of the relentless spread of the ever more formally rational and ever more substantively irrational historical social system in which we all find ourselves collectively trapped. They represent screams of pain against the irrationality that oppresses in the name of a universal, rationalising logic. Had we really been moving from *Gemeinschaft* to *Gesellschaft*, all this would not be occurring. We should instead be bathing in the rational waters of an Enlightenment world.

At one level, there is much hope. Our historical system, as all historical systems, is full of contradictions, of processes which force us to go in one direction to pursue our short-run interests and in another to pursue our middle-run interests. These contradictions are built into the economic and political structures of our system and are playing themselves out. Once again, I do not wish to repeat here analyses I have made elsewhere about what I call 'the crisis of transition' (Wallerstein 1982b), a long process taking perhaps 150 years, which has already begun and which will result in the demise of our present system and its replacement by something else, without, however, any guarantee that this something else will be substantively better. No guarantee, but a meaningful possibility. That is to say, we are before an historical, collective choice, the kind that comes rarely and is not the lot of every generation of mankind.

I would prefer to develop here the question of the possible role of the historical social sciences in this collective choice, which is of course a moral choice, hence a political choice. I have argued that the basic concept of 'society' and the basic historical myths of what I have called the liberal-Marxist consensus of the nineteenth century, which combined to form the framework of social science as the principal ideological expression of the world-system, are fundamentally offbase. Of course, this was no accident. The concept of society and the historical myths were part of the machinery that made the modern world-system operate so well in its heyday. In a period of relative systemic equilibrium, the consciousness of the intellectuals is perhaps the finest-tuned reflection of the underlying material processes.

However, we are no longer in a time of relative systemic equilibrium. It is not that the machine has been working poorly, but rather that it has been working only too well. The capitalist world-economy has showed itself over 400 years magnificently adept at solving its short-run and middle-run problems. Furthermore, it shows every sign of being able to do more of the same in the present and near future. But the solutions themselves have created

167

changes in the underlying structure, which are eliminating over time this very ability to make the constant necessary adjustments. The system is eliminating its degrees of freedom. I am unable here to argue this case. I simply assert it, and use it to explain the fact that, amid the constant hosannas to the efficiency of capitalist civilisation, we see everywhere the signs of malaise and cultural pessimism. The consensus has therefore begun to break down. And this is what is reflected in the myriad of anti-systemic movements that have begun to develop momentum and get out of hand.

Among the intellectuals, this malaise is reflected in the growing questioning of fundamental premises. Today we have physical scientists who are doubting the whole philosophical description of science as the 'disenchantment of the world', one that goes from Bacon to Newton to Einstein, and are asking us to understand that science is rather the 'reenchantment of the world' (Prigogine and Stengers 1979). And I am coming before you to express what many have come to feel, that it is futile to analyse the processes of the *societal development* of our multiple (national) 'societies' as if they were autonomous, internally evolving structures, when they are and have been in fact primarily structures created by, and taking form in response to, world-scale processes. It is this world-scale structure and the processes of its development that provide the true subject of our collective enquiry.

If I am anywhere near right, it has consequences for us. It means of course that we must collectively rethink our premises, and therefore our theories. But it has an even more painful side. It means we must reinterpret the meaning of our entire stock of slowly-accumulated 'empirical data', a stock whose constant growth is making our libraries and our archives bulge, and which serves as the historically-created and distorted basis of almost all our current work.

But why will we do this? And in whose name, in whose interest? One answer that has been given for at least 75 years now has been 'in the name of the movement, or the party, or the people'. I do not reject that answer because of some belief in the separation of science and values. But that answer is no answer, for two reasons. First, the movement is not singular. Perhaps at one time, the family of anti-systemic movements could lay claim to a semblance of unicity, but surely no longer. And in terms of world-scale processes, there is not merely a multiplicity of movements, but even of types of movements. Secondly, the collectivity of movements is undergoing a collective crisis concerning the efficacy of the strategy of change which emerged out of the nineteenth-century debates. I refer to the strategy of achieving transformation through the acquisition of state power. The fact is that the anti-systemic movements have themselves been the product of the capitalist world-system. As a consequence, they have by their actions not merely undermined the world-system (their ostensible objective, partially achieved) but they have also sustained this same system, most particularly by taking state power and operating within an interstate system which is the political superstructure of the capitalist world-economy. And this has created inbuilt limits on the ability of these movements to mobilise effectively in the future. Thus it is that, while the world-system is in crisis, so are its anti-systemic movements, and so I may add are the analytic self-reflective structures of this system, that is, the sciences.

The crisis of the movements has its locus in their collective increasing inability to transform their growing political strength into processes that could truly transform the existing world-system. One of their present constraints, though surely not the only one, has been the ways in which their own analyses have incorporated large segments of the ideology of the existing world-system. What the historical social sciences can contribute in this crisis of transition is therefore an involvement that is simultaneously engaged with the movements and disengaged from them. If science cannot offer praxis, it can offer the insights that come from distance, provided it is not neutral. But scientists are never neutral, and hence the science they produce is never neutral. The commitment of which I am speaking is of course the commitment to substantive rationality. It is a commitment in the face of a situation where collective choice is being made possible by the decline of the historical social system in which we are living, but where the choice is made difficult by the absence of a clear-cut alternative social force standing for a wise choice.

In this situation, in purely intellectual terms, it means we have to rethink our conceptual apparatus, to rid it of the nineteenth century's ideological patina. We will have to be radically agnostic in our empirical and theoretical work, while trying to create new heuristic frameworks which will speak to the absence, not the presence, of substantive rationality.

You will forgive me if, before a congress of German sociologists, I invoke Max Weber. We all know his passionate address to the students in 1919, 'Politics as a Vocation'. There is a deep pessimism in that talk:

> Not summer's bloom lies ahead of us, but rather a polar night of icy darkness and hardness, no matter which group may triumph externally now. Where there is nothing, not only the Kaiser but also the proletarian has lost his rights. When this night shall have slowly receded, who of those for whom spring apparently has bloomed so luxuriously will be alive? (Gerth and Mills 1946 : 128).

We must wonder if the polar night which did indeed come as Weber predicted is yet behind us or whether still worse is to come. Whether the one or the other, the only possible conclusion we should draw is the one that Weber did draw:

> Politics is a strong and slow boring of hard boards. It takes both passion and perspective. Certainly all historical experience confirms the truth - that man would not have attained the possible unless time and again he had reached out for the impossible. (Gerth and Mills 1946 : 128).

I have said that our concepts can be traced to the intellectual conundra bred by the French Revolution. So can our ideals and our solutions. The famous trinity, 'liberté, égalité, fraternité', is not a description of reality; it has not infused the structures of the capitalist world-economy, in France or anywhere else. This phrase was in fact not really the slogan of the so-called bourgeois revolution but rather the ideological expression of the first serious anti-systemic movement in the history of the modern world that was able to shape and inspire its successors. Liberty, equality, and fraternity is a slogan directed not against feudalism but against capitalism. They are the images of a social order different from ours, one that might one day be constructed. For this we need passion and perspective. It scarcely will be easy. It cannot be done without a fundamental reassessment of strategy on the part of the anti-systemic movements, another subject I have not been able to discuss here. (See, however, Wallerstein 1984, Part II.) But it will also not be done unless those who say that they strive to understand social reality, that is, we, the historical social scientists, will be ready to repeat, in science as in politics, Weber's final plea, 'in spite of all!'

Notes

1 The English translation is: 'the aggregate of persons living together under particular political, economic and social conditions' ... 'the bourgeois, socialist classless society'.

2 The English translation is: 'the aggregate of persons living together under homogeneous social and economic as well as political conditions' ... 'the development of (human) society...; the new socialist, communist society; the classless society...; the bourgeois capitalist society'... 'no plural'.

3 In the published English version we have two problems. One is the title which is rendered as *The History of the Social Movement in France, 1789-1850*. This omits from the title the fact that Stein was concerned with the *concept* of society. The passage is rendered as: 'Society is one of the most difficult concepts in political theory.' (1964, 43) This translates the untranslatable '*Staatwissenschaft*' into an imperfect equivalent, 'political theory'. It so happens that the point I am making, the *a priori* definitional link between 'society' and 'state', comes out even more clearly in the German version.

4 The English translation is: 'theory of evolution' ... 'economy and society'.

5 The English translation is: 'the cultural, societal, historical, political, economic, social development of our nation'.

6 The English translation is: 'theory of evolution' .... 'the theory of the development of all living beings from lower primitive organisms.'

7 The published English-language translation once again changes the title. It becomes *Industrial Evolution*. The three stages are translated as independent economy, town economy and national economy.

8 The English translation reads: 'National economy is the product of a development extending over thousands of years, and is not older than the modern State...' (1901 : 88).

Bibliography

BÜCHER, Carl. 1901. *Industrial Evolution*. New York: Henry Holt.
ÜCHER, Karl. 1913. *Die Entstehung der Volkswirtschaft*. Ninth edition. Tübingen: H. Laupp'schen Buchhandlung.
GERTH, H.H. and MILLS, C. Wright. 1946. *From Max Weber: Essays in Sociology*. New York: Oxford University Press.
GONZALEZ, José Luis. 1980. *El país de cuatro pisos*. Rio Piedras, P.R.: Ed. Huracán.
PRIGOGINE, Ilya and STENGERS, Isabelle. 1979. *La nouvelle alliance*. Paris: Gallimard. (English translation: *Order Out of Chaos* New York: Bantan, 1984.)
STEIN, Lorenz von. 1959. *Der Begriff der Gesellschaft und die soziale Geschichte der Französischen Revolution bis zum Jahre 1830*. Three volumes. Hildesheim: Georg Olms Verlagsbuchhandlung.
WALLERSTEIN, Immanuel. 1982a. 'Economic Theories and Historical Disparities of Development', in: *Eighth International Economic History Congress, Budapest 1982*, J. Kocka and G. Ránki, eds. B. 1: *Economic Theory and History*. Budapest: Akadémiai Kiado, 17-26.
WALLERSTEIN, Immanuel. 1982b. 'Crisis as Transition', in: S. Amin, G. Arrighi, A.G. Frank and I. Wallerstein, *Dynamics of Global Crisis*. New York: Monthly Review Press, 11-54 and London: Macmillan.
WALLERSTEIN, Immanuel. 1984. *The Politics of the World-Economy*. Cambridge: Cambridge University Press.

RENT-SEEKING OR DEPENDENCY AS EXPLANATIONS OF WHY POOR PEOPLE STAY POOR*

Erich Weede

According to the World Bank (1981 : 18), 'in 1980 about 750 million people lived in absolute poverty in the developing world, about 33 per cent of its population (these estimates exclude China)'. In a more optimistic scenario the World Bank hopes for a reduction of this number to 630 million in two decades or 18 per cent of the LDC population outside of China; in a more pessimistic scenario the Bank conceives of 850 million living in absolute poverty in the year 2000. Whether optimistic or pessimistic scenarios become true, the absolute number of poor people is likely to remain terribly high. Optimism amounts to hoping for a falling proportion of mankind suffering from absolute poverty and hardly at all to hoping for a reduction in numbers. Many truly poor people do stay poor. Why?

For some time dependency theorists have suggested that the persistence of Third World poverty is not accidental, that somebody makes or keeps poor people poor, that Northern affluence and Southern poverty are just two faces of a single coin. While dependency theorists disagree among themselves on exactly which mechanisms maintain Third World poverty, they tend to shift responsibility for poverty from the poor to the privileged. Since the general idea that the privileged make or keep poor people poor is so plausible, criticism of dependency theories – all of which (like dependency theory) comes from more or less privileged *persons* – sounds implausible, self-serving and even immoral. That is why I cannot imagine that dependency theories will lose their grip on the minds of people because of anomalies, falsification, or destructive criticism. Pointing to evidence which is incompatible with dependency theories is important, because it forces dependency theorists to

* *The formulation of the title has been inspired by Michael Lipton's book* Why Poor People Stay Poor. – *I am grateful to Edward N. Muller for his comments on an earlier draft of this paper. – More or less the same paper has previously been published in German: 'Warum bleiben arme Leute arm?'* Politische Vierteljahresschrift *26(3), 1985, 270-286.*

withdraw on this or on that intellectual front, but it does not suffice to overcome the paradigm. Only a competing paradigm can do so.

The theory of the rent-seeking society offers such a competing paradigm. Moreover, adherents of rent-seeking and dependency theories do agree on the general notion that the privileged make or keep poor people poor. Therefore the rent-seeking approach looks as plausible as the dependency paradigm. Of course, dependency theories and the rent-seeking approach do differ in many important respects. At best, dependency theorists demonstrate 'benign neglect' for micro-economic theory – despite the fact that economists find it easier to agree on micro-economic theory than on macro-economic theory (see Bell and Kristol 1981), and despite the widespread feeling that economics is the 'queen of the social sciences'. By contrast, the rent-seeking approach is not only compatible with micro-economic theory, but should be conceived of as a broadening and deepening of this theory.

In the next sections I shall outline what dependency and rent-seeking theories do assert, what evidence is available for a preliminary evaluation of these theories, what the policy implications of these theories are, and why I believe rent-seeking theory to be superior to dependency theories. Wherever possible, I shall give special attention to cross-national analyses of economic growth rates or income distribution. Given the scope and urgency of the global poverty problem there is little hope in reducing it without more economic growth in poor countries (Ahluwalia, Carter and Chenery 1979) or without equalising size distributions of income in many or most of them. Since I compare an older, and – albeit only outside of the discipline of economics! – more established paradigm, dependency, with a younger or even still nascent one, rent-seeking, the reader should not be surprised that there is more quantitative and cross-national evidence on dependency theories than on rent-seeking, that dependency theories tend to suffer from anomalies, while the rent-seeking approach tends to suffer from a dearth of evidence. Such a state of affairs is typical when a new paradigm aspires to replace an older one (see Kuhn 1962).

Dependency, growth and inequality

Dependency theorists agree with one another that poor people stay poor because privileged people contribute to and maintain their poverty, because privileged nations somehow benefit from the international economic order at the expense of poor nations. But they disagree with each other on exactly how worldwide inequity is created and maintained. I shall restrict myself to a discussion of those three dependency theories[1] which so far have received most scrutiny in quantitative and cross-national research on economic growth and income inequality: Galtungs's (1971) 'structural theory of imperialism', Wallerstein's (1974, 1979, 1980) world-system approach which has been translated into quantitative research designs by an adherent of the theory (Rubinson 1976, 1977), and Bornschier's (1980a, 1980b; Bornschier and

174

Ballmer-Cao 1979) view that investment dependence and penetration of LDCs by multinational corporations contribute to stagnation and inequality.

According to Galtung (1971), developing countries suffer from vertical trade and feudal interaction patterns. Vertical trade refers to the fact that most rich, industrialised and powerful countries tend to import raw materials, but to export processed goods, while LDCs demonstrate the reverse pattern. In Galtung's view, the production of raw materials in LDCs creates few positive spin-offs; sometimes the eventual exhaustion of mineral deposits will leave nothing behind but a hole in the ground. But production of sophisticated processed goods in the top-dog nations necessarily contributes to human capital formation. Workers and management learn new skills which tend to remain useful even when production is shifted from one good to another. In essence, the worldwide division of labour, which concentrates manufacturing and processing, and in particular sophisticated processing, in some nations and extraction and agricultural raw material production in others is the root cause of more privileged standards of living in wealthy industrial societies and of deprivation in LDCs. The need for a broad human capital base in sophisticated industrial economies exerts some equalising pressure in these countries. Since raw material extraction or production favours landed property owners, the global division of labour permits a very unequal distribution of income in LDCs.

Galtung's mechanism of vertical trade is supplemented by feudal inter-action patterns. By and large, export earnings of many less developed countries derive from a very small number of products; sometimes a single product accounts for most export earnings. Moreover, commodity concentration often is accompanied by partner concentration. For example, some Central American 'banana republics' do not only depend on the export of bananas, but also suffer from exporting most of them to the US market where they also buy most of their imports. Comparable degrees of dependency characterise the relationship between some former French colonies in Africa and France. Even where the pattern is less obvious, commodity concentration and partner concentration create opportunities for privileged nations to keep poor peoples poor.

This crude sketch of Galtung's theory suffices to raise a number of questions. Countries like Australia or Canada, and most important of all, the United States, do not really fit the theory. Australia, Canada and even the US do too well on exporting raw materials or agricultural products. So do some sparsely populated OPEC nations, which even enjoy (close to) tax-free welfare states. But I do not want to evaluate Galtung's 'structural theory of imperialism' by pointing to a couple of anomalies. After all, 'all theories are born refuted' (Kuhn 1962; Lakatos 1968 : 163). More important than the existence of anomalies is whether the independent variables of his theory, which Galtung already operationalised himself, do or do not contribute to the explanation of cross-national patterns of economic growth or income inequality. Does the import of (sophisticated) processed goods and the export of raw materials reduce the growth prospects of LDCs and simultaneously contribute to income inequality? Do export commodity concentration and partner concentration in trade decrease economic growth rates, but increase income inequality?

Before I attempt to summarise the empirical evidence on Galtung's theory, I want to continue my sketch of various lines of reasoning within a dependency paradigm. According to Wallerstein (1974 : 406), 'the functioning of a capitalist world economy requires that groups pursue their economic interests within a single world-market while seeking to distort this market for their benefit by organising to exert influence on states, some of which are more powerful than others but none of which controls the market in its entirety'. In this view, some groups and nations succeed in distorting markets and rigging prices to their own benefit and at the expense of other groups and nations.[2]

In his effort to translate this general idea into quantitative research designs, Rubinson (1977 : 7) argued that a strong state 'is able to control the activities of the population within its boundaries . . . one indicator of state strength is the government revenues of a state as a proportion of GNP . . . This indicator measures the degree to which the total economic resources of the country are available to the state'. In addition to a domestic dimension of state strength, there is an international dimension of it. While Rubinson (1976, 1977) discusses and applies a variety of indicators, some of the most potent ones are trade, ie. import and/or export, shares of GNP. To summarise the Wallerstein/ Rubinson perspective: states are most likely and able to promote economic growth and income equalisation, if they exercise much control of economic activities within their borders, as indicated by government revenue to GDP or GNP proportions, and if they depend little on the vicissitudes of the world market, as indicated by low trade to GNP shares.

Finally, there is a third perspective. According to Bornschier (1980a, 1980b; Bornschier and Ballmer-Cao 1979), multinational corporations (henceforth abbreviated MNCs) are the main culprits for Third World poverty. LDCs heavily depend on foreign investment, most of which is supplied by MNCs. In the short run, the inflow of MNC-capital contributes to investment and growth. In the long run, however, MNCs succeed in getting more out of LDCs than they put in, ie. in decapitalising Third World economies. Rigging of the terms of trade in *intra*-MNC, but simultaneously *inter*national trade is one of the mechanisms whereby such decapitalisation can be achieved. The more powerful MNCs are in a less developed economy, the worse its growth prospects become. But MNCs do even more harm than that in LDCs. Since MNCs apply capital-intensive production technologies, which do not need much local and unskilled labour input, since they tend to produce for the more privileged classes in LDCs only and ally themselves with them politically, MNC penetration reinforces income inequality too.

This crude sketch of three dependency explanations of why poor people stay poor has yielded a list of six independent variables: vertical trade (or export of raw materials and import of processed goods), export commodity concentration, trade partner concentration, low government revenues as a proportion of GDP, high trade to GNP proportions, and strong MNC penetration. According to the above discussed dependency theories, all of these variables should simultaneously decrease growth and increase inequality and thereby hurt the poor. Do they?

Adherents and opponents of dependency theories did a lot of cross-national and cross-sectional work. So, there is *some* evidence that LDCs, which are extraordinarily dependent on exporting raw materials and importing processed goods or which suffer from severe export commodity concentration and trade partner concentration, do indeed demonstrate greater income inequality and/or grow more slowly than other nations (Alschuler 1976; Galtung 1971; Rubinson 1977; Stokes and Jaffee 1982; Walleri 1978a, 1978b). But there are also studies which cast a much less favourable light on Galtung's (1971) 'structural theory of imperialism' (Bradshaw 1985a;[3] Delacroix 1977; Delacroix and Ragin 1978, 1981;[4] Kaufmann et al 1975; Ray and Webster 1978; Weede 1981, 1982; Weede and Tiefenbach 1981a, 1981b). Similarly, there is *some* evidence for a relationship between low government revenue/ GDP or high trade/GNP ratios, on the one hand, and less economic growth and more income inequality, on the other (Bornschier 1980a; Bornschier, Chase-Dunn and Rubinson 1978; Meyer and Hannan 1979; Rubinson 1976, 1977; Rubinson and Quinlan 1977). But there are also other studies which call these findings, and thereby the Wallerstein-Rubinson line of reasoning, into question (Landau 1983; Marsden 1983; Weede 1980, 1981, 1982; Weede and Tiefenbach 1981a, 1981b). Finally, there is *some* evidence for a negative impact of investment dependence, or MNC penetration, on economic growth and income equality (Bornschier 1980a, 1980b, 1981a, 1982; Bornschier and Ballmer-Cao 1979; Chase-Dunn 1975; Gobalet and Diamond 1979). But again there are studies which do not support these contentions (Bradshaw 1985a : 202, 1985b : 93-94; Delacroix and Ragin 1981; Jackman 1982; Muller 1984; Weede 1981, 1982; Weede and Tiefenbach 1981a, 1981b). Even a recent study by Bornschier (1985) himself concedes that the negative effects of MNC penetration on economic growth are no longer significant in the late 1970s.

Since these studies differ in sample size, period of observation, operationalisation of variables, and specification of regression equations, it is difficult to explain their inconsistent findings. In my view, it is not essential to do so for the purposes of this paper. The mere fact of contradictory findings, instead of robust support in favour of dependency theories, justifies some doubt. Moreover, most studies neglect competing explanations of cross-national differences of growth rates or income inequality and thereby risk some specification error. If one takes into account that income inequality and economic growth demonstrate curvilinear and non-monotonic relationships with the level of economic development, that human capital formation (as assessed by literacy, school enrolment ratios or even military participation ratios) contributes to growth and equality, that investment contributes to

177

growth, then empirical support for dependency theories tends to wither away (Weede 1981, 1982; Weede and Tiefenbach 1981a, 1981b).[5] While the research strategy outlined above suffices to call dependency theories into question, this strategy is not necessary in order to arrive at similar conclusions (see Delacroix 1977; Muller 1984; Ray and Webster 1978). Although it is always conceivable that a research programme in trouble – as dependency currently is – may recover and score better and more lasting explanatory success in the future than in the past, looking for alternative and possibly better explanations of why poor people stay poor seems justified.

Rent-seeking, growth and inequality

Economists (Buchanan, Tollison and Tullock 1980; Tollison 1982 : 577) define rent as 'a payment to a resource owner above the amount his resources could command in their next best alternative use'. In a truly competitive market where everyone is a price-taker rents do not exist. Therefore rent-seeking is an attempt to distort markets and to evade competition. Where rent-seeking is on the rampage, we refer to rent-seeking societies. The fundamental problem of rent-seeking societies is that they suffer from a serious distortion of incentives. There are strong incentives to engage in distributional struggles and to seek contrived transfers, but comparatively weak incentives to engage in productive and growth-promoting activities. While rent-seeking decreases growth, there is no reason to expect the poor to be particularly successful in distributional struggles.

In order to elaborate on rent-seeking, let us look to monopolies. Typically, monopolists maximise their profits by supplying smaller quantities at higher prices than a competitive market would do. Buyers pay more than they should and the monopolist enjoys his rent. The monopoly implies three important effects. First, there is a transfer of income from buyers or consumers to the monopolist. Since buyers or consumers are often poorer than the monopolist, this transfer of income tends to be regressive. Second, some people will suffer a welfare loss because of the monopoly without a corresponding improvement for someone else. Some people who would have bought a product at competitive prices simply stop buying it at higher monopoly prices. While these people suffer a welfare loss – technically labelled deadweight loss – not even the monopolist gains from it. He is unable to exploit those who stop buying. Finally, there is the third and probably worst effect of monopolies. Since monopolies are profitable for those who can gain them, many would-be monopolists invest resources in attempts to become monopolists. Most of these attempts must be in vain. Still, even unsuccessful attempts to become a monopolist consume resources which thereafter are no longer available for productive purposes. The fiercer the fight among monopoly contenders, the more resources are wasted for the only purpose of neutralising the efforts of other contenders.[6]

Cartels are little better than monopolies. The purpose remains the same: to maximise profits by selling (lower quantities) at higher prices. In general, there still is the regressive transfer from poorer buyers or consumers to richer cartel members. The consumer surplus of those who are ready to pay competitive prices, but not cartel prices, still disappears. In particular if illegal, cartelisation still requires resources. But, in contrast to monopolies, cartels require collective action. Seen from the perspective of a group of producers of a particular good, a cartel provides a collective good. If higher prices can be imposed on consumers, every producer receives some rental income. For simplicity's sake, let us assume that cartelisation is illegal and requires bribing politicians and bureaucrats into looking the other way.[7] Then there is a free-riding tendency. Every producer would like to benefit from the cartel, but to make other producers pay for it. According to Olson (1965, 1982), the prospects for the provision of collective goods and for overcoming free-riding tendencies are much better in small groups than in large groups.[8] That is why oligopolists should find cartelisation easier than a multitude of small and scattered producers. Elitist interests always enjoy a headstart in the cartelisation game. Equalisation by cartelisation is extremely unlikely. Since cartelisation consumes resources and interferes with an efficient allocation and growth, it is a collective bad for society as a whole.

Trade unions are a special type of distributional coalition or cartel. Since workers belong to large groups, there are strong free-riding tendencies. Therefore workers need skilful political entrepreneurs (Frohlich, Oppenheimer and Young 1971) to guide them[9] and the application of selective incentives and coercion. Moreover, it takes time to organise a union (Olson 1965, 1982). But explaining how trade unions come into existence is not the purpose of this paper. Here the concern is to understand their effects.

Trade unions try to increase the wages or salaries of their members. Since workers are usually poorer than their employers, a transfer of income from employers to workers is progressive. In this respect, unions seem better than most other cartels. In other respects they are not. If workers succeed in obtaining higher wages than they could in a competitive situation, then employers are likely to offer less jobs. Would-be employees in the unionised sector of the economy are thereby driven into the informal sector or even into involuntary unemployment (Hayek 1960; McKenzie and Tullock 1978 : 256; Olson 1982 : 201). In order to obtain wages which are inflated by the inclusion of a rental component, workers need to invest resources, ie. they organise themselves, prepare for strikes and prevent their employer from maintaining production with the assistance of non-unionised and possibly previously unemployed labour. Since employers dislike excessive wages and a profit squeeze, employers are likely to invest some resources in cancelling out the effects of workers' efforts. Whoever wins this struggle, some resources will simply be wasted.

Rent-seeking requires government acquiesence or, 'better' still, support. Most monopolies or cartels are organised at the national level, not on a global scale. Therefore national governments could easily restore competition by abolishing all tariffs and non-tariff barriers to international trade. Foreign

179

producers could and would sell below monopoly or cartel prices and cause these prices to collapse and corresponding rents to disappear. Similarly, wide open borders for foreign labour would contribute to undermining union power. While governments *could* decrease rent-seeking, they often contribute to it by granting monopolies, by organising cartels, by helping trade unions, by subsidising some activities and applying discriminatory taxation against others, by interfering with international trade and migration. That is why Tullock (1980 : 211) deplores: 'One of the major activities of modern governments is the granting of special privileges to various groups of politically influential people'. Similarly, Buchanan (1980 : 9) claims: 'Rent-seeking activity is directly related to the scope and range of governmental activity in the economy, to the relative size of the public sector'.

Rent-seeking is not only wasteful. It is contagious. Imagine that there is a monopoly or cartel in some sector of the economy which produces goods, like steel, which serve as important inputs to the production of other goods, say cars or trucks. Expensive inputs tend to make domestic industries uncompetitive compared with foreign rivals. If the government has condoned a monopoly or cartel of steel producers, it is likely to come under pressure from steel-consuming industries to protect domestic markets and/or to subsidise exports. In granting protection, the government makes it easier or more worthwhile for the industries concerned to become cartelised too. So the evil spreads.

The fundamental problem in rent-seeking societies is that economic actors and groups invest too many resources in capturing rents and too little in productive activities. While rent-seeking is obviously harmful to growth and prosperity, there is no reason to expect it to contribute to equity or equality. For small, elitist, privileged groups enjoy a headstart in the game. The strong are likely to win distributional struggles and the poor are likely to lose them. Olson (1982 : 175) puts this proposition in these words: 'There is greater inequality . . . in the opportunity to create distributional coalitions' – whose purpose is rent-seeking (author's comment) – 'than there is in the inherent productive abilities of people'.

So far the discussion of rent-seeking has been rather abstract and removed from the problems of less developed countries. This need not be so. Without using the term rent-seeking, Lipton (1977) in his seminal book *Why Poor People Stay Poor* nevertheless analyses the phenomenon. In his view, there is a conflict of interest between urban and rural populations in LDCs which urban dwellers tend to decide in their favour. In a conflict of interest between groups the recipe for successful collective action and overcoming resistance is to generate concentrated gains for a relatively small group and diffused and preferably invisible losses for a much larger group (Olson 1965). In most LDCs, by far the largest group is the rural population tilling the land. In general, this rural-agrarian population is poorer than the urban population. If the smaller, relatively more privileged, urban population could succeed in rigging the urban-rural terms of trade, the recipe of concentrated gains and diffused losses would be realised.[10] That is why an incentive for urban exploitation of their rural brethren exists.

It is much easier for urban people to organise themselves for the promotion of their collective interests than for scattered rural-agrarian people. Karl Marx (1852, 1969) knew it long ago. Urban interests are concentrated in small, but densely populated, areas. Rural interests in LDCs are widely scattered and often suffer from poor transportation and communication facilities. The higher cost of collective action in the underdeveloped countryside makes a rural defence of agrarian interest less likely.

A comparatively small number of urban producers in the LDCs finds little difficulty in creating an informal cartel if the law should not permit a formal one. It is much easier for urban factory workers to unionise than for scattered rural people, some of whom may be tenants or sharecroppers. Nevertheless, these different rural people do share an interest in high prices for whatever they sell. Finally, the largely urban public sector with its bureaucratic structure tends to be born organised for collective action. Aggregation of these somewhat organised urban interests is relatively easy. Urban employers and manufacturers, urban workers and largely urban civil servants and politicians do share an interest in cheap food to be supplied from the rural hinterland to the cities. Obviously, distorted urban-rural terms of trade – ie. artificially low prices for food and artificially high prices for urban products – depend on governmental policies and some degree of state interference with international trade. If farmers were free to sell their products to highest bidding buyers from anywhere inside or outside the country, then food prices could not be distorted downwards. But prohibition of exports or state-buying monopolies may prevent such harmful getting in the way of urban interests. Differential degrees of unionisation and corresponding urban-rural wage differentials also contribute to the distortion of urban-rural terms of trade and simultaneously decrease the labour absorption capacity of unionised, urban sectors.

Why should ruling politicians contribute to or at least tolerate some distortion of urban-rural terms of trade in LDCs? There are a number of reasons. First, but possibly least important, such a distortion benefits themselves by reducing their cost of living. Second, it is much easier for a political entrepreneur to build a power base from better organised groups than from amorphous groups. The costs of resource mobilisation for political action can be dramatically cut by assembling a coalition of previously existing interest groups or organisations compared with calling them into existence in the first place (Oberschall 1973). Third, most rulers prefer poverty, disorder and violence to occur out of sight, if they cannot prevent it. They prefer starvation in remote villages to an urban riot in front of the presidential palace. Fourth, since unorganised rural-agrarian groups in remote parts of the country cannot effectively fight back (short of guerilla war, which probably requires some foreign help; see Gurr 1968; Gurr and Duvall 1973), it may even be politically stabilising to redistribute from the rural poor to the somewhat better-off urban dwellers.

Sometimes low food prices and government action to achieve them are rationalised by state support for agriculture such as subsidising pesticides or fertilisers. In theory this is fine. In practice it often is not. Subsidisation makes inputs appear cheaper than they are. So demand is bound to increase. In LDCs it usually cannot be met. Then somebody has to decide which farmers obtain the subsidised inputs and which ones do not. This somebody is likely to be a bureaucrat or local politician. Even if honest – and that is a big if – allocation is likely to be discriminatory. Bureaucrats want to be properly approached. They like written applications or might even be legally required to insist on them. The smallest and poorest farmers in the remotest areas are least likely to pass this hurdle. Richer and bigger farmers are more likely to find somebody in their family or among their personal friends who is able to write an application or to fill out a form. Since Third World bureaucrats or local politicians rarely enjoy affluence, even if their incomes are *much* higher than those of ordinary peasants, tenants or share-croppers, there must be a strong temptation to accept gifts or bribes for allocations of subsidised fertilisers or pesticides. If the worst comes to the worst, what has been intended as a subsidy for agriculture turns into a subsidy for bureaucrats and/or politicians and into an incentive for corruption.

Overvaluation of the domestic currency is a useful tool for rigging urban-rural terms of trade. It automatically reduces farmers' export prospects and simultaneously benefits mostly urban consumers of imported goods. Since overvaluation necessarily reduces the competitiveness of urban industries and tends to suck in imports, a poor country with an overvalued currency is likely to experience some balance of payments problems. To handle it and to protect domestic industry, what an Indian newspaper once termed 'permit, license, quota Raj' is created. Such regulations boost bureaucratic employment and promotion opportunities to the benefit of some urban people. They provide gratifying rents for those who obtain them. Take an import licence, for example. Even after illegal payments to bureaucrats or politicians, such a licence may still be a source of nice profits. The licensed importer and bureaucrats or politicians in regulatory agencies share the rent which has been created by the regulation of foreign trade.

As Lipton (1977, 1984) pointed out, distorting the urban-rural terms of trade in LDCs is closely related to inefficient development strategies. Often investment is characterised by an urban bias which neglects factor scarcities in LDCs. Except for capital surplus oil exporters, most LDCs suffer from a scarcity of capital, but command an ample supply of unskilled or even semi-skilled labour. Urban investments often outperform rural investments in raising labour productivity. But rural investments generally outperform urban ones in capital productivity. Where capital is scarce and labour is not, it is more important to maximise productivity per unit of capital than per unit of labour. Nevertheless, many LDCs prefer urban investments as a matter of principle and neglect rural ones. Therefore, they get lower rates of growth than they could.

While a capital-intensive strategy of industrialisation retards development, it pleases some industrialists and unionised urban labour aristocracies, who succeed in obtaining higher wages. Simultaneously, such higher wages slow down the labour absorption capacity of the modern industrial sector and thereby condemn those not yet employed there to remain in the agricultural or in the urban-informal sector, both of which contain the bulk of absolutely poor people in LDCs.

Rent-seeking is bad for society and growth since it distorts incentives and interferes with efficient resource allocation. In LDCs most rents benefit urban groups and harm rural-agrarian ones because the latter find it hard to organise themselves for collective action and to become included in prevailing distributional coalitions. In rent-seeking societies there is a protracted distributional struggle where the poorest rural groups are destined to become losers. Equity loses alongside efficiency.

In my view, all societies are to some degree afflicted by rent-seeking. After all the generation and distribution of rents is what makes politics and government attractive for many (or most?) active participants.[11] But societies differ in the degree to which they tolerate or encourage rent-seeking. Is there any quantitative evidence that those LDCs, which permit more rent-seeking, grow more slowly than others without at least generating a more equal distribution of income? While there is not much evidence, the existing evidence is fairly strong.

There is no rent-seeking without price distortion. Therefore an index of price distortion is simultaneously an index of rent-seeking. For the 1970s and 31 LDCs the World Bank (1983 : 57-63) provides such an index. The Bank's price distortion index 'concentrates on distortions in the prices of foreign exchange, capital, labour, and infrastructural services (particularly power)'. If the trade-weighted exchange rate of an LDC currency appreciates or does not depreciate despite higher inflation at home than abroad, if competitiveness is thereby eroded, this is simultaneously a cue to the presence of price distortions and a cause for interfering with international trade, which is another cue to the existence of price distortions. Distortion of capital prices is assumed to exist wherever real interest rates are negative. Minimum wage laws, high social security taxes and cheap provision of infrastructural services by state agencies are further indications of price distortions and rent-seeking.

In the 1970s the World Bank's (1983 : 57-63) price distortion index alone explains about one third of the variance in GDP growth rates. But price distortion is *not* significantly correlated with income inequality. While certainly in need of replication in larger samples and for different periods of observation,[12] the reported correlation is much stronger than what dependency theory can offer. Moreover, if one introduces those control variables, which make effects hypothesised by dependency theorists wither away, then the negative impact of price distortions on growth remains essentially as it was in bivariate analysis and the relationship between price distortions and equality remains close to zero and insignificant (Weede 1986a).

183

All societies are likely to be somewhat afflicted by rent-seeking, but not to an equal degree. Political system characteristics should be expected to influence the amount of rent-seeking in societies. Political democracy offers civil liberties and political rights to everyone. Necessarily this includes the right to create distributional coalitions or to participate in them. Because of its egalitarianism and liberty, democracy *may* increase the number of players in the rent-seeking game. But I do not want to argue that democracy *per se* retards economic growth and development in LDCs, as many previous writers have argued (Adelman and Morris 1967 : 202; Andreski 1969 : 266; Huntington and Dominguez 1975 : 61; Huntington and Nelson 1975 : 23; Marsh 1979 : 240). If one properly controls for the level of economic development, for investment and human capital formation, then democracy is not significantly related to economic growth rates (Weede 1983a, 1983b), nor to income inequality (Weede and Tiefenbach 1981a).[13]

If political democracy *enables* more people to participate in the rent-seeking game than authoritarian or totalitarian systems do, how can democracies avoid retarding growth? The answer must be that many people even in democracies resist the temptation to join distributional coalitions and to seek contrived transfers. But there might be important differences among democracies in this respect. While democracy *per se* need not retard growth, democracy in combination with some other characteristic, which reinforces rent-seeking, still might do so.

The incentive to seek rents does not only depend on governmental tolerance for interest groups and their activities, but also on the degree of state interference in the economy (Buchanan 1980 : 9). By and large, capturing rents needs some governmental assistance by establishing barriers to entry for domestic or, probably more often, foreign competitors. That is why rent-seeking requires not only a permissive environment for the formation of distributional coalitions, but simultaneously strong government control of and interference in the economy. Among those nations or LDCs where government revenues exceed 20 per cent of GDP and thereby indicate an economically strong state, democracy does slow down growth (Weede 1983a, 1983b). This is another piece of quantitative and cross-national evidence which fits a rent-seeking approach. Finally, Singh (1985) reports some cross-national regressions of economic growth rates on a general state intervention index and concludes that state intervention in the economy significantly reduces growth rates.

Rent-seeking in global perspective

Even where a discussion of rent-seeking focuses on the domestic context, it is unavoidable to refer to the world economy as a whole. The deadliest blow to the rent-seeking society, which I can imagine, is to open wide the doors to foreign competition. In essence, rent-seeking requires barriers to entry in order to avoid competition. While international borders are not the only conceivable barriers to entry, they constitute probably the most powerful and persistent ones that actually exist. International borders do not only enable some domestic distributional coalitions to capture rents at the expense of other groups *at home*, but also at the expense of other groups *abroad*. Moreover, the winning group at home may be fairly inclusive, and the losers or losses may be scattered worldwide or nearly so.

Some core insights which have been first developed by a dependency theorist, Emmanuel (1972), may be retained, if one replaces his Marxist or theory of value assumptions, with a rent-seeking perspective. Emmanuel makes four major observations. First, wages in industrialised democracies are much higher than in the Third World, even when different skill levels or work intensities are accounted for. Second, capital is fairly mobile from country to country. That is why capital yields similar returns everywhere, leaving out risk premiums in some politically unstable places. Third, labour is much less mobile than capital is, despite Mexicans pouring into the United States, Algerians into France, Indians or Pakistanis into Britain and Turks into West Germany. Fourth, labour is much better organised in the more developed countries than in the less developed countries. As Emmanuel claimed, these facts are interdependent.

One may improve one's understanding of worldwide rent-seeking, if one applies a similar line of reasoning to Emmanuel's major observations as Becker (1971) did in his work on the economics of discrimination or as Krauss (1983) did more recently. From a global perspective the best solution would be to overlook the Northern (or OECD) or Southern (or Third World) origin of capital and labour; ie. no nation-state would interfere with movements of capital or labour and newly arrived labour could compete on an equal footing with others.[14] Capital and labour would move to places where the outlook for high returns is best. Obviously, much Southern labour would move to the North and some Northern capital would move to the South. These movements of capital and labour would exert globally equalising pressures on capital and labour returns. In this scenario, some people would gain and others would lose compared with the current status quo. By and large, unskilled and semi-skilled Northern labour would suffer great losses and Southern labour would score major gains. Just imagine the pain in Chicago or Paris and the joy in Calcutta or Lagos, if the gap in wages for, say, garbage collection, started to close, since no one any longer prevented garbage collectors from poor countries from threatening the job security of garbage collectors in rich countries.

Whether the Southern capital would lose and the Northern capital would win depends on one's assessment of the effectiveness of current restrictions on international capital movements. I am inclined to accept Emmanuel's (1972) belief that current restrictions on capital movements are by and large ineffective. Consequently, dismantling them would not make much of a difference. Thus it is evident that the overriding effect of abolishing all state interference with capital and labour movements would be beneficial to Southern labour (or parts of it) and quite harmful to Northern labour.[15]

185

The above sketched scenario, if it ever came true, would do much more to fight absolute poverty on a global scale than the welfare states in industrialised democracies. As Tullock (1983 : 64) and Krauss (1983) observed, Northern welfare states cater for, or redistribute within, the most privileged decile or quintile of mankind and simultaneously their redistributive efforts depend on keeping the less fortunate majority of mankind out. But the above sketched scenario is unlikely ever to become true for the obvious reason that relatively well organised and unionised rental income receivers in the North will prevent it from happening.[16]

A brief look at South Africa may clarify the general issue. In South Africa there is job reservation for white citizens and tight control over the influx of blacks and others. Undoubtedly unskilled and semi-skilled whites gain from this at the expense of comparably skilled, but much poorer, blacks. While the South African economy grows more slowly than it conceivably could without discrimination, a bigger slice of the cake easily compensates white rental income receivers for the slower expansion of the cake. OECD citizens may be more like their white South African brethren than most care to think.

OECD welfare states do little to help the poor in LDCs. The efficiency of their aid is questionable (Bauer 1981; Bornschier, Chase-Dunn and Rubinson 1978; Krauss 1983; Singh 1985). The biggest economies (USA and Japan) are niggardly donors. Moreover, they do not concentrate their aid on the poorest countries. On top of this one may even argue with Krauss (1983) that OECD welfare states slow down LDC growth rates *by being welfare states*: first, the welfare state distorts incentives and reduces allocative efficiency and growth (Bernholz 1982; Weede 1984, 1986b). Less growth in rich countries simultaneously impedes the growth prospects of poor countries. Second, the transformation of a capitalist country into a welfare state affects the structure of demand. Public demand partially replaces private demand. Public demand is less likely than private demand to improve the export prospects of LDCs. It is possible that American and Japanese hesitation to become full welfare states according to the Scandinavian model helps LDCs more than generous Scandinavian aid does.

The very existence of a multitude of states on the globe and state interference in the world economy is closely related to the problem of why poor people stay poor. State-supported or state-tolerated price distortions within domestic economies are supplemented by state-generated price distortions within the world economy. Both kinds of distortion keep poor people poor. Now I find myself in partial agreement with a dependency theorist whom I critically evaluated above. Therefore I quote Wallerstein once more:

> The functioning of the capitalist world economy requires that groups pursue their economic interests within a single world-market while seeking to distort this market for their benefit by organising to exert influence on states, some of which are more powerful than others but none of which controls the market in its entirety.

> (Wallerstein 1974 : 406)

I agree with Wallerstein on the harmful impact of price distortions and on the state's role in generating these distortions, although I do not classify these observable aberrations as functional requisites of a capitalist world economy. Nor can I conceive of avoiding the negative effects of price distortions by manipulating these distortions to the benefit of the poor, as Wallerstein (1974, 1979, 1980) seems to imagine.

'Policy implications' and conclusion

Recently, Olson deplored that:

> in these days it takes an enormous amount of stupid policies or bad or unstable institutions to prevent economic development. Unfortunately growth-retarding regimes, policies, and institutions are the rule rather than the exception, and the majority of the world's population lives in poverty.

(Olson (1982 : 175)

From a global perspective, rent-seeking at the expense of other groups at home or abroad is indeed incredibly wasteful and – if one wants to call it so – stupid. Losers always lose much more than winners gain. Still the game looks gratifying to those who win it. The 'stupidity' of the game serves winners well. Privileged people keep poor people poor, and must do so if they want to protect their rental incomes because rents rest on barriers to entry. Of course, even without rent-seeking, inequality and poverty would persist, but probably less inequality and almost certainly less poverty.

What can be done about it? In theory, providing a list of policy recommendations is deceptively simple. LDC governments should stop distorting prices for domestic currencies, for food, for capital and for labour. They should open their economies and be less tolerant of the efforts of monopolies and distributional coalitions to distort prices than they are. Industrialised democracies should improve the prospects of the poor by eliminating agrarian and industrial protectionism and discrimination against low wage exporters, by interfering less with worldwide capital and labour flows than they do, by eliminating discrimination between citizens and foreign labour and discrimination between those who already hold some job for some time and new, and possibly foreign and usually poor, applicants. While such reforms are incompatible with welfare states for the most privileged quintile of humanity (Krauss 1983; Tullock 1983), they could help the truly poor, almost all of whom live in the Third World.

But I am aware that provision of *this* list of 'policy recommendations' comes close to implying a pessimistic prediction: the poor will not get the help they need. It is possible that there will be some marginal improvements but no wholesale renunciation of rent-seeking. If economic man is a self-interested utility-maximiser, he will always prefer competition among others and rents for himself. The general fulfilment of such human desires is inconceivable. But our uncoordinated efforts do maintain domestic and global rent-seeking societies.

187

While I do not know how to overcome the rent-seeking society, how to achieve the equivalent of general disarmament in distributional struggles, I do think that an obvious strategy does not work. The poor cannot as easily unite, exert political pressure or compel revolutionary change and obtain a better deal as more privileged groups can.[17] As Bauer (1981 : 138-150) has elaborated in somewhat different words, such a strategy may serve the rent-seeking purposes of some already privileged persons better than those of the poor. Politics, and the price distortions thereby created, is at least as much, if not more, closely related to the causes of poverty than to their cure. If the poor only unite, they have no chance to prevail. If *some* poor groups receive an offer to participate in some winning coalitions, they will accept it. The winning coalition will aim at concentrated gains for their members including previously poor ones and dispersed and preferably invisible losses for others who cannot fight back – for example, because they are not yet organised and still poor.

It is possible that the true heroes of human history and improvement are those who aim for minor but useful reforms, who never get tired in an uphill struggle against rent-seeking. But to ask for this is to ask for a kind of altruism. The trouble with altruism is that it is so rare that we should not trust some self-confident group to enforce it on others. Most guardians of morality are likely to defect and look for rents.

Notes

1   There are other dependency approaches. One of them is incompatible with rent-seeking theory in its economic foundations, but is similar to it in its analysis of distributional conflicts (Emmanuel 1972). This approach is discussed later.

2   Wallerstein's (1974, 1979, 1980) focus on government-sponsored distortion of markets is compatible with rent-seeking theory. Much of his theorising and Rubinson's (1976, 1977) interpretation of it is not.

3   Bradshaw (1985a : 202) does not even refer to Galtung or his theory. But he reports a weak *positive* effect of primary product specialisation on growth and an equally weak *negative* effect of commodity concentration on growth in black Africa. While the former result flatly contradicts Galtung's expectations, the latter provides some extremely weak support for it.

4   Some readers may object to my listing of the studies by Delacroix and Ragin (1978, 1981) among those who call Galtung's ideas into question. The *older* study was mainly concerned with different issues. But it did control for human capital formation, ie., secondary school enrolment. In my view, this is useful and other studies should have done so, too. Therefore, one should note that the older study does *not* find a negative effect of primary product exports and manufactured imports. The more recent study maintains that the export of primary products and commodity concentration obstructs development in 'advanced peripheral countries'. Most LDCs are not classified by Delacroix and Ragin with this category, but countries like Japan, Israel, Italy, Austria, the Soviet Union, Poland, Czechoslovakia, East Germany and some time LDCs are. Given the heterogeneity of the 'advanced' category, the important result seems to be that neither the export of primary products nor commodity concentration hurts the growth prospects of the so-called 'poor periphery', which still contains nations like Brazil, Turkey or South Korea among its members.

5   The relationship between military participation and human capital formation is discussed in Weede (1983c). By and large, negative findings on dependency propositions do *not* depend on inclusion or exclusion of military participation ratios as control variables. Still, *some* results are fairly sensitive to one's point of view on a number of technical issues. See the

188

debate between Bornschier (1981b, 1982), on the one hand, and Weede and Tiefenbach (1981a, 1981b, 1982), on the other.

6   With Schumpeter (1942) one may argue that this treatment of monopolies rests on oversimplification. Monopolies may produce positive rather than negative effects because they permit economies of scale or provide incentives for innovation. The hope to achieve a temporary monopoly may provide one of the most important incentives to innovate. Therefore innovators deserve and receive legal protection, although such protection limits competition. While I admit the validity of these arguments, I contend that *on balance* the negative effects of monopolies which are described in the main text predominate. – Whether competition among would-be monopolies is harmful or not, depends on how they compete. Price and quality competition may be desirable. Competition for political influence and legal protection of monopoly rights is always undesirable. Unfortunately, monopolists *must* aim at such protection because otherwise monopoly profits will be limited by the fear that fat profits attract challengers and renew competition.

7   It may be that reality is sometimes even worse where there are *no* bribes. Lobbying, dining with bureaucrats, entertaining legislators and offering electoral support may be even more costly than outright bribes (and do some recipients less good) and still result in similar policies.

8   Unequal size of group members also makes the provision of collective goods more likely. Simultaneously it may create the interesting phenomenon of the exploitation of the strong by the weak.

9   While workers need political entrepreneurs and leadership, leaders are likely to exact a price which Michels (1910, 1962) has described in his iron law of oligarchy.

10 By and large we can observe a mirror-image phenomenon in contemporary industrialised democracies. Here rural-agrarian minorities succeed in distorting the urban-rural terms of trade in their favour and at the expense of urban consumers and taxpayers. Again, the recipe of concentrated gains and dispersed losses is met.

11 One may dispute this statement in so far as rich industrialised democracies are concerned. In the United States, entering public service or politics often implies major income losses. Not so in LDCs, where politics or state employment come close to being the only available paths to personal advancement. That is why politics in poor countries without vigorous private enterprises so easily degenerates into what Andreski (1969 : 64) aptly termed 'kleptocracy'. Possibly one may minimise (not abolish) 'kleptocracy' by limiting government revenues or governmental control of the economy.

12 In some respects, Bradshaw's (1985b, 1986) cross-national studies present an alternative approach to the World Bank's index of price distortions and studies based on it. Bradshaw focuses on 'urban bias' only, ie., on the disparity (ratio) between output per worker outside and inside agriculture. He thereby captures a much narrower range of rent-seeking phenomena than the World Bank does in its index of price distortions. But data are more easily available, thereby permitting different and larger samples. Unfortunately Bradshaw's work has been focused on urbanisation rather than on growth or inequality. While the direct effect of urban bias on growth appears weak and sometimes insignificant in Bradshaw's regressions, he does support a positive effect of urban bias on overurbanisation which indirectly contributes to lower growth rates. For the purposes of my paper, a summary measure of direct *and* indirect effects of urban bias on growth rates would be more interesting than the information Bradshaw provides.

13 *All* results reported on the democracy-inequality relationship should be treated with caution. The quality of inequality data leaves much to be desired. Results may depend on the data set used (see Weede and Tiefenbach 1981a for a demonstration).

14 In this scenario nobody would enjoy job security or tenure. Such privileges are inherently discriminatory.

15 As Emmanuel (1972) claimed, worldwide unity of labour movements is unrealistic. Whatever the declared policy of Northern unions is, their actual policy must aim at defending their privileges against Southern competition, whether by protectionism, migration control or by impeding the outflow of capital and technology. For a more recent treatment, see Krauss (1983).

16 It is hard to imagine how one can make a humanitarian case for local welfare states in rich countries without implicit or explicit recourse to ethnocentric or racist arguments. Why

189

should rich people in OECD countries be taxed in order to enable their less fortunate *fellow citizens* to buy used cars or to enjoy Mediterranean holidays instead of saving truly poor *fellow men and women* in LDCs from abject proverty and starvation?

17   For a systematic treatment of revolutions from an economic perspective, see Tullock (1974).

References

ADELMAN, I. and MORRIS, C.T. 1967. *Society, Politics, and Economic Development.* Baltimore: Johns Hopkins University Press.

AHLUWALIA, M.S., CARTER, N.G. and CHENERY, H.B. 1979. 'Growth and Poverty in Developing Countries'. *Journal of Development Economics* 6 : 299-341.

ALSCHULER, L.R. 1976. 'Satellization and Stagnation in Latin America'. *International Studies Quarterly* 20(1) : 39-82.

ANDRESKI, S. 1969. *Parasitism and Subversion: The Case of Latin America.* New York: Schocken.

BAUER, P.T. 1981. *Equality, the Third World and Economic Delusion.* London: Weidenfeld and Nicholson.

BECKER, G.S. 1971. *The Economics of Discrimination.* Second edn. Chicago: Chicago University Press.

BELL, D. and KRISTOL, I. 1981. *The Crisis in Economic Theory.* New York: Basic Books.

BERNHOLZ, P. 1982. 'Expanding Welfare State, Democracy and Free Market Economy: Are they Compatible?' *Zeitschrift für die gesamte Staatswissenschaft* 138 : 583-598.

BORNSCHIER, V. 1980a. *Multinationale Konzerne, Wirtschaftspolitik und nationale Entwicklung im Weltsystem.* Frankfurt/Main: Campus.

BORNSCHIER, V. 1980b. 'Multinational Corporations and Economic Growth'. *Journal of Development Economics* 7 : 191-210.

BORNSCHIER, V. 1981a. 'Dependent Industrialization in the World Economy'. *Journal of Conflict Resolution* 25(3) : 371-400.

BORNSCHIER, V. 1981b. 'Comment' (on Weede and Tiefenbach 1981a). *International Studies Quarterly* 25 : 283-288.

BORNSCHIER, V. 1982. 'Dependence on Foreign Capital and Economic Growth'. *European Journal of Political Research* 10(4) : 445-450.

BORNSCHIER, V. 1985. 'World Social Structure in the Long Economic Wave'. Paper delivered at the 26th Annual Meeting of the International Studies Association, Washington, DC.

BORNSCHIER, V. and BALLMER-CAO, T.-H. 1979. 'Income Inequality: A Cross-National Study of the Relationships between MNC-Penetration, Dimensions of the Power Structure and Income Distribution'. *American Sociological Review* 44 : 487-506.

BORNSCHIER, V., CHASE-DUNN, C. and RUBINSON, R. 1978. 'Cross-National Evidence of the Effects of Foreign Investment and Aid on Economic Growth and Inequality: A Survey of Findings and a Reanalysis'. *American Journal of Sociology* 84 : 651-683.

BRADSHAW, Y.W. 1985a. 'Dependent Development in Black Africa'. *American Sociological Review* 50 : 195-207.

BRADSHAW, Y.W. 1985b. 'Overurbanization and Underdevelopment in Subsaharan Africa'. *Studies in Comparative International Development* 20(3) : 74-101.

BRADSHAW, Y.W. 1986. 'Urbanization and Underdevelopment: A Global Study of Modernization, Urban Bias and Economic Dependency'. Paper delivered at the 27th Annual Meeting of the International Studies Association, Anaheim, CA.

BUCHANAN, J.M. 1980. 'Rent-Seeking and Profit Seeking', in Buchanan, J.M., Tollison, R.D. and Tullock, G. (eds.), *Toward a Theory of the Rent-Seeking Society.* College Station: Texas A and M University Press, pp.3-15.

BUCHANAN, J.M., TOLLISON, R.D. and TULLOCK, G. 1980. *Toward a Theory of the Rent-Seeking Society.* College Station: Texas A and M University Press.

CHASE-DUNN, C. 1975. 'The Effects of International Economic Dependence on Development and Inequality'. *American Sociological Review* 40 : 720-738.

DELACROIX, J. 1977. 'Export of Raw Materials and Economic Growth'. *American Sociological Review* 42 : 795-808.

DELACROIX, J. and RAGIN, C.C. 1978. 'Modernizing Institutions, Mobilization, and Third World Development: A Cross-national Study'. *American Journal of Sociology* 84 : 123-150.

DELACROIX, J. and RAGIN, C.C. 1981. 'Structural Blockage: A Cross-national Study of

Economic Dependency, State Efficiency, and Underdevelopment'. *American Journal of Sociology* 86 : 1311-1347.

EMMANUEL, A. 1972. *Unequal Exchange: A Study of the Imperialism of Trade.* New York: Monthly Review Press.

FROHLICH, N., OPPENHEIMER, J.A. and YOUNG, O.R. 1971. *Political Leadership and Collective Goods.* Princeton: Princeton University Press.

GALTUNG, J. 1971. 'A Structural Theory of Imperialism'. *Journal of Peace Research* 8 : 81-117.

GOBALET, J.G. and DIAMOND, L.J. 1979. 'Effects of Investment Dependence on Economic Growth: The Role of Internal Structural Characteristics and Periods in the World Economy'. *International Studies Quarterly* 23 : 412-444.

GURR, T.R. 1968. 'A Causal Model of Civil Strife'. *American Political Science Review* 62 : 1104-1124.

GURR, T.R. and DUVALL, R. 1973. 'Civil Conflict in the 1960s'. *Comparative Political Studies* 6 : 135-169.

HAYEK, F.A. von 1960. *The Constitution of Liberty.* Chicago: Chicago University Press.

HUNTINGTON, S.P. and DOMINGUEZ, J.I. 1975. 'Political Development', in Greenstein, F.I. and Polsby, N.W. (eds.), *Handbook of Political Science. Vol. 3: Macropolitical Theory.* Reading, Mass.: Addison-Wesley.

HUNTINGTON, S.P. and NELSON, J.M. 1976. 'No Easy Choice: Political Participation in Developing Countries'. Cambridge, Mass.: Harvard University Press.

JACKMAN, R.W. 1982. 'Dependence on Foreign Investment and Economic Growth in the Third World'. *World Politics* 34 : 175-196.

KAUFMAN, R.R., CHERNOTSKY, H.I. and GELLER, D.S. 1975. 'A Preliminary Test of the Theory of Dependency'. *Comparative Politics* 7 : 303-330.

KRAUSS, M.B. 1983. *Development without Aid: Growth, Poverty and Government.* New York: New Press (McGraw-Hill).

KUHN, T.S. 1962. *The Structure of Scientific Revolutions.* Chicago: Chicago University Press.

LAKATOS, I. 1968/69. 'Criticism and the Methodology of Scientific Research Programmes. *Proceedings of the Aristotelian Society* LXIX : 149-186.

LANDAU, D. 1983. 'Government Expenditure and Economic Growth'. *Southern Economic Journal* 49 : 783-792.

LIPTON, M. 1977. *Why Poor People Stay Poor.* London: Temple Smith.

LIPTON, M. 1984. 'Urban Bias Revisited'. *Journal of Development Studies* 20 (3) : 139-166.

MARSDEN, K. 1983. 'Steuern und Wachstum'. *Finanzierung und Entwicklung* (HWWA-Institut für Wirtschaftsforschung, Hamburg) 20(3) : 40-43.

MARSH, R.M. 1979. 'Does Democracy Hinder Economic Development in the Latecomer Developing Nations?' *Comparative Social Research* 2 : 215-248.

MARX, K. 1852 (1969). 'The Eighteenth Brumaire of Louis Bonaparte', in Marx, K. and Engels, F., *Selected Works.* 2 vols. London: Lawrence and Wishart.

McKENZIE, R.B. and TULLOCK, G. 1978. *Modern Political Economy.* Tokyo: McGraw-Hill Kogakusha.

MEYER, J.W. and HANNAN, M.T. eds. 1979. *National Development and the World System: Educational, Economic and Political Change.* Chicago: Chicago University Press.

MICHELS, R. 1910 (1962). *Political Parties.* New York: Collier.

MULLER, E.N. 1984. 'Financial Dependence in the Capitalist World Economy and Distribution of Income within Nations', in Seligson, M.A. (ed.), *The Gap between Rich and Poor.* Boulder, Colorado: Westview, pp.256-282.

OBERSCHALL, A. 1973. *Social Conflict and Social Movements.* Englewood Cliffs, N.J.: Prentice-Hall.

OLSON, M. 1965. *The Logic of Collective Action.* Cambridge, Mass.: Harvard University Press.

OLSON, M. 1982. *The Rise and Decline of Nations: Economic Growth, Stagflation and Social Rigidities.* New Haven: Yale University Press.

RAY, J.L. and WEBSTER, T. 1978. 'Dependency and Economic Growth in Latin America'. *International Studies Quarterly* 22 : 409-434.

RUBINSON, R. 1976. 'The World Economy and the Distribution of Income within States'. *American Sociological Review* 41 : 638-659.

RUBINSON, R. 1977. 'Dependence, Government Revenue, and Economic Growth, 1955-1970'. *Studies in Comparative International Development* 12 : 3-28.

RUBINSON, R. and QUINLAN, D. 1977. 'Democracy and Social Inequality'. *American Sociological Review* 42 : 611-623.

SCHUMPETER, J.A. 1942. *Capitalism, Socialism and Democracy*. New York: Harper.

SINGH, R.D. 1985. 'State Intervention, Foreign Economic Aid, Savings and Growth in LDCs'. *Kyklos* 38(2) : 216-232.

STOKES, R. and JAFFEE, D. 1982. 'The Export of Raw Materials and Economic Growth'. *American Sociological Review* 47(3) : 402-407.

TOLLISON, R.D. 1982. 'Rent-Seeking: A Survey'. *Kyklos* 35(4) : 575-602.

TULLOCK, G. 1974. *The Social Dilemma: The Economics of War and Revolution*. Blacksburg, Va.: University Publications.

TULLOCK, G. 1980. 'Rent-Seeking as a Negative-Sum Game', in Buchanan, J.B., Tollison, R.D. and Tullock, G. (eds.), *Toward a Theory of the Rent-Seeking Society*. College Station: Texas A and M University Press.

TULLOCK, G. 1983. *Economics of Income Redistribution*. Boston/The Hague/London: Kluwer-Nijhoff.

WALLERI, R.D. 1978a. 'The Political Economy Literature on North-South Relations: Alternative Approaches and Empirical Evidence'. *International Studies Quarterly* 22 : 587-624.

WALLERI, R.D. 1978b. 'Trade Dependence and Underdevelopment'. *Comparative Political Studies* 11 : 94-127.

WALLERSTEIN, I. 1974. *The Modern World System: Capitalist Agriculture and the Origins of the European World Economy in the Sixteenth Century*. New York: Academic Press.

WALLERSTEIN, I. 1979. *The Capitalist World Economy (Essays)*. Cambridge: Cambridge University Press.

WALLERSTEIN, I. 1980. *The Modern World System II: Mercantilism and the Consolidation of the European World-Economy, 1600-1750*. New York: Academic Press.

WEEDE, E. 1980. 'Beyond Misspecification in Sociological Analyses of Income Inequality'. *American Sociological Review* 45 : 497-501.

WEEDE, E. 1981. 'Dependenztheorien und Wirtschaftswachstum'. *Kölner Zeitschrift für Soziologie und Sozialpsychologie* 33(4) : 690-707.

WEEDE, E. 1982. 'Dependenztheorie und Einkommensverteilung'. *Zeitschrift für die gesamte Staatswissenschaft* 138(2) : 241-261.

WEEDE, E. 1983a. 'The Impact of Democracy on Economic Growth'. *Kyklos* 36(1) : 21-39.

WEEDE, E. 1983b. 'Das Verhältnis von Demokratisierung und Wirtschaftswachstum in Entwicklungsländern', in Hartwich, H.-H. (ed.), *Gesellschaftliche Probleme als Anstoss und Folge von Politik*. Opladen: Westdeutscher Verlag, pp.154-168.

WEEDE, E. 1983c. 'Military Participation Ratios, Human Capital Formation, and Economic Growth'. *Journal of Political and Military Sociology* 11 : 11-19.

WEEDE, E. 1984. 'Democracy, Creeping Socialism, and Ideological Socialism in Rent-Seeking Societies'. *Public Choice* 44(2) : 349-366.

WEEDE, E. 1986a. 'Rent-Seeking, Military Participation and Economic Performance in LDCs'. *Journal of Conflict Resolution* 30(2) : 291-314.

WEEDE, E. 1986b. 'Catch-up, Distributional Coalitions and Government as Determinants of Economic Growth or Decline in Industrialized Democracies'. *British Journal of Sociology* 37(2) : 194-220.

WEEDE, E. and TIEFENBACH, H. 1981a. 'Some Recent Explanations of Income Inequality'. *International Studies Quarterly* 25(2) : 255-282 and 289-293.

WEEDE, E. and TIEFENBACH, H. 1981b. 'Three Dependency Explanations of Economic Growth'. *European Journal of Political Research* 9 (4) : 391-406.

WEEDE, E. and TIEFENBACH, H. 1982. 'A Reply to Volker Bornschier'. *European Journal of Political Research* 10(4) : 451-454.

WORLD BANK 1981. *World Development Report 1981*. London: Oxford University Press.

WORLD BANK 1983. *World Development Report 1983*. London: Oxford University Press.

AN OPERATIONAL ANALYSIS OF THE PHENOMENON OF THE OTHER UNDERDEVELOPMENT IN THE ARAB WORLD AND IN THE THIRD WORLD*

Mahmoud Dhaouadi

The Forgotten Other Underdevelopment

In dealing with the phenomenon of underdevelopment in the Third World, Western social scientists have tended to *confine* themselves to the socio-economic[1] sides of underdevelopment. The accumulated quantity of Western social sciences literature on underdevelopment since the Second World War is impressive. Yet there is hardly any reference to the other sides of underdevelopment (*The other underdevelopment*), that is, the psycho-cultural underdevelopment! The latter is measured in underdeveloped societies by such manifestations as the desire to imitate the West, suffering from an inferiority complex, using Western languages (English, French etc.) instead of native ones, the Third World's heavy dependency on modern Western science and knowledge, the wide diffusion of Western cultural values in developing countries etc. As such 'the other underdevelopment' is seen as having largely resulted from Western imperial domination[2] of Asian, African and Latin American societies in contemporary times. In response to this academic and intellectual silence vis-à-vis 'the other underdevelopment', we have set out here to explore this 'forgotten underdevelopment' (see Dhaouadi 1983, 1986b) in a rather *operational* systematic framework. As expected, one can hardly seek

*This paper is an extension of the theme developed in two previous papers which were published in Arabic entitled 'The Other Underdevelopment in the Maghreb' (published in 1983 in *The Journal of Al Mustagbal Al Arabi* 47) and 'The Other Underdevelopment as a Research Notion both in the Arab World and the Rest of the Third World' (published in 1986 in a book entitled *Toward an Arab Sociology*, Beirut: Centre for Arab Unity Studies, pp. 163-84).

any direct help from Western or Western-oriented social sciences in going about defining, conceptualising and theorising in this field of research. The silence of these social sciences on 'the other underdevelopment' constitutes in itself a *phenomenon* which needs an explanation. We shall attempt to do that in the last part of this study.

'The Other Underdevelopment's' Dualistic Nature

As a phenomenon, 'the other underdevelopment' is considered here as having *two* major components: (1) the cultural underdevelopment component, and (2) the psychological underdevelopment component. 'The other underdevelopment' is, thus, a psycho-cultural underdevelopment in nature as will be argued throughout this essay. In order to do that we discuss, on the one hand, the nature of each one of them and, on the other, attempt to look at them as *two interdependent* components which interact ultimately with each other in a *reciprocal* pattern. 'The other underdevelopment' can be looked at, therefore, as a *psycho-cultural system*.

Cultural Underdevelopment

Culture is seen, especially by modern anthropologists and sociologists, as a vital force in the existence of human society. Society's dynamics depend greatly on the state of its cultural forces.

Understanding Third World underdevelopment remains incomplete and shortsighted without paying adequate attention to its cultural aspects of underdevelopment. Third World cultural underdevelopment is but one dimension of its global (socio-economic dimensions, etc.) underdevelopment and it can be measured by *three* manifestations:

1. *Linguistic underdevelopment.* We define linguistic underdevelopment as, on the one hand, the widespread use of one or more foreign languages in a given society and, on the other, the *under*-usage (the less than full use) of society's own native language(s) (spoken/written or both).

In today's Third World linguistic underdevelopment can best be illustrated by the African continent case.

(a) *Black Africa's linguistic underdevelopment.* As a result of Western imperialism in Africa since the fifteenth century, English, French, Portuguese and Spanish have become the *official* languages of most countries of today's Black Africa. There are nearly as many independent African states which use English as there are states that use French as *official* languages. The total number of those countries amounts to 38 which constitutes the majority of the African states of the Black continent (Frags 1984: 164-83). It is because of this *linguistic fact* that Africa is so often divided today into *two* Africas: (1) English-speaking Africa, and (2) French-speaking Africa. To name just a few of these countries, we can mention Uganda, Ghana, Nigeria, Liberia and Sierra Leone which belong to English-speaking Africa, while Senegal, Chad, Guinea, Congo and Zaire are representative of French-speaking Africa. Portugal's earlier colonisation in the continent has led to the widespread use of Portuguese in such countries as Mozambique, Angola and Guinea-Bissau, where Portuguese (ibid.) is still the *official* language of these independent states. Compared to the wide use of English and French in Black Africa, Portuguese use is very limited. It is adopted only in five countries as an official language. Finally, Spanish as an official language is found only in Equatorial Guinea. As such, the *widespread* use of these languages, particularly in various modern sectors of these societies, constitutes a linguistic underdevelopment. In other words, native languages are not given the opportunity to be *fully* used in all walks of life. Their growth and their maturity are, therefore, bound to be hampered and *underdeveloped*.

The general acute linguistic underdevelopment in Black Africa should not, however, be explained only by Western imperialism, but also by in-built difficult internal linguistic situations which characterise most of these countries. On the one side, there is hardly any common language/dialect in each of those societies which is understood and acceptable to all clans, tribes and groups. On the other, the language(s)/dialect(s) is often limited to the *oral* form. As such, its *full* usefulness falls short of meeting the modern aspirations of the new African states like the self-management of modern structures and institutions in their own societies. This delicate linguistic state in today's Black Africa should be made meaningful in any rigorous attempt to understand the *special* nature of the complex problems of underdevelopment facing those nations. That is to say, the challenges they face in the battle against underdevelopment are not limited only to the socio-economic dimensions. Their underdevelopment is global in nature. Their psycho-cultural underdevelopment is a fundamental component of their broad underdevelopment as this study attempts to make clear.

(b) *North Africa's linguistic underdevelopment*. Furthermore, the North African societies (Algeria, Tunisia and Morocco) cannot be exempted either from the phenomenon of linguistic underdevelopment. The post-independence constitution of each of these countries explicitly affirms that Arabic is the national *official* language. Yet the special use of French (spoken and written) is still a prevailing common phenomenon in these societies, particularly in the various modern sectors. One manifestation of linguistic underdevelopment is the widespread use of the Franco-Arabe[3] (spoken Arabic mixed with spoken French) among nearly all groups of today's Maghrebian societies.

National government policies of Arabisation have not yet been entirely able to promote the status of Arabic to a fully used language (spoken and written) in all sectors of these nations. As such, the societies of North Africa suffer, though to a considerably lesser degree, like the majority of Black African societies from linguistic underdevelopment. However, Algeria, Tunisia and Morocco have, on the whole, a much better chance than the rest of the African states in ending linguistic underdevelopment. This is for the following reasons:

First, Arabic is spoken and understood by the vast majority of the population of these three countries. Second, Arabic is the sacred language of the Holy Book

195

(*The Koran*) of the Islamic faith to which the Arabs and the Berbers of the Maghreb adhere. Third, as a language Arabic is well developed. It had already proved its great vitality during the Golden Age of Arab-Muslim civilisation. The enormous movement of translation undertaken by this civilisation, especially under the Califa El Maamun's rule, illustrates very well the capacity of the Arabic language in integrating Greek philosophy, Persian and Indian sciences and wisdom into the Arabic-Islam cultural heritage.

Based on this, the relative linguistic underdevelopment in Algeria, Tunisia and Morocco has mainly resulted from the French linguistic and cultural colonisation and *not* from inherent linguistic handicaps which afflict Black Africa as referred to earlier.

Thus, successful Arabisation becomes here the key for dealing with linguistic underdevelopment. However, social policies, enthusiasm and determination of the post-independence regimes in those countries have not unanimously[4] been in favour of Arabisation. This attitude is likely to contribute to the delay of linguistic underdevelopment eradication in these independent countries, in spite of the Arabic language's great potentialities.

(c) *Linguistic underdevelopment in Asia and Central America.* The case of linguistic underdevelopment in Africa presented here is far from being confined only to this continent. Linguistic underdevelopment can be equally found in Asia and the Central American countries, particularly where English and French imperialism have ruled. English as the official or semi-official language in India and Pakistan has created foundations for the development of linguistic underdevelopment of the Hindi or the Urdu language, so has the use of French in the state of Haiti similar implications[5] on native languages and dialects.

2. *The Third World's Underdevelopment in Modern Science and Knowledge.* *Two* manifestations are used here as indexes of the Third World's underdevelopment in modern science and knowledge:

 – Developing countries' *acute* dependency on Western science and knowledge.
 – The Third World's scientists and intellectuals of Western educational background often have *poor* knowledge of their own civilisation and cultures' past contributions to the fields of science and knowledge.

(a) *Western monopoly in modern science and knowledge.* There is no question that today's Western (capitalist and socialist) advanced societies have an overall monopoly on modern science and knowledge (Mendelsohn 1976). In the contemporary period, the Third World has not *only* been dependent on the West in the fields of the exact sciences – such as physics, medicine, biology, computer sciences etc. – but also in the corpus of the social sciences, like sociology, economics, political science, psychology, etc.

(b) *The Third World's past contribution in science/knowledge and their present dependency on the West.* This does not mean, however, that non-Western civilisations have had no recorded contributions to science and

196

knowledge. Chinese, Indian, Persian and Arab-Muslim civilisations are known for their significant accumulated heritage of knowledge and science. European contact late in the Middle Ages with Muslim centres of science and knowledge, especially in Spain and Sicily, is considered by many as the triggering spark of Western European Renaissance which had set the scene for the great Western achievements in modern times in science and knowledge (Randall 1976: 208-9; Landan 1976). Underdeveloped societies' *actual* heavy dependency on Western science and knowledge may be seen as the *most* damaging handicap that blocks their capacities to exploit their potentialities for self-development. Human societies can hardly aspire to continuous progress and development without good standing in scientific and knowledge achievements. Science and knowledge play a similar role to that of natural selection as far as the survival and the progress of human societies is concerned. The more science and knowledge they have, the more successful the adaptation societies can make to their environment. It is because of this that an increasing number of experts see the *real* gap which separates the developed from the underdeveloped nations as lying in the domains of science and knowledge and *not only* in the differences in economic growth rates. Thus, winning the battle against underdevelopment and catching up with the advanced industrial countries becomes a hopeless target for today's Third World without the self-mastery of science and knowledge. The transfer of Western science and knowledge to developing nations can hardly be the alternative to the self-development of science and knowledge in the Third World.

(c) *Western vision and practice of science/knowledge are not the only model.* Furthermore, the Third World's self-creative process in science and knowledge does not mean that the developing countries must *blindly* abide by the Western modern vision in these vital fields. The nature of human science and knowledge is far from being free from the influences of history, socio-economic conditions, cultural value systems etc. of a given society or civilisation. Thus, the forces which have shaped the modern outlook of Western science and knowledge are not necessarily the same forces which may or should affect the Third World's ethics and visions of its new self-developed science and knowledge. Arab-Muslim civilisation's philosophy, vision and practice of science and knowledge may be cited as an illustration of this difference from that of Western civilisation. Islamic science and knowledge differ in their epistemological/ethical premises and practices from their Western counterparts. This can be shown in the following five points of comparison.

(d) *The anatomy of two visions of science and knowledge.*

The ethic of Western science and knowledge:
1) The Prometheus principle: conflict between Man and God over the possession of knowledge.
2) Prometheus' struggle for knowledge is human-centred. That is, human use of that knowledge is either indifferent or hostile to non-humans. God's existence, presence etc. is denied outright or marginalised and Nature is

197

considered an enemy. So it has to be conquered and mastered. Such unnatural fragmentation of the universe's interrelated and inseparable various phenomena is the result of this egoistic human vision of the world.

3) Because Prometheus-inspired knowledge is human-centred, its negative impact on non-human elements of the universe is to be expected.

4) Promethean human self-centredness has led nonetheless, in the West, to a greater narrowness in the notion of humanity. The ethic of Promethean-based Western science and knowledge has in the last centuries selected a few privileged groups, while exploiting many more others of the same human race at large.

5) Modern Western science and knowledge have restricted their sources to tangible sense data. They are *uni-dimensional* (materialistic) in nature. In doing so, they have become hostile or, at best, indifferent to revelation or spiritualism as source of information in the making of human science and knowledge.

The ethic of Islamic science and knowledge:
1) No such conflicts exists between Man and Allah. The *Koran*, for instance, over-encourages Man to learn through science and knowledge. But Allah's knowledge is infinite, while Man's is always limited (limitation and humility).

2) All creatures of the universe are Allah's. A firm belief in Him and devoted worship imply a conscious and a categorical respect for all of Allah's creatures including Nature. The result is an ever conscious awareness of the intimate interrelations that brings all the world's phenomena together (respect for the subject and object of study).

3) The deep global moral religious world vision of the Muslim scientist or scholar is expected to stand against the harming of any of Allah's creatures.

4) Because all humans are equal before Allah, the ethic of Islamic science can tolerate neither exploitation nor discrimination against other humans because of their colour, genus, ethnic origin, etc.

5) Islamic science and knowledge rely on *two* sources. On the one hand, there is the sense data source, on the other, there is the extra sense-data source symbolised in divine revelations, personal psychological states, etc. Thus the Islamic base of science and knowledge is *multi-dimensional*.

(e)   *The Third World's major obstacle to self-developed science and knowledge.* The widespread monopoly of Western science and knowledge in the Third World has been consolidated by the colonial educational system which was put in place by the colonising powers in these countries. English and French imperialism not only spread their languages in their colonies but also exposed the natives, those who went to school, to the ethics and the practice of Western science and knowledge. The result of this educational acculturation has led to the emergence of Western educated groups[6] who have a *poor* or distorted knowledge of their own civilisation's cultural heritage in the domains of science and knowledge. Algerian, Tunisian, Moroccan scientists or intellectuals with a French academic background can be cited as an example. With their ignorance, on the one hand, of the Arab-Muslim civilisation's contribution in science and knowledge, and, on the other, with their French training in Western science and knowledge, they become themselves a sort of an *internal system* capable, because of its power, of diffusing Western vision, philosophy and practices of science and knowledge in their own societies. The widespread hold of this cultural infrastructure is bound to sustain the Third World's heavy dependency on Western science and knowledge for a long time to come and, thus, hampers those countries from becoming self-creative, self-productive and self-assertive in these crucial domains.

(f) *The role of self-made science and knowledge in development.* Without the self-creative process in science and knowledge taking place both the independence and the future of development and growth in developing societies are (and will be) seriously compromised. Self-development in science and knowledge is of fundamental importance for human societies to achieve maturity and self-managing capacities.

Self-made science and knowledge are essential acquisitions for society's authentic dynamism. The self-innovation and use of science and knowledge make the latter more relevant and valid to society's use. With this, society can help itself to consolidate its own autonomy and, thus, put itself in a firm position for reliable development and growth.

Being *dominated* by the West in recent history, Third World nations tend to be great imitators of their *superiors* in many fields. The domains of science and knowledge are no exception. Western educated elites of underdeveloped societies are unlikely to take a serious critical stand towards certain aspects of the Western outlook in science and knowledge. This attitude should be no surprise at all. On the one hand, their educational acculturation process into the vision, the philosophy and the practices of Western science and knowledge leaves little room for dissent or criticism. On the other hand, their *poor* or *falsified* knowledge of their civilisations's heritage in science and knowledge can hardly enable them to formulate or seek to establish new alternatives to the philosophy and ethics of modern Western science and knowledge. In contrast to this general apathetic position of Third World scientists and intellectuals, the number of intellectual and scientific publications on 'the crises of knowledge' (Boudon 1984, 1955) in the West has been on the increase in recent years. Questions are addressed to the epistemology, the materialism, the coherence, the ethics, of modern science and knowledge.

Thus, attacking a non-Western civilisation's outlook to these critical issues of modern science and knowledge would certainly encourage Third World scientists and scholars to undertake the indigenisation process of science and knowledge in their own countries. With this, the scene would be set for the undermining of developing nations' underdevelopment in science and knowledge.

3. *The Third World's Underdevelopment in the Cultural Value System*

(a) *The general and the subtle rules of cultural exchanges.* The contact, in modern times, between the *dominant* West and the *dominated* Third World has enabled the former to impose the spread of its own cultural values, particularly those of *modernity* in the underdeveloped societies. The phenomenon of the

199

Westernisation of Third World customs and morals is largely a result of this type of balance of power between the *two* parties (see Manzoor 1985). This is in line with the spirit of a quasi-universal law which tends to regulate the nature of the process of cultural exchanges during human civilisations' encounters. This law stipulates that the weaker (the conquered, the dominated, the subordinate, etc.) is often inclined to more or less imitate the stronger (the conqueror, the dominant, the superior, etc.). Ibn Khaldun, the famous Arab historian-sociologist of the Middle Ages, had explicitly stated the principles of *who imitates whom* in his *Muqaddimah* (1974: 116).

Contemporary social science research literature (Devos 1976: 5) disagrees only in certain nuances with the author of the *Muqaddimah* on this point. For instance, the diffusion of the Western cultural value system in developing societies is a fact which cannot be denied. However, the nature and the degree of this cultural diffusion is far from being uniform among the different social groups of Third World countries. On the one hand, groups of a Western educational background as well as urban citizens are more likely to be more exposed to and, thus, affected by the spread of Western cultural values. On the other hand, the illiterate, as well as non-urban population, of the Third World is understandably the least influenced by Western culture. Furthermore, Western acculturation of urban residents and those groups with Western educational training does not have an identical impact on all dimensions of the acculturation process. While the French language is a widespread cultural feature in today's Algeria, Tunisia and Morocco, Christian religious values have hardly received any sympathy among those Muslim groups during the French colonisation.

The cultural exchange process between people has, therefore, its own subtleties and nuances. In cultural matters, it seems, it is *not* only the dominant party's *sheer superiority* which dictates what the dominated party will adopt from the culture of his or her superior. This is true not only of the interaction of the North African culture with its French counterpart in modern times, but also of other previous cultural encounters between civilisations. Though the Arab Muslims were the *dominant* power in the Middle East in the earlier spread of Islam, they were not able, however, to spread Arabic and the Islamic values (as cultural components) *evenly* among the population they ruled. While Arabic has become the language of the area called the Arab world today, Christianity has survived among significant minorities there. The Persian civilisation's encounter with Islam had resulted in a different cultural exchange pattern. The majority of Persians had adopted Islam (Shia Islam) as their new faith, while the adoption of the Arabic language has remained very limited in this new land of Islam.

(b)   *The disorganising effect of Western culture in the Third World.* The Third World's contact with the dominant modern West has, in contemporary times, led to some erosion or *disorganisation* in its own cultural value system. Modern Western cultural values have their greatest impact, as pointed out earlier, on those groups with a Western educational background and residents of urban centres. But even among the most Westernised of these groups, complete Western acculturation has hardly ever occurred. In many cases, Western cultural values never took root in the infrastructure of the cultural value system of the Third World countries. They have remained *superficial* because of their superimposed nature on those societies. A scholar like Ali Mazrui sees that one of the greatest dilemmas of today's Africa is 'a direct consequence of the fact that its institutions and ideologies are alien, lacking any African roots whatsoever' (Noor 1986: 76-7). Political instability and widespread authoritarianism in the Black continent are considered by Mazrui to be the result of *cultural disorganisation* which has been brought about mainly by Western colonialism in modern times.

What is at stake here is the clash between *tradition* (Third World cultures) and *modernity* (the new cultural values and visions of Western civilisation since the nineteenth century). This is a theme which is often covered ethnocentrically by contemporary Western sociologists. Most of their studies do not hesitate to side (theoretically or empirically) with modernity (Westernisation) against tradition (non-Western cultures) (Lerner 1964; Inkeles and Smith 1974).

(c) *The impact of tradition/modernisation on Tunisian society.* Tunisia's attempts to modernise (Westernise) since independence (1956), under Bourguiba's pro-Western leadership, have probably led it to undergo the most acute conflict of cultural values when compared with its neighbours, Algeria and Morocco. The modern Western outlook on the drinking of alcohol, sexuality and women's equality/freedom is bound to clash with the Tunisian Islamic-Arabic Mediterranean cultural value system. This *dualistic* cultural heritage can often lead to what modern social scientists have called anomie, cultural disorganisation, confusion and tension[7]. This situation can hardly help the Tunisians consolidate their cultural identity or promote their own cultural value system. Such critical cultural confusion is a principal source for the hardening of cultural underdevelopment as defined in this study. Furthermore, Westernisation has practically taken over, especially among the younger Tunisian generation, in the area of dress. For young Tunisians, the wearing of Western dress rarely constitutes any conscious feeling of internal conflict. In other words, wearing traditional clothing is *no* longer a *real* alternative to the self-imposed Western one. Western dress for them is therefore a *fait accompli*. This does not mean, however, that modern and modernising Tunisians do not wear their traditional dress any more. They do, but in a *ritual* manner; that is, on special occasions. During the summer, a great number of men dress up in Tubba. At wedding or circumcision celebrations modern Tunisian women may be seen in traditional or semi-traditional clothing. Thus, as a cultural heritage, the traditional Tunisian dress has been seriously marginalised. As such, it is another feature of cultural underdevelopment in this North African country. In brief, the *three* categories of cultural underdevelopment discussed in this section on the whole represent an impoverishment, a disruption or disorganisation of these main cultural components (language, science/knowledge and cultural value system) of the cultures of the New Nations.

The Psychological Underdevelopment in the Third World

(a) *The definition of psychological underdevelopment.* Psychological under-development is used here to mean *the deterioration* of the basic foundations of psychological well-being of the Third World individual's personality as a result especially of contemporary imperial Western *cultural domination*. Syndromes like loss of faith in one's self, the strong desire to imitate the Other (the West), the spread of the inferiority complex, feeling of alienation, increased rate in mental insanity, and deviant and criminal behaviours are considered to be possible symptoms of this 'psychological underdevelopment' in today's underdeveloped countries.

(b) *Cultural domination and the deterioration of self-esteem.* The *three* aspects of cultural underdevelopment just outlined make it clear that Western colonialism and imperialism of the nineteenth and twentieth centuries in the Third World has not been limited to military, economic and political domination. It has also been a *cultural* one. Some of today's developing countries experienced *total* Western domination under Western colonialism. The French style of occupation of Algeria is a case in point.

This interaction between *unequals* has often led, on the one hand, to the development of complex symptoms of inferiority among the *dominated* people of the Third World and, on the other, to the development of a superiority complex among the *dominant* Western societies. Western cultural domination in its *two* forms (1 and 2) spelled out earlier has shown its *detrimental* effects on the self-esteem of the culturally dominated individual of underdeveloped countries. French colonial cultural domination of the North African societies is an example. The French had made serious attempts to deculturise the North Africans from their Arabic-Islamic heritage and acculturise them instead to the French language and its culture. The result of this process has been the creation of *cultural alienation* among Algerians, Tunisians and Moroccans who have had a predominantly French education. On the one hand, these Maghrebians[8] have had high admiration for the French language and culture. Their widespread and frequent use of French[9] is a good indicator of their compulsive attachment to the French culture in general. On the other hand, they are found to consider Arabic and its culture as traditional (outdated) and, thus, unsuitable for modernity (Westernisation). Their acculturation into the dominant French culture has made them feel *uneasy* with regard to their relations with the Arabic language and its culture. Knowing one's language and culture becomes, therefore, a *source of feeling inferior* instead of feeling proud as usually occurs under normal circumstances.

(c) *The inferiority complex and linguistic avoidance response.* There has developed, among this *type* of educated North African, what we call a 'linguistic avoidance response' phenomenon vis-à-vis Arabic.

In Tunisia, for instance, this author has repeatedly observed, even among the post-independence generation of students of high school as well as of university, that they tend to use the term '*l'arabe*' (Arabic in French) while speaking in Arabic, instead of '*al-arabiyya*', when referring to the Arabic language course. Avoiding the use of Arabic is well conveyed by the example of these Tunisian students and so is their admiration for the use of French even when speaking about Arabic! The connotations of this linguistic behaviour suggest that these

Tunisians are hardly proud of Arabic as their national language. The negative image they have held of Arabic is bound to be, to a large degree, the outcome of hostile French colonial ideology towards the Arabic language and Arab culture. The phenomenon of 'linguistic avoidance response' is symptomatic of a psycho-cultural crisis. On the cultural side, the French acculturation of these Tunisian students appears to be overwhelming and, thus, their alienation from their cultural heritage (Arabic language and its culture) is quite visible. On the psychological side, there is a deterioration in one's self-esteem, one's faith in one's identity, etc. (psychological underdevelopment 1). In other words, the psychological dimensions of the basic personality of those Tunisians are somewhat eroded and undermined. In short, what is involved here are: (1) the development of false (distorted) cultural identities, and (2) the appearance of manifest symptoms of an inferiority complex.

(d)   *The cultural value system and disorganised personality*. The acute state of cultural conflict between the traditional cultural value system and its modern Western counterpart is expected to have certain side-effects on the personality structure of the Third World acculturised (to Western culture) individual.

Some modern sociologists have referred to this type of personality as *'disorganised personality'* (Znaniecki and Thomas 1958) (psychological underdevelopment 2). This disorganisation of the cultural value system (cultural underdevelopment 3) is often associated in human societies with *socio-behavioural* manifestations, such as social tension, protest, socio-cultural change, deviance and rise in crime, and an increase in mental illness (Kisker 1982: 103-6). The latter is accounted for by the fact that cultural value conflicts expose the person to psychological strains, stress and tension due to the adjustment he or she has to make to the polarising nature of his or her cultural value system. As we have seen, the self-imposed Western cultural values have intruded practically into nearly all Third World societies. The study of the confrontation between the *two* cultural value systems and their implications constitutes a potentially *rich area* of social science research which is yet to be fully explored, especially by Third World social scientists. In putting their efforts in this new vista of research, Third World scientists will unravel in a more systematic and scientific manner not only the nature and the variety of the psycho-cultural impact on underdeveloped countries, but they will also push forward the social science indigenisation process in their own societies.

The Other Underdevelopment as a Psycho-Cultural System

As shown throughout this essay, the 'other underdevelopment' appears to be a phenomenon of a psycho-cultural nature. Its *two* components are mutually interacting in a reciprocal manner. We have seen, on the one hand, that linguistic underdevelopment (1) and science/knowledge underdevelopment (2) are likely to lead to the development of inferiority complex symptoms (psychological underdevelopment 1) in the personality of the *Western* acculturised individual of the Third World. On the other hand, psychological

Figure 1

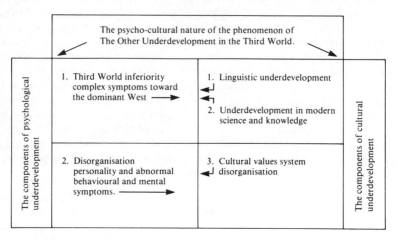

underdevelopment *predisposes* the individual's personality to learn and use the language(s) and the culture(s) of dominant societies. Furthermore, the inferiority complex becomes a strong force causing the development of a *negative* perception of one's national language and culture. Psychological inferiority complex symptoms (psychological underdevelopment 1) appear, thus, to harden the *two* dimensions (1 and 2) of cultural underdevelopment and, consequently, contribute to the making of *cultural alienation*, a phenomenon which is widespread in underdeveloped countries, especially among those groups with a Western educational background.

What we have called disorganised personality (psychological under-development 2) contributes, in turn, to the degree of breakdown of cultural values (cultural underdevelopment 3). In other words, conflicts of cultural values are likely to make the personality structure of the individual of the Third World more vulnerable to *further* breakdowns and, thus, more receptive or less resistant to the adoption of Western cultural values. All this would tend to lead to a deeper disintegration of the personality structure and, consequently, to confusion in one's cultural identity. Figure 1 illustrates the main components of the phenomenon of the 'other underdevelopment' as well as the nature of their interaction.

The Roots of the Silence of Modern Western Social Science
on the Other Underdevelopment

It must be clear by now that the existence of the phenomenon of the 'other underdevelopment' in the Third World is not based on mere speculation or imagination. We have defined the 'other underdevelopment' and spelled out its psycho-cultural components which convey its very nature. In spite of this, modern Western (liberal capitalist or socialist Marxist) social sciences have in general remained *silent* as far as the 'other underdevelopment' is concerned.

This silence, as we stated at the outset of this study, requires an explanation. The assessment we offer below would account, in our opinion, for the mute modern social science negligence of the study of the psycho-cultural underdevelopment in the Third World. The causes of that can be classified into *two* categories:

(a) *Causes derived from Western ethnocentrism*:

1. There is a generally widespread attitude, particularly among Western liberal social scientists concerned with the study of development/underdevelopment, which hints or claims implicitly or explicitly that the cultural heritage (values, traditions, religions etc.) of underdeveloped societies is largely an obstacle to the development process in those countries. This should explain why *cultural underdevelopment*, as defined by us, has *no* place in their studies of development/underdevelopment in the Third World.

2. The Western ethnocentric vision of development/underdevelopment has made modern specialists and researchers in the social sciences tend to think that Third World countries cannot achieve development on their own. Thus, Third World dependency on external help (preferably Western in nature) is recommended by them. The spread, therefore, of modern Western languages (English, French etc.) and cultural values into Third World societies is expected to be endorsed or even encouraged, especially by modern Western social scientists (see Lerner 1964; Inkeles and Smith 1974). For the latter it is quite obvious that Western cultural diffusion in underdeveloped countries is a process which helps the promotion of cultural development and *not* a process which leads to the 'other underdevelopment', as we have outlined it in this study.

3. Western liberal capitalist social scientists have hardly made any link between the phenomenon of *underdevelopment* in the Third World and *Western colonialism* of the latter (ibid.). When underdevelopment in all its forms (economic, social, psycho-cultural, etc.) is not related somehow to imperial Western classical or new colonialism in the last two centuries, then the 'other underdevelopment', seen by us as resulting largely from Western domination of the Third World, is unlikely to be recognised and, subsequently, studied by those social scientists.

4. Western social scientists' conceptualisation, understanding, theories, etc. of development/underdevelopment are bound to be *westerncentric*. This is only natural. The social scientist, whatever his or her nationality may be, is inclined to *rely heavily* on the realities of his or her own social/civilisational milieu in analysing social phenomena as well as theorising about them. In doing so, it is difficult not to be, at least partially, biased in going about research endeavours including his or her own choice of what phenomenon to study. Western social scientists' negligence of the study of the 'other underdevelopment' is a case in point. In other words, advanced Western capitalist and socialist societies, to which most modern social scientists belong, are *not* known to have *seriously* suffered, if at all, from the 'other underdevelopment' syndrome described in this work. Thus, the 'other underdevelopment' has remained an alien phenonemon which has failed to seriously attract their scientific curiosity.

205

(b)   *Causes of an epistemological nature*:

1. Generally speaking, Western liberal as well as Marxist social scientists' conceptualisation of the development/underdevelopment phenomena is materialistic in nature. If development/underdevelopment is conceived basically in terms of economic, social, scientific and technological indicators, then it becomes understandable why psycho-cultural underdevelopment has received little or no attention at all from those social scientists. It is well known that Marxist social thinkers have spoken more about Third World economic exploitation by the capitalist West, but they have given *no more* than lip service to Third World cultural exploitation.[10]

2. As pointed out, the 'other underdevelopment' constitutes an underdevelopment which focuses mainly on the factors leading to the *deterioration* (underdevelopment) of the psycho-cultural components of *the individual's personality* in the Third World. Thus, psycho-cultural underdevelopment is not materialistic in nature. If development/underdevelopment is conceived by Western social scientists primarily in terms of structural-materialistic variables, then the whole issue of the 'other underdevelopment' can hardly find any attention among structuralist-materialistic social scientists. By neglecting the study of the 'other underdevelopment' as an *essential* feature of society's development/underdevelopment dynamics, modern Western sociologists and economists in particular have put into *serious question* the integrity as well as the validity of their paradigms and theories about development/underdevelopment in the Third World.

Notes

1. As an example, consult the list of books, articles, etc. which have been written about development/underdevelopment in Jacquemot et al. (1981).

2. Fanon is probably the only Third World intellectual who has written with clarity and depth about the psycho-cultural scars, caused by Western imperialism, to the personality of the dominated people of the Third World. He has referred to French policy which attempted to alienate the Algerian Arab from his country and reduce him to a state of 'absolute de-personalisation'. The Algerian was a victim of an abortive attempt to de-cerebralise a whole people. For him, as for us, colonialism is a global phenomenon, as argued in this study, including psycho-cultural dimensions. To *undo* colonialism, Third World nations *must* eradicate the manifestations of the 'other underdevelopment'. For Fanon, the process of de-colonialisation is not only national in form, it is violent in content. Colonialism is violence, political, military, *cultural* and *psychic*. Only counter-violence operating in the same spheres can eradicate it – see Fanon (1967, 1963). Our effort here is to systematise and make the phenomenon of the 'other underdevelopment' *measurable* by concrete reliable indicators. In doing so, we are hoping to dissipate all vagueness which may have been one of the excuses used by some social scientists, in order *not* to put the phenomenon under rigorous scrutiny.

3. See the author's study in French (1984); and also that in Arabic (1986b).

4. The former President Bourguiba of Tunisia had criticised Arabisation for the deterioration of the level of the Tunisian educational system (Noor 1986: 19-20). The implications of this may lead to the comeback of French in the Tunisian scene. If this happens, linguistic underdevelopment in Tunisia will probably survive longer.

5. Westerners often form their own *wrong* impressions about educated Third World groups with Western educational backgrounds. This is particularly true of North Americans. In their encounter with Third World students, in particular, in their countries, Americans and Canadians are frequently impressed by those foreign students' fluency in English or French (or both). Their

amazement becomes stronger when they believe that those students must know and master their own languages *better*. In many cases this perception is entirely *false*. Had they been aware of *linguistic underdevelopment* in the Third World, as described here, they would have avoided being naive about the nature of Western domination and its global impact on dominated countries.

6. They are often those who have more *power* in running their countries after independence. Traditionally educated groups have hardly had much power in Third World societies since independence. The indigenisation process of science and knowledge in these countries remains difficult to achieve in these circumstances. Attempts to Islamise modern knowledge – carried out by the late great Muslim thinker Ismail Al Faruqui and the Institute of Islamic Thought (Washington) – are, in our opinion, far from being the natural solution to the self-development of *authentic* Islamic science and knowledge. The *real* Islamisation of knowledge can really take place only when it is initiated and self-developed by Muslim scientists and intellectuals whose socio-cultural milieu and ethics are *Islamic* in nature. See Al-Faruqui (1982) and Davies (1986: 54-8).

7. The conflict between traditional Islamic values and modern *adopted* Western ones appears to be *one* important factor for political tension at the highest level in Tunisia during Bourguiba's rule.

8. Maghrebians = Algerians, Tunisians and Moroccans. The word Maghreb encompasses, therefore, the three countries.

9. The frequent use of French in these countries takes essentially *two* forms: 1) The widespread *exclusive* use of French is common particularly among educated groups with French training where dealing with modern scientific and intellectual subjects; 2) the *Franco-Arabe* (mixing Arabic with French in speaking) is much more widespread among the general population of these three societies. North African educated women, in particular, appear to *mix* their Arabic with French more than their Maghrebian male counterparts. See Dhaouadi (1986b).

10. Writings on development/underdevelopment of Marxist authors, such as Amin (1973), Frank (1969) and Baran (1960) reflect their silence on the psycho-cultural underdevelopment as an integral part of the greater phenomenon of underdevelopment in the Third World.

References

AL-FARUQI, I. 1982. *Islamization of Knowledge: Principles and Work Plan*. Washington: IIIT.
AMIN, S. 1973. *Le développement inégal*. Paris: Minuit.
BARAN, P. 1960. *The Political Economy of Growth*. New York: Mentor.
BOUDON, R. 1955. 'Savoir en crise'. *Revue Internationale d'Action Communautaire* 15.
BOUDON, R. 1984. *La place du désordre*. Paris: P.U.F.
DAVIES, M. 1986. 'Islamising the Behavioural Sciences'. *Inquiry Magazine* 3 (7): 54-8.
DEVOS, G.A. 1976. *Responses to Change: Culture and Personality*. New York: Van Nostrand.
DHAOUADI, M. 1983. 'The Other Underdevelopment in the Maghreb' (in Arabic). *The Journal of Al Mustagbal Al Arabi* 47.
DHAOUADI, M. 1984. 'Les racines du franco-arabe féminin au Maghreb'. *Arab Journal of Language Studies* 2 (2).
DHAOUADI, M. 1986a. 'The Other Underdevelopment as a Research Notion both in the Arab World and the Rest of the Third World' (in Arabic), in *Toward an Arab Sociology*. Beirut: Centre for Arab Unity Studies. pp. 163-84.
DHAOUADI, M. 1986b. 'Language Borrowing as a Linguistic Behavior of the Dominated North Africans' (in Arabic). *The Arab Journal of Humanities* (Kuwait University) 6 (22).
FANON, F. 1963. *The Wretched of the Earth*. London: Présence Africaine.
FANON, F. 1967. *Black Skin, White Masks*. New York: Grove Press.
FRANK, G. 1969. *Capitalism and Underdevelopment in Latin America*. New York: Monthly Review Press.
FRAGS, K.L. ed. 1984. *Encyclopedic Atlas of the World*. London: Apple Press.
INKELES, E. and SMITH, D. 1974. *Becoming Modern*. Cambridge, Mass.: Harvard University Press.
JACEQUEMOT, P. et al. 1981. *Economie et sociologie du tiers-monde: guide bibliographique*. Paris: L'Harmattan.
KHALDOUN, I. 1974. *The Muqaddimah*. Princeton, N.J.: Princeton University Press.
KISKER, G. 1982. *The Disorganized Personality*. London: McGraw-Hill.

LANDAN, P. 1976. *The Arab Heritage of Western Civilization*. New York: Arab Information Centre.
LERNER, D. 1964. *The Passing of Traditional Society*. New York: Free Press.
MANZOOR, P. 1985. 'Cultural Autonomy in a Dominated World'. *Inquiry Magazine* 2 (6): 32-7.
MENDELSOHN, K. 1976. *Science and Western Domination*. London: Thames and Hudson.
NOOR, S. 1986. 'The Sacking of Mzali. *Inquiry Magazine* 3 (8): 19-20.
RANDALL, J.H. Jr. 1976. *The Making of the Modern Mind*. New York: Columbia Press University.
ZNANIECKI, F. and THOMAS, W. 1958. *The Polish Peasant in Europe and America*. New York: Dover.

OCCIDENTAL REASON, ORIENTALISM, ISLAMIC FUNDAMENTALISM: A CRITIQUE*

Mona Abaza and Georg Stauth

Introduction

Inter-cultural relations and the pattern of exchange between Islam and the West have been prominent topics of many academic studies of which one may single out Albert Hourani's *Europe and the Middle East* (1980) and Jacques Waardenburg's *L'Islam dans le miroir de l'Occident* (1963), not necessarily as the most prominent ones but as the most extended and detailed. In addition, orientalist approaches to understanding the Islamic world have found an early prominent critique in the works of Arkoun (1964) and Abdel-Malek (1963).

These critiques of classical orientalism and underlying orientalist assumptions of modern social theory continued to attract considerable attention in the late 1960s and 1970s among both students of Islamic culture and Western sociology and philosophy. It might be helpful in this context to note the studies of Rodinson (1968), Laroui (1973), Djait (1974), Arkoun (1970) and Turner (1974, 1978). However, only since the appearance of Said's book (1978) has orientalism become a major theme of inter-cultural research (the extensive reception of this book deserves a study of its own right). Finally, we should

*Parts of this paper have been presented at the EIDOS Meeting, 15-16 May, 1987 in Bielefeld. We thank all the participants of this meeting and, especially, Hans-Dieter Evers for his valuable comments. Other parts have been presented and discussed at the Middle East Research Seminar, at the Free University of Berlin, in January 1988 by invitation of Friedemann Büttner. We are grateful to the participants of this seminar and, especially, to Friedemann Büttner, Baber Johansen and Fritz Steppat who, with their comments, encouraged us to redraft this paper. Bryan S. Turner has commented substantially on an earlier version of this paper and we would like to extend our grateful thanks to him.

note Schluchter's publication on *Max Webers Sicht des Islam* (1987) which seems to be little worried by any reflection of the 'Orientalism' debate. In his introduction to this collection of articles on Weber, Schluchter reaffirms the traditional interpretation of Weber's texts on Islam, namely, that the Islamic religious ethic is directed toward world domination by means of world conquest, and as a result of this toward adaptation to the world and of inner-worldly affirmation.

In this paper we do not wish to explore the scope and the impact of Said's *Orientalism* (1978). Rather we attempt to demonstrate how a reductionist Foucaultian discourse on epistemes of cultural classification of the Other, his paradigm of knowledge/power and attempts at better and deeper understanding of the Other, and thus of doing less injustice to the local, indigenous people, brings about a false framework of indigenous culture and religion which denies a long history of productive cultural exchange. Within the 'indigenous' discourse Third World sociologists, but also cultural anthropologists and feminist students of local cultures, apply such paradigms, providing a new imagination of what is supposedly the 'essence' and the 'real' of the culture of the Other (or of their own cultural traditions). This trend in cross-cultural debates is, in fact, leading to a new type of 'Orientalism in reverse' (al-Azm 1981).

Our argument here is that a new trend of 'going native', both among Western academics as well as among local ones, is to be observed. On the practical level this is manifested by an apologetic attitude vis-à-vis Islamic fundamentalism.[1] This attitude is, in fact, the logical consequence of the Western sociological tradition attempting to understand the religious phenomenon. We propose here that, in order to evaluate the discourses produced about fundamentalism, an understanding of Max Weber's impact on the sociology of religion is of crucial importance. It is interesting to note how post-modern discourses in sociology and social thought are now penetrating the field of inter-cultural studies and developmentalist approaches in social research. Thus, attempts at 'essentialising' – to use a word which has recently been applied in this debate – the real needs and thoughts of people together with a new post-modern understanding of social reality as a mere 'world of floating signs' (Baudrillard 1978) encompasses a new stage in the construction of an 'iron cage' in inter-cultural discourse and exchange.

It was the declared aim of early nineteenth century anthropologists and orientalists (Bachofen and Nöldecke might be quoted here as examples) to understand more deeply the 'soul' of the cultural Other. This, however, did not prevent anthropology and oriental studies from undergoing a process of internal 'sociologisation' and with this a classificatory externalisation of alien cultures. Here, it might be important to note that the formalisation and institutionalisation process of the cultural sciences in nineteenth century Germany, for example, also brought about a systematised apparatus of social categorisation which then formed the background to Weber's cross-cultural comparative studies and his attempts at the construction of a value-free universal history (Stauth 1988).

It has recently become fashionable in inter-cultural studies to link Foucaultian discourse with hermeneutics and, in doing so, to praise the failures of Marxism, nationalism and institutional structures in Third World countries (Hobart 1986; Etienne 1987). It follows from this type of reasoning that local cultures have failed to be compatible with the modern structures of the nation-state. It also follows that indigenous people would have, indeed, different conceptions of power, of communism, and socialism. Mystical interpretations are thus given to explain malfunctions within structures while economic analysis is totally ignored. The failures of structures are here utilised to argue that the alternative should be a religious one.

In fact, we would like to show how Foucaultian discourses and the theorists of failures are leading to an epistemological deadlock which has serious political consequences. Here the issue of Islamism is a point for study in its own right.

These approaches could be labelled as a new type of 'going native' sociology which 'essentialises' the cultures of the Other by penetrating them with hermeneutic methodology. On the other side, and coinciding with the spread of the above mentioned approaches, an increasing claim is being made for the 'indigenisation' of social sciences both in the Middle East and in South-East Asia instead of 'distorted' Westernisation and imported social sciences. A claim for the purity of cultural traits has been recently established. Those, however, who claim authenticity by 'indigenisation' might not yet be aware of the fact that the local knowledge, upon which they want to construct an alternative, has long since been part of global structures; or of the fact that they play a part in a global cultural game which itself calls for the 'essentialisation' of local truth. The new apologetics for Islamist trends are a derivation of the new Western 'essentialism' in inter-cultural studies. In promoting Islamist groups they have thus launched a fierce attack on secular Third World intellectuals.

The Paradox of Western Secularism

Orientalists have often reproduced standard arguments concerning secularism and Islam which need attention here. Firstly, they argue that Islam is a religious community which has not - or rather not yet - created a separation between a private sphere of belief and the secularised sphere of public affairs, an important factor in the division of labour in modern society (e.g. Endress 1982: 91 f.).

Secondly, it is argued that Islam is the religion of obligation, not of confession and creed. Orientalists have understood Islam as a religion that does not relate the inner confession of the believer to the religious dogma as a whole. Rather they have argued that the ritual observation of rules related to the Islamic law (*Shari'a*) is the focal point in the social behaviour of Muslims.

Thirdly, it has been argued that there is no inherent opposition between religious law and everyday practice which could create the necessary tensions for further practical rationalisations of religious beliefs. The *Shari'a* law, however, is understood to entail a certain flexibility in the forms of its application. The *Shari'a* has never been fully codified and the formation of different legal schools led to a stagnation of theological disputes and rational thought.

Finally, we are told that the Islamic understanding of the world remains superficial. In opposition to Western attitudes of world mastery, such as self-restraint and science, Islam calls for the conquest of the world and thus also adapts to the cultures of the conquered. This adaptation process in integrating or loosely assimilating the cultures of the conquered – for example, for over three centuries Islam left relatively untouched the administrative and cultural apparatus of the Byzantines – has also accounted for the world affirmative character of the belief system in Islam. Moreover, it is argued, that Islam has no calling for the understanding of the 'inner' logic of the cosmos. Islam is seen to contradict and to remain incompatible with a modern scientifically founded world-view. Against these interpretations which are also present in Weber's *Sociology of Religion*, Rudolf Peters, in a recent article (1987), has argued that prior to modern developments, which could be viewed as being dependent on influences of Western thought, there have been fundamentalist movements in the eighteenth and nineteenth centuries, originating from pure Islamic traditions. Peters follows the steps of Maxime Rodinson's *Islam and Capitalism* (1968). In fact, for Rodison, Islam developed motives and religious elements which are similar to those which Weber had traced in Protestantism and which Weber understood - in spite of their being present in Islam - as decisive 'inner' dispositions of occidental rationalism and capitalism. Peters attempts to prove that the fundamentalist movements of the nineteenth century contributed considerably to introducing rational thought among their followers. He argues,

> that all the teachings and motivations which are characteristic for Calvinist Protestantism and which Weber has seen to be conclusive with the development of capitalism, can also be discovered in fundamentalist Islam.
>
> (Peters 1987: 229)

In fact, there is a new wave of literature which argues for a Weberian re-evaluation of Islamic fundamentalism (e.g. Freund 1987). Fundamentalism takes here a similar historical role as Protestantism and is seen to bring about similar cultural achievements as those of the calvinist movement of the sixteenth and seventeenth centuries. This new trend in oriental studies could be considered as the result of a Marxist critique of *Die orientalische Despotie* (Wittfogel 1962) and of critical reviews of traditional orientalist literature. The view, however, that Marxism has put an end to orientalism (Turner 1978) remains a rather preliminary judgement. Here, the critique of 'orientalism' has created a rather new facet of the cultural perception of the Other. These attempts to integrate Islam into a general pattern of 'modernisation' and universal culture are, in fact, eliminating all cultural critical motives of

212

medieval Islam (against Christianity) and of orientalism (in search of the cultural Other) toward Western modern rationalism. But more decisively they deny the paradox of religion and modernity in Western civilisation, namely, the rise of secularism brought about by religious fundamentalism.

Max Weber, in his *Protestant Ethic and the Spirit of Capitalism* (1952) discovered a fascinating paradox in occidental reason, namely, that the secular modernisation of society is brought about by a fundamentalisation of religion. We can clearly identify this paradox in Weber's metaphor of the '*Doppelgesicht*' (double face) of the Calvinist and Puritanist ethic which ties '*Diesseitsinteresse*' (practical interest in this world) to '*Jenseitsschicksal*' (fate in the Beyond) together in an indissoluble relation (Weber 1920: 540).

For Weber – and for Friedrich Nietzsche who contributed to Weber's insight in this respect (Stauth and Turner 1986) – this paradox remained a unique product of occidental cultural development and of modernity. Strikingly enough, many recent observers of the Islamic fundamentalist movements have claimed that these movements could be seen as an alternative for the social development of the region. Islamic fundamentalism which developed – in many ways as a reflection of the youth and student movements of the West – in nearly all Middle Eastern countries since the late 1960s is now seen to serve as a functional equivalent to secularisation.

In opposition to these assumptions, it is the intention of this paper to recall, in the light of the knowledge of the religious foundations of modernity, the secular foundations of modern trends in Islam. Furthermore, we believe that the secular calling of modern persons can only be understood as a disguised form of their essential religious commitments. Perhaps it is helpful to remind ourselves of Ernst Troeltsch's understanding of modern secularism in terms of a cultural transposition of Christian Protestant forms of valuation. But Carl Schmitt (1922) has also taught us to understand the most crucial concepts of the constitution of the modern state in terms of secularised theological terminology. The religious foundation of modern secularism has been widely disguised and neglected in cross-cultural studies. The classical interpretation of Weber's *Sociology of Religion* (1956) has positivistically universalised the 'inner' relation between practical reason and religious ethos, but in doing so it denied the religious Christian foundation of the scientific apparatus of cultural analysis which it established. In the final instance in the developmental interpretations of Weber, the West appears to be secular, while the East seems to continue to be religiously inspired. The particular relation between secularism and religion in Islamic history has been totally ignored. In fact, what has been described as a continuation and a re-awakening of religious spiritualism in the Middle East could be explained in terms of a derivation from modern Western developmentalist concepts. But more decisively, Islamic fundamentalism shoud be seen to be a result of mass culture, as an Eastern facet of projected Western imagery of 'religious spirituality'. This 'one-dimensional' promotion of Islamism ignores the historical roots of knowledge and reason in science, philosophy and political theory of Islamic civilisation.

213

Finally, we should be aware of the fact that for the 'modern man', the 'scientifically trained' and 'highly professional' (state-)official, the state has replaced religion. This substitution has led to a pluralistic culture, through which the individual is given the freedom of choice of diverse religious beliefs. With the growing artificiality and fragmentation of modes of living within a universal cultural framework of consumer culture (Featherstone 1987), and particularly with mass holidays, sports and other leisure activities, the 'body' enters into the field of social battles. Baudrillard's observation that the body as an object of salvation has replaced the ideological function of the soul (1970) is of importance here. This new encroachment on physical appearance, symbolic division of space, on architecture and life-style, also entails a continuous reference to the domain of moral and religious questions. Cosima Wagner's call for religion in art, which Friedrich Nietzsche so vehemently refused as an attempt to fabricate a state-, a mass-culture, for the German Reich, is of significance for any understanding of modern nation-state culture and the various forms of intellectual production taking place within it (cf. Janz 1981, Vol. 3, passim). Today social anthropology, which attempts to understand more deeply what the 'natives" belief is, has created a new language of understanding the cultures of the Other in terms of aestheticising the religious symbolism. Aesthetisation, we wish to argue, is a new form of cross-cultural exchange which is specifically enhanced by the 'going native' attitude of the anthropologist. Perhaps Geertz's *Islam Observed* (1968) represents an important contribution in terms of comparative studies of religion in Third World countries. Geertz elaborates an interpretative perspective by tracing the evolution of Islam in two totally different cultures: Morocco and Indonesia. In these societies the intrinsic cultural and historical dimensions have had a radical impact upon the nature of rule and legitimation of the newly created states. According to Geertz, the evolution of collective life is the factor which transformed Moroccan Islam into 'activist, rigorous, dogmatic, more than a little anthropolatrous' (Geertz 1968: 20), while Indonesian Islam became rather 'syncretic, reflective, multifarious and strikingly phenomenological' (ibid.). By reference to both history and folk beliefs Geertz has extended his comparison to modern leaders in the respective countries. Thus, the legitimacy of King Mohammed V is dependent on traditional symbols, 'the sultan as the chief marabout of the country' (ibid: 77), while the Indonesian President Sukarno is viewed as a highly scientific man, possessing great knowledge in different areas and arguing that politics, art, science and religion are indissoluble (ibid.: 117).

Geertz's comparison, although very illuminating, is still inappropriate. In fact, his perspective falls into a general distinction between different paths of development of Islam in various regions (e.g. dogmatic/rigorous vs. syncretic/reflective) without giving close reference to the interplay between class and religious style of life practice. In *The Religion of Java*, Geertz develops at length the difference between the Santri and Abangan syncretic vs. puristic Islam (Geertz 1960, 1976a: Chs. 10–12). More importantly, a Geertz reading of Islamic trends in the Arab world presupposes the availability of some general or absolute method of judgement from which a valuation of how certain patterns of tradition operate within the 'cultural unit' observed; this valuation is then used to analyse the system of action and behaviour of the so-called 'natives'. With this attempt to figure out matters from the natives' point of view, Geertz puts himself into a competitive position with the natives over the interpretation of what really is the natives' point of view. We might shortly refer to an example that in our view is most significant. In asking, what is the perception of the self in Moroccan society, Geertz 'by searching out and analyzing the symbolic forms – words, images, institutions, behaviours – in terms of which, in each place people actually represent themselves to themselves and to one another' (Geertz 1976b: 224 f.), points to the Arab linguistic form of the term *nisba* as a 'symbolic means by which to sort people out from one another and from an idea of what it is to be a person' (ibid.: 231). Geertz, in consulting the dictionary, is very much aware that the term refers to 'kinship'. He also elaborates on a *nisba* as a term of distinction by reference to a person's locality. He remains, however, fully unaware that the term – more specifically in Geertz's own interpretation – corresponds to distinctions of con-sanguinity and co-residence, both the most essential concepts of primordial relations, generally from the view of all anthropologists. Why then should a person in Morocco be distinguished and self-defined merely on the grounds of a concept of *nisba*? Obviously, Geertz 'essentialises' an informant's loose description into a deep concept on the grounds of his professional perspective on primordial relations.

Geertz's anthropological models are, as he states, 'moving from local truths to general visions' (1973: 23), but his own attempts of replacing 'positivism' with hermeneutics might easily lead to the conclusion that the local truths are mere shadows of his own general visions.

The floating character of Geertz's cross-cultural interpretations become even more vague, becoming merely a rather shadowy background for symbolic reference where hermeneutics are linked with a 'political economy of symbolic exchange' of the Baudrillard type. In his 'Elixir of Morality' (1987), Hobart proposes that we read the Balinese economy in terms of an economy of death. Hobart argues that economics is a positivist science, and that 'the stress on material production, especially the social relations of production, has itself become a fetishizing of the nineteenth century Bourgeois pre-occupations' (Hobart 1987: 2). With this statement, Hobart summarises Baudrillard's earlier critiques of Marx's 'Law of Exchange Value' (Baudrillard 1972). By using the idea of economy as a metaphor, however, Hobart attempts to show that value in Balinese culture entails a variation of meanings; e.g. the concept of *merta* (which we would in a common-sense translation understand as blessing) varies from what gives one energy to degeneration which is built in the notion of *merta* itself to poison and various other interpretations (Hobart 1987: 3). From the notion of value he goes on to argue:

Organic metaphors seem to play a far lesser part in Balinese discourse. Not only are complex agents not referred to by analogy to humans (as we talk of corporations as 'bodies' and their activities in pseudo-organic terms), but images of growth, continuity and survival are restricted to living beings. The language for talking about the state, the economy and so on are quite disjunct from that used of its members. The connection lies not so much in shared metaphor as in the presupposition of decline and transformation.

(Hobart 1987: 10)

Hobart's linguistic metaphors to describe his 'Economy of Death' and the cremation process in Bali seems to mix up two levels of analysis, namely, that social interaction is interpreted in terms of myths and metaphysics while at the same time all dimensions of practical reason in everyday social life become disconnected and, in fact, non-existent or hidden on the back-stage of the metaphoric theatre. Like many hermeneutic studies undertaken by anthropologists (see e.g. Rosen 1984 for Morocco) Hobart reduces the universal logic of practical reason (e.g. Sahlins 1976; Bourdieu 1980) to a negligible position.

Nietzsche, Weber, and the Modernity of Islamism

As a critique of the misleading attempts at interpreting the Islamist phenomenon we would like to question whether modernisation, both in Europe and in the Arab world, did lead to a total process of secularisation. Although many historical and political observers still claim that Islamism is a true movement of the masses against a secular and corrupt state, devoid of any legitimation, a closer look at Egyptian history reveals that the superstructure was never totally secularised and the discourse on the legitimation of state power was always used as a playground for religious argumentation and symbolism (Roussillon 1988). This observation allows us to reverse the question: fundamentalism thus does not appear as a reaction against too much modernisation and secularism, as many Western observers have argued. Rather it is a reaction against an incomplete and false transposition of religious language into the language of 'modernity'. This false transposition relates essentially to the fact that the construction of the colonial powers in Europe remained profoundly tied to religious discourses and the official ceremonies of state churches. Furthermore, by looking into the Western sociological tradition, and particularly to Troeltsch and Weber, what really distinguished and differentiated Europe from the rest of the world was its essentially Christian foundation which was tied to a rationalisation process and to capitalism. Thus, Carl Schmitt – the famous political philosopher of the German Right – had clearly argued that the legal and political terminology developed with the rise of the nation-state in Europe has deep roots in the theological discourses of the Middle Ages and Enlightenment (Schmitt 1922: 9). Weber's modern, scientifically trained *Fachbeamter* in his inner consciousness is a Christian man. But what interests us here is the fact that Weber's explicit, scientific comparison of world religions, which is based on his concept of 'economic

216

ethics', not only implies an exposed position of modernity, as Habermas (1985) puts it, but in fact it also implies a hidden consolidation of a model of 'Christianised modernity'. Weber himself crystallizes the achievement of a transposition of Christianity into modernity. But first, contrary to Weber, Nietzsche criticised modernity and Christian methods of ethical devaluation which it brings to rule. He discovered that Christianity and its method of rationalisation leads to a combination of practical interest and ultimate ends. This combination, for Nietzsche, crystallizes a process of nihilism and decadence of Western culture giving the Christian method of tying, what he calls, the lowest interests to the highest purposes.

Weber essentialised, simplified and reversed the argument: 'No', he said, 'not only Christianity devalues culture, in the final instance disenchants nature, but all world religions do so'. In fact, one could claim that Weber's definition of religion comes exactly close to the point of disguising practical interest through the use of ultimate ends. While all world religions may ultimately combine these two separate spheres, they do not do it as cleverly as Christians do. In Weber's terms other religions do not achieve this combination so essentially, i.e. they do not tie their internal (e.g. external) existence to their practical attitudes in everyday life in a similarly radical way as Christianity. From this point of view it becomes clear that what distinguishes modern man from all others for Weber is his 'essentialistic' attitude towards all prevalent spheres and territories of social action. While this 'essentialistic' and ambiguous attitude of practicality and sacredness was seen by Nietzsche as the most disastrous and nihilistic one, for Weber it remained a most powerful tool of world domination. This essentialising attitude, which is achieved by the individual interested in self-preservation and distinction alike, indicates a real process of construction of modernity, of modern man (Stauth and Turner 1986). For all this it becomes clear that the problem of Islamisation has to be reviewed in terms of cross-cultural and global impacts of this process of creating modernity.

From Schlegel to Weber the pathway of the merging occidental rationalism encompassed a variety of subtle distinctions over what 'true' religion means and how simulative and ritualised practices may betray the depths of religious feeling. In modern occidental rationalism Islam has the connotation of superficiality, ritualised and simulative-obligatory religious leadership. For Weber, Calvin is a priest. He relates his inner, his eternal fate, to pragmatic, calculable ends in this world. With this essential internal attitude he transforms the drudgery of this world into a sacred existence in the Beyond. Calvin's conception of world mastery was directed accordingly against evil, the devil, the threat of fate, sex, and nature. In opposition to Calvinism, for Weber, Islam is the religion of accommodation. The true Muslim is affirmed by the will of God and not constantly threatened and controlled. Mohammed, the warrior, wanted world mastery. His warrior ethics were directed towards the physical conquest of this world. His desire was directed to the appearance, the 'physics' of things, not to the depth of metaphysics. In fact, all quotations of Weber on Islam and Mohammed, the

217

prophet, point to the belief that Islam is a religion of obligation and ritual, and not of understanding and reason (Turner 1974).

Going Native: Nativism and Legitimacy

Most sociological explorations of religious fundamentalism in the Third World, and specifically those undertaken with an anthropological or cultural theory perspective, tend to assume explicitly or implicitly that these fundamentalist movements are of a 'nativist' character. Mühlmann (1964) has made a cross-historical and cross-cultural study of such movements, which for him are to be described as 'reactive' against alien suppression and entail a self-reflective re-evaluation of traditional cultural values and a reverse interpretation of 'the world' aiming to destroy a given order of political power. Within such a perspective not only various Christian and even pagan African movements seem to be comparable, but also the various movements that have emerged in the legacy of Islam. In Germany, Mühlmann's approach to socio-religious movements was influential not only in the study of the Muslim-Brotherhood-Movement (Kandil 1983), but also in the study of Islamic revivalism in general (Tibi 1981). Thus, both the Mahdist and the more recent Shi'a movements in Iran have been compared as nativist and entailing a 'localist' character (Dekmejian 1980: 2; Johnson 1987). All these views on the Arab social movements seem to be significantly influenced by H.A.R. Gibb who relates the Muslim-Brotherhood-Movement of the 1930s and 1940s to Mahdism:

> In contrast to the modernists and the nationalists, who represent differing applications of Western concepts to the political problems of Islam, this is a popular movement, reflecting the native impulses of the Arab and Muslim mind. It is the true product of primitive Islamic romanticism with an emotional reason of its own. It is not a rational assertion that one type of political organisation is more desirable than another, but a revolt against what is felt to be in some particular relation an intolerable state of affairs.
>
> (Gibb 1947: 113)

It is interesting to note that the argument promoted by Gibb was never requestioned. Contemporary studies analysing the Islamic movements tend to repeat the same argument. Al-Banna, but also the Al-Jihad group are thus again understood as nativistic, chiliastic, and as a return to Islamic rules (see Dekmejian 1980; but also Hanafi 1982; Lutfi Al-Sayyid-Marsot 1984). Not to mention here that irrationality and nativism in this logic seem to bear a certain similarity. One could easily claim that these perspectives are leading to rather elitist assumptions because they deny the strong religious foundations of the modern Western world and of its social and political inclinations. But they also deny and overlook the strong secular commitments of such movements in overstressing the fundamentalist, nativist, chiliastic foundations of social movements and social action in these countries.

On the other side of the coin – although stressing exactly its local and reactive stance against Western sociology and its limitations – a remarkably similar movement of essentialising in the social sciences can be observed:

the 'going native of natives' (Semsek and Stauth 1987). In the case of the Arab world, regional strategies of 'indigenisation of the social sciences' have been proposed by various authors. Mursy et al. (1987) have pointed to the fact that these attempts have not yet produced an alternative position to Western methodology. The indigenous or native anthropology, which was born out of the dilemma related to the decolonisation problematic and the questioning of the very epistemological premises of the discipline, today creates a counter-reaction (Mursy et al. 1987). Mursy et al. have argued that so far this trend has not succeeded in producing a distinctive 'indigenous alternative', since it is closely related to the epistemological, methodological, and the political/ideological critique of Western social science. More often, those who have followed the 'indigenisation' perspective have substituted the epistemological with the political critique (ibid.: 6). Thus, as a whole, Western political science was entirely rejected to be replaced by Arab/Islamic sources. One might, however, be tempted to add that the 'indigenisation perspective' falls into the very trap of cultural globalisation against which it wants to stand up: the claim for cultural and scientific authenticity in local traditions is in itself a production of modernity. To reject modernity and to search for alternatives in tradition already presupposes participation in and knowledge of modern culture.

In Egypt one of the most representative figures of this intellectual attitude is the Egyptian economist 'Adil Hussein. 'Adil Hussein was previously a Marxist and wrote a widely read book about Egypt's dependency on the world market. He now argues that there exists an epistemological and conceptual break between East and West. This break runs parallel to the break between Islam and secularism (*dunyawiyya*). In defining this break, 'Adil Hussein puts 'faith' as the classificatory mechanism between East and West. What distinguishes the East from the West is the maintenance of faith. By borrowing the notion of *'umran* (the Ibn Khaldunian notion for fundamental, all-embracing civilisation) 'Adil Hussein attempts to furnish us with solutions to the crucial problem of Middle Eastern societies, namely, the problem of economic dependency.[2] According to 'Adil Hussein, the Islamic faith could be the guiding principle for economic development and for the control of consumerism ('Adil Hussein 1987: 354 f.). His thesis of the material West and the spiritual East is, of course, not new; it is an underlying pattern of argumentation of all discourses which attempt to reverse the orientalist perspective. This affirmative argument is maintained regardless of the same underlying pattern being part of many orientalist statements about the internal logic of Islamic religious attitudes. However, as a reaction to 'Adil Hussein's usage of this classificatory pattern, we could also take into consideration descriptions brought forward by an Egyptian thinker like Hussein Amin, who gives us a clear-cut picture of his confrontation with Islamic groups in a Western world, namely, fundamentalist groups in Houston, Texas, which confronted him with nearly the same classificatory pattern. Amin states:

...only that our thinkers are of that rudeness to talk about the materialism of the West and the spirituality of the East: the materialism of the West which produced to humanity

219

the music of Bach, the literature of Tolstoy, the paintings of Van Gogh, and the writings of Toynbee in history, and the spirituality of the East which created the adored by the masses *A.'A.* and *fadikha hanim harakat.*

(Amin 1978: 312)[3]

Within the perspective of indigenisation, various concepts that had been formally applied in the social and cultural life of the Middle East were now denied as being dubious and Western. Thus, the concept of a political party was denied as being appropriate for the Middle Eastern Islamic society. Likewise, the usage of the concept of *'umran'* replacing any concept of development and progress, has been revitalised as an indigenous expression in the Arab social sciences of the 1980s. This 'going native attitude' of Arab intellectuals, however, should be given a cautious analysis. There is no serious attempt to analyse the process of sociological production in Third World countries and in the West, while historical settings and relations between the two, such as confrontation, interaction or mutual influence are neglected.

One could point here to Bourdieu's call for the need to objectify the profession of the objectifiers (Bourdieu 1987: 44-5). Bourdieu suggests that we can reduce the field of intellectual production to a market where there exists a layer for competing forces and internal strategies. This market also has its own rules which define the game as a competition for social positions (ibid.). As for the Middle Eastern and, in particular, the Egyptian case, we could observe an immense liberalisation of academic life and social research during the 1970s and 1980s. This liberalisation brought Middle Eastern intellectuals into a position of strong competition with Western colleagues. However, their economic and social position never reached the affluent and dominating positions which Western colleagues might enjoy. Here arose the crucial point of a process of establishing an own competence in a position of bargaining for the 'real'. The bargaining process over resources of information became very important within this competition. One has to re-evaluate the attacks on foreign research and foreign scholarship, which have been put forward by Egyptian social scientists in the early 1980s, in the light of this competitive game. Here the 'indigenisation of social concepts' gave the social scientists of the region a new stance towards Western dominance.

The Decomposition of Secular Intellectualism

One of the striking elements of inter-cultural discourses in the social sciences in recent years is the phenomenon of Western admiration for the political spiritualism of the East. It was no other than Michel Foucault, the French social philosopher, who, in observing the mass protests against the modern instruments of death, expressed his deep admiration for what he called a new 'spiritual dimension in the political life' (Foucault 1978). For Foucault the revolutionary forces created by this religious spiritualism have marked a new stage of resistance against modern rationalism and power based on science and technology. Western social scientists and intellectuals, who were similarly impressed by Muslim revivalism, have too crudely and too quickly evoked perspectives and arguments which aimed at a decomposition of secular intellectualism in the Middle East. There exists, however, a strong tradition of secular critique of religion in the Middle East which is widely neglected. But, more specifically, intellectuals who have recently attempted to attack religious ideologies on the grounds of materialist and historicist critiques, have had little response among Western colleagues. In fact, they have even been criticised by Western social scientists. Here Etienne's book *L'islamisme radical* (1987) is a case in its own right. This disenchanted Marxist, who claims that his old methodology and scientific perspective led him to misunderstand the social and cultural developments of the Middle East, is now trying to construct a new 'Orient', where the time of social interaction and social space are reinterpreted in terms of a new religious symbolism: 'The Koran as the Practice' (1987: 49). Here, radical Islam is presented as the salvation of society. Etienne considers the Islamists as 'radicals' by their re-reading of the history of the Orient and the West (ibid.: 20). He considers Islam as the religion of mass mobilisation. He argues that the construction of an Islamic society in agreement with its religious morality remains the only civilisatory project in the Middle East (ibid.: 67). Again his underlying argument is that nationalism has failed as a secular ideology because of its incapacity to relate to the historical forces inherent in the region. This is, however, a deep misunderstanding of the significant role of the nation-state. The symbolic and discursive patterns and the power games related to the nation-state culture are much more important than Etienne suggests. As Aziz El-Azmeh puts it:

> Islam cannot be regarded as filling a gap created by the failure of nationalism. Nationalism never failed, it was transformed, incorporated within the state, its deeper appeal is still alive among some of the groups which it formerly mobilized.
>
> (El-Azmeh 1979:6)

Islamism has to be understood mainly as a new turn in the discourses of power and nation-state within the framework of an inter-cultural exchange between East and West.

Middle Eastern secular intellectuals who claim to scientifically observe the internal motion of their societies easily become victims of an 'essentialist' understanding of the social forces behind 'Islamism'. For example, Afaf Lutfi Al-Sayyid-Marsot (1984) argues that in contrast to all other political movements of the early and the middle twentieth century in Egypt, the Muslim-Brotherhood-Movement, with its strong religious involvement, was the only political force which referred to an indigenous cultural tradition. Lutfi Al-Sayyid-Marsot is in agreement here with Western observers who would interpret any reference to religion as a form of revitalisation of cultural traditions. In fact, what Lutfi Al-Sayyid-Marsot and Western observers forget, is that the Muslim-Brotherhood-Movement emerged precisely in the period when Italian and German fascism increased. In fact, many of the Muslim Brothers had been deeply inspired by the aestheticism and structures of Nazi organisations (Heyworth-Dunne 1950:58).[4] Here, we do not want to deny the strength and popularity of the Muslim Brothers before 1952. However, to

221

reduce this political trend to an 'indigenous' and 'nativist' one would devalue their efficient organisational structures and political claims.

Both Western and Eastern secular observers have developed an attitude toward Islamism as if it were the only authentic alternative that is able to create a 'real' or 'true' form of political legitimation. To return to Lutfi Al-Sayyid-Marsot:

> ... the question one needs to ask is whether the involvement in these movements was (and is) a truly religious one. If one looks upon religion as *din* and *dunya*, then all aspects of life are matters of religion. Men's relationships with men are as much matters of religious interest as men's relationship with God. When the laws of a Muslim society, such as Egypt, are built on caprice, whim, or the interests of the few – as many of the more recent laws were – then an alternative source of legitimacy will be sought. Those who are disadvantaged and ask for justice will do so on the basis of the *sharia* and of religious principles, since the *sharia* stands above the ruler and his cohorts. To say, that a law passed by the People's Assembly is unjust, is a matter of opinion and open to dispute. To say, that a law passed by the People's Assembly [is] in contrast to the *sharia*, is to render it nil and void.
>
> (Lutfi Al-Sayyid-Marsot 1984: 551)

Here again, an important statement is made without attempting to understand that the whole discourse over Islam (both within the Nasser period as well as during the Sadat regime) was embedded in the central state discourse. In Egypt, it was not the masses who called for the introduction of the *shari'a islamiyya* as a matter of social justice; but rather the fact that the Muslim Brothers would have strongly backed the application of the Islamic *shari'a* even if it would have been promoted by Sufi Abu Taleb, a man of the regime (see Zaqariyya 1986: 87).[5] The initial policies of the Sadat regime intended to re-erect religious symbolism as a part of the state discourse in order to deconstruct Nasserist and communist appeals to the masses. Here, the state made itself a social movement, as Baber Johansen (1981) put it, and competed over the social conditions for the definition of the 'true' religious involvement of the 'real' social masses. Religious language, therefore, overflowed official discourses, but also affected the disputes of the opposition.

In coming to a judgement on 'the real religious involvement of these movements', we could take into consideration the statement of Abdallah Laroui, who argues 'that orientalists and salafists have both agreed that Islam is a theocracy. However, they have not defined whether this is a reality or a utopia. Islam, they say, is *din wa dawla* (religion and state). The importance, of course, is to define the sense of the conjunction which does not imply a total identity' (1987: 33f.). Laroui argues that thinkers like Ibn Khaldun were realists in seeing the brutality of the state which was based on military coercion. Here, for him, arises the concept of the state as a necessary evil, an indispensable means of life of man as a natural, animal being. But these thinkers have always clearly stated that humanity can improve and develop itself spiritually only outside the framework of the state. For Ibn Khaldun the state was not to be moralised or religiously rationalised. For him the state is a reality, and thus a necessity, but it never can acquire a religious form of legitimacy. Laroui argues that in Islamic orthodoxy – different from any European understanding of state legitimacy – *'umma* and state (community and state) are, in fact, contradicting themselves, they totally ignore each other (Laroui 1987: 33 ff.). Contrary to Al-Sayyid-Marsot's argument, which is also supported by Lewis and many other Arab and Western social scientists, namely, that Islam is state, religion and power, community and polity (Lewis 1984: 11–2),[6] it becomes clear from the writings of Laroui, but also from Arkoun (1984), that there always existed separations and nuances betwen *din*, *dawla*, and *wa duniya* (religion, state and life, i.e. civil matters), and that these separations have been systematically neglected by all Western orientalists.

It would, indeed, be a rather complex task to show in this context and in detail that the rationalisation process associated with the rise of the nation-state in Europe was always closely linked with religious fundamentalism. But we should be aware that underlying patterns of this religiously founded state discourse in the West might lead us to misunderstand the nature of 'modernity' in social movements and to trace them in an 'Islamic' tradition.

Against the Politics of an Islamic Imagery

Where then can we today trace the reasons and causes by which Muslims 'essentialise' their religious feeling, their religious traditions, and all spheres of social cultural interaction and of public space? How can one explain the public attitude of defending an 'essentialist' usage of Islamic symbols, gestures, and cultural meanings? Our argument here is that the types and forms of cultural valuations employed by the new fundamentalist movements cannot be explained by an analysis of the tradition of Islamic religion and history; it has to be seen as an effect of inter-cultural exchange which is fundamentally based on a Western understanding of Islam as the culture of the Other. To speak today about Islamic fundamentalism also means to speak about the emergence of a new 'orientalism' which attempts to reconstruct new images of the East. The habitus of the individual, and the many time and space relations are now re-interpreted in a Bourdieu-type analysis of religious symbolism, constructed over sacred and profane social spheres. Thus, the veil, the mosque, the public bath, the magical and mystical usage of space, the rediscovery of the 'old men' of true Islam, who are not understood by the young generation, are drawn into our consciousness. Here again, in a way similar to the politics of Islamism, religious symbols are used, but in a purified aesthetic way. The symbolic conquest of social space is idealised within a religious imagery.

In the West, Gilsenan's book *Recognizing Islam* (1982) is fascinating to read, but the new reading of Islam on the aesthetic and mysticised level coincides with the political conquest of public space by religious movements in the semi-industrial societies of the East. The politics of Islam coincide with the symbolic aestheticisation of the 'Orient' in the West. The causes and effects in the first instance still have to be discovered. Which came first: The politics of imagery or the Islamists' politicisation? Foucault's of the religious spirituality of the Iranian Revolution as perhaps the only adequate form of revolution in a totalised modernity can also be interpreted as a re-translation of the historical message which was brought into Islam. Foucault translated the appearance of a bodily resistance of the masses against a coercive military machinery in terms of the religious spirituality of the West.

In this framework of Foucault's analysis of the Iranian Revolution (when he worked as a journalist during 1978 and 1979 for European newspapers), the new interpretations of Islamic movements in Egypt and North Africa by Kepel (1984) and Etienne (1987) took on a new dimension. In fact, both Etienne's and Kepel's reinterpretation of fundamentalist groups could be understood in the light of Foucault's readings of the Iranian Revolution and its impact upon the French left. Kepel's understanding of the *Jihad* and the prisoners of *Takfir wal Higra* remained linked to an image of the 'organic intellectual' who, only through his religious spirituality, is able to resist the coercive apparatus of an unjust regime. Both Western and national observers have thus started to exaggerate the historical mission of these groups as a historical alternative to an illegitimate regime. Some intellectuals have only recently raised their voices in demystifying the so-called progressive character of both the Islamic 'revolutionaries' and the Islamising trends within the society as a whole. Although these voices could be labelled as both Muslim and liberal secular[7] thinkers, they have been strongly attacking the wave of fundamentalism and have put stress upon its terrorist dimension. Both Fuda and Zaqariyya have pointed to the danger of confusing between what people think of as revolutionary Islam and petro-Islam, which has very little to do with progressive thoughts.

Authors like Hussein Amin (1987), Fuad Zaqariyya (1986, 1987), and Farag Fuda (1985, 1986), although differing in their political thought, are presenting interesting critiques of the new movements based on both the secular and religious facts and texts of Islamic history. Thus, authors raised their voices against the widespread interpretations of a Western trained intellectual, like Hassan Hanafi.[8] He argued that the al-Jihad group takes the same historical stance as the scholars of Muslim law, the *fuqaha*, 'in defending the authentic (*'asil*) against the newly introduced (*dakhil*), the "doctrine" against polytheism, and the pure text (*al-nass al-kham*) against new interpretation (*ta'wil*). These *al-Jihad*-groups are, like the *fuqaha*, people of imitation of tradition (*ahl al-naql*) and not people of reason (*ahl al-aql*). He says that even if these groups are fanatical and narrow-minded, they still express an Islamic authenticity' (Zaqariyya: 1986: 51-2).[9] Against Hassan Hanafi's arguments, Fuad Zaqariyya has expressed serious reservations. He poses the question: Why does Hanafi relate imitation to authenticity and refuses to relate reason to authenticity? Zaqariyya also poses the question: Why does Hanafi relate the *fuqaha*, the people of imitation, to the nation-state, as the defenders of the *'umma* and orthodoxy, while all the rational traditions of Islamic history and, specifically of Islamic philosophy, remain totally suppressed? In other words, why is Islamic philosophy not used as a possible source of authenticity? Hanafi, who himself claims to be a translator of Islam into a modern revolutionary perspective, is demystifyed here as merely posing questions in terms of a reactionary, historical tradition of Islamic orthodoxy.

It is a well-known fact, both in orientalist and in Islamic studies of social history, that the *fuqaha* have essentially been linked with the dominating state powers and the classes organised within it. According to Fuad Zaqariyya, if one reads the text of the al-Jihad very closely, *The Absent Pillar (al-farida al-gha'iba)*, one would realise that Hanafi has given very little notice to the most frightening passages of this text, which relate to methods of employing violence against the enemy, the ambiguity of the definition of the enemy through a broad interpretation of *dar al-kufr* (the house of the non-believers) and the sectarian language they use in general.[10] As Zaqariyya and others have put it, the Islamic movement cannot be understood as a pure reaction to the Westernisation of the Sadat era, but rather as its own mirror. It is seen that its limitations and oblivion to history has led it to take the same discursive nihilism which was present in this era. It is the mediocrity of the state which created such a mediocre resistance, argues Zaqariyya:

> The phenomenon is indeed a direct expression revealing that the intellectual decadence has reached its peak and that the authoritarian tendency which has for thirty years demystified consciousness has come to its natural end. The same intellectual atmosphere which made Tharwad Abaza Egypt's first novelist, Anis Mansur and Mustafa Mahmud the most important thinkers and Ahmad 'Adawiyya the most popular singer, is the one which also produced Islamic militance and made them the most popular movement among the youth.
>
> (Zaqariyya 1986: 115)

With these discussions, Zaqariyya points to a general observation which is very important in this context. It is, in fact, not only Hassan Hanafi, but also many Western observers, who point to various political and social trends within the region as authentic if they have an Islamic and oriental appearance, notwithstanding in this context the fact that the 'Islamic' or 'oriental' appearances in most cases have already been produced in a sphere of inter-cultural exchange between the West and the East; they have been largely a product of global mass cultural relations. The search for authenticity within the creation of modernity is, however, not only an Islamic phenomenon. It is a topic of its own right which has been witnessed and discussed at length in the discourse of modernity as arising in the European social philosophy of the 1920s.

Conclusion

We have attempted to demonstrate that the so-called 'indigenisation' and 'Islamisation' of the social sciences have their equivalent in Western anthropology and Middle Eastern studies. The critique of traditional orientalism and the attempts to 'do less injustice to people' have – opposite to what they intended – contributed to a new form of orientalism. The corollary of this 'going native' attitude is that it does refuse to analyse its conceptual elaboration within the framework of the general field of sociological production. Many of the concepts used by Islamism were, in fact, created by orientalists. For example, it is often argued that the Salafi movement today, being confronted with modernity, is in search of an identity. It is interesting to note that this attempt at a decolonisation process does, indeed, fall into the same epistemological impasse which orientalists have faced. Here Laroui is quite right in ranging orientalists and Salafis on the same level of reasoning (Laroui 1987). Against the orientalist tradition, which explains contemporary phenomena with dogma and relates to history in an ahistorical way, we argue that we cannot understand religious fundamentalism today in terms of nativism and chilialism. Indeed, further research is needed in order to compare such movements with analogous ones in South-East Asia, where different religions are witnessing similar forms of 'revivalism'. There we can easily recognise the similarity existing between such movements as well as the non-specificity of Islamic fundamentalism.

We have to recognise the fact that we live in a global world today, which has already shaped and transformed 'traditional' structures and values. The paradox of Western secularism, namely, that it was brought about by religious fundamentalism, should not lead us to assume a universality of deeply rooted Christian connotations. In fact, one cannot deny that the Christian/Islamic confrontation led to a mutual negation of the Other, but we also have to consider that this process of negation implied mechanisms of 'essentialising' the imagined past.

Authenticity, the return to tradition, is in modern times no less modern than modernity itself. It can only lead to the mythologising of the past. In order to establish a critical historical analysis of Islam, it is necessary to take such processes of cross-cultural interpretation into consideration. In this context, we should consider that Said's knowledge/power concept (1978), which led to rather nihilistic consequences, should be re-evaluated in the light of Mohammad Arkoun's statement:

> Knowledge is to foresee, in order to obtain power. However, to be powerful, one should start by knowledge, and one cannot know without the condition of liberating oneself from the obsession of power.
>
> (Arkoun 1984: 49)

Postscript

It is not by pure chance that after having concluded our article we refer to Sivan's *Radical Islam* (1985) who, strikingly enough, has argued that the dangerous potentialities of Islamic radicalism could be rooted in the 'rise of a selective receptivity to modernism permeated by a spirit of essentialism (or orientalism in reverse, to quote Sadiq Jalal al-'Azm)' (Sivan 1985: 181).

Sivan's assessments of the potentialities of the Islamic movement are, nevertheless, too simple, in that he eliminates the distinctions between the social forces expressed in secularism, popularism, and popular culture and the Islamic tradition. Sivan again bases Islamic radicalism on the bedrocks of traditionalism and, thus, completely ignores the role of the nation-state in shaping and influencing the religious discourse as well as its religious opponents.

Notes

1. This study will tackle some, but not all, of the discourses produced about Islamic fundamentalism.

2. 'Adil Hussein was previously a Marxist who wrote a very important book about Egypt's dependency on the world market. Today he identifies himself with the Labour Party *Hizb al'Amal*, which is an extension of the young Egyptian Party *Misr al-Fatat*; this party manifested populist fascist tendencies but also socialist ones. 'Adil Hussein is now the chief editor of the newspaper *al-Sha'ab*.

3. Which could be named Ahmad 'Adawiyya, an Egyptian folk mass cultural singer, beloved by the masses, but known for a very vulgar tongue, and also beloved by the millions which Amin calls *fadikha hanim harakat*, *fadikha* standing for scandal, *hanim* standing for madam and *harakat* standing for the belly dance movements.

4. Although it is often argued that Hassan al-Banna was strongly inspired by Sufism, he, however, clearly differentiated himself from them and created a new type of organisation. 'I did not want to enter into competition with the other orders, and I did not want to be confined to one group of Muslims or one aspect of Islamic reform, rather I sought that it be a general message based on learning, education and Jihad' (Mitchell 1969: 215). In fact, both Heyworth-Dunne and Mitchell demonstrate that Hassan al-Banna was a brilliant orator and organiser. He acquired both Western and Islamic methods of propaganda and employed modern microphone techniques. The organisation of the party, conference, ceremonies, and press propaganda reveal that the rationalisation of the organisation did not differ from any Western or Egyptian political party during that period (Heyworth-Dunne 1950: 16, 30, 58, 59; Mitchell 1969: 163-84).

5. For a similar argument, see Ibrahim (1982) and Hanafi (1982) who, due to the success of the Iranian Revolution, have started to re-read the history of the Muslim Brotherhood as representing the only authentic oppositional movement in the political arena. Within the framework of this argument Islam, as a revolutionary alternative, was also brought forth.

6. It is interesting to note that there exists on the discursive level a divorce between previous studies undertaken by political scientists and economists, which analysed the development and changes of the colonial and new independent states, and the recent works analysing the role of the state vis-à-vis the fundamentalist dilemma. These recent studies basically refer to the static ideal notion of the state in Sunni Islam as an absolute category and totally ignore the changes which occurred in the infrastructure of the economy. Here, again, most of the observers encountered the problem of historical analysis.

7. We would like to point here to the secular tendency which also includes many journalists and writers who in recent times have courageously expressed their thoughts in the official press. We could mention here Yussif Idris, Makram Mohammad Ahmad, Ahmad Baha'a ad-Din and 'Abdel Rahman al-Sharqawi. The debate has been polarised with the flourishing of the Islamic investment companies. Rosa al-Yussuf, but also al-Ahram, al-Iqtissadi, are periodicals which have recently conducted a fierce attack against these companies as being engaged in semi-criminal activities (hashish-dealing, smuggling hard currency, Mafiosi-type activities of monopolising the property market), and against the economist 'Adil Hussein who has reported these companies as serving the national interest (see e.g. Rosa al-Yussuf 1987).

8. Hassan Hanafi has introduced to Egypt the writings of the Imam Khomeini and A'li Shariati. He was among the first intellectuals to claim the progressive Islamic trends for the Left Islam (see Al-Yasar al-Islami [The Islamic Left], Cairo 1981).

9. Zaqariyya quotes Hanafi without specifying the reference. However, a more subtle and and more developed elaboration of Hanafi's argument can be found in Hanafi's recent study on *From Belief to Revolution* (1988, Vol. 1: Chs. 1 and 2).

10. Similarly, Sa'ad ad-Din Ibrahim has argued that during the Sadat period the Muslim Brothers were (according to him) the most important resistance and critical group

of '*al-Da'wa*'. The magazine published virulent articles on Sadat's visit to Jerusalem and the peace treaty with Israel (Ibrahim 1982: 85). However, in referring to that, Ibrahim does not comment upon the language used by the Muslim Brothers. They seem, in fact, to understand the Arab-Israeli conflict as a war of religion. Strongly anti-semitic but also anti-communist tones are manifested. Western states are portrayed as imperialist crusaders. They are thus simplifying the socio-economic dimensions of the conflict.

References in Arabic

'AMIN, Hussein. 1987. *Dalil al-muslim al-hazin* (Guide of the Sad Muslim), 2nd Edn. Cairo: Maktabat Madbuli.

FUDA, Farag. 1985. *Qabl as suqut* (Before the Collapse). Cairo: Dar al-Kutub.

FUDA, Farg. 1986. *al-Haqiqa al-gha'iba* (The Missing Truth). Dar al-fiqr lid-dirasat wan-nashr.

HANAFI, H. 1981. 'ad-Din wal-tanmiya fi-misr' (Religion and Development in Egypt), in *Misr fi rub'a qarn 1952-1977* (Egypt in 25 Years, 1952-1977). Beirut: Ma'had al-inma' al-'arabi.

HANAFI, Hassan. 1988. *min al-aqida ila-thawra* (From Belief to Revolution), 2 vols. Cairo: Maktaba Madbuli.

HUSSEIN, 'Adil. 1985. 'al-Turath wa mustaqbal al-tanmiya' (Heritage and the Future of Development), in *Tiknulugia tanimiyat al-mugtama' al-'arabi* (Technology of Development of the Arab Society), al-Marqaz al-iqlimi al-'arabi lil-buhuth wal w/tawthiq fil-'ulum al igtima'iya al-'arabiya lil-dirasat wal nashr. Cairo, November 9–10.

rosa al-yussuf. 1987. 'intiqadat li-ra'is tahrir ash-sha'ab, bi-sabab difa'ihi 'an sharikat tawdhif al-amwal' (Islamic investment companies are threatening the national security). September, 28.

ZAQARIYYA, Fu'ad. 1986. *al-Haqiqa wal wahm fil-haraqa al-islamiya al-mu'asira* (Reality and Fiction in the Contemporary Islamic Movement). Cairo: Dar al-fikr lid-dirasat wal nashr wal tawzi'.

ZAQARIYYA, Fu'ad. 1987. *as-sahwa al-islamiya fi mizan al-'aql* (Islamic Revivalism in the Light of Reason). Cairo: Dar al fikr al-mu'asir.

References in European Languages

ABDEL MALEK, A. 1963. 'L'orientalisme en crise'. *Diogène* (Oct./Dec.): 109–142.

AL-'AZM, S.J. 1981. 'Orientalism and Orientalism in Reverse'. *Khamsin* 8: 5–26

ARKOUN, M. 1964. 'L'islam vu par le professeur G.E.V. Grunebaum'. *Arabica* 2. Leiden.

ARKOUN, M. 1970. *Contribution à l'étude de l'humanisme arabe au IV-IX siècle, Miskawayh philosophe et historien*. Paris: J. Vriu, Librairie philosophique.

ARKOUN, M. 1984. *Pour une critique de la raison Islamique*. Paris: Maisonneuve et Larose.

BAUDRILLARD, J. 1970. *La société de consommation, ses mythes, ses structures*. Paris: S.G.P.P.

BAUDRILLARD, J. 1972. *Pour une critique de l'économie politique du signe*. Paris: Gallimard.

BAUDRILLARD, J. 1978. *Die Agonie des Realen*. Berlin: Merve.

BAUDRILLARD, J. 1982. *Der symbolische Tausch und der Tod*. Munich: Matthes und Seitz.

BOURDIEU, P. 1980. *Le sens pratique*. Paris: Les Editions de Minuit.

BOURDIEU, P. 1987. *Choses dites*. Paris: Les Editions de Minuit.

DEKMEJIAN, R.H. 1980. 'The Anatomy of Islamic Revival: Legitimacy, Crisis, Ethnic Conflict and the Search for Islamic Alternatives'. *Middle East Journal* 34.

DJAIT, H. 1974. *L'Europe et l'Islam*. Paris: Seuil.

EL-AZMEH, A. 1979. 'Islam Histories, Icons, Politics'. Unpublished paper.

ENDRESS, G. 1982. *Einführung in die islamische Geschichte*. Munich: Beck.

ETIENNE, B. 1987. *L'Islamisme radical*. Paris: Hachete.

FEATHERSTONE, M. 1987. 'Consumer Culture, Symbolic Power and Universalism', in Stauth, G. and Zubaida, S. (eds)., *Mass Culture, Popular Culture and Social Life in the Middle East*. Boulder, Colo.: Westview Press.

FOUCAULT, M. 1978. 'A quoi rêvent les Iraniens?'. *Le Nouvel Observateur*. October 16.

228

FREUND, W. 1987. 'Jüdischer und islamischer Fundamentalismus: Entsprechungen, politische Konsequenzen'. *Der Orient* 28 (2): 216–228.

GEERTZ, C. 1968. *Islam Observed: Religious Development in Morocco and Indonesia.* Chicago: University of Chicago Press.

GEERTZ, C. 1973. *The Interpretation of Cultures, Selected Essays.* New York: Basic Books.

GEERTZ, C. 1976a. *The Religion of Java.* Chicago: Chicago University Press.

GEERTZ, C. 1976a [1960]. *The Religion of Java.* Chicago: Chicago University Press. Understanding', in Basso, K.H. and Selby, H.A. (eds.), *Meaning in Anthropology.* Albuquerque: University of New Mexico Press.

GIBB, H.A.R. 1947. *Modern Trends in Islam.* Chicago: Chicago University Press.

GILSENAN, M.R. 1982. *Recognizing Islam.* London: Croom Helm.

HABERMAS, J. 1985. *Der philosophische Diskurs der Moderne.* Frankfurt: Suhrkamp.

HANAFI, H. 1982. 'The Relevance of the Islamic Alternative in Egypt'. *Arab Studies Quarterly* 4 (1/2).

HANAFI, H. 1985. 'Des idéologies modernistes à l'Islam révolutionnaire'. *Peuples méditerranéens* (Oct./Dec.): 3–15.

HEYWORTH-DUNNE, J. 1950. *Religions and Political Trends in Modern Egypt.* Washington: Brentano.

HOBART, M. 1986. 'Introduction: Context, Meaning, and Power', in Hobart, M. and Taylor, R. (eds.), *Context Meaning and Power in Southeast Asia.* Ithaca, N.Y.: Cornell University Press.

HOBART, M. 1987. 'The Elixir of Morality: Towards a Balinese Economy of Death'. Paper presented at the EIDOS Workshop: The Economy as a System of Meaning, Sociology of Development Research Centre, Bielefeld, July 10-11.

HOURANI, A.H. 1980. *Europe and the Middle East.* London: St. Antony's.

IBRAHIM, S.E. 1982. 'An Islamic Alternative in Egypt. The Muslim Brotherhood and Sadat'. *Arab Studies Quarterly* 4 (1/2).

JANZ, C.P. 1981. *Friedrich Nietzsche: Eine Biographie,* 3 vols. Munich: Hauser.

JOHANSEN, B. 1981. 'Islam und Staat im Kapitalismus'. *Das Argument* 129/130: 690–703 and 787–811.

JOHNSON, N. 1987. 'Religious Paradigms of the Sudanese Mahdiya'. *Ethnohistory* 25 (2): 159–178.

KANDIL, F. 1983. *Nativismus in der Dritten Welt. Wiederentdeckung der Tradition als Modell für die Gegenwart.* St. Michael: Bläschke.

KEPEL, G. 1984. *Le prophète et le pharaon. Les mouvements Islamistes dans l'Egypte contemporaine.* Paris: La Découverte.

LAROUI, A. 1973. 'For a Methodology of Islamic Studies'. *Diogenes* 83: 12–39.

LAROUI, A. 1987. *Islam et Modernité.* Paris: La Découverte.

LEWIS, B. ed. 1984. *The World of Islam.* London: Thames and Hutchinson.

LUTFI AL-SAYYID-MARSOT, A. 1984. 'Religion or Opposition: Urban Protest Movements in Egypt'. *International Journal of Middle East Studies* 16 (4): 541–552.

MITCHELL, R.P. 1969. *The Society of the Muslim Brothers.* Oxford: Oxford University Press.

MURSY, S., NELSON, C., SAAD LUKA, R. and SHOLKAMY, H. 1987. 'Anthropology and the Call for Indigenization of Social Science in the Arab World'. Unpublished paper.

MÜHLMANN, W.E. 1961. *Chiliasmus und Nativismus.* Berlin: Reimer.

MÜHLMANN, W.E. 1964. *Rassen, Ethnien, Kulturen.* Berlin/Neuwied: Luchterhand.

PETERS, R. 1987. 'Islamischer Fundamentalismus: Glaube, Handeln, Führung', in Schluchter, W. (ed.), *Max Webers Sicht des Islam.* Frankfurt: Suhrkamp.

RODINSON, M. 1968. *Islam and Capitalism.* London: Penguin.

ROSEN, L. 1984. *Bargaining for Reality: The Construction of Social Relations in a Muslim Community.* Chicago: University of Chicago Press.

ROUSSILLON, A. 1988. 'Islam, Islamisme et démocratie: la recomposition du champ politique en Egypte'. *Peuples Méditerranéens* 41–42: 303–341.

SAHLINS, M. 1976. *Culture and Practical Reason.* Chicago: University of Chicago Press.

SAID, E.W. 1978. *Orientalism*. New York: Vintage Books.
SCHLUCHTER, W. 1987. 'Einleitung: Zwischen Welteroberung und Weltanpassung. Überlegungen zu Max Webers Sicht des frühen Islam', in Schluchter, W. (ed.), *Max Webers Sicht des Islam*. Frankfurt: Suhrkamp.
SCHMITT, C. 1922. *Politische Theologie: Vier Kapitel der Lehre von der Souveränität*. Munich: Duncker & Humblot.
SEMSEK, H.-G. and STAUTH, G. 1987. *Lebenspraxis, Alltagserfahrung und soziale Konflikte in Kairoer Slums*. Stuttgart: Steiner.
SIVAN, E. 1985. *Radical Islam, Medieval Theology, and Modern Politics*. New Haven: Yale University Press.
STAUTH, G. and TURNER, B.S. 1986. 'Nietzsche in Weber oder die Geburt des Genius im professionellen Menschen'. *Zeitschrift für Soziologie* 15 (2): 81–94.
STAUTH, G. 1988. 'Innerlichkeit und Fremdkultur. Das Islambild im okzidentalen Rationalismus' ('Essentialism' and the Culture of the Other. The Image of Islam in Occidental Rationalism). Mimeograph. University of Bielefeld.
TROELTSCH, E. 1966. *Aufsätze zur Geistesgeschichte und Religionssoziologie*. Edited by Hans Baron. Aalen: Scientia Verlag.
TURNER, B.S. 1974. *Weber and Islam*. London: Routledge and Kegan Paul.
TURNER, B.S. 1978. *Marx and the End of Orientalism*. London: George Allen and Unwin.
WAARDENBURG, J. 1963. *L'Islam dans le miroir de l'Occident*. The Hague: Mouton.
WEBER, M. 1920. *Gesammelte Aufsätze zur Religionssoziologie*. Tübingen: J.C.B. Mohr.
WEBER, M. 1956. *Sociology of Religion*. Boston: Beacon Press.
WEBER, M. 1958. *The Protestant Ethic and the Spirit of Capitalism*. New York: Scribner's.
WITTFOGEL, K.A. 1962. *Die orientalische Despotie*. Cologne: Kiepenheru & Witsch.

WORLD MOVEMENTS

If now we can affirm the existence of one world society, not simply as the ideal of humanity but as a material fact, it follows that the full range of social processes which sociologists have identified may be studied in their global extent.

In consequence, 'international sociology' no longer refers only to the activities of the international community of sociologists, it also takes on a much more substantive content as a branch of the discipline which deals with global processes.

Globalisation is a more comprehensive concept than the older one of internationalisation and better expresses the most recent trends in the creation of one world. Certainly an international sociology, in the sense of a branch of the discipline, deals with the facts of internationalisation, relations between states, the creation of supra-national bodies, migration across national boundaries and the growth of an international class. But it also deals with processes which do not merely cross national boundaries or link states, but which rely on worldwide communication in commerce, science, journalism and entertainment. For this reason we can speak of the globalisation of consciousness.

We have chosen social movements as an illustration of the content and direction of the newly emerging international sociology because they have always had an ambiguous relationship with sociological paradigms which posit societies as the units of analysis. Their character in relation to social institutions, their often inchoate organisation and shrouded origins and the mysteries of individual commitment, have all suggested social psychological explanations might be the most fruitful.

But additionally movements, in their aspirations to realise values and promote ideal states, have regularly found national boundaries either irrelevant or obstacles to be surmounted. 'Internationalism' and 'movement' were two terms which were soon associated with each other after their widespread reception in the nineteenth century and found their most prominent joint usage in the 'International Workingmen's Movement'. However, there is a growing sense among sociologists that in the last decade movements have undergone a change which we may possibly sum up as the shift from internationalism to globalism.

It was probably the student movement and events of 1968, in particular, which resensitised sociologists to the international dimensions of movements. Broadly similar events seemed to occur relatively independently in widely dispersed centres, but whether by diffusion of ideas, or through similar responses to like structural conditions, or some combination of both, has never been agreed. But it was no longer possible to ignore the international dimension.

More recent movements in the eighties, in particular the latest form of the women's movement, the peace movement and the green movement have manifested such levels of cross-national contact and consciousness that diffusionist/structural alternatives are no longer adequate for grasping the change. The three papers which follow indicate the new directions in which analysis may be pursued.

Johan Galtung's analysis of the Green Movement in Western Europe comprises some of the more traditional approaches, i.e. he identifies the relative strength of the movement in different countries and also the sources of recruitment and here crucially Galtung identifies marginalised groups, outside the mainstream of society. At the same time, he argues that the Western social formation is undergoing a transformation.

It is in this transformational context that the main feature of Green thought, namely holistic thinking, takes on its full significance as an umbrella for all kinds of more partial movements and as something which transcends particular interests. Galtung suggests this was anticipated by socialist humanism, but the impression he conveys is that this is a feature which is much more central to the Green movement than the old idealism was to the socialist movement. In this way, he effectively identifies a consciousness which relates to the social formation as a whole and not to individuals' various positions within it.

Artur Meier's account of the Peace Movement shares with Galtung's an emphasis on the umbrella nature of the movement and its non-class basis, but he gives even more explicit expression to the view that it is a qualitatively new phenomenon, not a mere summation of different national movements, but a genuine international actor, the counterpart and adversary of the worldwide military-industrial complex. It has a global social network, creates a new political culture and becomes a factor in the transformation of world society.

This sense of the emergence of qualitatively new forms of social movement incites Zsuzsa Hegedus to seek for a new conceptual framework beyond what she considers the outdated formulations of the seventies. She argues that there has been a 'planetarisation' of practices which had hitherto been thought to be confined to the first world, and that in the West it is the international arena which is the focus for the new movements.

From her own research Hegedus finds that the key point in the new movements is the assertion of citizen empowerment to manage individual and collective destinies, both with respect to domestic and transnational issues. With the new movements 'by their genuinely new manner of *individualising* planetary problems, they "*globalise*" individuals throughout the world' (269).

The lessons we can draw from these accounts of the new social movements are profound for the direction of our scientific activity. The boundaries of nation-states are even less appropriate for setting limits to our search for explanations than they were. The universalism of sociology is now faced with the reality of international society. Only the collected and cooperative activities of the world community of sociologists could possibly measure up to its interpretation.

THE GREEN MOVEMENT: A SOCIO-HISTORICAL EXPLANATION*

Johan Galtung

1. A Problem, Three Approaches

The Green Movement is puzzling people today, particularly when it takes the form of a Green Party, and most particularly in connection with the German party, by far the most important one, *Die Grünen*. They are said to be unpredictable and unable/unwilling to make any compromises with any other actors on the party-political scene; consequently they are not really in politics, they are only political. For a party launched in 1981, to break through the 5% barrier (they made 5.6%) already in the elections of March 1983 and then move on to 7, 8 and 9% in subsequent elections, is already an achievement and leads to three obvious hypotheses about the future: the Greens will continue their comet-like career; they will find their natural level as a party below 10%, but possibly still above 5%; they will dwindle down to zero again which is where they belong.

The following is an effort to explore the phenomenon, particularly directed at listeners and readers very used to conceiving of politics in terms of blue and red; market forces, protected by conservative parties, and *étatiste* forces with planning and redistribution protected by socialist parties; both of them found in democratic and dictatorial versions. The Greens are obviously different, neither blue nor red, neither dicatatorial nor democratic in the parliament-arian sense of that word. In spite of participating in parliamentary elections,

* Originally presented as a lecture at FLACSO, Santiago, Chile, December 1984 and at the Gujarat Vidyapith, Ahmedabad, India, January 1985.

mass action, direct democracy, local autonomy, self-reliance and so on are obviously closer to their heart.[1]

Hence, what do they stand for, where do they come from, and who are they? This paper does not claim to have conclusive or any novel answers to these questions, but they are certainly worth exploring: the Greens have probably come here to stay, and to expand. Hence, three analytical approaches: *ideological, historical* and *sociological*; not necessarily compatible, not necessarily contradictory, but well suited to shed some light on the phenomenon.

2. The Green Movement: An Ideological Characterisation

The reader will find on the next page 'A Survey of Green Policies', divided into twenty points, organised in packages with four points each. The mainstream characteristics in First World societies are then confronted with their counter-points, Green policies and movements. The list is self-explanatory, suffice it here only to add some remarks about how the list came into being.[2]

The point of departure is a simple model of mainstream society with an economic basis, a military basis and a structural basis. The latter is particularly important for this is where the pillars of the Western social formation are found: the State with its bureaucracy and its plans, Capital with its corporations and its markets, and the Intelligentsia with its research, serving both of them. In addition to that there is a peculiar selection of people for these institutions: middle-aged males with university education from the dominant racial/ethnic group (MAMUs) being preponderant almost everywhere. It is this structure, then, and composed in that particular manner that organises the economic and military basis of society. And all of this is done, manifestly, in order to achieve what is here called the 'Bourgeois Way of Life' with its four characteristics, and the somewhat empty, 'Chemical Way of Life' with booze, with *panem et circenses*, in ways known to everybody in the First World. The BWL/CWL complex.[3]

Let me now formulate two assumptions about the Green Movement:

(1) The Green Movement is an umbrella movement for a number of partial movements, each one of them attacking one or more elements on this list.

And,

(2) The Green Movement differs from many other social movements in denying that basic social problems can be solved attacking one single factor; a much more holistic approach is needed.

236

A SURVEY OF GREEN POLICIES

Mainstream Characteristics		Green Policies, Movements
Economic Basis	1. Exploitation of external proletariat	Cooperative enterprises, movements; labour buyer/seller difference abolished, customers directly involved
	2. Exploitation of external sector relations; liberation movements	Co-existence with the Third World; only equitable exchange
	3. Exploitation of nature	Ecological balance Person-Nature; building diversity, symbiosis; complete or partial vegetarianism
	4. Exploitation of self	More labour- and creativity-intensity; decreasing productivity in some fields; alternative technologies
Military Basis	1. Dependency on foreign trade	Self-reliance; self-sufficiency in food, health, energy and defence
	2. Dependency on formal sector, BCI-complex	Local self-reliance, decreasing urbanisation, intermediate technology; defensive defence policies with less destructive technology, also non-military non-violent defence.
	3. Offensive defence policies, very destructive defence technology	
	4. Alignment with superpowers	Non-alignment, even neutralism de-coupling from superpowers
Structural Basis	1. Bureaucracy, state (plan) strong and centralised	Recentralization of local level; building federations of local units
	2. Corporation, capital (market) strong and centralised	Building informal, green economy: - production for self-consumption - production for non-monetary exchange - production for local cycles
	3. Intelligentsia, research strong and centralised	High level non-formal education, building own forms of understanding
	4. MAMU factor; BCI peopled by middle-aged males with university education (and dominant race/ethnic group)	Feminist movements, justice/equality and for new culture and structure; movements of the young and the old; movements for racial/ethnic equality

237

A SURVEY OF GREEN POLICIES (Cont'd)

Mainstream Characteristics   Green Policies, Movements

		Mainstream Characteristics	Green Policies, Movements
Bourgeois Way of Life	1.	Non-manual work, eliminating heavy, dirty, dangerous work	Keeping the gains when healthy, mixing manual and non-manual
	2.	Material comfort, dampening fluctuations of nature	Keeping the gains when healthy, living closer to nature
	3.	Privatism, withdrawal into family and peer groups	Communal life in bigger units, collective production/consumption
	4.	Security, the probability that this will last	Keeping security when healthy, making life style less predictable
Chemical, Circus Way of Life	1.	Alcohol, tranquilisers drugs	Moderation, experiments with non-addictive, life-enhancing things
	2.	Tobacco, sugar, salt, tea/coffee	Moderation, enhancing the body's capacity for joy, e.g. through sex
	3.	Chemically treated food, panem, natural fibres removed	Bio-organic cultivation, health food, balanced food, moderation
	4.	Circenses, TV, sport, spectatorism	Generating own entertainment, moderate exercise, particularly as manual work, walking, bicycling

Thus, the Green Movement is a federation of constituent movements and aims at an alternative society roughly characterised by the right hand column in the survey of the policies. Many such lists can be made. This is one of them, not necessarily better or worse than most others; probably somewhat more comprehensive. To be a 'Green,' one does not have to subscribe to all of these ideas; one probably has to agree with more than just one of them, however. There is a correlation in the ideological universe and not only because ideas happen to be held by the same people. There is some kind of internal consistency. For one's inner eye is conjured up the vision of a decentralised society, probably some kind of federation, with strongly autonomous units using the local bases in a self-reliant manner, trying not to become dependent on the outside, including for military purposes. Inside this social formation an Alternative Way of Life is supposed to come into being, more or less as described here.[4]

There is no doubt that ideologically the Green Movement is in neither the liberal/conservative/capitalist nor the marxist/socialist traditions, but in the anarchist tradition, and more particularly in the non-violent part of that tradition. Two great names from the Third World in this century, Gandhi and Mao Zedong are now overshadowing the great French and Russian thinkers of the nineteenth century, St Simon and Proudhon, Bakunin and Kropotkin. There is much to draw upon. But this is not necessarily a philosophically deeply reflective movement. It is rather, as pointed out above, a more or less tightly knit federation of single-issue movements, some of them with relatively low life expectancy, but then possibly to be revived within a more general Green setting. Thus, I doubt that there is much to learn about the ideology of this movement from the study of the six names mentioned; I doubt that the members of these movements themselves have even been much inspired by those books. Rather, *the Green Movement is a general reaction to the malfunctioning of the Western social formation*. It is a reaction to the generally lamented 'crisis' and purports to bring into society a number of initiatives that when realised on a large enough scale together would constitute a solution.

3. The Green Movement: A Historical Characterisation

However, this is a much too rational way of looking at a phenomenon like the Green Movement. It is also a part of a socio-historical dialectic, like any other social movement, and should be understood in the light of that dialectic. About the basic dialectic of the Western social formation, there are many opinions. My perspective is one, and runs as follows.[5]

Let us take as point of departure the classical European social formation, often referred to as 'feudal', which is acceptable if that word is understood to transcend the Middle Ages. In that formation the clergy was on top, then came the aristocracy, then the merchants (and some artisans), then the peasants (and some workers) and at the bottom were the totally marginalised people: gipsies, Jews and Arabs, women.[6]

Let us now see each of these five groups as the carrier of successive social transformations. *First*, the revolt of the aristocracy against the clergy, secularising the social order, separating State and Church. *Second*, the revolt of the merchants against the top two, claiming a place in society that could be legitimised neither as God's servants, nor by noble birth, invoking such instruments as human rights to promote social and geographical mobility. *Third*, the revolt of the fourth layer, workers of all kinds, basically men, in order to have a better share in the social product they themselves were largely responsible for bringing into being, and in order to benefit from the social mobility channels opened by the bourgeoisie. Socialist parties, social democrats, trade unions - and communists.[7]

And then, the *fourth* transformation spear-headed by the bottom layer, by what today would be the foreign workers, by the women, by everybody marginalised by the social order set up by the other four (with the clergy transformed into intellectuals, the aristocrats into bureaucrats and the commercial people, the capitalists remaining capitalists so that the three together constitute precisely the BCI complex, populated by MAMUs, many of them taken from the working classes). Logically, socio-logically, socio-historically there is not the slightest reason why they should not also claim their right to come into the society created by the other four, to open that society for foreign workers and women alike, thus constituting a pressure on the Western social formation.[8]

However, there is no social movement that only wants to fill positions in the existing structure. It also wants to change that structure. If this is not the case, the movement is no longer social; it is just a number of parallel individual movements to promote their own social careers on an individual basis, into slots already prepared in the structure. Social change is used to legitimise striving for individual career; individual careers may be used 'inside the system' to promote social change - either approach may be more or less successful. The preceding social transformation by the working class probably changed the workers more than the social order they wanted to transform, but in so doing also changed that social order. Neither the fifth group nor the fourth group in this image of the classical Western society were alone in what they were doing; they were always aided by enlightened/disgruntled individuals from the other groups. Nor did everybody in the group participate in the transformation. Social history is never that neat.[9]

Let us now try to translate this into very concrete terms, the terms of party politics. Let us assume that the first two groups, the clergy and the aristocracy with their institutions, Church and University, Land, Military and Law constitute the backbone of conservative society, and also the basic carriers of conservative parties. Of course they have many more followers than their own numbers should indicate, among other reasons because they command institutions that reach deep down in society, to its very end, the outcasts (particularly true for Church and Military), serving as vacuum cleaners to scoop up even the social debris at the very bottom, putting them at the disposal of the top, at least as voters.[10]

Given that image, it is clear that *the conservative parties* have received three basic challenges, corresponding to transformations No. 2, 3 and 4 respectively.

The *first* challenge came from the second transformation, from the merchants/burghers, strongly individualistic, human rights oriented and in favour of free circulation of production factors, goods and services, of labour skilled and unskilled, capital and nature. In other words: *the liberal parties.*

The *second* challenge came from the third transformation: the mass movements of the working classes, backed up by their strong institution, Trade Unions, in other words *the socialist/workers parties.*

And then the *third* challenge corresponding to the fourth transformation: the Green wave, ultimately and necessarily also organised as one or more political parties, *the Green Parties.*

The second basic hypothesis in this connection would be that the conservative parties tend to remain although they transform their content: their task is always and invariably to resist the social transformation demanded by those challenging the social order. The first challenge, the liberals, came, broke through the conservative barrier and formed their own governments, declined and are now by and large disappearing from the scene.[11] On the way down it made electoral alliances in many countries with the next party on the way up, the working class parties. They were then able to liberate themselves from the liberals, broke through the conservative barrier (of which the liberals may now have become a part) made their own governments, started declining and are now in all likelihood on their way out. One basic reason for that, incidentally, is that the trade unions are on their way out as major social forces, simply because they do not muster adequate numbers of sufficiently exploited workers who think collective action with major strikes will bring more benefit than the skilful use of individual career opportunities.[12]

Working class parties on their way down would then be coalition material for Green wave parties on their way up in spite of everything that is now so often being said about their incapacity as political partners. We shall enter a period of *red-green alliances* and by then see the Green Parties break through the conservative barrier with the help of such alliances (later on perhaps alone), until they reach their climax, start declining and ultimately disappear. In other words, the idea is not that the Green Party is the end of the political history of the Western social formation, nor that the social formation is doomed in advance to a lasting Green future.[13]

Everything is an episode, including the Green wave. What is claimed, however, is that the phenomenon will increase in importance, the working class parties decrease, but it is in the interest of both of them to form alliances so that for some period they may break through the basic conservative pattern and constitute something new. That prediction, like any prediction, may be right or wrong - I would tend to believe in it because it seems to fit the logic of Western social history relatively well.[14]

However, there is another danger with this kind of perspective. The focus is on the Green Party rather than the Green Movement, simply because the Green Party is more in the mass media, in the public eye. Yet, the Green Party can only make politics (as opposed to politicking) when supported by the Green Movement.

4. The Green Movement: A Sociological Characterisation

Who, then, will tend to join the Green Movement? Above two categories have been mentioned: foreign workers, and the whole 'ethnic' complex within any country, marginalised because of their ethnicity, and women - certainly not all members of these groups, but sufficient numbers to make the movement grow. But many of them would tend to vote with the parties that represent preceding social transformations, having no wish at all for new social transformations only for stability and security and possibly some advancement within the status quo.

However, there are many other groups that might be interested in the Green Movement according to the type of analysis made above. They can be seen by looking at the list of Green policies presented above, especially if one makes use of two simple criteria: is the subjective *motivation* to feel concerned strong enough? And is the subjective sense of *capability* strong enough to make the person feel that it matters if he or she joins? Or, would an individual solution be preferable?

Thus, take the issue of cooperative enterprises. To be interested in this, today a major aspect of the Green Movement, one definitely has to be interested in some kind of production, but basically in doing things together, closeness, overcoming feelings of isolation, alienation. And this immediately concerns a considerable number of the citizens of the contemporary Western social formation. Work as therapy becomes a major slogan, work together as a group therapy even better.[15]

When we move on to the point about the Third World, the members of the Green Movement would be sympathisers with those in the Third World suffering the consequences of 'modernisation' and those in the liberation movements suffering the consequences of continued or renewed repression. But they would be relatively few and relatively ideological; the people really hit are found outside any First World society.[16]

This is not the case with the ecological sub-movement of the Green Movement, however - the one that has given rise to the name of their movement, 'Green'. At this particular point in the Green Movement the motivation will only increase with the growing perception of impending disaster, right now particularly in connection with the dying out of forests in Central Europe (starting in Northern Europe, as well). At the same time, there is increasing frustration in people feeling that there is very little they can do

242

individually; the matter is in the hands of big corporations and big bureaucracies. Individuals may cut down on electric consumption and save water in their private households. They may also change their dietary habits, but they feel helpless facing such macro-phenomena, and that helplessness will increasingly be translated into demonstrations and mass movements and be the kind of material of which political party formations can be made.[17]

New work styles, however, is more a question of capability than motivation. Many people seek more artisanal modes of production simply because they are capable of doing so; others may sense a strong motivation but feel totally incapable. The search for alternative technologies will continue but it may also be that the momentum of the 1970s is no longer there, or at least not so forcefully. There may be a new cycle, however.[18]

But then, on the other hand, there are the points associated with another major component in the Green Movement: the peace movement. This is a broad movement not only concerned with such military matters as decreasing dependence on offensive weaponry, particularly nuclear arms; and trans-armament in the direction of social defence, or defenisve defence in general (including conventional military defence and paramilitary defence).[19] The peace movement is also concerned with such issues as non-alignment/ neutrality, various forms of decoupling from super-powers, at least in the sense of denying them bases, particularly with nuclear 'tasks', and of withdrawing from their command structure in times of war. Moreover, the peace movement is concerned with both local and national self-reliance, with making countries stronger so that they can resist economic blackmail, and also by making local communities stronger, much more capable of standing up for themselves, being less dependent on the centre of the country. In short, the peace movement does not only stand for international transformations with trans-armament and transformation of the alliance system; the peace movement also stands for changes at the national level to make national and local societies stronger. The peace movement will probably continue growing, in depth and quality if not in mass demonstrations and quantity - the latter was more typical of the anti-missile movement which no doubt has played a considerable role for consciousness formation, political mobilisation and even confrontation. Neither the blue, nor the red, nor the pink, seem to be capable of solving these problems, hence the motivation will still be there, although frustration may also have a paralysing impact.[20]

When it comes to the structural changes envisaged by the Green Movement, such as decentralisation with more power to the local level and trans-formations from centralised to more (con)federate structures; the building up of informal, Green economies (more locally based, less monetary, more for the quality of life and less for money); decentralisation of knowledge production to very many and much smaller universities, I think the motivation will continue to be there, also the capability, particularly in the form of Green economy and non-formal Green education. When it comes to changes in the heavier structures, the State formation itself, it goes without saying that this can only be done by using central political machinery, possibly through parliaments and political parties. Individual capability is almost nil, and I am not so sure that the motivation is as strong as it was in the 1970s.

But the third major part of the movement, the feminist movement, has had considerable success. It is obviously split into two: the 'fifty-percenters' wanting social positions to be gender-blind, meaning 50 women in positions so far dominated by men and 50 men in positions so far dominated by women (including domestic life); and on the other hand, those who think and act in terms of a specific feminist culture that could serve as a model for social relations at large.[21] I think it is useful to conceive of the feminist movement in terms of both - and, and not either-or when it comes to this split, and that both types of momentum are terribly important in the on-going social transformation. Of activist women there are many: many men will join them and many women will not, but it is hard to believe that motivation and capability will not increase rather than decrease in the years to come. It may also be that the movement for the older generation, the *troisième cycle*, retired people, will be of significance as well as the lasting significance of racial/ethnic equality in heterogeneous countries and that means, increasingly, all countries today. In principle, the Green Movement will be an umbrella for all of them, depending on the extent to which it is capable of articulating their demands in a politically relevant direction.

Finally, there are the two 'ways of life'-packages, more relevant individually. Again, it may be that the big wave of the 1970s with communes, kitchen gardens, health food, etc. has flattened out to some extent, in some quarters even decreased. But, on the other hand, it may also be that the days of fundamentalism are over, that the movement is penetrating all sections of society (with very expensive health food for those who only feel well when they spend a lot of money), in smaller packages, less densely packed, more pragmatic. The transformation of individual ways of life may also have an impact on the political outlook although it is not at all certain that this will lead to votes for Green Parties; it could also lead to the greening of red, pink and blue parties. Like the feminist movement, these may be signs of successful social transformations, changing the essence of what it means to be a First World inhabitant during the last decade of the twentieth century.[22]

I think the net conclusion of what has been said above is that the Green parties will continue to grow. The reasons are simple: there are so many issues generated by the present Western social formation; there is so much frustration around; there is so little capability in the blue, red and pink parties to bear upon these issues in a forceful manner; many people are hit by the problems; the motivation is high; and individual level solutions are insufficient. Obviously, to feel motivated by a social evil not directly hitting oneself, both social knowledge and social compassion are indispensable, together with the sense of individual frustration, 'there is nothing I and my family can do for ourselves to solve the problem'.

These two conditions should point in the direction of people with a certain level of education, which would mean middle class and upper class people; but at the same time away from upper class people who, because of their resources, usually will be able to find a solution for themselves and their family - like moving out of polluted cities to non-polluted countryside, combining work and leisure, affording the transportation/communication expenses involved. At the same time, any transformation movement would appeal more to the young and the middle aged, than to the old: the latter might say, why bother, we shall not be around very long anyhow. Finally, the movement will appeal more to women than to men, both because women are worst hit by the system, because the feminist movement is an important component of the total Green Movement, and because women are, presumably, more capable of holistic thinking. So much for the sociological portrait.

But holistic thought is almost a condition for Green Movement behaviour in general, and Green Party behaviour in particular. Look again at the issue catalogue: there is no simple, all-encompassing formula like 'the interests of the entrepreneurs/employers' or 'the interests of the workers/employees'. If society is a layer cake, these issues do not necessarily mobilise one layer against the other. Rather, the metaphor would be layer cake with some poisoned almonds, raisins and what not distributed all over, visible only to those who have a vision of the cake as a whole. Unfortunately, they have to be removed, something has to be done about it, otherwise the whole cake will be poisoned, those on the top, those in the middle and those at the bottom. The happy message is that the poisoned items do not all have to be removed at the same time. Removal of one of them already makes sense for that environment. The sad message is that there is no method by which one can remove all at the same time, nor does removal of one guarantee that all the others will disappear. 13 Well-coordinated, synchronous work is recommended, as mentioned above.

It may be objected that we have now come a long way from the theory of the fifth layer in the preceding section. But that is a historical theory of social dynamism, of major social forces that may carry on their shoulders much of the movement. It is like the preceding movement of the working class. There were the obvious interests of the working class. But the socialist wave contained considerably more than that, there was also 'socialist humanism', an international peace movement, and so on. As a matter of fact, many of the tasks today taken on by the Green Movement can be seen as parts of the socialist programme, the preceding wave of social energy left unsolved.[24]

And that gives us an important additional interpretation of the Green Movement in general and the party in particular as a meeting ground of frustrated people from the blue parties (conservatives, nationalists, even with a Nazi past) and from the red parties (1968 generation) finding nowhere else to go. Strange bedfellows these: the Green Party seems to have some transformative capacity, making Green people out of the most diverse raw material. How lasting these transformations are, and how lasting the cohabitation will prove to be, is another matter.

5. Conclusion: The Green Movement has come to stay

I think it is very difficult to arrive at any other conclusion. Like any political movement, it will have ups and downs, and although it is a child of the Western social formation, the geographical variation inside the West will be considerable.

Take the case of the Federal Republic of Germany. Why is the movement so strong there? The problems of one half of humanity, the women, are not particularly worse in that country than in other Western countries. The peace problems are more acute, the ecological problems about the same with the exception of the dying forests. The reason is probably historical: the Green Movement is also a rupture with the Nazi past, a past that encompassed almost all of German society, leaving the communists relatively alone as a nucleus of solid resistance. But anti-Nazism cannot be built on communism in Western Europe in general, and Western Germany in particular. Marxism was tried, from the mid-sixties to the mid-seventies, the student revolt, with terrorism (RAF) as an extreme form of expression. The Green Movement with its focus on non-violence is also a rejection of terrorism and single factor, Marxist determinism.[25]

Take France as another example. The Green Movement is inconspicuous, the ecological party made only 0.5% in the cantonal elections Spring 1985. Why is that?

One reason, very conspicuous in the eyes of a foreign observer like the present author, would be the sharp distinction in France between a *classe politique* with not only decision monopoly but also, practically speaking, knowledge monopoly, and for that reason, interest monopoly. The population at large is simply uninterested in a wide range of political phenomena, and uninformed. It is not like Western Germany (and GDR also, for that matter) where one can travel to almost any little town or village and find people deeply concerned, well-read, and articulate about the points on the Green agenda. In France disinterest is the rule.[26]

But this, of course, is also begging the question: why is that so? Maybe one reason is to be found in an extremely strong French individualism. The French love 'freedom', meaning the right of the individual with his/her nuclear family to do more or less what they want to do, a right which is also expressed in the somewhat particular way of driving and parking cars. In the Green Movement there are strong collectivist elements, togetherness beyond the confines of the nuclear family and very much concern for the society as a whole, for collective solutions. French individualism would point in the direction of interest parties rather than interested (or for that matter, interesting) parties. The layer cake model with one layer against the other, perhaps agreeing on cake expansion to counteract the poisoned cake model![27]

Still, another difference relative to Germany would be the shared feeling, right or wrong, that there is no past to reject, no sins to atone for. The old parties may not be perfect but they can do the job. They have been with us for a long time; if the Left doesn't make it, then the solution will by definition have to be with the Right and vice versa. This may be totally irrational reasoning. Economic problems may depend on changes in the world system and be totally beyond reach of Left or Right; the many problems of contemporary French society may also be outside the paradigms for political action shared by Left and Right. In either case, the Green formulae may be relevant, but if they are not seen as such in a French setting then that does not help much.

Still another reason may be the strong reaction against the undeniable Puritan elements in the Green Movement. The French are very tied to their *cuisine*. The *cuisine* is meatist rather than vegetarian, as such it is of course excellent, one of the two best in the world (the other being Chinese). To challenge meatism is to challenge French *cuisine*. Not to go in for the bourgeois style of life, including some elements of elegance in the clothing, is un-French activity and can probably only be legitimised if one is aesthetically elegant in some other field, for instance by being an artist. The Germans have no *cuisine* to defend, hence there is no problem of that kind. And although the ordinary German looks very bourgeois, there is no *haute couture* to defend either. National pride is not at stake, only bourgeois feelings.

Finally, Germany is a neighbour, watched relatively closely by French politicians. The inroads made by the Green Movements in German politics must have given them a shock: this must not happen here. The calumnies coming out of the French press against the peace movement and the ecological movement are telling signs of irrational fear, not the invitation to reasoned debate that should characterise democratic society. On the other hand, the French feminist movement is strong and relatively successful although they have a very long way to go with the remnants of feudalism. But then, *la femme française* is also a part of the national pride. She is not un-French activity, she is French. And yet France will probably sooner or later have to follow suit with the other countries also in this regard.

The countries of Southern Europe, however, will not follow suit. They are still in the throes of the third social transformation, even the second, even the first for that matter (Spain, Italy). On the other hand, in the countries of Northern Europe one may even talk of a general greening of all political parties - with conservative parties picking up ecological and feminist issues, but (certainly) not peace issues.

So the picture is mixed, as it should be. But there are Green points all over that picture. Anyone wanting to understand the First World today would do better not pretending that they are not there. They may commit all kinds of 'mistakes'. But the problems of the Western social formation do not disappear even if Green Parties or movements should decline. The historical forces are undeniable. And individuals as well as collective motivation and capability will produce sufficient mobilisation from sufficiently many corners of Western society. In short: the Green phenomenon is here to stay.

Notes

1 The elections 1985 in the Federal Republic of Germany did not work so well for *Die Grünen*; but ups and downs are to be expected as well as internal conflicts over persons and issues.
2 The paradigm underlying this list is developed in some detail in the first volume of a forthcoming set of books on development theory and practice - *Development: Goals, Concepts and Theories*.
3 The 'chemical/circus way of life' is then seen as something accompanying the basic form, the bourgeois way of life, to alleviate some of the loneliness and meaninglessness that may be the way the person experiences BWL.
4 Two basic issues discussed inside any Green Movement, viz. - does one start changing the social formation or engaging in alternative ways of life, at the individual and micro social levels - or both? - is a micro level change possible at all without a macro level change?; simply opting out of industrial society as the Green fundamentalist Rudolph Bahro would and does advocate.
5 For a discussion of this, see Volume 2 in the set mentioned in footnote 2 above: *Development and Social Processes* (forthcoming).
6 There is probably something universal in this; any social order needing specialists in cultural, force and economic production and reproduction, although the relative order of these groups in the power structure may vary from one formation to the other and over time - with occasional breakthroughs for the underdog subjects. The Indian philosopher P.R. Sarkar bases reflections of this type on a theory of four types of personality, corresponding to the four classical castes and has, like Sorokin, a cyclical theory of history where the groups take power in the order Force-Culture-Economy-People-Force. He forgets, however, and strange for an Indian, that there are two groups of people: low class and marginalised. The Green Movement will mobilise the latter rather than the former. The marginalised include women, and *die Grünen* are to a large extent a woman's party, essentially being founded by one woman (Petra Kelly) and presently (1985) steered by a directorate of three women.

For Sarkar's very important theory, see R.N. Batra. 1978. *The Downfall of Capitalism and Communism, A New Study of History*. London: Macmillan.

[7] In Sarkar's thinking this is the *shudras*, the masses of working people, breaking through the crust provided by the other three. But where are the *pariahs*?

[8] All of that is actually happening today around us, living in the societies of the Western social formation, all the time. No doubt it will be classified as a revolution in due course of time. But it does not conform to our standard image of revolution, with *one* relatively well-defined group exercising tremendous pressure on *one* particular point in the social structure and at *one* short interval of time.

[9] The French Revolution must have been equally confusion to the contemporaries; it is only afterwards, when intellectuals have processed the raw material, that the period gains sufficiently in coherence to be upgraded as a revolution.

[10] Western societies still retain much of the verticality of feudal organisation, particularly as related to the great organisations of the classical Western social order, Church, Land and Military (police) and Commerce, making it natural for underdogs in these institutions to exhibit conservative political profiles.

[11] For the time being the Liberal Party in Great Britain is doing well in its alliance with the Social Democrats - perhaps exactly for that reason: the element of social democracy.

[12] Of course, the dwindling of the secondary sector in post-industrial societies is also a major factor here. The structure keeping workers as an exploited proletariat has to a large extent been demolished by the labour movement; and, while retaining the gratitude and solidarity of the first generation of workers liberated, their offspring may use the transition from structure to actor to design highly individual-centred careers and/or to play on the market.

[13] Of course, new cleavages will appear, new contradictory values and/or interests. Green ideas may also be co-opted by older parties, as to some extent happened in Saar to the Social Democratic Party under the skilful leadership of Oscar Lafontaine, leading to a sweeping victory - the voters liking the new wine, but preferring the old bottles to Green Party style marketing. The basic point, however, is that with the Green Movement the conflict potentials of the traditional Western social formation has been acted out - according to the model presented here.

[14] See Galtung, Heiestad and Rudeng. 'On the last 2,500 years of Western History, With Some Remarks on the Coming 500'. Final chapter in the companion volume, 1979, *New Cambridge Modern History*. London: Cambridge University Press, pp. 318-361.

[15] See the chapters by the Danish authors in Friberg and Galtung (eds.) 1985. *Alternativen*. Stockholm: Akademisk Förlag - consistently stressing the theme of closeness as basic to an alternative way of life.

[16] And these societies, mainly in the Third World, may be in other phases in their history of social transformation. The worst hit may be the marginals who may not even dream of being actors in any transformation, meaning that the Green Parties will tend to cooperate with the upper classes in the Third World countries (particularly with the intellectuals), who may have very different interests.

[17] The basic point in our ecological predicament is probably very simple: the joint transformation from cyclical to linear ecological processes and from limited to highly extended economic cycles - due to massive industrialisation and world trade - leads to depletion and pollution, on the one hand, and lack of direct control, on the other. The individual may engage in some protective measures at the micro level, but they may easily come to naught through the harmful operation of macro level processes.

[18] In many Third World countries, such as Malaysia, a certain fatigue effect with modern technology is already discernible - simply because the costs seem to outweigh the benefits.

[19] For an analysis, see Johan Galtung. 1984. *There Are Alternatives*. Nottingham: Spokesman. Sections 5.1-2, pp. 162-183.

[20] But then a new escalation of the arms race, such as the SDI, may lead to a new explosive burst of peace movement activity.

21 For a good example, see Anne Wilson Schaef. 1981. *Women's Reality*. Minneapolis, particularly Chapter 5, 'The Female System and the White Male System: New Ways of Looking at Our Culture', pp.99ff.

22 This brings out the point of not confusing the Green Movement with the Green Party: whether the latter is the most adequate carrier of the basic ideas of the former is an empirical question, not to be decided by semantics alone.

23 This point goes deeper than political strategy. It is not merely a weak movement advocating change through the synergy of multiple small attacks; this is also the expression of a philosophy/epistemology favouring synchronicity to causality based on a single lever approach to social transformation.

24 If that is the case it should affect the recruitment profile: not many workers but the same (over-) educated, urban middle class that flocked to the Socialist Parties earlier in this century should join 20 the Green Movement. In fact, what happened to the SPD in the March 1983 elections in the Federal Republic of Germany was precisely that they lost (probably three million) workers to the CDU/CSU, and a high number of the country's intelligentsia to *Die Grünen*.

25 It should be pointed out that the RAF was also engaged in a large-scale social experiment, testing the hypothesis that their terror would lead to the uprising of the working class with the anti-terrorist terror of the state as the intervening factor. The hypothesis has been disconfirmed, and the fascist nature of a group killing others in a social experiment has been confirmed in its place. This is one factor underlying the rise of the Green Movement: the fall of the ultra-reds.

26 This disinterest should not be confused with loyalty to country/state/government - if that were the dominant sentiment the French would have produced a *levée en masse* against the German invasion in 1940. Rather, it could be seen as profound concern for individual and family welfare over and above the issues affecting society as a whole - except when they touch on the private sphere directly, limiting what the French call 'liberté'. The Green Peace case is an example.

27 Thus, the French Socialist Parties can be seen as a party of state employees securing their interests, failing because of low economic growth.

THE PEACE MOVEMENT: SOME QUESTIONS CONCERNING ITS SOCIAL NATURE AND STRUCTURE*

Artur Meier

Sociology in the past has been, unfortunately, little concerned with war and peace. Among the founding fathers of the discipline, Marx's references to war, particularly civil war (1962a), and Engels' interest in militarism (1962b), are exceptions as well as – within the non-Marxist sociological mainstream – Weber's studies of violence and war (1980). Only after World War II did the critical essay of C.W. Mills on the power elite in the USA (1959) become a starting point for intensive and widespread research on the military-industrial complex which promoted in the subsequent two decades a harvest of both theoretical concepts and empirical findings about social groups with interests in the profitable arms race and in tensions beween states (for example, Rose 1973; Senghaas 1972; Autorenkollektiv 1981). But in sociological textbooks or dictionaries, even from the 1970s or early 1980s, it is hard to find articles on the global problem of peace, international security, the threat of a nuclear catastrophe or the hindrances to social change and development through the increasing expenditure on the deadly destructive potential. The study of these areas has been for a long time evidently the domain of historians, political scientists, philosophers and economists. Sociologists seem to be latecomers to this field, though there exists an established sub-discipline, the sociology of the military, which, however, remained in the past rather narrow in scope compared with the global significance of the war-and-peace issue (Harries-Jenkins and Moskos 1981).

But the situation is changing just now in the 1980s. In view of the current state of international affairs, the acute danger of a nuclear holocaust and the opportunities for socio-economic development that are rapidly being lost by the wildly running arms race, on the one hand, and the immense efforts that are made by people throughout the world to maintain peace and to relieve

*This paper was presented to Symposium VI:2 at the XI. World Congress of Sociology, New Delhi, August 1986.

251

humankind from the growing threat of nuclear self-destruction, on the other, sociologists have given increasingly more professional attention to the peace-and-war question on a global dimension. Among the international community of sociologists we witness a marked interest in the study of the causes of war and the conditions for peace. It is – in my opinion – one of the most encouraging phenomena in the development of the discipline on the international level that a growing number of sociologists coming from different national and social backgrounds recognise their responsibility, as humanistic researchers, for the world in which they and future generations will live. To contribute to peace-building by its own research work requires not only concern about the danger of war, but also serious and appropriate investigations devoted to the dynamics of peace-keeping processes.

From this aspect it seems to be relevant to raise – on the foundations of the sociological discipline – some questions concerning the peace movement as a possible agent of social change, and to put forward some hypotheses in order to stimulate a lively professional debate, and to increase our knowledge about the social nature and social structure of the current peace forces.

Is the peace movement already a subject of sociological research?

The answer to this simple question is not easy. If only genuine sociological concepts and investigations of the movement are taken into account, and if only established standards and criteria of the discipline are applied, then one might tend to a more negative judgement about the 'state of the art' in this particular field.

Certainly, the considerable scope of the peace movement in the 1980s and also its many campaigns have prompted speedy analyses of its political and ideological structure. Our minds have been directed towards the examination of some general political features and ideological tendencies of the movement. But, as far as I can see, there are only a few descriptions portraying the present peace movement in its sociological aspects (for example: Parkin 1968; Shibata 1980; v. Bredow 1982; Harms 1982; Schmid 1982; Galtung 1984; Mitev 1985; Meier 1986a; Hegedüs 1986). What is true of sociology, in respect of the lack of a systematic account of peace-and-war relations as a whole, is also the case in the study of the peace movement in particular: sociologists have long relied on the work of scholars in such established and allied disciplines as political science and history. This need not necessarily be a disadvantage. The subject may be studied, of course, from many perspectives and by various methods. Furthermore, the cooperation and links between scholars coming from different social sciences have not only established peace research very early as a fruitful interdisciplinary field of study but also widened the potential boundaries of each discipline engaged (Meier 1986b). However, the inter-disciplinary character of peace research, that of the movement included, do not excuse sociologists from their task of specialist studies. The inherent tendency to develop professional specialism, and a more refined internal division of peace research in order to increase its efficiency, suggest that we have to remind ourselves of basic areas of sociological interest when analysing the peace movement.

The common areas of concern, which sustain an integrated sociological approach to this particular subject and which simultaneously relate it to other topics of sociological peace research are, to my mind, the following:

– the conceptualisation of the peace movement in the framework of the emerging sociology of *social movements*;
– the study of the *global character* of the peace movement and of its *social peculiarities* in different regions, nations and societies;
– the analysis of the *social structure* of the movement;
– the investigation of the *social aims, values and orientations* of the movement;
– the examination of the movement's *capacity for effecting social change.*

If we fail to elaborate the sociological aspects, we are left with a diffuse area of study which becomes so broad in scope that our understanding of one of the most important social phenomena of our time might be weakened instead of enriching the body of sociological knowledge (Weidig and Winkler 1986). In other words, studying the peace movement from a genuine sociological viewpoint means, therefore, exploring new territory for the discipline.

Can the peace movement be regarded as a type of modern social movement?

The peace movement of the 1980s shows, compared with those preceding it in the decades before, some new features, the most significant of which is its broad popular base. Larger and smaller social groups throughout the world, social, political and cultural movements representing other fields and aspects of social struggle, a wide range of non-governmental organisations but, in some cases, even states with their political leaders: that is, then, groups and invididuals stemming from different professions and social origins, ageing and elderly people, but also, to a significant degree, particularly major parts of the younger generation have joined and participate in today's peace movement. These social actors from around the world have, of course, attracted sociologists to analyse the new type and the changing structure of the movement.

We can identify, as far as I can see, three interpretations of the current peace movement. Quite a number of analyses and considerations of the movement have over the last few years derived, firstly, from the evident fact of the overrepresentatively large participation of young people and provided explanations based on concepts of crisis and social change, or of the evaluations of particular effects of prolonged education and/or a shift to post-materialist values among the young generation (Inglehart 1977; Jugend-protest 1981; Küchler 1981). The commitment to peace is seen as part of the wider youth protest. Secondly, as the essence of the few relevant studies indicates, the latter-day peace movement is explained by some authors mainly in terms of strata concepts. In this light, the movement turns out to be one expression of the latest rebellion of the younger groups from the intellectual and well-educated middle class or stratum which can look back already on certain traditions of democratic struggle in the last two decades (Küchler 1981; Harms 1982). Thirdly, and sometimes related to the former interpretation, the peace movement is definitely conceptualised as an element of the new social movements which emerge only in our time and challenge the technocratic powers as well as their dominant value systems. The opposition and fight against the madness of the arms race are interpreted, from this aspect, as one form of an overall protest of the growing 'alternative base' in society against large-scale technological change with its destructive potentials (Brand, Brüsser and Rucht 1983).

However, one of the outstanding experts in the field of studying the new social movements, Alain Touraine, is quite reluctant to define the peace movement as a social movement, because it is based essentially on a critical attitude toward the state (1985). As we know, he has always rejected the 'new political science of change', as he labelled it, created today by the analysts of the state, and declared his support for a sociology of classes and social movements. Social movements are, in his conception, much more than mass protest against the state. For the first time, social movements struggling for the control of 'historicity' now are becoming the main actors of society, the principal agents of history. The emergence of a new generation of social movements indicates, in Touraine's view, the transition from industrial to programmed society. The new social movements, therefore, will tomorrow take over the central role that the workers' movement held in industrial capitalist society (Touraine 1981). The anti-nuclear ecological movement fighting against the technocracy represents, in Touraine's opinion, the prototype of the new social movements linking social struggle with fundamental cultural innovations (Touraine 1982).

I think one must share his doubts about simply classifying the peace movement as a component of the so-called new social movements. Marxist researchers in the Federal Republic of Germany, for example, also came to the conclusion that it would be a mistake to define the peace movement in these terms (Reusch 1986). One can, indeed, argue that the peace movement is clearly of a political nature rather than a struggle on the 'cultural front', as is so often typical of the alternative groups. What makes it, in my view, very different from the movements on which Touraine focuses when looking at the agents of a possible transition to the so-called programmed society is its lack of counter-cultural protest and innovation (or, positively spoken, it does not suffer to any signficiant degree from the 'programmatic ballast' of many middle-class dominated alternative protest movements). Moroever, its most characteristic features, compared with other movements, are its very heterogeneous social composition and its real global dimension. The social base of the present peace movement goes far beyond the recruitment fields of any other of the 'new' social movements.

However, it seems to me absolutely inappropriate to exclude by definition the peace movement simply by the argument that it differs in some respect from the so-called new movements. On the contrary, *my thesis is that the world peace movement represents the broadest and strongest social movement in our time.* It meets, consequently, all the main criteria on which consensus can be reached among sociologists who nowadays deal with this kind of social force:

- it is a mass movement, a collective actor, with a broad popular base and a heterogeneous, fluent social structure linking very different social entities, small groups as well als worldwide organisations, through a social network of global extension;
- its adversary can be identified clearly: it may be called the 'great technico-economic apparatus' (Touraine), because it is formed by the established armament complex of social interest groups and represented by the monopolistic state machinery;
- manifesting a new kind of thinking in the nuclear age, the peace movement creates also a new political culture with innovative norm or value-oriented strategies for action;
- the peace movement of today, articulating the needs of people in many countries, is becoming a factor in transforming world society, provided it survives nuclear annihilation, at least to a new stage of relations between states, nations and social classes worldwide.

Peace movement – one or many?

Some writers in the field of both political science and sociology stress the national, or sometimes regional, peculiarities of the peace movement and deny its universal character (v. Bredow 1985). In their view, the movement should be understood and defined mainly as a national phenomenon. They point to the specific forms and structures, aims and strategies of the movement among Western nations, to the significant differences between the movement in East and West, and (last but not least) to a gap between the people of the so-called First or Second World and the Third World countries, adopting in this case usually the super-powers doctrine in its many ideological variants.

I cannot share these reduced views of the world peace movement and would like to reject the concept of a multitude of smaller or bigger national movements which have in common only some general ideas and feelings about peace and seem to be unable to form a transnational community. Of course, nobody will ignore the fact that the peace movement has striking national or regional features due to different traditions and societal circumstances. Furthermore, nobody can deny that Third World people experience peace and war in their very own way under the conditions of a tremendous lack of resources for economic and social development and for the satisfaction of their basic needs and under the pressure of military conflicts and regimes in their regions. And finally: it would certainly be a great misunderstanding of the peace movement in the socialist countries to define it dogmatically only

255

according to the measures of the Western peace movement, leaving aside the differences of the societal structures within which the movement acts.

Nevertheless, despite evident national, regional and societal peculiarities, the peace movement is of a truly international character and of global extension.

Since movements always represent a combination of structure and process (Gusfield 1981; Neidhardt 1985), the boundaries and structural forms of the peace movements are really fluent with a rich variety of organisational and institutional social networks within each particular nation, but more than that: between them on a worldwide dimension. Unprecedented in history, this kind of global mass movement, which wages the struggle for the maintenance of world peace, operates on different levels, in this way uniting heterogeneous social forces on the widest possible scale.

In my view, the international peace movement of the 1980s represents the historical response of people throughout the world in the name of the productive forces of world society to the deadly challenge stemming from the alarming increase in destructive nuclear-weapon arsenals which might be deployed in connection with a military conflict. The threat of a global nuclear catastrophe originated – in the opinion of many people all over the world – through the uncontrolled arms race stimulated by social interest groups which are, irrespective of their national origins, also transnational in their extension and influence. The powerful adversary of the peace movement, the multinational military-industrial complex with its deadly destructive potentials for the whole of mankind, can only be countered by an international movement which by all means and on a global dimension tries to change the situation away from the danger of extermination of all forms of life and society to a more peaceful world. In my opinion, *the counterparts, the trans- or multinational military-industrial complex, on the one hand, and the world peace movement, on the other, are both parts of the larger socio-economic and political structure of the global order* which is interdependent but at the same time contradictory in its elements. *Therefore, both of the adversaries are international in character and operate on a worldwide scale.*

Who are the people forming the movement and where do they come from?

Comparing the present-day peace movement with the social structure of its forerunners we can discover significant differences. The peace movements before World War I and II were more or less class-based, the former depending on the social-democratic workers' movement, the latter on the radical socialist movement with some allied groups of intellectuals united by the idea of an 'anti-fascist people's front', both evidently restricted to regional dimensions. Ever after the Second World War the concept of an international alliance against fascism and imperialism, broader in scope, of course, but in general still in the tradition of the people's front thinking, seemed to provide the understanding of the peace movement.

The massive peace movement of the 1980s, by contrast, is free from these limits: *really global in its existence, it is significantly non-class based.* The broad popular social recruitment basis consists of many other grass-roots movements, of a diversity of organisations, some important states included, as well as associations, social groups and individuals coming from very different, sometimes even divergent, political, cultural and social backgrounds. Broad, popular-based, means non-class based but certainly not classless.

Perhaps through a more detailed look at the social structure of the present movement in the context of the different societies within which it is operating, we can learn more about its specific social components. Why do all classes and strata of socialist societies participate nearly to the same extent in the movement and why is the mainstream of the peace forces in these countries supported by their governments and vice versa? Who acts as the social and political hegemon and who are the 'followers' of the peace movement in the non-aligned or Third World countries? Why are so many peace activists in the West intellectuals and what are their relations to the workers' movements? How can it be explained that in some of those countries the workers' movement is a source for the peace movement and not in others?

There are too many questions to be discussed here. Therefore, I only want to draw my attention to an actual trend in broadening the social recruitment basis of the movement, namely to the significant tendency among scientists just now to leave their ivory tower and to join the peace movement.

The reasons for the intelligentsia, particularly the young, to take an active part in the struggle for peace have to some extent already been discussed in sociological articles. Some authors in the West believe that a changing of the guards is now taking place between the leading generations, a conflict between the old elite with its established power and values, and a new well-educated one coming from the universities which forms the avant-garde of broad protest movements like that struggling against the armament complex (Küchler 1981; Szabo 1983). Other experts in the field point also to the increasing size of the intelligentsia, or so-called new middle class, due to the outputs of the dramatically extended educational systems (Galtung 1984), and ascribe to the members of these strata a particular sensitivity to the threat to mankind's existence and sometimes also the ability of looking through state-monopoly manipulation as a result of their easier access to information (Harms 1982).

It is a striking fact indeed that in many Western countries peace activists are primarily masses of students, teachers and people of other adjoining socialisatory professions, representatives from the media intelligentsia, a considerable number of doctors and other holders of social welfare and therapeutic jobs, and groups of what are called the social service professions. Nowadays the peace movement is enriched by natural scientists who come mainly from public research institutes or universities (take, for example, the broad movement at United States universities to resist SDI). The trend among natural scientists signals a new phenomenon of intellectuals' attitude to the movement, in so far as in the beginning peace activists came over-representatively from the socio-cultural intelligentsia (Meier 1986a).

If we now look for a common criterion of the social existence of these groups representing the social core of the peace movement in important Western countries, we can find that nearly all of them not only belong to the educated strata but also depend to a considerable degree and in a very direct way on the state in terms of their living conditions and life prospects. The young people who attend educational establishments, the students of secondary schools and universities, are under almost complete governmental control. The wage-dependent intelligensia working in the civil service or related professions within the state sectors of education, health care and social welfare, or in the public media, are suffering a similar fate. Compared with their predecessors the members of this stratum experience the loss of the relative independence of their social positions, and more than that: many of their jobs are under threat. Many who are enrolled or try to find a job in the state and public sectors are beginning to realise that the burden imposed by the armament complex under the hegemony of the state apparatus gives rise to the present economic and social hardships. Fairly large groups of the intelligentsia stratum, therefore, oppose the state and its policy, particularly in the field of armament.

My hypothesis is, therefore, that the overrepresentative involvement of some groups of the intelligentsia in the peace movement is not only a result of its educational or information level but is also, probably mainly, the outcome of the worsening of their real living conditions under state-monopolistic rule. The peace movement seems to be chosen among the different present-day protest movements because it is precisely the one that most clearly attacks the power establishments in essential fields of policies.

Digging deeper and discussing the real living conditions of wage – and at the same time state – dependent segments of the working classes and strata, we can find further groups among them which support the peace movement because of its character as a catchment basin for the politically largest common denominator of protest against the ruling powers. Ideological (including educational) factors play a mediating role but cannot serve to explain fully the real sources of the protest.

Morever, I assume that the considerable geographical variation of the movement's social structure among Western countries can also be explained in a better way if the strata groups whose living conditions are more or less dependent on state monopoly are identified and the question answered as to whether they tend to oppose the ruling powers by joining the broadest social movement against armament policy. This might also lead at least to new interpretations of the different relations between the peace movement and the workers' movement in several countries.

In terms of 'movement sociology', the social structure of the present peace movement is still very much 'in a state of flux'. That is why some of its contours are easily blurred. But one thing is unmistakeably clear: *that today's worldwide peace movement goes beyond the limits of certain classes and strata, and that its structure is characterised by social heterogeneity.* The broad social base will allow, in future too, new political alliances to be entered into and new lines of action to be taken – with changing topics, however, against the same persistent adversary.

The peace movement – an agent of social change?

The global peace movement is an expression of the crisis in the so-called international order which has become extremely grave since the beginning of this decade. People all over the world are deeply concerned about the acute threat to world peace, and are increasingly articulating their fears that modern weapons of mass destruction under the twin pressures of politico-military strategies, on the one hand, and an uncontrolled technological momentum, on the other, might possibly be employed and lead to a nuclear catastrophe. Facing, for the first time in history, the possibility of a total nuclear destruction of world society which would be simultaneously, of course, the absolute end of any kind of social development or change, many people – irrespective of their national or social origin – call into question the given state of international relations and challenge the established order with its deadly destructive dynamics. If world society is to be prevented from extermination, a radical change of the present international order must be achieved. The special crisis of international affairs in the 1980s creates global problems of 'inter-social' dimensions (Sagladin and Frolow 1982) and requires a new kind of inter- and intra-social relations on a worldwide scale that will encourage the functioning of a less violent and less dangerous international order.

From this point of view, the peace movement is an important symptom of mass aspirations for a more secure and equitable world focusing through collective action on changes which might build a new international order. At the global level it represents the central social movement fighting for control over the main direction of mankind's development against social forces which promote the irrational, but profitable arms race and undermine, in effect, the existence of the planet's social life. The antagonistic contradiction between the multinational military-industrial complex and the world peace movement might be defined as the central social conflict on the global level.

The process of changing the established system of international and, in some cases, intra-national power relations will only take place through a combination of several types of collective action. Far-reaching effects could only be achieved by the interaction of different, particularly social, movements of change following their own course towards transformation but, at the same time, interweaving with the broader social movement which is centred around the most crucial problem of global society, peace. The world peace movement provides the basis for several kinds of political, social and cultural struggle of a larger number of groups being mobilised for different types of social change. How the components of the peace movements define themselves must be explored by accurate research on their orientations and dynamics. Yet if one regards peace not only as the absence of war and violent, military conflicts but as something more positive, viewing it from the postulate of social justice (as Johan Galtung has done, nearly two decades ago [1969], with his much quoted attempt to reach an extended concept of peace), then this aim of the peace movement can be brought to a point in the multi-dimensional complex of tasks for social change which clearly involves social development. *If we talk about peace in this broader sense, the movement against the armament complex is obviously linked with the struggle for social progress.* The study of disarmament and development has emphatically stressed that the arms race and social progress are in a competitive relationship. Taking a global perspective, this study views development as a universal requirement, including the need for sustained and stimulated economic growth for the developed countries and accelerated socio-economic performance by the developing countries (United Nations 1983). This perspective needs to be incorporated into the discussion about the capacities of the peace movement as a possible agent of social change and development.

References

Autorenkollektiv 1981. *Militarismus heute*. Berlin, GDR: Dietz Verlag.
BRAND, K.-W., BRÜSSER, D., and RUCHT, D. 1983. *Aufbruch in eine andere Gesellschaft. Neue soziale Bewegungen in der Bundesrepublik*. Frankfurt, Main/New York: Campus Verlag.
BREDOW, W. von 1982. 'Zusammensetzung und Ziele der Friedensbewegung in der Bundesrepublik Deutschland'. *Aus Politik und Zeitgeschichte* B/24 : 3-13.
BREDOW, W. von 1985. 'Friedensbewegung – international'. *Das Parlament* 13 : 11.
ENGELS, F. 1962b. 'Anti-Dühring', in Marx, K. and Engels, F., *Werke* 20. Berlin, GDR: Dietz Verlag.
GALTUNG, J. 1969. 'Violence, Peace and Peace Research'. *Journal of Peace Research* 6 (3).
GALTUNG, J. 1984. *Es gibt Alternativen!* Opladen: Westdeutscher Verlag.
GUSFIELD, J.R. 1981. 'Social Movements and Social Change. Perspectives of Linearity and Fluidity', in Kriesberg, L. (ed.), *Research in Social Movements, Conflict and Change*, Vol. 4. Greenwich and London: Jai Press.
HARMS, T. 1982. 'Probleme der neuen Friedensbewegung'. *Marxistische Studien. Jahrbuch des IMSF* 5 : 201-12.
HARRIES-JENKINS, G. and MOSKOS, C.C. Jr. 1981. 'Armed Force and Society'. *Current Sociology* 29 (3).
HEGEDÜS, Z. 1986. 'Orientations et dynamiques du mouvement de paix en Allemagne de l'ouest et aux Etats-Uni'. Paper present at the XI. World Congress of Sociology, New Delhi, 18-22 August.
INGLEHART, R. 1977. *The Silent Revolution – Changing Values and Political Styles among Western Publics*. Princeton: Princeton University Press.
Jugendprotest im demokratischen Staat 1981. 'Bericht und Arbeitsmaterialender Enquetekommission des Deutschen Bundestages'. *Schriftenreihe der Bundeszentrale für politische Bildung* 196.
KÜCHLER, M. 1981. '18 bis 35 Abitur Aktivgruppe' – Professor Manfred Küchler über das Potential der Friedensbewegung. *Der Spiegel* 48 : 65-70.
MARX, K. 1962a. 'Der Bürgerkrieg in Frankreich', in Marx, K. and Engels, F., *Werke* 17. Berlin, GDR: Dietz Verlag.
MEIER, A. 1986a. 'Warum gerade die Jugend? Zur Sozialstruktur der westlichen Friedensbewegung'. *Jahrbuch für Soziologie und Sozialpolitik*.
MEIER, A. 1986b. 'Peace Research versus Military R & D – Young Intellectuals at the Crossroads'. Paper presented at the International Conference of ISA-RC 34, Varna, Bulgaria.

MILLS, C.W. 1959. *The Power Elite*. New York: Oxford University Press.

MITEV, P.E. et al. 1985. *Youth and Peace*. Sofia:

NEIDHARDT, F. 1985. 'Einige Ideen zu einer allgemeinen Theorie sozialer Bewegungen', in Hradil, S. (ed.), *Sozialstruktur im Umbruch*. Opladen: Leske Verlag & Budrich.

PARKIN, F. 1968. *Middle Class Radicalism. The Social Basis of the British Campaign for Nuclear Disarmament*. Manchester: Manchester University Press.

REUSCH, J. 1986. 'Überlegungen zur Zukunft der Friedensbewegung in der BRD'. *Jahrbuch für Soziologie und Sozialpolitik*.

ROSE, S. ed. 1973. *Testing the Theory of the Military-Industrial Complex*. Toronto/London: Lexington.

SAGLADIN, W. and FROLOW, I. 1982. *Globale Probleme der Gegenwart* Berlin, GDR: Dietz Verlag.

SCHMID, G. 1982. 'Zur Soziologie der Friedensbewegung und des Jugendprotestes'. *Aus Politik und Zeitgeschichte* 24 : 15-30.

SENGHAAS, D. 1972. *Rüstung und Militarismus*. Frankfurt/Main: Suhrkamp.

SHIBATA, 1980. 'International Discussion: For Human Survival'. *Hiroshima Peace Science* 3.

SZABO, F. 1983. 'Generationswechsel in Europa: Auswirkungen auf das westliche Bündnis'. *Europa-Archiv* 2 : 37-44.

TOURAINE, A. 1981. *The Voice and the Eye. An Analysis of Social Movements*. Cambridge/Paris: Cambridge University Press & Editions de la Maison des Sciences de l'Homme.

TOURAINE, A. 1982. *Die antinukleare Prophetie. Zukunftsentwürfe einer sozialen Bewegung*. Frankfurt, Main/New York: Campus Verlag.

TOURAINE, A. 1985. Letter to Artur Meier regarding the XI. World Congress of Sociology, February 14, 1985.

UNITED NATIONS 1983. *Economic and Social Consequences of the Arms Race and of Military Expenditures*. New York: United Nations Publications.

WEBER, M. 1980. *Gesammelte Politische Schriften*. Tübingen: J.C.B. Mohr.

WEIDIG, R. and WINKLER, G. 1986. 'Soziologie und Frieden'. *Jahrbuch für Soziologie und Sozialpolitik*.

SOCIAL MOVEMENTS AND SOCIAL CHANGE IN SELF-CREATIVE SOCIETY: NEW CIVIL INITIATIVES IN THE INTERNATIONAL ARENA

Zsuzsa Hegedus

No period in the post-war era has witnessed such a massive and unexpected emergence of new movements on a global scale as has the eighties. And rarely has the discrepancy between the practices and analysis of new social movements been so acute.

The eighties can be characterised, first, by the 'planetarisation' of practices formerly identified with new social movements in the West; that is, by the massive emergence throughout the world of collective actions which are non-violent and pragmatic in their methods, non-integrated and multiple in their structures, anti-hierarchical and networking in their organisations, heterogeneous (cross-class, cross-ideology, cross-age) in their constituencies, non-coercive in people participation and non-exclusive in their adherence – such as Solidarnosc in Poland, the anti-apartheid movement identified with Desmond Tutu in South Africa, and even the People Power in the Philippines. Secondly, as these practices began to emerge in the Second and the Third World, in the First, the movements of the eighties acquired a new, genuinely global, dimension – as did the campaign against hunger and also the campaign for disinvestment in South Africa – and they extended the 'traditional' field of new social movements to such 'old' issues as hunger and poverty. Finally, especially in the Western world, the eighties can be characterised by the massive emergence of new movements which intervene directly in a field traditionally considered as exterior and closed to social movements: the international arena:

as do the peace movement and the campaign against the apartheid system.

As for the analysis of these practices, these new movements are usually not even integrated in the field of 'new' social movements. And when they are – as the peace movement – it is often in a problematic manner.

The first point I will try to outline concerns this discrepancy between these practices and the theories of new social movements – a discrepancy which I think is due to the application of the conceptual framework worked out for the movements of the seventies to the movements of the eighties. Secondly, through an analysis of the contemporary peace movement, I want to establish an analytic field which embraces both the peace movement and the various other movements of the eighties in the West. My basic point is to show that if one focuses on the practices of the movements of the eighties, it is possible to outline a new approach to the question: what is the unity of these movements, and, more generally, what is social movement in contemporary society, called alternatively 'post-industrial' (Touraine 1969; Bell 1973), 'programmed' (Touraine 1973), 'informatic' (Naisbitt 1982), and what I term 'self-creative society'?[1]

Social Movements in the Eighties: A New Challenge

1. *From crisis to pessimism.* At first sight, to characterise the eighties by the emergence of new movements throughout the world might seem surprising. The period normally associated with 'new' social movements is not the eighties but the seventies. In fact, the 'history' of new social movements usually starts with the student movement in the late sixties, and the list of these movements is almost definitely established by the end of the seventies. For some, the list is even closed when – shocked by the various 'crises' provoked by the post-industrialisation of the world-system – the West lost confidence in its capacity for change and, the 'new' social movements of the seventies (women's, anti-nuclear, ecological and regionalist movements) seemed to lose momentum if not their '*raison d'être*'. Moreover, most theories of the new social movements do not include collective actions outside of the area of developed countries as part of their field. As a matter of fact, 'new' social movements are usually considered as a Western phenomenon, which they actually were, but only until the end of the seventies.

The very restrictive dimensions of this image indicate, on the one hand, that the seventies did not leave us a 'sceptical' (Melucci 1985) but a quite 'pessimistic' paradigm. Especially in Europe, the theories of new social movements lost their optimism and, according to these theories, the movements lost their counter-offensive/transformative character, at least on a societal level.[2] Of course, over and above the 'disenchantment' of intellectuals, this pessimistic paradigm reflects a creative crisis. This led us to definitely abandon the 'old' paradigm we inherited from industrial society and which, during the seventies, more or less influenced all the theories of new social movements. Nevertheless, however creative it was, this crisis led to a kaleidoscopic and highly problematic image of new social movements. Some opted for a low profile solution and accorded, in different manners, a more limited significance to social movements by focusing on their innovative dimension at a basically organisational and/or institutional level (Gundelach 1984; Kriesi and van Praag 1987). Hence the recent success in Europe of the theories of resource mobilisation (see, especially, Gerlach and Hine 1970; McCarthy and Zald 1973; Oberschall 1973). Others try to find a new 'base' for social movements which, in contrast to industrial actors, do not have any class dimension but directly connect individual emotion and collective actions. For some, new social movements are carried by an alternative sensibility (Melucci 1985), for others by a collectively shared *Angst* (Japp 1986) generated by the risks inherent in modern society (Beck 1986). But neither the first, symbolic and individualistic, nor the second, anxious and collective interpretation allows social movements to acquire a transformative capacity on a societal level.[3] However innovative, they are on a cultural-individual and/or on a collective-political level (Offe 1984): in the first case, new social movements can hardly challenge central issues, in the second, they are definitely defensive (Beck 1986; Japp 1986) and unavoidably reactive (Offe 1986). Presumably limited to their opposition to irreversible options, social movements are supposedly unable to acquire a capacity to challenge what actually *is* at stake in self-creative society: the 'technocratic' *single-optional problem-solving* which generates risks and engenders irreversibility (see Hegedus 1987a), that is, the 'systemic' (Habermas 1981) or 'technocratic' – but in both cases single-optional and reductionist – rationality which commands the realisation of a new modernity.

2. *The model of the seventies and the movements of the eighties.* However, the very restricted character – not only in space but also in time – which used to be accorded to the phenomenon of new social movements brings to light a less obvious but more important conceptual problem. This is not related to the old paradigm and its crisis, but to the decisive influence of the seventies on the conceptual framework of theories of new social movements, which accounts, in my opinion, for the striking discrepancy between the practices and prevailing theories of today's social movements. The sharp contrast between the globalisation of the movements and the narrowness of research fields reveals, in fact, that however different these theories are one from the other – in their analytical assumptions as well as in in their methodological consequences – they reflect and conceptualise the characteristics of new social movements in the seventies.

Now, without any doubt, the movements of the eighties are basically similar, in their practices and in their orientations, to those of the seventies. More importantly, they 'capitalise' on the experience of former movements, that is, they take part in a very *complex process of social learning and communication with a multiple time-space perspective* which is the *new matrix* of a social movement in self-creative society (Hegedus 1984a, 1984b, 1985). Effectively, at least in the conceptual framework I propose to develop through the analysis of the peace movement, a social movement is neither a being nor

265

a feeling but a doing. It cannot be fixed in time and space, and it cannot be identified with any specific 'base': neither with an alternative sensibility nor with a collectively shared anxiety, not even with a 'new' middle class (Offe 1985) and even less with some particular interest. The involvement in an action is a matter of conscience *and* emotion, of responsibility *and* intention, of reflection *and* (com)passion,[4] it is basically *moral*, global *and* individual (Hegedus 1985, 1987a).

However, partly because they capitalise on the experience of former movements, the movements of the eighties are also significantly different from those of the seventies. As a matter of fact, in several crucial aspects they simply do not fit into the conceptual frameworks patterned after the characteristics of social movements in the seventies.

First of all, the movements of the seventies were characterised by their basically cultural dimension. Beyond their different and multiple significances, they were the 'agents' of a major cultural change: the shift from industrial to 'post-industrial' values. Theoretically, this led to an essentially and often exclusively cultural definition. In contrast, without having lost this cultural dimension, the movements of the eighties are characterised by their basically ethical dimension. They do not appeal to alternative sensibility, and even less to collective interest, but to personal responsibility for a collective future at a local, national and planetary level (Hegedus 1987a).

Secondly, the movements of the seventies intervened in 'new' fields, formerly belonging to the private rather than the public sphere. Hence these movements were easily 'sectorised' and it was difficult to define their unity not only at a symbolic and individual (cf. Melucci 1985), or at an organisational and political,[5] level but at a practical and societal[6] level. Moreover, the 'newness' of the field of intervention became often an important element in defining 'new' social movements (Offe 1985). Now, as a matter of fact, most of the movements of the eighties appeared not in 'new' – nor specifically cultural – fields. Neither peace nor hunger nor poverty could be characterised as specifically new and/or cultural issues.

Thirdly, while the movements of the seventies were undoubtedly transnational in their scope and effects, the actions and practices were not. Even if they simultaneously emerged throughout the Western world and generated major changes in values and behaviour on a global scale – as the women's and the ecological movements did – the movements of the seventies only intervened within the political framework of nation-states and not beyond it. This explains the cultural-political interpretation of these new social movements. They were presumably 'global' and/or 'utopian' in their values, but actually they were presumed national in their field and political in their intervention. In contrast, the movements of the eighties are basically global, planetary and transnational not only with regard to the issues they address but, above all, in their interventions. 'Thinking globally, acting locally', the slogan of the peace movement, reflects exactly the genuinely new and multiple dimension of these practices which act simultaneously at an infra- and transnational level, and challenge the very framework of nation-states as well as the basic paradigm of an international world order, structured on the

266

exclusive relations between states, blocs and military super-powers (Hegedus 1984b, 1986, 1987a).

Finally, the movements of the seventies reflected the 'transitional' character of the period. New in their values and practices, they were, still, 'old' in their discourses and in their more or less ideological, 'leftist' or counter-cultural character. This basically gave a minority constituency to these movements and an essentially 'exemplary' character to their practices. This explains the basically cultural significance accorded to these new practices. Some prevailing theories emphasise the innovative dimension of these practices at an individual and/or micro-social level (Freeman 1983), others at an organisational and/or political level (Offe 1984), but they do not assess these same practices in their transformative dimension at the very societal level.

This last point explains the inadequacy of the theories on new social movements in the face of the massive emergence of the same practices, to which the movements of the eighties assign a majoritarian and anticipative-transformative vocation throughout the world: as do, in the West, the peace movement, the campaign against hunger in Africa and that against domestic poverty, the campaign against apartheid in South Africa and that against racism at home; as do Solidarnosc in Poland and the different autonomous civil initiatives – for human rights and peace, against environmental destruction and domestic poverty – which are going to multiply in Eastern Europe as well as in the USSR...

Hence also the inability of these theories to grasp the major transformations these movements engender simultaneously at individual and collective, local and national, infra-, trans- and, also, international levels by their *autonomous intervention* on *different issues* in the *same transformative-anticipative manner*.

A New Pattern of Social Movements: Analysis of the Peace Movement[7]

1. *Controversialisation of issues as definition of social movements*. Rarely has social protest provoked so many passions and controversies as has the unexpected and unexpectedly massive emergence of a new peace movement in 1981.

The unprecedently large range of questions – strategic, economic, political and ethical – which within a few months became controversial public issues, indicates the effective *conflictualisation* of the security issue in all its possible aspects. And the very existence of this multi-faceted controversy well illustrates the basically *democratic-transformative* character of this transnational protest which, by opening public debate on the security issue, in fact transformed the field of international security, dominated by nation-states, into an informal and 'mediatic' but undoubtedly *transnational public area* (see Hegedus 1984a, 1984b, 1987a). (The term 'mediatic' refers to the 'media' and to the articulation of a new area by the means of TV, radio, etc.)

And, while the campaign of French intellectuals against 'pacifism'[8] illustrates - somewhat caricaturally – the acuteness of passions concerning the

267

peace movement, the very lack of consensus as to the name of this six year old protest, and the relative scarcity of sociological studies on the present mobilisation, indicate both the controversial and problematic character of the question: what *is* this movement?

As a matter of fact, the controversial character of this debate used to be considered as obviously legitimate with regard to the issue at stake. Moreover, arguments against the peace movement are systematically presented as being a priori justified by the controversial nature of the problem addressed by the peace movement.[9] Undoubtedly passions and controversies are legitimate with regard to the security issue. And they are easy to understand with regard to the complexity of this huge popular mobilisation, which emerged around single-issue campaigns and engendered a real explosion of citizens' and professional initiatives as well as other actions at local, national, transnational and transcontinental levels. In a word, this 'new' movement does not fit any of the usual interpretations but challenges our way of representing social movements as well as our vision of social change. So do, for that matter, all the other 'new' movements which have emerged recently throughout the world around different issues but in a very analogous manner, and which are not even included in the field of investigation on new social movements.

Now, however legitimate they are, *none* of the arguments on the peace movement can be justified by the controversial 'nature' of the security issue. Simply because, far from being controversial by 'nature', the security issue was not even a public concern, but a military state's affair par excellence, exterior to public debate and to democratic control, until the emergence of today's peace movement. In other words, the usual assumption is not only wrong, but should be *reversed*. Instead of explaining the controversial character of the question 'what is the peace movement?', the present controversial nature of the security issue – that is, the opening of a *new transnational public sphere* outside, and that of a *new multi-optional field* inside the up to then single-optional realm of the arms-race – suggests that the very '*controversialisation*' of this issue answers this question and, more generally, outlines a new approach to the real problem of 'what is a social movement?' in self-creative society. And, first of all, what are the other movements which emerged recently around various issues, and transformed the formerly esoteric and/or ignored problems of hunger, poverty, apartheid into a more or less controversial but undoubtedly public concern at a transnational level? This applies to the campaign against hunger in Africa and that against poverty in our own countries, as much as no doubt the campaign against apartheid and, to a certain extent, that against racism in France.

2. *Addressing the security issue: the new characteristics of the peace movement.* The question 'what is the peace movement?' involves two problems: 1) what is the nature of the present mobilisation – in comparison with the 'new' social movement of the seventies, as well as earlier peace and anti-war mobilisations?, and 2) what is the unity of these various campaigns and mobilisations, so diversified in their objectives and in their time/space

perspectives but basically similar in structure, organisation and 'methods' on both sides of the Atlantic?

The first point to stress is the basic similarity between the peace and other 'new' social movements in respect of *practices*: in respect of the grass-root and non-hierarchical character of the organisations, the non-violent and pragmatic character of the modes of action, and also with regard to the diversity, the cross-ideological and heterogeneous character of the constituencies. The analysis of the peace movement's practices – in fact 'patterned' after those invented by the new social movements of the seventies – brings to light the similarity of these movements with regard to their methods as well as their original relation with the political system, parties and institutions. Like other new social movements, the peace movement is characterised by its autonomy vis-à-vis the established parties, by its innovative, direct relationship with public opinion, media and institutions, and by the same new manner of 'doing politics'.

At the same time, this investigation reveals some significant differences which partly account for the unprecedentedly massive dimension of the peace movement. Unlike the movements of the seventies – characterised by their essentially cultural dimension and also by their minority constituencies – the peace movement is characterised by its basically *ethical dimension* and its self-assigned *majoritarian* vocation. By appealing to direct responsibility – of citizens, professionals, Christians etc. – it addresses individual consciences and the mainstream population. The *new character* of the current peace movement reveals the *practical unity* of this highly diversified mobilisation which is based, in fact, on the multiplicity and similarity of autonomous practices essentially related to the grass-root and local character of their organisation, the ethical dimension of their argumentation, the individual character of people's commitment and participation, and the autonomy and pragmatism of their interventions.

Like the earlier peace movements, mobilisations against war and/or nuclear weapons, the present protest emerged as massive opposition to the deployment of new missiles and to the acceleration of the arms-race. However, unlike earlier peace and anti-war movements, the current mobilisation is neither limited to the question of weapons nor even focused on peace. On the one hand, far from being reduced to their limited objectives, the single-issue campaigns (especially the Freeze) challenged directly the prevailing security policy in the name of alternative solutions aimed at the *reversal* of the arms-race. On the other hand, however dominant these campaigns were at the beginning of the mobilisation, the present peace movement has never been reducible to these single-issue actions. Beyond the umbrella of the Freeze and anti-Pershing campaigns, the movement includes a multitude of civil initiatives addressing the security issue in its diverse aspects and connecting the problem of the arms-race with different domestic and international, economic and financial, social and political issues (military budget and deficit, poverty and unemployment, defence and foreign policy, arms-race and intervention etc.). Unlike former mobilisations, focussed effectively on the question of weapons or on war and peace, the present protest focused immediately on the *problem of security* and directly addressed the *manner* in which this problem was *treated*. Beyond peace and disarmament it raised the question of *human security* in its unavoidably *double dimension*: one's security in a world of conflict, and the security of this world in the nuclear era. And it immediately associated this fundamental concern with the exigency of inventing a new way of dealing with the problem of security which does not subordinate the protection of humanity against nuclear weapons to the defence of the West against the East.

The centrality of the security issue allows us to define the *analytic unity* as well as the *area* of this movement. The conceptual unity is that of a *problem*, and the area of the movement includes all the *civil initiatives* which address the security issue in an *autonomous manner*. This definition anticipates the conceptual framework I propose to define the unity and the autonomy of social movements in self-creative society. The *unity* of each particular movement is that of a specific *problem*, and their *autonomy* is not dependent on their relation to political parties, but on their *capacity to address a problem in an autonomous manner*.

As for the peace movement, this definition allows the integration of the whole spectrum of very diversified actions related to the security issue in one analytic field. And it outlines the *three-dimensionality* of this transnational movement, which (a) in its objectives addresses the security issue; (b) in its practices challenges the dominant patterns of citizens' participation in the political decision-making process; (c) in its appeal to individual/professional responsibility, transforms the dominant values and behaviour not only with regard to citizens' responsibility for a collective future but also with regard to personal responsibility for transnational issues and for international conflict resolution.

3. *Centrality of the security issue and conflictualisation of its treatment.* Despite its defensive and oppositional postures, the peace movement of the eighties engendered an entirely new capacity to challenge the whole process responsible for the arms-race. Seen in this light, the standard interpretations – which reduce the peace movement to a mere rejection of nuclear weapons (like the ban-the-bomb movement of the fifties), to a single-issue campaign (like the test-ban movement of the sixties), to a matter of political pressure on states (in the United States) or to an opposition to the United States (in the Federal Republic of Germany),[10] or to a basically symbolic, utopian or cultural movement (Melucci 1985) – simply overlook the most significant and innovative aspect of a movement which also transcends also the traditional opposition between single- and multi-issue actions. Rather, as a *problem-centred* movement, the contemporary peace movement addresses the security issue in its complex and multiple dimensions; through a loose system of networking, it connects a multitude of civil initiatives which address the same problematic in all its diverse aspects and at different levels, but always in an *autonomous and anticipative manner*.

As the *key item* on the agenda of today's peace movement, the security issue plainly exposes the real stakes lying behind the different objectives, the

270

question of weapons and, even, the problem of the peace. Furthermore, it reveals the underlying *unity* of this heterogeneous movement which, through a wide spectrum of actions at local, national and transnational levels, addresses the *same* problem inside and across national boundaries: *how security should be dealt with domestically and internationally*.

At the same time, the analysis of the different ways these autonomous civil initiatives effectively address the security issue and challenge its treatment brings to light the *multi-dimensional* character of this *problem-centred* movement and the three interdependent but often competitive orientations which are operative in it: (a) a *democratic protest*, which challenges the state monopoly as well as the very framework of the dominant decision-making process regarding security on the *domestic level*; (b) a *'peace' movement*, which challenges the dominant problem-solving process in the security field at the *international level*; (c) an *emancipatory movement*, which challenges the prevailing patterns of citizens' participation in the political process and, above all, the dominant models of conflict resolution at the *collective and interpersonal* and at the local, national and transnational level.

Initially, the peace movement was dominated by the strains – on both sides of the Atlantic until 1984 – between the single-issue campaigns (Freeze, anti-Pershing II) and other, more complex, campaigns and more radical actions (nuclear free zones, Jobs with Peace, nuclear disarmament campaigns, civil disobedience, tax refusal). However, beyond the difference of objectives, these tensions in fact reflect the intrinsic conflictuality *and* substantive complementarity between two autonomous logics which translate two strategies, *two different ways* to address the same problem: how to create significant modifications in the dominant decision-making and problem-solving processes in the security field. However different these strategies are in their dynamics, they proceed in the same *autonomous manner to create and anticipate* these modifications. They associate opposition *and* alternative proposals to prevailing policies and *directly* intervene in the autonomous sectors of the security field through a multitude of civil initiatives on local, national and transnational levels.

In the first place, the strains reflect the unavoidable tensions between a political logic focused on coalition building and a social logic focused on making connections between different issues related to the security question (military budget and deficit, investment, unemployment and poverty connections, disarmament – foreign policy – interventionism and Third World connections). The first is aimed at creating *political* capacity to *reverse* the orientation of prevailing national security policies ([a] 'democratic protest'). The second is aimed at creating a *social* capacity to *challenge the whole problem-solving process* accountable for the arms-race, as well as for the blocs system and the militarisation of conflict resolution, especially in the Third World ([b] 'peace movement').

But beyond these tensions, all these campaigns and actions proceed in the *same manner*: by means of autonomous actions which directly intervene inside and outside existing institutions and the legal framework of the decision-making process at local, national and transnational levels (Freeze and nuclear free zones referenda, effective denuclearisation of individual homes, towns, countries and continents, peace initiatives and civil disobedience, Jobs with Peace budgets and non-cooperation in IDS research, peace studies and nuclear disarmament campaign) ([c] 'emancipatory movement').

In other words, an analysis of the tensions between a political and a social logic, reveals the conflictual complementarity between the 'democratic protest' and the 'peace movement' orientations, and brings to light the *centrality* of the third *'emancipatory'* dimension in the present peace movement.

Empowerment and Problem-Solving – Social Movement and Social Change

1. *Emancipatory process and social change in the security field.* All these civil initiatives, campaigns and actions – the most limited and the most radical – share the same concern for citizen autonomy and the same vision of direct individual responsibility for the future. They not only demand change, but intervene directly in the security field by means of *autonomous civil practices* which set *social limits* that condition security policy and propose *alternatives* which challenge prevailing policies. As a result, these practices not only influence security policy. They effectively *transform* the basic character of civil society/state relations in the field of international security. And in so far as these practices infringe on the normal political process and enhance both individual and collective control at local, national and even transnational levels, they engender a movement of citizen *empowerment*.

This key point, consistently stressed in the interviews, reveals the underlying unity of a movement which surpasses both the framework of a democratic protest and the field of a 'peace' movement. In a very pragmatic way, it addresses the basic question of *people's empowerment* to enter the political process directly and to 'control their own history': that is, *to manage in an autonomous manner their individual and collective destiny with respect to domestic and transnational issues*.

This emancipatory dimension has become an increasingly important aspect of the peace movement and it is a key component of the recent campaigns and initiatives around different international issues.

More significantly, the analysis of these autonomous civil practices, especially their manner of modifying the framework of the decision-making and problem-solving processes by creating social limits and alternatives to state policies, opens an entirely new perspective which exposes the *mechanisms of social change in the security field*. This new perspective suggests the whole scale of on-going transformations created by the peace movement with respect to the security issue, as well as with respect to civil society/state relations. It indicates that even if the peace movement failed to achieve its immediate objectives (Freeze) and (temporarily) lost political momentum, it nonetheless initiated four, partly complementary, *long-term processes*: (a) a *democratisation* process on the domestic level ('socialisation' and conflictualisation of the security issue by its integration in the public sphere); (b) a *'civilisation'* process on the transnational level (denuclearisation of defence policy, demilitarisation of foreign policy); (c) an *emancipation* process on the planetary level (demilitarisation of conflict resolution, depolarisation of the world system, de-statisation of transnational relations); (d) an *empowerment* process on each level (empowerment of citizens and civil societies at local, national, transnational level).

2. *Emancipatory process and social change in the international arena.* The recent emergence of new movements around international issues – anti-apartheid, anti-famine campaigns – underlines the larger significance of this *emancipatory process.* At the same time, the unprecedentedly large and rapid impact of these movements on a transnational – and even trans-bloc – scale (disinvestment campaign, Live Aid, multiplication of unofficial peace groups in the GDR, Hungary, Poland and USSR) emphasises the importance of assessing the new mechanisms by which these movements now directly intervene in international issues and effectively modify the framework of policy formation on a world scale.

My basic proposal is that all these new mobilisations are parts of the same phenomenon and can be analysed in the theoretical framework I outlined through the analysis of the peace movement. My key point is that, like the peace movement, the anti-apartheid and anti-famine campaigns are *autonomous problem-centred actions* which, by their direct intervention in state-managed international issues, 'participate' in the same process of democratisation–civilisation–emancipation–empowerment. In this way, they challenge the dominant organisation, decision-making and problem-solving process in the international arena in three different but interdependent areas: (1) security issue (peace movement); (2) foreign policy issue (anti-apartheid and sanctions movements); (3) development issue (campaign against hunger in Africa).

This analytic proposal is based on the *similarity* of these movements with respect to their *practices* and to the *autonomous manner* in which they intervene in state-managed international issues. Without any doubt, the peace, anti-apartheid and anti-hunger movements significantly differ with regard to the complexity of the issues they address and, also, to the complexity of the approaches they take. The peace movement challenges the whole problem-solving process in the security field through strong protest and opposition to prevailing security policy. The anti-apartheid campaign is basically a protest movement but it is centred on a limited issue, while the anti-hunger campaign addresses a highly complex problem without any obvious oppositional posture. However, beyond the obvious differences, these movements are genuinely *similar* with respect to: (1) the international character of their issues; (2) the transnational dimension of their actions; (3) the autonomy and pragmatism of their intervention; (4) the way they 'socialise' state-managed issues by appealing to individual *responsibility and solidarity* on the transnational level ('We are the world'); (5) their method to call for immediate, local actions for intervening directly in international issues (disinvestment campaign – acting locally, thinking globally); (6) their new manner of making connections between international issues and domestic questions (hunger and domestic

273

poverty, see the role of the USA for Africa in 'Hands across America', apartheid and domestic racism, Third World problems and increasing xenophobia against immigrant workers in Europe).

More importantly, these movements are basically the *same* in their ethical dimension, in their non-violent and expressive modes of action, in their grass-root and anti-hierarchical organisation, as well as in the way they mobilise heterogeneous, single-issue constituencies on a local and transnational scale. At the same time, they are *similar* in the way they intervene and create transformations in the international arena: by addressing individuals and mobilising public opinion beyond national boundaries and creating *new civil solidarities across boundaries*; by opening public debates on state-managed international issues and creating *new* – informal and mediatic but undoubtedly *transnational – public spheres*; by transforming prevailing international policies into *controversial issues* and setting *social limits* to their realisation; by raising the social, political and even economic price of contested policies and by inventing/generating *alternative* approaches.

Auto-Creativity and Self-Determination: The Double Challenge

1. *Social movement in self-creative society: a new paradigm.* The thrust of my argument above suggests the shape of the conceptual framework with which I propose to analyse social movements and the process of conflictual creation in a society characterised by its *'auto-creativity'*: by its genuinely new capacity to *invent and realise*, and therefore to *choose*, its own *futures* in an *autonomous manner*.

There is no doubt that contemporary society can be characterised by its complexity, by the generalisation of science and of politics as well as by the new and unprecedented dimension of risks (Beck 1986), by its new way of proceeding by programmation (Touraine 1973) and/or by symbol- and information-processing (Naisbitt 1982). We are undoubtedly in a computer and communication age which could even be termed 'post-material', in the sense that the centre of production is not in the manufacturing but in the knowledge industries.

However, none of the usual terms enables one, in my opinion, to grasp the real challenge of contemporary society consequent to the *reversal* of our relation not only to environment but, also, to the future. As a result of the new paradigm of science (Moscovici 1973; Prigogine and Senghers 1979), nature has effectively ceased to be a 'territorial' exteriority, and the future is no longer a temporal posteriority (Hegedus 1985). The point I want to stress with the term of 'auto-creativity' – and the *'raison d'être'* of this new term – concerns precisely the consequences of this reversal. If nature is 'interiorised' (Moscovici 1973; Beck 1986), the future is 'humanised': it ceases to be a destiny and becomes an option. It is the product of a self-creative process which proceeds from the invention of new possibilities (paradigms) to the formalisation of problems and to their resolution: two interdependent but autonomous phases of a very complex process with a multiple time/space perspective. The key point of my definition is that what is at stake in self-creative society is nothing other than the *choices* which will be formalised and the *finalities* which order the whole problem-solving process.

In effect, my first proposal is that, however complex it is, this self-creative process is not commanded by an autonomous logic engendering risks and auto-destruction (Beck 1986), nor is it a system of self-regulation (Von Foerster and Zopf 1962; Morin 1973), and/or auto-poetic (Luhmann 1982). It is structured around a *'dynamic tension'*[11] between these two autonomous phases which are usually identified with fundamental research, on the one hand, and with engineering, on the other. Of course, this *central tension* cannot be fixed in space and it is multiple in time. Nevertheless, it is perfectly localisable: it is at the *junction* of the constitutive phases of the whole process of auto-creativity, where the *choices* which *command the realisation of possible futures* intervene in every possible sphere of activity; that is, the choices of options. In other words, my second proposal is that, though it is complex and polycentric, this self-creative process is structured around a 'central point', which cannot be identified in space, and which is multiple in time. Nevertheless, this 'point' is not only symbolic but perfectly real. It is the moment where the decisions concerning the options intervenes and, at least potentially, it is the 'moment' of the *conflictual creation of these options*, that is, the 'moment' of a *structural* and *central conflict* which characterises self-creative society.

Hence, my basic proposal is that what is *at stake* in a self-creative society is not the 'what to do' but the *'how to do'* of the whole process of problem-solving; that is, the *method* of elaborating and realising possible options. Consequently, self-creative society is neither unified nor disintegrated. It is a binary system of actions which is structured around a *central conflict* between *two methods* of problem-solving, competitive in their means, opposed in their finalities and procedures, and antagonistic in their consequences. In contrast to industrial society, this conflict cannot be identified with any specific problem, and it cannot be fixed in space and time. It does not oppose specific groups (classes), or masses and individuals to the technostructures[12]. This conflict cannot be 'personalised', and it does not correspond to any adversity. It is the *permanent conflictuality of two ways of dealing with problems*.

The dominant method of problem-solving assigns the finality of maximising efficiency, proceeds with the concentration of means on one single option, which is presented as the only possible solution. Hence a selective rationalisation (Habermas 1982) and the concentration of powers: the legitimisation of one single option by a systemic rationality (Habermas 1982), the concentration of cognitive, scientific, technical and financial means on the elaboration and realisation of one option, and the concentration of information – by secrecy and opacity – in order to ensure the exclusivity of this option. The consequence of this single-optional 'technocratic' problem-solving is, on the one hand, the *monopoly* of conceptors over the *choices* of solutions[13] and, on the other, the *reduction of possible choices and options*, which engenders risks and endangers the future, and leads unavoidably to irreversibility.

In self-creative society, a social movement is, in my definition, nothing else than the permanent invention of autonomous capacities to *challenge* –

across time and space boundaries – the *finality* and the *procedures* of the dominant method of problem-solving by *setting social limits* to the realisation of a contested single option (protest side) and by *inventing/engendering alternative approaches* and options (counter-offensive transformative side). A social movement is a very complex process – with a multiple time/space perspective – of *empowerment* and *alternative problem-solving* which assigns the finality of maximising the *possibility of choices* on all levels and in every aspect of social life, and *creates this possibility* by its capacity to engender new (multiple) options. In this sense, self-creative society can be characterised as multi-optional (Naisbitt 1982), but only potentially. Its effective multi-optionalisation depends on the capacity of social movements to *conflictualise* the issues; that is to challenge the single-optional-technocratic orientation of the dominant problem-solving process, and in this way to open up the field of possible options.

In other words, what is at stake in self-creative society, characterised here by the permanent invention of new possibilities and the realisation of possible futures, is not 'the' power but *empowerment*: the capacity of people to intervene directly in problems they are concerned with and to 'control' the choices of their own futures; that is, to decide their collective and individual destiny or, simply, the choices concerning different aspects of their own lives.

2. *Empowerment and globalisation: a world pattern of conflictual creation.* The movements of the eighties plainly bring to light the procedures involved in these processes of *conflictualisation* and *empowerment*, protest *and* transformation; that is, the *new pattern* of social movements in self-creative society. In contrast to the seventies, the recent movements definitely lost their minoritarian character. They do not only intervene in new fields but address different issues and share, throughout the world, the same moral and grass-root dimensions as well as the same autonomous practices. Basically similar in their ethical and democratic orientations, they address individual consciences and appeal to direct responsibility for a collective future. Above all, they share the same purposive orientation, aimed at *self-determination*, which – from a national-political concept – has become an individual-collective issue with a basically ethical, but also cultural, social and political meaning. Effectively, what *is* at stake in self-creative society is neither autonomy (Gorz 1980) nor self-realisation, but nothing other than *self-determination*; that is, the capacity of people to control their own destiny and to choose their own future at any level and in every aspect of their personal and collective life. More importantly, these new movements do not ask for change but proceed, throughout the world, in the same *autonomous-anticipative* manner to *create transformations* by setting *social limits* to the realisation of contested policies (hence the major role of civil disobedience in the new movements throughout the world) and by *inventing/generating alternative approaches*.

In other words, the new pattern of social movement in self-creative society has a double dimension. The 'identity' of each single movement is *thematic*, its singularity – or 'specificity' – is that of the *problem* it addresses, and its *autonomy* is related to its capacity to challenge the dominant problem-solving process in its own field. And the unity of these movements – that is, the *unity of social movement in self-creative society* – is not simply symbolic and/or theoretical, neither is it at the level of a collectively shared *Angst* or an alternative sensibility. It is at the level of the same *conflictual-alternative approach* to problem-solving and the same *empowering-transformative procedures*.

Moreover, the eighties are characterised by the eruption of social practices, public opinion campaigns, and civil initiatives in the international arena. By their very existence, these challenge the conceptual exclusion of social movements from the international arena, that is the traditional assumption concerning the basic separation between the domestic field of social relations and the exterior field of international relations. The international field has long been seen as: (a) solely reserved for state intervention; (b) entirely structured by intei-state relations; and (c) inherently *exterior* to civil society and citizens' interventions, to the arena of the democratic process, as well as to the fabric of social relations (conflicts and actors) both presumed to be confined to the political framework of nation-states.

This separation, which reflects historical practices on a multiple time/space scale, no longer corresponds to social practices in the West. The traditional paradigm is invalidated by the emergence of new movements which: (a) address international-planetary issues, (b) intervene directly in the international arena; (c) effectively act at a transnational level. Unlike former peace and anti-war mobilisations, the recent movements around international issues are not limited to national boundaries, nor to actions which merely pressure governments or oppose states. They now intervene in a newly autonomous manner in the international arena by directly addressing different issues formerly managed by states in the framework of inter-state relations (as the security issue used to be managed until the emergence of today's peace movement). Whatever the mode and the level of intervention (local, national or transnational), these movements challenge the state's monopoly over international issues, as well as the dominant organisation of problem-solving processes in the international arena.

In other words, in contrast to the seventies, the movements of the eighties directly address planetary issues and challenge the dominant problem-solving process at a global level: they proceed in an autonomous manner to the *democratisation*, to the '*civilisation*' and *multi-optionalisation* of this *self-creative* – and polycentric – *world-system*. By their capacity to *conflictualise* global issues, they open up the field of *possible choices* at a *planetary* level. And, by their genuinely new manner of *individualising* planetary problems, they '*globalise*' individuals throughout the world, engendering a new way of thinking and acting; that is, a *new ethic of responsibility* and a *new practice of self-determination and solidarity*. This could be perfectly summarised by the simple idea we owe to rockers, who alone have succeeded in effectively integrating the world into one single community of conscience for the time of a concert: 'We are the world'.

Notes

1. Several points of the theoretical framework which underlies this term – especially those concerning 'auto-creativity' and the new role of science, the multiple time-scale perspectives and the transnational character of this society and of the new social relations and movements – were developed in different articles and in a former book. It will be developed in a more systematic manner in a forthcoming volume. See Hegedus (1985, 1987a).

2. The aim of this section is to highlight the crucial points which reflect the characteristics of the movements of the seventies in different new social movements' theories. Consequently, it is not a comprehensive nor, even less, a critical summary. More importantly, the references in this section do not pretend to be representative but only illustrative.

3. Moreover, none of these interpretations allow us to cover the whole phenomenon of new social movements. The women's movement cannot be characterised by a collectively shared *Angst*, and the movements of the eighties are rarely characterised by an alternative sensibility. Even in the case of the peace movement, the alternative sensibility cannot be considered as a dominant feature and certainly not as the dominant motivation and/or a condition for involvement.

4. The recent crusade of French intellectuals against Live Aid and other mobilisations piloted by rockers, churchmen and other personalities of great moral credibility (Glucksman and Wolton 1986; Finkelkraut 1987) illustrates perfectly the total misunderstanding between the 'new' movements and an 'old', basically ideological, 'interpretation'. Effectively, in contrast to the past, the characteristic of these new movements is precisely their capacity to overcome the traditional opposition between rationality and emotion, reflexivity and passion. They do not appeal to collective interest and they do not refer to any ideology, and even less to a 'cause'. They address individual consciousness by provoking emotion; they appeal to personal responsibility and global solidarity by addressing people's hearts and minds by way of provoking reflection and (com)passion.

5. As more or less do the different versions of the theory of resource mobilisation.

6. As we unsuccessfully tried to do in our study on the anti-nuclear movement (Touraine et al. 1981).

7. The problematic, as well as the analytic orientations I develop here, are based on the study of the peace movement I conducted in the United States and the Federal Republic of Germany (between 1982-85). The results were presented in several articles (see Hegedus 1984a, 1984b, 1986, 1987a) and communications, and will be published in a forthcoming volume.

8. This question and the highly ideological character of French intellectuals' hostility to the peace movement were analysed in a former article (Hegedus 1984c). The basic reason for this adversity is the totally ideological, non-critical and – in this sense – 'totalitarian' character of the shift of ex-leftist intellectuals in the mid-seventies from what I call 'the myth of the revolution to the mysticism of human rights'. The main point is that the defence of human rights is presented by these intellectuals (A. Glucksman, B.H. Levy, A. Finkelkraut) in exactly the same intolerant-totalitarian manner, i.e. as the only exclusive 'cause', as was presented formerly – and by the same intellectuals – the defence of the revolution, i.e. of revolutionary-totalitarian regimes (USSR, China, Cuba, Vietnam). Human rights became the only exclusive 'cause' one is authorised to defend. Moreover, it is presented as the only single criterion around which the world is definitely divided into two empires in war with each other for and against freedom. In other words, this 'mysticism of human rights' maintains the same ideological division of the world into two 'camps', which sustained the leftist ideology and the myth of the revolution. Except that the former God – socialist or communist but always revolutionary (Stalin, Mao, Castro) – became the new 'evil'; while the former 'evil' imperialist-capitalist-colonialist super-power (United States) became the new God, more or less conservative but always actively anti-communist (Reagan). Hence the extreme popularity of Reagan and his arms-race and interventionist policy among French ex-leftist intellectuals who actively supported his fight against the Congress – for aid to the Contras.

9. See especially Glucksman (1983); Heller and Fehér (1983); Bosquet (1981). More generally, this is the dominant position of the special issue of *Telos* on 'pacifism' (1982) as is pointed out by S. Benhabib in the same issue.

10. Regarding the critics of the different interpretations of the peace movement, see Hegedus (1984a, 1984b, 1986).

11. I use the term 'dynamic tension' in the sense of Hofstadter (1979).

12. J.K. Galbraith, the father of the concept 'technostructure' (1967), himself criticises this unified image and proposes a new, less integrated, plural image of power structures in contemporary society in his recent book (1983).

13. One the best analyses concerning the procedures by which the conceptors or 'technicians' acquire this monopoly over the choices of solutions – in the field of security – is given by S. Zuckerman (1983). He brings to light the fact that, far from justifying new steps in the arms-race, the famous gaps – or windows of vulnerability – between the super-powers were systematically invented by the 'technicians' in order to make governments accept and decide on the production of new weapons systems which were already planned and designed.

References

BECK, U. 1986. *Risikogesellschaft: Auf dem Weg in eine andere Moderne*. Frankfurt: Suhrkamp.

BELL, D. 1973. *The Coming of Post-industrial Society*. London: Heinemann.

BENHABIB, S. 1982. 'The West German Peace Movement and its Critics'. *Telos* 51 (Special issue).

BOSQUET, M. 1981. 'Plutôt rouge que mort'. *Nouvel Observateur*, Nov. 21.

FINKELKRAUT, A. 1987. *Le déclin de la pensée*. Paris: Fayard.

FREEMAN, J. ed. 1983. *Social Movements of the Sixties and Seventies*. New York/London: Longman.

GALBRAITH, J.K. 1967. *The New Industrial State*. Harmondsworth: Penguin.

GALBRAITH, J.K. 1983. *The Anatomy of Power*. New York: Houghton Mifflin Co.

GERLACH, L.P. and HINE, V.H. 1970. *People, Power and Change*. Indianapolis: Bobbs Merill.

GLUCKSMAN, A. 1983. *La force du vertige*. Paris: Grasset.

GLUCKSMAN, A. and WOLTON, T. 1986. *Silence on tue*. Paris: Grasset.

GORZ, A. 1980. *Adieu au proletariat*. Paris: Galilée.

GUNDELACH, P. 1984. 'Social Transformation and New Forms of Voluntary Associations'. *Social Science Information* 23 (6).

HABERMAS, J. 1981. *Theorie des kommunikativen Handelns*. Frankfurt: Suhrkamp.

HEGEDUS, Z. 1984a. 'The Dynamics of the Peace Movement in the United States and the Federal Republic of Germany', in *European Security: Nuclear or Conventional Defence?*. Oxford: Pergamon.

HEGEDUS, Z. 1984b. 'Une protestation démocratique à la recherche d'un nouveau modèle de sécurité. *Revue Internationale d'Action Communautaire* 12 (52).

HEGEDUS, Z. 1984c. '"Vague pacifiste" ou renouveau démocratique'. *Passé Présent*. 3

HEGEDUS, Z. 1985. *Il presente e' l'avvenire, nuove pratiche e nuova rappresentazione sociale*. Milano: Franco Angeli.

HEGEDUS, Z. 1986. 'Pacifismo, neutralismo o un nuovo movimento transnazionale per la pace?', in *Movimento sociali e sistema politico*. Milano: Franco Angeli.

HEGEDUS, Z. 1987a. 'The Challenge of the Peace Movement: Civilian Security and Civilian Emancipation'. *Alternatives* XII. Also, in *Towards a Just World Peace*. London: Butterworths.

HEGEDUS, Z. 1987b. 'Scienza e scienzati nella società programmata'. *Sociologia e Ricerca Sociale* 24.

HELLER, A. and FEHER, F. 'Les antinomies du pacifisme'. *Esprit* 2.

HOFSTADTER, D. 1979. *Gödel Escher Bach: An Eternal Golden Braid*. New York: Basic Books.

JAPP, K.P. 1986. 'Neue soziale Bewegung und die Kontinuität der Moderne'. *Soziale Welt* 4 (Special issue).

KRIESI, H.P. and VAN PRAAG, P. Jr. Forthcoming. 'Old and New Politics: The Dutch Peace Movement and the Traditional Political Organizations'. *European Journal of Political Science*.

LUHMANN, N. 1982. 'Autopoesis, Handlung und kommunikative Verständigung'. *Zeitschrift für Soziologie* 4.

McCARTHY, J.D. and ZALD, M.N. 1973. 'Resource Mobilization and Social Movements: A Partial Theory'. *American Journal of Sociology* 86.

MELUCCI, A. 1985. 'The Symbolic Challenge of Contemporary Movements'. *Social Research* (Winter).

MORIN, E. 1973. *Le paradigme perdu: la nature humaine*. Paris: Seuil.

MOSCOVICI, S. 1975. *Essai sur l'histoire humaine de la nature*. Paris: Flammarion.

NAISBITT, J, 1982. *Megatrends*. New York: Warner Books.

OBERSCHALL, A. *Social Conflict and Social Movements*. Englewood Cliffs, N.J.: Prentice Hall.

OFFE, K. 1984. 'Politische Legitimation durch Mehrheitsentscheidung', in Guggenberger, *An den Grenzen der Mehrheitsdemokratie*. Cologne.

OFFE, K. 1985. 'New Social Movements: Challenging the Boundaries of Institutional Politics'. *Social Research* (Winter).

OFFE, K. 1986. 'Die Utopie der Null-Option'. *Soziale Welt* 4 (Special issue).

PRIGOGINE, I. and SENGHERS, I. 1979. *La nouvelle alliance*. Paris: Gallimard.

TOURAINE, A. 1969. *La société postindustrielle*. Paris: Denoel.

TOURAINE, A. 1973. *Production de la société*. Paris: Seuil.

TOURAINE, A., HEGEDUS, Z., DUBET, F. and WIEVIORKA, M. 1981. *La prophétie antinucléaire*. Paris: Seuil.

VON FOERSTER, H. and ZOPF, G.W. eds. 1962. *Principles of Self-organization*. Oxford: Pergamon.

ZUCKERMAN, S. 1983. *Nuclear Illusion and Reality*. New York: Vintage Books.